C0-DNE-724

History of the

CHURCHES OF CHRIST

In Texas

1824 - 1950

•

By

STEPHEN DANIEL ECKSTEIN JR., PH. D.

•

FIRM FOUNDATION PUBLISHING HOUSE
AUSTIN, TEXAS

1963

COPYRIGHT, 1963,
BY STEPHEN DANIEL ECKSTEIN JR.

Dedicated to my beloved wife

MILDRED

whose untiring efforts in a large measure contributed to the successful completion of this work.

ACKNOWLEDGEMENTS

It is my earnest hope that this study will serve to inform the readers concerning what I believe to be an interesting and important phase of church history. For their assistance in providing, suggesting, and locating materials for use in making this study, I wish to express my appreciation to the personnel of the libraries at Texas Technological College, Lubbock, Texas, Abilene Christian College, Abilene, Texas, Texas Christian University, Fort Worth, Texas, and the University of Texas, Austin, Texas; to Claude Spencer, curator of the Disciples of Christ Historical Library, Nashville, Tennessee, C. E. W. Dorris, owner of a complete file of the *Gospel Advocate*, Nashville, Tennessee, and Reuel Lemmons, editor of the *Firm Foundation*, Austin, Texas. Most particularly I am sincerely indebted to Dr. Ernest Wallace, Professor of History, Texas Technological College, who, as director of the study, gave unstintingly of his own time throughout its preparation. Appreciation is hereby expressed to other members of the advisory committee, Professors S. S. McKay, C. D. Eaves, O. A. Kinchen, and J. W. Davis for their helpful suggestions. To James M. Tolle, Austin, Texas, who read the completed manuscript and made several valuable comments, Leona Head, Clovis, New Mexico who made the drawings, and a host of other individuals, I wish to express my deep gratitude for their encouragement and assistance in many ways.

Stephen Daniel Eckstein Jr.

TABLE OF CONTENTS

INTRODUCTION viii
Restoration Movement.

I. EARLY BEGINNINGS—1819-1836 1
Religious Conditions and Activities—Early Members of the Church of Christ—The First Congregation.

II. THE CHURCH DURING THE REPUBLIC ERA 1836-1845 11
Religion in the Republic—Preachers and Churches—Weaknesses and Needs—The Church at the End of the Republic.

III. CHURCH GROWTH IN THE EARLY STATEHOOD PERIOD 1845-1861 27
Early Influences—Pleas for Preachers—Cooperations—Initial Efforts in East Texas—Northwest Texas, the Wilmeths and B. F. Hall—Dallas, Fort Worth and Vicinity—South Texas—Houston, San Antonio and Uvalde—Tireless Evangelists—Spiritual Deficiencies—The Slavery Issue—Military Service and War—Church Status in 1860.

IV. AN ERA OF CONSIDERABLE ADVANCE 1865-1906 84
Post-War Conditions—Efforts in East Texas—Dallas—Fort Worth—North Texas—Central Texas—Gulf Coast—Southwest Texas.

V. BEGINNINGS OF CHURCHES OF CHRIST IN WEST TEXAS 154
Abilene and Vicinity—San Angelo and Westward—Lubbock and the South Plains—Amarillo and the Panhandle.

VI. EVANGELISM 177
Devoted Evangelists—T. B. Larimore, the Sherman Revivals—Camp Meetings—Debaters and Debates—T. W. Caskey—Evangelism Among Negroes—Missionary Efforts in Mexico—Indian Missions—Religious Periodicals—Educational Institutions—Weaknesses of the Evangelistic Method.

VII. CONTROVERSY AND DIVISION 229
   The American Christian Missionary Society—Texas State Meetings—The Texas Society—Instrumental Music—Rebaptism—Minor Issues—Authority, the Role of Religious Periodicals—Reconciliation Efforts—Basic Divergent Attitudes—Division and Names—1906 Religious Census.

VIII. THE CHURCHES OF CHRIST BECOME A
   MAJOR RELIGIOUS BODY 296
   Church Growth—Educational Media—Work Among Negroes and Mexicans—A Jewish Mission—Foreign Missions — Benevolent Work — Premillennialism and Cooperation—Comparative Statistics—Summary.

   BIBLIOGRAPHY 331

   APPENDIX 346

   STATISTICS 346

   MISCELLANEOUS 367

INDEX 369

INTRODUCTION

"No religious body is more definitely American than the Disciples of Christ (known as churches of Christ or Christian Churches). It developed on the frontier, and was an attempt to restore primitive Christianity." Thus, Anson Phelps Stokes, eminent church historian, has aptly characterized a religious movement born on the western border of a new nation and nurtured by its hardy, independent pioneers.

Developing in conjunction with the westward migration down the fertile Ohio valley in the first half of the nineteenth century, churches of Christ spread rapidly southwest into Kentucky and Tennessee, and west into Indiana and Illinois. A few members were in the trickle of enterprising frontiersmen who entered Mexican Texas before 1836. More came during the Republic era. When Texas became a state on December 29, 1845, a torrent of land hungry, opportunistic immigrants poured into the vast timber lands adjacent to the Sabine River, thence onto the grassy prairies, and finally onto its wide rolling western plains. Amid this stream were a considerable number of members of the churches of Christ, forerunners of a religious body which today has more of its members in Texas than in any other state. But one may ask, how and why did this church arise?

After the Declaration of Independence was promulgated, European traditions rapidly were replaced by fresh philosophies born of democratic free men. In the field of religion, chaos and confusion prevailed because of the multiplicity of existing sects. The lack of a predominant religion undoubtedly was the main factor which led to the incorporation of an article guaranteeing the freedom of worship in the constitution. Inspired by the unrestricted spirit of the "truth seeker," a number of preachers in several denominations began independent but virtually simultaneous efforts to arrive at a common authority in religion upon which all Christendom could unite. It was from this common effort that churches of Christ arose.

THE RESTORATION MOVEMENT

The restoration movement which began about 1790 was founded on the principle that the Bible alone could serve as sole authority in all religious matters. As a step toward their goal, the originators of the movement decided that all things pertaining to Christianity were to be designated by Biblical terms and names. There were several unrelated initial efforts in this direction. One significant movement was launched by evangelists James O'Kelly and Rice Haggard among the Methodists in the back country of Virginia and North Carolina in 1792. Rejecting the authority of Bishop Francis Asbury, O'Kelly and his followers withdrew from the Methodist Church. First calling themselves "Republican Methodists," they soon adopted the name "Christian" as the only Biblical term which they thought proper to denote a disciple of Christ. Within a few years, several thousand adherents had united with the new body.

Another group with somewhat similar views sprang up in New England. Abner Jones and Elias Smith, Baptist preachers in Vermont and New Hampshire, after concerted study of the Bible, in 1801-2 rejected certain Calvinistic doctrines and severed themselves from the Baptist Church. Repudiating all human names, they organized a "Christian Church." Soon, additional congregations were formed on a similar basis throughout New Hampshire, Vermont, and Massachusetts. Although the views of these men reflected in a measure the religious thinking of their day, it remained for three other movements initiated by other free thinking evangelists of the early nineteenth century to merge their beliefs and followers into the body known today as the churches of Christ.

The first group arose from the extraordinary religious fervor that swept the southern frontier, particularly in Kentucky, in the form of revivals from 1795 to 1804. Here, the spirit of the frontiersman was incited by accomplished orators who played upon pliable emotions, ready for free and forceful expression. Wooded groves became camping grounds for thousands of fellowship hungry pioneers. Tree stumps became pulpits for energetic preachers of all sects. In the ensuing services, especially in the evenings, fiery evangelists blazed forth with hell, fire, and brimstone tirades. The listeners expressed their emotional effects visibly by jerking, barking, or contorting their bodies into odd shapes, seemingly conclusive evidence that they had received the Spirit of God in full measure. Such was construed as eloquent testimony that they had been saved by Almighty God.

Sometimes participant, sometimes spectator, was Barton W. Stone, a talented Presbyterian preacher. Ordained in 1798, Stone proclaimed to one and all the salvation of God through his limitless grace and rejoiced as multitudes entered the fold. However, the Old School Presbyterians, steeped in traditional predestination theology, did not like what they saw or heard. Shocked by the preaching of such a "free salvation," the Kentucky Presbytery eventually summoned Richard McNemar, a revival preacher, before its august body in regard to this so-called "Armenian teaching." But they did not reckon with the frontier spirit which seemed to pervade and often supersede formal theological instruction. Before charges could be pressed, Stone and three others rallied to McNemar's support with a written document purporting their right to interpret the Scriptures as they saw fit. Denouncing the jurisdiction of the Presbytery, they formed the Springfield Presbytery, an informal band of independent Presbyterian preachers within the pale of the church in 1803. The attempt to establish a central organization for their own views was doomed to a short life, however, because the revivalists would tolerate no control from above. Within a year, the dissenters met under the leadership of Stone and dissolved the loose confederation with a pronouncement of the famous "Last Will and Testament of the Springfield Presbytery." The fundamental principle which expressed the sentiment of those signing the document was ". . . that the people henceforth take the Bible as the only guide to heaven; and as many as are offended with other books, which stand in competition with it, may cast them into the fire if they choose . . ."[1] Logically, at the same meeting, the assembly adopted the name "Christian" to the exclusion of all sectarian names. During the two decades 1805-1825, the Christians grew rapidly and probably numbered over ten thousand by the time Stone began publishing the *Christian Messenger* in 1826.

The second and most prominent group was the one gathered around Thomas Campbell and his more renowned son Alexander. Arriving at Philadelphia from Scotland in 1807, Thomas Campbell was assigned by the Presbytery to western Pennsylvania where the

---

[1] Charles A. Young, *Historical Documents Advocating Christian Union* (Chicago, 1904), pp. 21-22. Hereafter cited as Young, *Historical Documents*.

secessionists were in control of the Presbyterian Church. Within a few months, a minister charged that Campbell was publicly advocating open communion and other doctrines not consistent with Presbyterian tenets. The following year, Campbell withdrew from the Presbytery. On August 18, 1809, Campbell and a few followers formed the Christian Association at Washington, Pennsylvania, and adopted the following motto: "Where the Scriptures speak, we speak; where the Scriptures are silent, we are silent." On September 7, 1809, Campbell set forth the principles and objectives of the association in his noted "Declaration and Address." Decrying the existing religious division, he proposed what he deemed to be a workable plan for unifying all Christians. "Our desire for ourselves and our brethren would be, that rejecting human opinions and the inventions of men, as of any authority we might forever cease from further contentions returning to and holding fast by the original standards taking the divine word alone for our rule . . ."[2] The proposal was unanimously approved by the association.

At this momentous time, Alexander Campbell arrived from Scotland. Having studied diligently the views of the Haldane brothers and other Scottish reformers while attending school in Glasgow, Alexander had embraced some teaching foreign to traditional Presbyterian dogma. After exchanging ideas, father and son mutually agreed to expound the gospel only as it could be supported by scripture. At least such was the theory motivating subsequent labor.

When his first child was born, Alexander restudied the question of infant baptism. After exhaustive re-

---

[2]Young, *Historical Documents*, p. 73.

search, including a careful analysis of Greek and Latin texts, Campbell concluded that it was unwarranted by scripture. Therefore, he and his father and their families had not been Biblically baptized. Immediately, he persuaded Matthias Luce, a Baptist preacher, to administer adult immersion after a simple confession of faith in Christ. Father and son, their wives, and three others were baptized in Buffalo Creek on the Pennsylvania-Virginia border in 1811. Shortly thereafter, other members of Campbell's Brush Run congregation were immersed. Although not identical in doctrine with the Baptists, the Brush Run church was affiliated with the Redstone Baptist Association from 1813 to 1825.

A third southern frontier group was led by Walter Scott, a recent immigrant from Scotland. From the time of his arrival in 1818 till his meeting with Alexander Campbell in 1821-22, Scott diligently studied the scriptures to determine how persons attained salvation. As a result of his research, Scott evolved a "plan of salvation" to be obeyed by each candidate after instruction from the scriptures. The plan prescribed a belief in Jesus Christ as the Son of God, repentance or turning from sin, and immersion in water for the remission of sins. In 1827, Scott, a member of a Baptist Church in Pittsburgh, accepted a call to preach for the Mahoning Baptist Association. His assignment provided him with ample opportunity to declare publicly his "plan." Since this exclusive use of reason in essence invalidated any statement or testimony of divine experience, it soon caused a cleavage within the association. As a result, the Baptist churches disclaimed the "Scottites" as the followers of Scott were sometimes known.

While these three independent groups were propagating their respective views, two religious journals were tending to unite them. The *Christian Baptist* (Buffalo Creek, Pennsylvania, 1823-1830), edited by Alexander Campbell, and the *Christian Messenger* (Georgetown, Kentucky, 1826-1845), edited by Stone, disseminated their respective doctrines throughout the Ohio valley. Many readers, both ministers and members, discerned an amazing similarity of views expressed by the two editors. Ensuing discussions between adherents of the three groups usually terminated in union upon common ground. The most influential voice for union was Alexander Campbell. In 1830, he changed the name of the *Christian Baptist* to the *Millennial Harbinger* (1830-1870) and dedicated it to the cause of union and the new teaching fundamental to the Christian Churches (preferred by Stone), the Disciples of Christ (favored by Campbell), and the churches of Christ (often used by Scott). Before the end of the decade, the three had completed their union. All followers of Jesus Christ were urged to restore the first century order of Christianity. From the time of union, the names "churches of Christ" and "Christian Churches" were used interchangeably until the first decade of the twentieth century when a schism led to a technical division under the two names. It is with the history of the group which eventually adopted the term "churches of Christ" exclusively that this study deals.

The organization of churches of Christ is limited to the congregational level. Each church is supervised by a group of elders (bishops or pastors) approved by the congregation in accordance with qualifications stipulated in the New Testament. Other men may serve as deacons (servants) provided they meet the prerequisites outlined in the Bible. The minister (evangelist or preacher) is selected by the elders in harmony with Biblical principles. Although a nominal bond of fellowship exists among the congregations, each remains entirely autonomous.

The history of this church is difficult to uncover because no central agency of authority exists superior to the local congregation. There are no national, state, or local conventions or synods composed of church delegates to formulate doctrine or church policy. Therefore, the data for the history of the churches of Christ must be gathered from many sources. The most valuable information was found in the numerous religious periodicals published by members of the churches of Christ during the last century and a quarter. Additional information was obtained from newspapers, state, county, and city histories, historical journals, government records, personal interviews and letters, and some few extant church records. Only in recent years, primarily since World War II, have congregations begun to keep systematic accounts of all church activities. No full scale history of churches of Christ in Texas exists.

The state of Texas contains more congregations and members of the churches of Christ than any other state in the nation. The more than 2,600 local churches and an estimated 450,000 members comprise about 35 per cent of the total membership in the United States. A history of this body is of value to all, especially to the church itself which has little knowledge of its past. This study attempts to trace the history of the church in Texas from the time its first followers arrived in the Spanish colony, through the formative years in the republic era, its progress and expansion in the last half of the nineteenth century, its problems and schisms that formally split it at the turn of the century, and its maturity into a major religious body in the twentieth century.

CHAPTER I

EARLY BEGINNINGS, 1819-1836

Religious Conditions and Activities

The church of Christ did not make its first organized appearance in Texas until the outbreak of the Revolution. A few of its members, however, were among the Anglo-Americans who had settled in Texas before that date. Spanish and Mexican policies had discouraged Protestants from coming. Spain did not permit Anglo-Americans to settle in Texas until 1820, and before the first group arrived, Mexico had securely established its independence. Mexican law, like Spanish law, specifically required all immigrants to embrace Roman Catholicism. When the first Anglo-Americans arrived, therefore, the Roman Catholic church was the only religious group in Texas.

Spain had used the presidio and the Catholic mission to control the sparsely inhabited land. The presidio, manned by a small detachment of soldiers, symbolized the extent of Spanish authority. Paralleling the military was the mission, outpost of religion, the method employed by Spain to Christianize and control the Indians. Despite its isolation, the marauding Indians, and the proximity of the French in Louisiana, the Spanish by means of this colonial system had maintained jurisdiction over their Texas domain for more than a century. Americans began entering Spanish Texas illegally about 1800. Some were motivated by the westward movement of the American populace;

others by the weakness of Spain and the indefinite boundary provided in the Louisiana Purchase Treaty of 1803. The boundary problem was not resolved until the Adams-De Onis Treaty was ratified in 1821 when Spain, in her final stage of collapse, furnished new incentive for Anglo-American infiltration by adopting a liberal colonization policy. Before the end of the year, Mexico, including Texas, had achieved independence. Very few of the filibusters, if any, were members of the church of Christ.

The new Mexican nation, influenced by the Spanish liberal immigration policy, proceeded to enact its own colonization law of 1824 which was supplemented by the Coahuila-Texas law of 1825.[1] Attracted largely by cheap land on easy terms allowed under these laws, great numbers of Americans entered Texas. By 1835, approximately thirty thousand had possessed the land west of the Sabine River, and Texas resembled other American frontier states, except for the formalities of government and religious institutions.[2] The most prominent figure during this period of immigration was Stephen F. Austin. He had advertised widely in the United States the advantages to be obtained in Texas. Despite cultural barriers and political instability, Austin did much to insure continued immigration until the revolution. Since the Anglo-Americans had an entirely different environmental background from the Mexicans, it was only a matter of time until the resulting conflict erupted in violence and war. One of the important cultural conflicts was over religion.

Although the Mexicans encouraged immigration,

---

[1] Eugene C. Barker, *Mexico and Texas in 1821-1835* (Dallas, 1928), p. 10.
[2] *Ibid.*, p. 21.

EARLY BEGINNINGS, 1819-1836   3

they invoked certain restrictions, some totally foreign to American thinking. Significant was the provision in the colonization laws that only the Roman Catholic religion could be practiced. Since there were usually no Mexican officials present to enforce the requirement, most Anglo-Americans in Texas, nevertheless, continued to exercise privately their religious convictions. The democratic frontiersman refused to conform to a ritualistic religion which he both feared and detested. Only a few instances of open violation occurred. As a result of the proscription, Texans made material welfare their primary concern and showed very little interest in formal religion. As early as 1827, Sumner Bacon, a Presbyterian minister, came to Texas to distribute Bibles and tracts among American families. He found that only about one in nine families of the six hundred American and three hundred Spanish in the vicinity of Nacogdoches possessed Bibles. The percentage was much less in the interior, according to his report in 1834 after some seven years of activity.[3]

Nevertheless, a number of Protestant ministers proclaimed their beliefs publicly. William and Henry Stevenson came from the Missouri Methodist Conference in 1818-19 to Sulphur Fork near Clarksville, supposing they were still within the United States. Their preaching brought no evident reaction from Spanish authorities.[4] Joseph Bays, representing the Baptists, arrived at Camp Sabine June 30, 1820. While awaiting news from Stephen F. Austin, he went across the

---
[3]W. S. Red, *A History of the Presbyterian Church in Texas* (privately published, 1936), p. 2. Hereafter cited as Red, *Presbyterian Church in Texas*.
[4]Homer S. Thrall, *History of Methodism in Texas* (Houston, 1872), p. 1. Hereafter cited as Thrall, *Methodism in Texas*.

river and preached in the home of Joseph Hinds until Spanish authorities at San Augustine, about twenty miles away, compelled him to cease.[5] While preaching in the home of a Mr. Stafford near San Augustine in 1824, Henry Stevenson was stopped by the alcalde, Gomez Gaines. Nevertheless, he resumed preaching two days later nearby in a Mr. Thomas' home on Atoyac Creek.[6] The general effects of this prohibition were described by W. B. Dewees, son of a Baptist evangelist, who came to Texas in 1822. Dewees, in a letter to a friend in Kentucky in 1831, lamented the absence of divine worship and the desecration of the Lord's day by stock driving and breaking of mustangs. He claimed that he had heard no preaching since attending a camp meeting in Arkansas some nine years previously.[7]

Other efforts to conduct Protestant services were more successful. Daniel Parker, a Baptist minister, who visited Texas in 1832, concluded that the law did not forbid the immigration of a church. He returned to Illinois, organized a seven member congregation in 1833, and then migrated to Austin's colony the following year. About the same time, T. J. Pilgrim organized a Sunday School with thirty-two pupils at San Felipe de Austin.[8]

EARLY MEMBERS OF THE CHURCH OF CHRIST

Although not a preacher, Collin McKinney was the first known member of the church of Christ to arrive in Texas. Born in New Jersey, April 17, 1776, Mc-

---
[5]J. M. Carroll, *A History of Texas Baptists* (Dallas, 1923), pp. 19-20. Hereafter cited as Carroll, *Texas Baptists*.
[6]Thrall, *Methodism in Texas*, p. 18.
[7]Carroll, *Texas Baptists*, p. 17.
[8]*Ibid.*, p. 46.

EARLY BEGINNINGS, 1819-1836

Kinney came from a family outspoken in its desire for freedom. His father Daniel was one of the fearless men who participated in the Boston Tea Party. In 1780, the McKinneys moved to Virginia, then to a place near Crab Orchard, called "McKinney's Station," on the dangerous Kentucky frontier. Collin's numerous skirmishes with the Indians made him a seasoned frontiersman by the time he arrived in Texas. From 1818 to 1821 he was in charge of the vast estate of George W. Campbell, who resigned his Senate seat from Tennessee to become ambassador to Russia. He then moved to Elkton, Kentucky, where he renounced his Baptist faith and embraced the church of Christ under the teaching of Barton W. Stone.[9]

Described as a typical frontiersman—one hundred sixty-five pounds, six feet tall, full chest, possessing well developed muscles and small keen eyes—McKinney with his family arrived on September 15, 1824, near the present town of Texarkana.[10] Since the boundary lines had not been surveyed at the time, the residents of northeast Texas were uncertain as to whether they resided in Texas or Arkansas. McKinney was among those who settled in the questionable zone, according to John Henry Brown who wrote that "among the early and most worthy settlers at the extreme northeast corner of Texas on Red River, sometimes in Arkansas, line being unsurveyed, was Collin McKinney who reached there in 1824."[11] McKinney had intended to settle in Texas in Arthur G. Wavel's colony, his

---

[9] Jewell Matthews, "Historical Sketches of the Early Church in Texas," *Christian Courier*, XLVIII (April, 1936), pp. 1-2. Hereafter cited as Matthews, "Historical Sketches."
[10] John H. Brown, *History of Texas 1685-1892* (St. Louis, 1892), I, p. 14. Hereafter cited as Brown, *History of Texas*.
[11] *Ibid.*

son William E. McKinney claimed in 1874 in a letter to Colonel John Henry Brown:

> Collin Co., April 26, 1874
>
> Dear Sir:
>
> In the year 1826, Col. Benjamin P. Milam came to my fathers home on the South Side of Red River. Accompanied by E. S. Williams, John Martin and Jefferson Milam (Who was to be his surveyor). Said he and Arthur Wavel, an Englishman, had secured from Mexico right to colonize one section of country extending from Red River to Bois-d-Arc Fork. I was then 13 and saw much of Milam and heard many incidents of him.[12]

McKinney resided in the area until 1831 when he moved to Hickman's Prairie (McKinney's Landing), about fifteen miles west of Texarkana, where he lived until 1846. He was elected to serve in the provisional government of Texas in 1835 and was the oldest member present when the Consultation convened. In the convention which assembled on March 1, 1836, McKinney was a member of the committee that drafted the Declaration of Independence, and was an active participant in framing the Constitution prepared by that convention. During the Republic, he represented Red River County in four sessions of Congress, in which capacity he was instrumental in having the North Texas counties formed into thirty mile squares.[13] Although active in politics, McKinney did not altogether neglect his religious welfare. Prior to the revolution, he periodically encouraged his family and scattered neighbors to worship in his home, but made no effort to establish a church in defiance of Mexican

---

[12]*Ibid.*, p. 147.
[13]Matthews, "Historical Sketches," XLVIII (August, 1936), p. 1.

EARLY BEGINNINGS, 1819-1836

law. After the revolution, little is known of his religious activities until 1841.[14]

Another member of the church of Christ who came to Texas before the revolution was Jose Maria Carvajal. Although Carvajal was of royal lineage and a direct descendant of Geronimo Carvajal, an early settler at San Antonio who died in 1748, his date and place of birth are unknown. In 1823, he went to Lexington, Kentucky, to work as a tanner for two years. Later, he attended school at Bethany, Virginia, where he received instruction from Alexander Campbell. While there, he renounced Catholicism and was immersed by Campbell. Shortly thereafter, he wrote Austin for assistance in selling Spanish language Bibles in Texas. In addition, Carvajal asked for a map of Texas since many families of Virginia were interested in joining Austin's colony.[15]

When Carvajal came to Texas in 1830, he evidently lost his initial religious fervor. Seemingly, he made no attempt to sell Bibles, but through Austin's help, became the official surveyor for Martin De Leon, one of the early empresarios of Texas, and laid out the town of Victoria. Subsequently, he married Refugio. De Leon's daughter, and became one of the "41" land owners and settlers of De Leon's colony. During the Republic, Carvajal made a radical change in his thinking which profoundly affected the remainder of his life. He planned to lead military ventures primarily from Mexico against Texas, apparently for self gain. From 1851 to 1855 he led several unsuccessful expeditions along the Rio Grande, and in 1861-1862 fought

---
[14]*Ibid.*
[15]Ernest C. Shearer, "The Carvajal Disturbances," *The Southwestern Historical Quarterly*, LV (October, 1951), p. 201.

against the French in Mexico.[16] He died in 1874 without having served the church of Christ in any profitable way.

The first evangelist of the church of Christ to arrive in Texas was probably William P. Defee, a physician by profession. Defee was born about 1798 in North Carolina of Huguenot ancestry. As a youth, he served under Andrew Jackson in the Battle of New Orleans and after the war went to Tennessee where he entered medical school. He arrived in East Texas in 1833, settled in the De Zavala colony, and became a successful practicing physician. Defee, a former Baptist, embraced the church of Christ before coming to Texas. Little is known of his religious activities in the pre-revolutionary days other than a report which appeared in the *Christian Messenger* in 1833. Defee wrote from the region of Sabine, San Augustine and Shelby counties, "I have started a society on the Christian doctrine."[17] Apparently he assembled a group for religious instruction but did not organize a formal church of Christ. During the Republic, he preached throughout East Texas as indicated by reports he submitted to religious journals circulated among churches of Christ.

THE FIRST CONGREGATION

Mansil W. Matthews, a physician, teacher, and preacher, evidently established the first church of Christ in Texas. Matthews, just prior to the outbreak of the Revolution, recruited a band of adventurers from his home community in northern Alabama to accompany him to the "promised land." The group,

---
[16]*Ibid.*, p. 202.
[17]Winfred Ernest Garrison and Alfred T. DeGroot, *The Disciples of Christ, A History* (St. Louis, 1948), p. 318. Hereafter cited as Garrison and DeGroot, *Disciples of Christ*.

most of whom were members of the church of Christ, set out in the fall of 1835 overland by wagon and horseback. David Crockett, already nationally prominent as a political opponent of Jackson and who was to gain even greater fame in death at the Alamo a few months later, accompanied the party as far as Memphis. Since the group stopped each Sunday to rest and conduct worship services, it became known as the "church on horseback and wheels."[18] After crossing the Mississippi, Crockett with some sixty volunteers, impatient at the delays, rode ahead, leaving a "Hurrah for Texas" resounding in the ears of the campers.

On the first Sunday after their arrival at Ft. Clark (Clarksville), Texas, on January 17, 1836, Matthews and his comrades met for divine worship and constituted what is believed to be the first congregation of the church of Christ in Texas. Since all Mexican soldiers and officials had been withdrawn from Northeast Texas with the outbreak of the Revolution, the members of the newly organized church could worship without molestation although no religion other than Roman Catholicism was sanctioned by Mexican law.[19] Matthews and most of the men of his party hurried away to join Houston's army, leaving Lynn D'Spain, another minister among the immigrant group, in charge of church affairs. The congregation assembled for worship during the remainder of the winter in a long, low, rambling log building which was the main part of Ft. Clark. As soon as spring weather permitted, it gathered for services under a brush arbor.[20] Matthews reached the army in time to serve with dis-

---
[18]Matthews, "Historical Sketches," XLVIII (April, 1936), pp. 1-2.
[19]*Ibid.*
[20]*Ibid.*, XLVIII (May, 1936), p. 4.

tinction as a surgeon. After the war, he several times represented with eminence Red River County in the Texas congress.[21]

Only a few dozen members of the churches of Christ were among the energetic, enterprising Anglo-American frontiersmen who by revolution had wrested a vast and potentially wealthy country from hands that so long had held it dormant, and opened the gates to the tidal wave of their western moving kinsmen. However, many adherents from Tennessee, a stronghold of the followers of Campbell and Stone, soon migrated to the infant Republic. This influx of disciples insured the rapid growth of the churches of Christ so that they became a prominent religious body in Texas within a decade.

---
[21]*Ibid.*

CHAPTER II

THE CHURCH DURING THE REPUBLIC ERA, 1836-1845

Several weeks prior to their military triumph over Santa Anna at San Jacinto, the Texans had taken steps to establish a new form of government. The convention, meeting at Washington on the Brazos on March 1, 1836, adopted on the next day a Declaration of Independence, and fifteen days later it had drafted a Constitution for the Republic of Texas. Since many of the delegates had served in some public capacity in the United States before coming to Texas, they logically incorporated into the new document provisions from the United States federal and state constitutions. Among these was the guarantee of religious freedom. The article in the United States Constitution reads: "Congress shall make no law respecting an establishment of religion, or prohibiting the free exercise thereof; . . ." The wording in the Texas Constitution was changed only slightly: "No preference shall be given by law to any religious denomination or mode of worship over another, but every person shall be permitted to worship God according to the dictates of his own conscience."[1]

RELIGION IN THE REPUBLIC

The successful conclusion of the Revolution and the establishment of a liberal democratic form of govern-

---
[1] *Constitution of the United States of America*, Amendment I; *Constitution of the Republic of Texas*, Article I, Section VI.

ment provided increased inducements for Americans to migrate to Texas. Newspapers and journals portrayed the advantages of settling in the new Anglo-American republic—almost unlimited cheap lands, fortunes could be made virtually overnight, and adventure for the thrill seekers. Some religious journals, however, printed derogatory remarks about Texas and its people. Hasty conclusions derived from unreliable sources led some editors to label Texans as heathens, infidels and renegades. With typical Texas pride, the *Telegraph and Texas Register* denounced the misinformation. With clarity and candor it reminded its readers that Texans were what "Yankees" call Americans, and what other Americans and Europeans term Yankees, similar in language, manners, and customs to the citizens of all the frontier states. If Texans were more enterprising and adventurous than their kindred in the United States, it was because of the peculiar environment in which they were placed.[2] The editor blamed the Mexicans for the destitute spiritual condition in Texas but insisted that the situation was being rectified rapidly by the influx of Protestant settlers. This erroneous idea of Texas being a country inhabited by heathens persisted for several years. Reliable information substantiated by reports from growing churches finally convinced a skeptical public otherwise. But as late as 1846, Tolbert Fanning, editor of the *Christian Review*, a journal circulated primarily among churches of Christ in Tennessee, mistakenly dismissed Texas with a few words. "I should like to visit the brethren in Texas; but my opinion is, the climate is not favorable for the Chris-

---

[2]*Telegraph and Texas Register* (Houston), May 16, 1837.

tian religion."³ Little did he imagine that within a century there would be more members of the church of Christ within its borders than in any other state. Nevertheless, American colonists poured into Texas, and among these hardy pioneers were many Protestant ministers.

Methodists, Baptists and Presbyterians were the most numerous of the denominations represented. Soon after independence had been secured, the Methodist circuit riders arrived to serve their adherents and expound the gospel to all who would listen. In April, 1837, the missionary board of the Methodist Church in New York decided to send hardworking, consecrated Littleton Fowler and Robert Alexander to the infant republic. The following year, the Methodists erected church buildings at Washington, McMahon's settlement, and at San Augustine.⁴ A quarterly conference, organized in a meeting held near Clarksville, appointed John Denton and E. B. Duncan to the Sulphur Fork circuit.⁵ By 1845, one hundred Methodist ministers served about three thousand members.⁶ In 1837, the aggressive American Baptist Home Mission Society sent James Huckins, a successful agent in South Carolina and Georgia, to meet the call of Texas.⁷ By the end of the Republic, eighteen churches with a combined membership of about one thousand had been organized.⁸ Peter Fullinwider, who was the first Presbyterian preacher in Texas, began his

---
³Tolbert Fanning, "Communications from Texas," *Christian Review*, III (August, 1846), p. 191.
⁴Thrall, *Methodism in Texas*, pp. 42-43.
⁵*Ibid.*, pp. 51-52.
⁶*Ibid.*, p. 149.
⁷William Wright Barnes, *The Southern Baptist Convention*, 1845-1953 (Nashville, 1954), p. 15.
⁸Carroll, *Texas Baptists*, p. 174.

work in Austin's colony in 1834. The first Presbyterian church edifice was erected in San Augustine and dedicated June 2, 1838.[9] By 1845, three small presbyteries had been established with about seven hundred communicants.[10]

PREACHERS AND CHURCHES

At the beginning of the Republic, the church of Christ had only a few evangelists and advocates to propound its beliefs. Most of them preached only occasionally, as they were usually engaged in secular work such as teaching, farming, or business. As a result, only a few congregations were founded with any degree of permanence.

Lynn D'Spain, who had arrived with the "church on wheels" at Clarksville in 1836, ministered to the group for a short time. In addition, he conducted a school for settlers' children with the Bible as one of the textbooks. After most of the congregation had moved to other localities, D'Spain went to Nacogdoches County and established a church in the vicinity. Little is known of his later activities.[11]

Farther up the Red River Valley in Fannin County, O. I. Jackson established a church of Christ in 1840. Jackson, who was a member of the church of Christ near Kansas City, Missouri, arrived with his family in 1845 and homesteaded a few miles south of Bonham. Here on what was known as Jackson Creek, he erected a small log school house and conducted worship services in it on Sunday. The congregation, composed primarily of relatives, met regularly until 1885, when

---
[9] Red, *Presbyterian Church in Texas*, p. 3.
[10] *Ibid.*, p. 133.
[11] Matthews, "Historical Sketches," XLVIII (May, 1936), p. 4.

it moved to the newly organized town of Gober. O. I. Jackson, a grandson named in honor of his pioneer ancestor, related to his son Hulen L. Jackson how as a boy he sat on "split log pews" during worship services conducted in the log school house in 1885. This congregation has continued to assemble regularly for divine worship to the present and stands as a monument to "New Testament worship and work."[12]

In extreme east central Texas, William Defee, itinerant physician and preacher, organized a church in 1836 about four miles from San Augustine in the home of Rhoddy Anthony. Designated "Antioch" because the "disciples were first called Christians in Antioch" (Acts 11:26), this church selected Anthony to serve as an elder, in which capacity he labored about fifty years. The congregation met in a log building on his property until about 1870 when a new structure was erected. The new building was used for church services for the next seventy-five years.[13] Dr. J. W. O'Banion, former Assistant Superintendent of Education in Dallas, was born in the Antioch community in 1875. He remembers the aged Anthony as a small man with snow white hair, long beard, and stooped. Each Sunday, Anthony came to the building with a basket containing the communion ware on one arm, Mrs. Anthony on the other. After arranging the communion table properly, he sat down in his pew to await the beginning of the service.[14] Although Dr. Defee practiced medicine in the vicinity of San Augustine, he did not neglect to preach whenever and wher-

---

[12]Jackson, Hulen L. (Dallas), letter to Stephen Eckstein September 15, 1957. (Jackson serves now as minister to the Trinity Heights Church of Christ in Dallas.)
[13]Colby D. Hall, *Texas Disciples* (Fort Worth, 1953), pp. 46-47. Hereafter cited as Hall, *Texas Disciples*.
[14]*Ibid.*

ever possible. He established some churches during the republic era, but no record is available concerning them.[15]

In extreme northeast Texas, George Gates from Indiana arrived at McKinney's landing in December, 1841, in company with a band of immigrants from Louisville, Kentucky. Finding the area where Collin McKinney resided virtually destitute of organized worship, Gates immediately conducted a seven day revival, baptized nine, and established a church with sixteen charter members. McKinney and his son William were entrusted with the spiritual oversight of the new flock.[16] This church remained active until 1845 when the McKinney "clan" moved to Van Alstyne north of Dallas.

Although he owned a considerable number of slaves, all of whom professed the Methodist faith, McKinney apparently neglected to give them religious instruction. Gates had observed on his visit that these slaves loved their master "as they would a father."[17] With such piety and devotion openly manifest, it seems evident that had McKinney endeavored to convert his slaves to the church of Christ, he would have succeeded in some measure.

During the Republic, some of the most fruitful work was wrought in Bowie, Red River and Lamar counties in northeast Texas. Mansil W. Matthews, who had brought the "church on wheels" to Clarksville, returned after the war and remained in the vicinity until 1844 when he moved to Rockwall. After organizing

---
[15]George Gates, "News from the Churches," *Millennial Harbinger* (May 1842), p. 238.
[16]*Ibid.*
[17]*Ibid.*

a church of Christ in his new home, he served as its minister and began cooperative labor with evangelists E. B. Moore and Green Weaver.[18] Testifying to the partial success of their efforts was Abner Hill, a preacher from Jackson, Mississippi, who visited Texas for several months in 1844. Arriving in April, Hill contacted numerous churches throughout the area in various stages of organization. Shortly thereafter, Hill and John McCluskey joined Matthews, Moore and Weaver to form an "evangelistic team." Throughout the summer they conducted protracted revivals all along the Red River valley. Inactive churches were activated and new congregations were established. Former members were restored and new members inducted into the church by baptism. Numerically, the greatest success was achieved at Daingerfield where fifty-seven were immersed in a five-day revival, and seven additional members received on the following Sunday. Hill jubilantly declared: "I have never in any country seen the gospel wield an influence so universal as it does in this part of Texas."[19]

In south central Texas, the first church of Christ was established near La Grange about 1840 by Colonel John H. Moore, a famous Indian fighter. Moore, who founded the town of La Grange in 1831, settled on a plantation several miles north of town. His talent as an orator, story-teller and comedian did not detract from his profound interest in religion. Moore supervised the erection of a church building on his plantation and organized a church of Christ in which he

---
[18]Matthews, "Historical Sketches," XLVIII (June, 1936), pp. 1-5.
[19]Abner Hill, "News from Texas," *Christian Review*, I (November, 1844), p. 263. Hereafter cited as Hill, "News from Texas."

served as an elder. With Calvinistic decorum, Moore directed his little flock. He took his place on the rostrum by the side of the preacher in order to watch the audience with a judicious eye. Even though he demanded strict attention on the part of the assembly, the church grew. Pioneer families included the Moores, Hunts, Philips, Perjans, Killens, and Ligons. Baptisms were performed in the beautiful Rocky Creek nearby.[20]

In the spring of 1841, John Stamps arrived in Washington County, termed by Carroll, a Baptist historian, as the "cradle of Texas Baptists, Methodists and Presbyterians," for the purpose of establishing the church of Christ. On April 24, twelve brethren assembled in his home in Gay Hill. Six or eight others manifested a desire to unite with the group by "faith, repentance and baptism as soon as they are fully organized."[21] Stamps found the community to be receptive to the simple gospel. He and a Dr. Clow, reportedly a fine scholar and zealous disciple, alternated in teaching from the pulpit. Stamps, however, felt the urgent need of a more competent expounder of the gospel. In an appeal for assistance, he prophesied that "had we a talented speaker of the right spirit, I am confident that sectarianism could be nipt in the bud. There is a kind of manly independence among them here (all denominations) that you do not see in the United States."[22]

In the same area, the church of Christ was strengthened by the defection of a free-thinking Baptist

---

[20] Leonie Rummel Weyand and Houston Wade, *Early History of Fayette County* (LaGrange, Texas, 1936), p. 221.
[21] John Stamps, "News from the Churches", *Millennial Harbinger* (August, 1841), p. 381.
[22] *Ibid.*

preacher to its ranks. T. W. Cox came to Texas from Alabama in 1838 and became pastor of the Baptist Church in Independence the following year. Early in 1841, a deacon baptized candidate L. P. Rucker in the absence of the pastor, evidently with Cox's approval. Shortly afterward, W. M. Tyron, missionary of the Home Mission Society of New York, conducted a conference in the church. During the proceedings, a motion was made to declare Rucker's baptism null and void. After a heated discussion, the motion carried. Despite this setback, the majority of the congregation remained loyal to Cox, and he continued to fill the pulpit of the church until the Baptist association met that autumn at Clear Creek and after prolonged debate excluded him on the grounds of "Campbellism."[23]

Immediately afterward, Cox wrote a letter to evangelist Joel Ponton of the church of Christ concerning his recent excommunication. Without bitterness or dismay, Cox expressed his determination to "continue to receive applicants for baptism on a declaration of their faith." He asserted furthermore that "our desire is to restore the ancient order of things in the church as nearly as we can according to the New Testament." Since he wielded considerable influence among the Baptists, Cox apparently persuaded several Baptist churches to become churches of Christ as suggested by his report in 1842 that "there are now four churches resolved as above."[24] However, his initial

---

[23] Carroll, *Texas Baptists*, pp. 134-135. The Baptists contended no candidate could be baptized prior to his relation of a supernatural experience of conversion satisfactory to the pastor and the church. Campbellism, as defined by the Baptists, was the teaching that any candidate could be baptized after a simple statement of faith in Jesus Christ.

[24] Joel Ponton, "News from the Churches," *Millennial Harbinger* (June, 1842), pp. 275-276. Hereafter cited as Ponton, "News from the Churches."

zeal evidently waned as E. H. East reported in 1846 that Cox practiced law in Rutersville and did not preach except in his own neighborhood. L. P. Rucker, the convert about whom the controversy had arisen, taught school, preached for the congregation in Brenham twice a month and elsewhere the other two Sundays, and continued to evidence his religious ardor.[25]

Two other churches of Christ were established to the south along the Gulf Coast during the Republic. In a small settlement on the Rio Navidad, Joel Ponton organized a congregation of eight members on the last Sunday in October, 1841. In the ensuing two months, only one person was converted, but Ponton fervently vowed to obey Christ as much as had the Christians of the first century.[26] About a hundred miles to the southwest, a congregation of one hundred members assembled regularly at San Patricio on the Nueces River, approximately twenty-five miles northwest of Corpus Christi. Unfortunately, no information about its origin, growth, or leaders is available.[27]

WEAKNESSES AND NEEDS

Notwithstanding the development of the churches of Christ, other factors retarded its growth. Many of its difficulties were common with those in all churches on the American frontier. The relatively unstable and incomplete political attachment of Texas to the United States, poor communication, and the non-permanent population posed formidable obstacles to organized religion. A serious impediment was the state of tension which existed between Texas and Mexico. To over-

---

[25] E. H. East, "News," *Christian Review* (August, 1846), p. 191. Hereafter cited as East, "News."
[26] Ponton, "News from the Churches," pp. 275-276.
[27] Garrison and DeGroot, *Disciples of Christ*, p. 319.

come this hindrance, evangelist Ponton, in 1842, pleaded for a treaty to be effected between the two nations in order to attract many "respectable citizens from the United States."[28] Evidently he failed to see that annexation to the United States would be a greater incentive, and that the churches of Christ, because of their locally autonomous congregational arrangement, would be particularly benefited.

One of the most urgent needs was for numerous, competent preachers to set in order strong, stable, self-supporting churches. The dearth of preachers in all denominations is evidenced by several reports submitted during the Republic era. Daniel Baker, a renowned Presbyterian minister, reported after traveling in Texas for four months in 1840 that he had found only four Presbyterian pastors. With candor, he challenged, "O shame, where is thy blush? O love for souls, whither art thou fled?"[29] In the same year, James Burke listed less than forty clergymen of all denominations wholly given to the ministry, half being Methodists.[30] Homer Thrall, a Methodist historian, cited forty-four local Methodist preachers, only twenty-five of whom devoted full time in ministering to the seventeen hundred Methodists in Texas in 1840.[31] At the same time, churches of Christ had only about a dozen evangelists and teachers, most of whom served on a part time basis. They labored at a greater disadvantage than those of the denominations since they had no recourse to a national organization. No missionary society existed to dispatch missionaries; no central agency such as a synod, convention or

---

[28]Ponton, "News from the Churches," pp. 275-276.
[29]Red, *Presbyterian Church in Texas*, pp. 55-56.
[30]*Ibid.*
[31]Thrall, *Methodism in Texas*, p. 149.

hierarchy disseminated information concerning the needs of the Texas churches to their brethren in the United States. Therefore, each congregation relied upon the infrequent letters from relatives in Texas, bits of news from itinerant evangelists recently in Texas, or scattered reports which appeared occasionally in the few religious journals published by brethren.

Another factor retarding development was the spiritual lethargy which prevailed among the churches and scattered members. Abner Hill frankly suggested, "The churches in Texas need the gospel government and discipline exercised among them in order to their permanency and growth."[32] In 1845, Robert Walker of Huntsville, a recent immigrant from Tennessee, sought to rectify this glaring spiritual deficiency by dramatically appealing for "nineteenth century Pauls."

> There are but few disciples in this country, and there are no evangelists in this county (Montgomery); there is no church, and I firmly believe, never will be until we are succored by the brethren of the U. S. Brethren, help, help us, or many, I fear, will perish! Imagine our situation, bring your Christian means to bear on our deplorable situation! We are here scattered, like lost sheep, tossed to and fro by melancholy breezes, and are susceptible to many sensual impulses; and I sincerely believe it will awaken an insatiate suscutation of charity, which will never satiate till competent and efficient evangelists are sent across the Sabine to itinerate over the land of Texas, and proclaim the blessed gospel of our Lord Jesus Christ, to hospitable, though unconverted people.[33]

---

[32] Hill, "News from Texas," p. 263.
[33] Robert T. Walker, "A Call from Texas," *Christian Review* (August, 1845), p. 191.

Not completely discouraged by existing circumstances, Walker did his best in speaking frequently to large and respectable audiences. However, he asked Tolbert Fanning, editor of the *Christian Review*, to comment upon his preaching publicly without "legal authority." He need not have questioned his "legal authority" because churches of Christ make no distinction between clergy and laity. Any Christian man may preach publicly and as such is considered ordained by God.

Another deterrent to church progress was the failure of religious periodicals published by members of the churches of Christ to circulate among the Texas churches. The *Millennial Harbinger* (1830-1870), printed in Bethany, Virginia, by Alexander Campbell, began to publish news reports from Texas preachers after 1840, but the only copies seemingly in the Republic were those brought in by settlers. No Texan appears in the list of subscribers contained in the March, 1843, issue. Nearly all were from Virginia and surounding states.[34] The *Christian Review* (1844-1847), published in Nashville by Tolbert Fanning, carried a few accounts of Tennessee preachers who had recently gone to Texas. However, it was virtually unknown in Texas according to Abner Hill, who arrived in the Republic in April, 1844. He later wrote that he did not see a copy of the *Review* until he returned to Mississippi in September. Furthermore, he failed to obtain subscribers because of the uncertainty of the mail service, the scarcity of money in Texas, and the necessity of paying the subscription price in advance.[35] People also refused to subscribe because of

---
[34]"Subscription List," *Millennial Harbinger* (March, 1843), pp. 137-139.
[35]Hill, "News from Texas," p. 263.

The Church at the End of the Republic

the possibility that they might move to another home before their mail arrived from the United States.

Despite the difficulties encountered in the early years, the churches of Christ in Texas were in a relatively good position to enjoy considerable growth in the coming years. In May, 1845, David R. Stout of Live Oak Well, Fayette County, summarized the status of the churches throughout the Republic. A small congregation met at Brenham in Washington County with Samuel B. Giles and Lindsay Rucker as teachers; T. W. Cox taught a group meeting at Clear Creek, Fayette County; Joel Ponton ministered to the disciples in Gonzales and Colorado counties. In addition, churches were in working order in Montgomery, Nacogdoches, San Augustine, Jasper, Fannin, and Red River counties. Evangelists who were laboring in the field included William Stirman, Father Hill, Ephriam Deboore, J. A. Clark, Robert Walker, and a Brother Eldridge who had immersed seventy or eighty in the summer of 1844. Stout asserted that although few in number, "the members possess zeal, and are respectable in point of Christian knowledge, and are walking in love and harmony, and bearing a good testimony for the one faith."[36] Evangelist E. H. East said, "It affords me pleasure to be able to say, there are a few even in Texas, who reject all human creeds, and take the New Testament alone for their rule of faith and practice."[37]

At the close of the Republic period, churches of Christ had been firmly planted in Texas. About

---
[36] David R. Stout, "News Report from Texas," *Millennial Harbinger* (September, 1845), p. 247.
[37] East, "News," p. 191.

twenty-five churches were established in sixteen counties. Approximately twenty-five evangelists, teachers, and exhorters (seventeen—half of whom were working full time—appeared in news reports) ministered to the scattered churches. Fifteen churches reported a combined membership of 470; 160 conversions were listed in religious papers during the period 1836-1845. Allowing for the ten unreported churches, those unknown, and isolated members worshiping with other groups such as the Baptists, the total number of disciples probably approached one thousand. Thus, churches of Christ were the fifth ranking religious body in Texas, outnumbered only by the Roman Catholics, Baptists, Presbyterians, and Methodists.

Nationally, churches of Christ in Texas were in a favorable position for considerable growth in the coming decades. In 1836, D. S. Burnet had estimated a membership of one hundred thousand, constituting the churches of Christ as the fourth largest religious body within the United States.[38] Robert Richardson's 1844 estimate of almost two hundred thousand seems excessively high; but nevertheless, it reflects an amazing growth for the decade.[39] Although the main strength of the church was concentrated in Kentucky, Tennessee, Ohio, Indiana, Illinois, and Missouri, more members resided in Texas than in Vermont, New Hampshire, Rhode Island, Connecticut, Massachusetts or New York. This clearly indicates that churches of Christ appealed to the open-minded, free-thinking people of the frontier rather than to the more traditionally minded inhabitants of the northeast. Since the

---

[38] D. S. Burnet, "Progress of the Present Reformation," *Christian Preacher* (January, 1836), p. 21.

[39] Robert Richardson, "Disciples of Christ, Christians, Reformers," *Millennial Harbinger* (April, 1845), p. 189.

settled portion of Texas was still a frontier and the major portion was yet unsettled, it is quite logical to expect churches of Christ to experience a relatively larger growth during the period of early statehood than would be true nationally.

CHAPTER III

CHURCH GROWTH IN THE EARLY STATEHOOD PERIOD, 1845-1861

December 29, 1845, was a memorable day in the history of both the United States and Texas. By a legislative act, the Republic of Texas was formally annexed to the American republic. Texas stretched some eight hundred miles from the heavily timbered lowlands of the Sabine River valley across the deep blacklands of Central Texas and the luxurious rolling plains of the western prairies halfway to the shores of the Pacific Ocean. The wandering Indians who roamed the sumptuous grassy western plains could not long withstand the energetic whites to the east who coveted free land and fortune. Immediately after annexation, many eager and visionary inhabitants of the states south of the Ohio River began making hasty preparation for the long and arduous but alluring trip to Texas. Within days, long lines of covered wagons wended their way westward. In the vanguard of these land-hungry pioneers were Tennesseans, more numerous than those from any other state. By 1860, more than fifty thousand had migrated to Texas. Other states with considerable representations were Alabama, Kentucky and Mississippi. Comparatively few came from states north of the Ohio River.

EARLY INFLUENCES

Churches of Christ undoubtedly benefited from this influx of settlers because of their large membership in

Kentucky and Tennessee. One authority estimates that Kentucky had 45,000 Disciples and Tennessee 12,000 prior to the Civil War.[1] This represents about 2.5 per cent of the combined populations of the two states in 1860. Although no figures are available relative to the number of church members who came to Texas, subsequent reports appearing in religious papers indicate approximately one thousand members of churches of Christ were among the more than seventy thousand immigrants who came from Tennessee and Kentucky before 1860. Using the 2.5 per cent average, about 1750 members of churches of Christ probably migrated to Texas. When allowance is made for several hundred immigrant members unaccounted for in reports in religious journals, the estimate is almost obtained.

During early statehood, the character of the churches of Christ was molded largely by its religious periodicals. While most denominations in the United States depended on their national organizations to evangelize the frontier, churches of Christ relied almost entirely upon the printed page to serve as a common agent to arouse the churches to evangelistic efforts. It was the one universal medium through which preachers could report church progress and solicit assistance. Because of the autonomous nature of the congregations, the religious journal was to churches of Christ what the printing press was to the Reformation.

The *Millennial Harbinger* (1830-1870), ably edited by Alexander Campbell, was the most influential journal circulated among churches of Christ during their formative years. A master penman with a brilliant mind, fortified with extensive knowledge of history,

---

[1]Garrison and DeGroot, *Disciples of Christ*, pp. 328-329.

languages and other pertinent fields, Campbell achieved a position of national prominence among the churches. Although printed in Bethany, Virginia, and read primarily in adjacent states, the *Harbinger* was most assuredly national in scope. Its column, "News from the Churches," contained dispatches of church work from evangelists in all parts of the nation.

The oldest, most prominent and widely distributed religious periodical among churches of Christ in the South is the *Gospel Advocate*. Begun in Nashville in 1855 by Tolbert Fanning, this paper has been published for over a hundred years with the exception of a short interim during the Civil War. Through Tennessee immigrants who located in Texas, the *Advocate* has in a great measure shaped the thinking and character of the churches of Christ in the Lone Star state. Its reception was favorable from the outset. "The brethren here are much pleased with the style and spirit of the Advocate," wrote A. M. Dean of Dallas in the fall of 1855.[2] In the same year, T. M. Sweeney of Bell County commented, "The *Gospel Advocate* is welcomed by all and I think will prove a very instructive companion."[3] Further substantiation came from W. B. Burditt of Austin and J. A. Clark of Madison County who supplemented their expressions of approval with promises to do all they could to extend its circulation. In 1857, J. B. Wilmeth of Pleasant Grove expressed "satisfaction and gratitude" for the good impression the *Advocate* was making upon its readers and for its discussion of important subjects.[4] Indica-

---
[2]A. M. Dean, "News and Notes," *Gospel Advocate*, I (October, 1855), p. 123.
[3]T. M. Sweeney, "News and Notes," *ibid.*, I (December, 1855), p. 190.
[4]J. B. Wilmeth, "Texas Department," *ibid.*, III (November, 1857), p. 360.

tive of its penetration even to the westernmost communities was the report in 1859 of J. J. Boyter of Carolina, Texas, who rejoiced that it was read in "far off Uvalde."

An important step was taken in 1856 to augment the appeal of the *Advocate* to Texas churches. Evangelist Carroll Kendrick of Salado, who evidently published the first religious journal for churches of Christ in Texas, suspended publication of the *Christian Philanthropist* in 1856, less than a year after its beginning. At once, editor Fanning suggested, "Since our list is quite large in that state, we have thought it proper for Kendrick to occupy a Texas Department in the paper."[5] This arrangement advertised the paper throughout the state and was reflected in increased subscriptions submitted by preachers. Thus, linked to Tennessee through numerous settlers and the *Advocate*, churches of Christ in Texas were confronted by a problem of the first magnitude, a shortage of ministers. Consequently, many congregations were without formal organization and often without any church services for weeks at a time. Some children grew into adults without having attended a formal religious service. With such conditions existing, it is not surprising that the moral fibre of the churches deteriorated. Many slowly wasted away; others mechanically performed church rituals. It was evident that more trained, dedicated preachers were needed to serve a rapidly increasing population, but incentive for their coming was slight indeed. Small churches, little or no remuneration, opposition from sects, poor living and traveling conditions comprised some of the dis-

---

[5]Tolbert Fanning, "News and Notes," *ibid.*, II (September, 1856), p. 286.

advantages of being a minister in Texas. Only those with a burning zeal for the cause of Christ were likely to surmount them.

PLEAS FOR PREACHERS

The dearth of preachers was emphasized by the incessant pleading letters from Texas residents. E. H. East deplored the scarcity of ministers in a report sent to the *Christian Review* in 1846. In 1848, Kendrick forwarded to the *Millennial Harbinger* an impassioned letter from Ann F. R. Williams, who lived near Houston. With a sad heart she urgently begged for volunteer missionaries:

> O! my dear brother, when I look around me upon the many precious souls that are in heathenish darkness, without the knowledge of the Christian religion, living as though there were no God, no Judge, no hereafter, but like the brutes that perish, my soul is melted within me, and I am constrained to say, O where are our missionaries? Where are these that preach the gospel of peace, and bring glad tidings of good things? And what are our brethren doing for the spreading of the gospel in this dark and benighted corner of our fair Republic? Should they not take this young and growing state into consideration immediately, and endeavor to supersede the sectarian denominations . . . Where are our Pauls, our Silases, our Barnabases? Have we none to obey the Macedonian call? I trust in the Lord we have and that the subject of "Mission to Texas" will so engage the feelings and attention of our able brethren, that they will not give "sleep to their eyes or slumber to their eyelids" until they have accomplished that great and good work. It would cause thousands to rejoice through time and eternity, raise on earth shouts of praise from the low prairies of the South to the northern border of our American possessions. . . Let them

send able and efficient proclaimers to the rapidly increasing cities of Galveston and Houston, that the gospel may grow with their growth and flourish with their strength. . .[6]

Equally urgent seemed the plea from William Defee in the same year from the vicinity of San Augustine. Eighty had been baptized into the church but were characterized as "sheep without a shepherd, gone astray. Oh! that the good Lord would send some faithful one to plead his cause! I am here alone . . ."[7]

With no national headquarters available to provide succor, J. B. Wilmeth in 1848 urged Alexander Campbell to send some "efficient young men" to the field. S. B. Giles and Lloyd Rucker offered to pay three hundred dollars to an evangelist who would labor a year in Washington and Austin counties. They requested Campbell to assist in procuring a man of "ability and zeal, indefatigable and fearless; one who is able to encounter and withstand strong opposition . . ." and would work for that modest amount.[8] In 1849, B. F. Hall, who visited North Texas on business, asked Campbell to encourage young men to go to Dallas, Collin, Red River and Hopkins counties to teach school and devote the rest of their time to preaching.[9] Evidently impressed by the opportunities in Texas, Dr. Hall returned in 1851 and settled in Grayson County. He immediately suggested that two missionaries evangelize the eastern part of the state, another two the western. He claimed that people flocked to hear the

---

[6] Ann F. R. Williams, "News from the Churches," *Millennial Harbinger* (August, 1847), p. 480.

[7] William Defee, "News from the Churches," *Millennial Harbinger* (August, 1847), p. 480.

[8] E. H. East, "A Call from Texas," *Christian Review* (October, 1847), pp. 357-358.

[9] B. F. Hall, "Things in Texas," *Millennial Harbinger* (February, 1850), pp. 103-104.

gospel in Texas. With typical Texas bigness, Hall sounded the clarion call for "men with big souls, touched with benevolence of the gospel, who are willing to imitate as far as possible, the self-sacrificing example of our adorable Lord; who are willing to forego the pleasures of earth, and battle for God and the souls of men—these are the preachers for Texas." To incite some young men to respond, Hall told of an eighteen year old lad who had to borrow a pony or else walk to meet his preaching appointments and received no monetary compensation for his efforts. When his pious mother could furnish him no longer with clothes, "he wore his old, worn out, patched home-spun clothes as long as he could and then worked for more! We want such young men now." Concluding with a ringing appeal, he challenged old and young alike, "Who are willing to fall fighting under the one starred banner of the Prairie state?"[10]

In 1850, John Stamps of Moulville compared the work of the churches of Christ to that of several denominations. He was acquainted with eight Baptist missionaries who possessed "respectable talents"; the Cumberland Presbyterians had sent in several men; the Methodist preacher was far in advance of the "Yankee Clock Peddler," but churches of Christ had only three ministers serving in the vast area west of the Brazos River.[11]

With commendable initiative, Stamps outlined a unique plan designed to saturate Texas with evangelists from the United States. He proposed that each

[10] B. F. Hall, "News," *Christian Magazine*, IV (August, 1851), pp. 251-252.
[11] John Stamps, "Missionaries for Texas," *Millennial Harbinger* (March, 1850), pp. 174-175. Hereafter cited as Stamps, "Missionaries for Texas."

member of every congregation in the Union contribute a dime, or more, to his local church for the "Texas Missionary Fund." Each year, churches would pool their collections and select one or more ministers to be sent to Texas. Musing hopefully, Stamps reflected, "This will be a small matter to each individual, but may be collectively, a sufficient sum to send several evangelists to Texas annually. . . May the Lord of all goodness prosper it!"[12] Theoretically sound, the plan was impractical because no central channel existed through which all churches could be informed. Evidently Stamps' suggestion attracted little attention.

Cooperations

Simultaneously, some Texas churches took concerted action to evangelize local areas more effectively. With vision and vigor, they formed cooperations, a type of district associations or conferences. These were simply gatherings of members from a group of adjacent churches, usually preachers and leaders, to discuss local needs, appoint evangelists for designated areas, and support them with church funds.

The first cooperation held in Texas assembled in Lamar County in the fall of 1845. John Crisp was dispatched as the messenger to contact brethren in Red River, Hopkins, and Fannin counties. Although several preachers attended, including Abner Hill, Green Weaver, Ephraim Moore, John McCluskey and William Stirman, evidently accompanied by his fifteen year old son Valentine, no formal organization apparently was forthcoming.[13]

In September, 1850, a cooperation met in Rusk

---

[12]*Ibid.*
[13]V. I. Stirman, "News," *Gospel Advocate*, XXX (May 16, 1888), p. 8.

County with forty-two present. Although no organization was formed, the group decided to meet again. A year later, 162 Disciples convened at Christian Union in Rusk County and an organization was effected with J. R. Hooten as secretary. The following constitution was approved unanimously:

> Article 1. This association shall be called the Christian Co-operation of Eastern Texas.
>
> Article 2. It shall have as its objects, the sending of the gospel where it is not, and sustaining it among ourselves.
>
> Article 3. It shall be composed of messengers from the churches, and of individuals who may wish to unite with us in the work of the Lord.
>
> Article 4. Its officers shall be a President, Vice-President, Secretary, Treasurer and a board of managers.
>
> Article 5. These officers shall be elected at each annual meeting; they shall continue in office till others are elected.

The delegates resolved to meet the following year in Mt. Enterprise.[14] Sam Henderson was appointed to evangelize the cooperation area for one year. Henderson, who was paid three hundred dollars for his labor, reported eighty-nine baptisms at the 1852 annual meeting. At this conference, the corresponding secretary was instructed to invite all known churches of Christ in East Texas to send representatives to the 1853 annual conference to be held at Millville. When Henderson declined to "ride the circuit," the managers were asked to secure "suitable laborers" in the near future.[15] In 1854, the group again met in Mt. Enter-

---

[14] Anonymous, "Eastern Texas Co-operation," *Christian Magazine*, IV (December, 1851), p. 377.

[15] C. Kendrick, S. Henderson, C. Vinzent, "Co-operation in Texas," *Millennial Harbinger* (December, 1852), p. 712.

prise, but reported nothing other than thirteen additions.[16]

Other cooperations were formed in East Texas on a similar order. In 1856, the managers of the Shelby, San Augustine and Nacogdoches cooperation appointed P. F. Southern to preach for the conference during 1857. He was uniquely commissioned to compile statistics as to the "number of miles traveled, sermons preached, additions and how many prayed in their families."[17] Unfortunately, no record of these data is available. In 1857, James Baird called for a cooperation at Forest Grove, seven miles west of Clarksville, in an effort to awake the churches from their lethargy.[18] In September 19, 1857, delegates from nine churches assembled and selected Baird to work full time, Asher Gough part time, in evangelizing Titus, Cass, Red River, Hopkins, and Lamar counties.[19]

In Dallas on June 7, 1856, a county cooperation was formed by the following representatives: Amon McComas, Henry Gale and A. G. Collins of the White Rock church; L. J. Sweet of the Lancaster church and A. M. Dean of the Dallas church. Sweet was requested to devote his full time to the ministry in the county until the "backslidden have been re-instated into the Church of our Heavenly Father." Viewing the languishing condition of the church, the group covenanted to "use all diligence to revive pure Christianity in our midst . . . watching over one another for good, and

---

[16] T. F. Campbell, "News from the Churches," *Millennial Harbinger* (January, 1854), p. 57.

[17] A. Oliver, "Co-operation in Texas," *Gospel Advocate*, III (April, 1857), pp. 123-124.

[18] James M. Baird, "News from the Churches," *ibid.*, III (August, 1857), pp. 267-268.

[19] H. L. Williams, "Northeastern Texas Co-operation," *ibid.*, III (November, 1857), p. 363.

striving to arouse the lukewarm from the state of indifference into which they have fallen."[20]

The most effective and widespread cooperation constituted in Texas was organized near Austin in 1851 with Henry Thomas of Austin as its evangelist. In November, 1853, some 167 delegates from six churches met at Georgetown. The conference secured A. P. H. Jordan as its evangelist. Jordan apparently was quite successful for he reported 107 additions to the church for the period June-November, 1854. Because of his fruitful ministry, the cooperation, which met in Lockport in October, 1854, appointed three other preachers, not named, to evangelize "Western Texas."[21] The high point of the cooperation was the fifth annual meeting which convened in Austin October 22, 1856. An informative and encouraging statistical report portrayed the size and growth of the seventeen member churches:

Church	County	Additions	Membership
Austin	Travis	12	52
Bastrop	Bastrop		15
Belton	Bell		
Berea	Washington		26
Caldwell	Burleson		25
Cedar Creek	Bastrop		7
Darr's Creek	Bell		
Elm Creek	Washington		38
Georgetown	Williamson	8	54
Hamilton	Burnet	62	97
Hickory Grove	Milam		71
Lockhart	Caldwell	23	89
Mountain	Gillespie	14	50
Post Oak	Washington		

---
[20]A. M. Dean, "Dallas County (Texas) Co-operation," *ibid.*, II (August, 1856), p. 246.
[21]S. B. Giles, "News from the Churches," *Millennial Harbinger* (March, 1855), pp. 178-179.

San Marcos	Hays	14	43
Sempronius Academy	Austin	9	34
Shiloh	Dewitt	63	167
	Totals	205	768

To augment the future work of the cooperation, the conference recommended that all evangelists fervently teach the necessity and scriptural obligation to support the ministry. If such instruction failed to elicit liberal contributions from all churches, the ministers were advised to devote their time to those who did contribute "since those who are unwilling to sow should reap no harvest."[22]

The scattered and intermittent efforts to evangelize Texas through cooperations were the exception rather than the rule. Most preaching was done on a "hit and miss" basis. Itinerant preachers spoke wherever the opportunity was afforded; others, engaged in business, preached from time to time in various localities on Sundays; a few local ministers endeavored to visit a group of churches once each month; some zealous members assumed responsibility for teaching to the best of their ability. As a result, converts were baptized, churches founded in all sections of the state, and in due time some houses of worship were erected. Thus, the members throughout the state found ways to circumvent the shortage of ministers.

INITIAL EFFORTS IN EAST TEXAS

The growth of churches of Christ in Texas prior to the Civil War was slow but continuous. To simplify

---

[22] Henry Thomas, "Minutes of the Fifth Annual Meeting of the Christian Co-operation of Western Texas," *Gospel Advocate*, II (December, 1856), p. 371.

a survey of that growth, the state is arbitrarily divided into four areas: East Texas; Northwest Texas with McKinney and Sherman as focal points; the Dallas-Fort Worth vicinity; and the triangular region with vertices at Huntsville on the northeast, San Saba on the northwest, and Beeville on the south, with a few isolated points lying outside the triangle included. The early efforts of churches of Christ in East Texas were characterized by attempts to proselyte members from several sects. In some instances, denominational barriers were eliminated and unity established on the basis of the Bible as the sole authority in religion. In 1847, William Defee and W. K. Withers founded the first church of Christ in Shelby County in the home of Richard Hooper, a former Baptist whose wife was a former Presbyterian. The eight charter members agreed to subscribe to the following declaration: "We, the Christians of the church called Zion, have met together this day, the 18th of July, 1847, and give each other our hearts and hands and all agree to take the Bible as the only infallible rule of faith and practice."[23] After a decade of faithful work, Hooper proudly reported that "the cause of Christ is advancing here."[24] In nearby Sabine County, Peter Eldridge and G. E. Slaughter, Baptist preachers, united with Defee and Withers upon "one Lord, one faith, one baptism for the remission of sins," using as a basis for such conclusions Acts 2:38 and Ephesians 4:4.[25] In 1851, a year after its establishment by S. B. Giles and N. Rutherford, the Boston Church of Christ and Baptist

---

[23] William Defee, "News," *Christian Review*, IV (October, 1847), pp. 358-359.
[24] Kendrick, "Texas Department," *Gospel Advocate*, III (April, 1857), p. 128.
[25] Defee, "News," *Christian Review*, IV (October, 1847), pp. 358-359.

Church with a total of twenty-one staunch members agreed to "live together and take the word of God as their sole guide."[26] W. P. Matteson of Indian Creek, Angelina County, reported the conversion of a Missionary Baptist preacher of "good talent, who is now preaching the faith he once endeavored to destroy."[27]

The church of Christ in Palestine was started about 1850, seemingly in conjunction with a Baptist church which apparently had denied its previous doctrine. Early in the year, Dr. A. P. H. Jordan, a Baptist pastor, arrived in the community and, upon finding seven people who had letters from Baptist churches, organized a Baptist church with ten charter members on the basis of the usual confession of faith. In a business meeting of the church about a year later, a member arose and inquired whether they should retain "our" confession ("I believe that God for Christ's sake pardoned our sins"), or the one in the Bible ("I believe that Jesus Christ is the Son of God." Acts 8:37, KJV). Immediately, all voted to accept the Bible statement, whereupon Dr. Jordan arose and said, "I have preached for the Baptists for thirty years but can't see wrong in swapping a human confession for a divine one, so I'll go along with you."[28] Shortly thereafter, a small log building was erected to serve the defected Baptist congregation and members of the church of Christ who united with them.

The cause of Christ was advanced in other East Texas towns because some sects manifested kindness toward ministers of the churches of Christ. D. L.

---

[26]John R. McCall, "News," *Christian Magazine*, IV (May, 1851), pp. 156-157.
[27]W. P. Matteson, "News and Notes," *Gospel Advocate*, V (October, 1859), p. 305.
[28]*Firm Foundation* (Austin, Texas), September 6, 1910.

D'Spain at first found that in Henderson the sects "are saying all manner of evil against us . . ." and denied him the use of their houses of worship and even the courthouse. However, by April, 1852, he had overcome prejudice to the point that the Baptists permitted him to preach in their building. D'Spain then publicly clarified his position in regard to faith, repentance, baptism, and the Holy Spirit, and organized a church with fourteen charter members.[29] Although numerous members of the church of Christ lived in Marshall and Jefferson in 1854, towns of about two thousand population each, they owned no church buildings. With surprising courtesy, the Baptists and Cumberland Presbyterians in both places tendered their buildings to A. Padon who conducted a series of meetings and baptized two. Padon aptly remarked, "The moral and religious aspects of the society here are highly favorable to the ultimate success of the gospel."[30]

Additional churches were planted in other East Texas communities. In September, 1849, Cyrus H. Randolph reported that over sixty had been immersed in Crockett, Houston County, since April, and that the cause had been firmly established.[31] W. B. Holloway, who moved from Georgia to Rusk County in the fall of 1846, finally gathered enough Disciples together to organize a church in 1849. Its building was a crude log house near Holloway's home. Holloway served as an

---

[29] D. L. D'Spain, "News," *Christian Magazine*, V (June, 1852), pp. 175-176.

[30] A. Padon, "News from the Churches," *Millennial Harbinger* (December, 1854), pp. 711-712.

[31] Cyrus H. Randolph, "News," *Gospel Proclamation*, II (September, 1849), p. 705.

elder of the church until his death in 1859.[32] By 1852, three other congregations had been established in the county and were "doing as well as could be expected in a new area." In July, 1851, J. W. Blackwell assisted thirty scattered members to form a church in Rusk, Cherokee County.[33] The "talented, zealous and intelligent" brethren of the Pleasant Grove church in Anderson County erected a "commodious house of worship" in 1852. Kendrick, who conducted a revival and received nineteen converts in a few weeks, felt that the whole community afforded one of the most promising fields for evangelical labor in the state.[34]

Numerous other congregations were "loosely formed" in rural sections where rough clapboard houses, wrought from native timbers, furnished with split logs for serviceable but uncomfortable seats, served not only churches of Christ but usually all denominations. H. C. Barnes gathered together scattered Disciples near Clarksville; thirty-three members began to meet regularly in Pine Tree, Upshur County, after a protracted meeting in June, 1856; W. P. Matteson and James Power converted and assembled about forty in Nacogdoches County in early 1859.

Notwithstanding the successful establishment of some congregations, churches of Christ in East Texas, especially along the Louisiana border, were few in number and spiritually weak. Preachers were virtually non-existent. In 1847, Dr. Defee, a physician who sometimes preached, told of the "cold state" of

---
[32]James Vernon, "News and Notes," *Gospel Advocate*, V (February, 1859), p. 64.
[33]J. W. Blackwell, "News," *Christian Magazine*, IV (August, 1851), p. 251.
[34]Carroll Kendrick, "News from the Churches," *Millennial Harbinger* (June, 1852), p. 354.

religion in general with whole churches of some denominations vanishing in a short time. His plea for help evidently went unheeded as he reported in 1852 that Sabine, Nicolin, Jasper, Angelina, Augustine, Shelbyville (probably meant Shelby) and Nacogdoches counties were entirely devoid of evangelists of the churches of Christ.[35] By 1860, there were fewer congregations and members of churches of Christ in East Texas than in any other section of the state. This comparative status has remained relatively unchanged to the present.

NORTHWEST TEXAS—THE WILMETHS AND B. F. HALL

Meanwhile, in Northwest Texas on the western fringe of the frontier, churches of Christ were slowly but steadily being established. In the forefront of evangelistic labor was the talented, courageous and influential Wilmeth family. Joseph Brice Wilmeth, whose grandfather had left Ireland in search of religious freedom, was born in North Carolina in 1807. While a small lad, he moved with his parents to Tennessee where as a youth of nineteen he married Nancy Ferguson, granddaughter of Colonel Patrick Ferguson, famous for his part in the battle of King's Mountain. In 1831 he arrived in Smithville, Arkansas, with several other families and subsequently farmed, raised livestock, served as a soldier, village blacksmith, clerk of a court, and escort of the Choctaws and Chickasaws from Mississippi to Indian Territory. Of greater importance was his conversion to the church of Christ and decision to preach the gospel. At first he con-

---

[35]Defee, "News from the Churches," *Millennial Harbinger* (January, 1852), p. 60.

ducted worship services in his home with friends and neighbors in attendance.

In 1845, Wilmeth received a pamphlet which portrayed the broad and fertile prairies in the Three Forks of the Trinity River, located in Peter's Colony, as an ideal home for immigrants, and offered a section of free land to every head of a family who would settle there. The Wilmeths and two other families with "six wagons—some with oxen, some with four horses, and some with horses and oxen combined . . . forty head of loose stock and one hundred sheep . . ." began the long and arduous journey. With commendable foresight, the pioneers packed their wagons with guns, ammunition, a complete set of farm tools, heavy homemade bed clothes, a spinning wheel and loom, and a six months supply of food. After proceeding to Paris, then called "Pinhook," the last outpost of civilization, the small caravan struck out along a dim wagon road designated as the "Military Trail." After a tedious three-month journey, the weary travelers arrived on December 26, 1845, in Dallas, a virtually uninhabited village of three houses, many residents having left because they presumed the county seat would be located elsewhere.[36]

Moving on to what is now Grand Prairie, then the very edge of the frontier, the family erected a house of hewn logs and dedicated it February 14, 1846. Since Indians were numerous in the vicinity, no lights were used at night. However, the red men visited the home in the daytime and often took the two youngest children out on the prairie without opposition from the fearful mother. In the evening, they returned the

---

[36]Matthews, "Historical Sketches," XLVIII (October, 1936), p. 1.

"Much brave woman"

children unharmed and grunted, "Much brave woman." Within a few months, increasing fear of the Indians caused Wilmeth to abandon an excellent stand of corn, new home and headright, and drop back to the east bank of the Trinity River. Although he wished to return to Tennessee, his brave wife with true pioneer spirit and tearful eye flatly refused. The Wilmeths thereupon moved to a point two miles north of present McKinney and purchased the claim of Moses Wilson for six hundred dollars.[37]

J. B. Wilmeth immediately began his evangelistic efforts in the community. About twelve miles north, near Van Alstyne, a few Disciples often met in the spacious home of Carroll McKinney, a devout but courteous and broad-minded Methodist. Under the supervision of Wilmeth, a church called Old Liberty was organized on the second Sunday of September, 1846, with eighteen charter members including Wilmeth, his wife Nancy, the McKinney family, Eliza S. Milan, and four colored slaves.[38] Although unable to read or write, Hannah, one of the slaves, could quote scripture better than most of the other members of the church. For several years the congregation met in the homes of members and was served by itinerant evangelists. Finding the distance to Old Liberty too far to travel each Sunday, Wilmeth in 1847 moved an old blacksmith shop into his yard, furnished it with split logs, and established a church. Later, with commendable ingenuity, he added an upstairs to his house, equipped

---
[37]*Ibid.*
[38]Members from the McKinney family were William C. McKinney, Margaret McKinney, Sarah McKinney, Ashley McKinney, Collin McKinney Sr., Marcus S. McKinney, D. L. McKinney, Polly McKinney, Collin McKinney, and Bettie L. McKinney. The colored slaves were Polina, Ninah, Hannah, Anderson, and Lucinda.

it with crude chairs, and constructed an outside stairway leading up to the porch, thus constituting a "true frontier church building." Visiting preachers often stopped to proclaim the gospel when Wilmeth permitted. On one occasion, an evangelist of a denomination exclaimed during the course of his sermon, "There are infants in hell, not a span long!" Immediately, Wilmeth arose and angrily shouted, "Stop that! You cannot preach that under my roof."[39] Churches of Christ maintain the Bible teaches that babies are saved or at least are in a state of innocence. In August, 1848, twenty-one new members were added to the church during a revival conducted by Wilmeth.[40] Two years later the church, now numbering sixty-nine, settled at Liberty and reorganized. A. Cartwright, a recent immigrant physician and preacher, William McKinney and B. W. Vernon were appointed as elders. Its first house of worship was erected at Mantua in 1854.[41]

Wilmeth continued to travel, preach, baptize hundreds, and establish new churches all over North Texas. His devoted sons, J. R. and C. M. (Mack), assisted him and endeavored to preach. J. R. seemingly was always before the public; Mack, a "veritable knight of the saddle bags," spoke in every house where an opportunity was presented. On January 15, 1892, one day after his beloved wife had passed away, Joseph Brice Wilmeth, an aged soldier of the cross, laid down his spir-

---

[39] Matthews, "Historical Sketches," XLVIII (October, 1936), p. 1.

[40] J. B. Wilmeth, "News from the Churches," *Millennial Harbinger* (December, 1848), pp. 705-706.

[41] Matthews, "Historical Sketches," XLVIII (July, 1936), pp. 1-5.

itual sword that he might receive the crown from the Captain of his salvation.[42]

Supplementing the energetic Wilmeths was colorful Dr. B. F. Hall, a traveling dentist and preacher from Kentucky. Hall, who arrived in Sherman in 1850, conducted services in a brush arbor near the log cabin courthouse and organized a church. Later, he preached in the lodge building at the corner of Travis and Pecan streets, used by all Protestant denominations in Sherman on designated Sundays.[43] In April, 1855, W. P. Torance reported that although the church had been without preaching for six months, it continued to meet every first day of the week "to read, pray and break the loaf."[44]

In August, Torance wrote that evangelists Goodnight and Beebe had preached in the vicinity, baptized a number of converts, and successfully organized several congregations.[45]

Meanwhile, Hall was evangelizing North Texas. During a short revival he conducted at Oak Grove in October, 1850, he received seventy-three additions to the church. Forty-three new members were added to the McKinney church during a meeting he held in 1857. Such large crowds attended that very few, other than the ladies courteously tendered seats, were able to press into the meeting house for the services. These

---

[42]*Ibid.*, XLVIII (October, 1936), pp. 1-4.
[43]*Sherman Democrat*, September 19, 1948.
[44]W. P. Torance, "Sherman," *Christian Evangelist*, VI (June, 1855), p. 287.
[45]Torance, "News," *Christian Evangelist*, VI (October, 1855), p. 479.

overflowing crowds apparently inspired Hall to laud North Texas as the best section of the state, settled by the best population, and as having presented the largest and most attentive audiences.[46]

Hall's most fruitful evangelistic efforts were held near Hallonia in the summer of 1859. Although a church had been planted here previously, it had withered away under the attack from a Baptist minister of the community and for lack of regular preaching. A Reverend Cotton, who was pastor to a strong Baptist church, recently had decried the so-called error of "Campbellism," and its resultant curse to the community. When Hall arrived in July, he promptly requested use of the Baptist house in order to refute Cotton's allegations but was refused. Thwarted but undaunted, he retired to a nearby grove where he elucidated Campbell's arguments as a rebuttal of Cotton. Hall spoke twice daily for a week in an arbor to audiences in excess of five hundred. Using military phraseology, Hall exclaimed, "We unfurled the banner of the lone star—the star of Bethlehem . . . a few faithful soldiers rallied round it . . . at length a breach was made; the ranks of the enemy commenced giving way. Four surrendered . . . and gave their allegiance to Prince Messiah. After that they fell, wounded at every fire." Referring to his apparently vanquished foe as having "discharged his filthy missiles and shot his envenomed darts till his resources were exhausted," Hall triumphantly announced the reorganization of the church augmented by thirty-one converts and nineteen reclaimed members.[47] In response to his call for building funds, the revitalized congregation pledged seven hundred dollars in one hour and proposed to erect a

---

[46]B. F. Hall, "Texas Department," *Gospel Advocate*, III (November, 1857), p. 362.
[47]Hall, "Progress of Reform," *Millennial Harbinger* (November, 1859), pp. 656-657.

house thirty-six by fifty feet. The discourse was generally called the "Cotton Picking," and one resident remarked that "he thought he had a good gin, but that was the cleanest picking he had ever seen done."[48]

DALLAS-FORT WORTH AND VICINITY

In the Dallas-Fort Worth vicinity, destined to be a stronghold of the churches of Christ in Texas a century later, several evangelists labored with some success. According to one authority, Elder Amon Mc-Comas, lately from Kentucky and of the "Christian faith," preached the first sermon in the small village of Dallas in 1845.[49] However, in 1909, an old pioneer citizen claimed that "the first Campbellite sermon preached in Dallas was at the house of a Mr. Cole in 1845. Preacher's name was Corder."[50] A year later, William Rawlins probably established the first church of Christ in Dallas County at Lancaster. The congregation, now known as Cold Springs, has continued meeting regularly since its organization. He settled in the community but described his initial evangelistic efforts as "dark and discouraging." In March, 1849, however, Rawlins, aided by a Brother McVey, in a ten-day meeting at Pleasant Run, two miles east of Dallas, baptized ten and organized a church of fifteen members.[51] By June, the congregation numbered forty-one.[52] In September, 1854, evangelists L. J. Sweet and N. O. Polly baptized twenty-nine during a

---

[48]Hall, "News and Notes," *Gospel Advocate*, V (December, 1859), pp. 338-340.
[49]*Dallas Morning News*, October 1, 1935.
[50]T. R. Burnett, "News Reports," *Burnett's Budget*, IX (July 15, 1909), p. 4.
[51]William Rawlins, "News," *Christian Record*, VII (July, 1849), p. 30.
[52]*Ibid.* (September, 1849), p. 90.

seven-day revival. Moving to Prairie Creek, they preached five days, immersed four, and had one indefinite addition. A lady, who was over seventy, made the confession, twice postponed being immersed, and apparently never submitted to the ordinance of baptism.[53]

Some uncertainty exists as to when the first church of Christ was organized in Dallas. According to the *Dallas Morning News,* a church of fifteen members was established in 1852, but no contemporary record validates this claim.[54] Melvin J. Wise, former minister of the Pearl and Bryan Church of Christ in Dallas, in his four-page history of the church stated that it began in 1855.[55] Wise apparently erred in his date for there is no available supporting evidence. Evangelist A. M. Dean in a letter dated February 29, 1856, gives the details of what he claims to have been the first. "We have succeeded in organizing a respectable congregation in this place of some twelve members, though much opposed," wrote Dean. He further stated that the church met only once a month because the house (apparently the courthouse) was used by others the rest of the time but that he preached every Sunday.[56] Some of the charter members were the Shepherd, Miller, Cole, Heard, and Peak families.[57] Captain Jefferson Peak, a former Kentuckian who fought in the Mexican War, brought his wife, three sons and three daughters to Dallas in 1855 and erected the first brick

---

[53]L. J. Sweet, "News," *Christian Evangelist,* VI (March, 1855), pp. 141-142.
[54]*Dallas Morning News,* October 1, 1935.
[55]Melvin J. Wise, *A History of the Pearl and Bryan Church of Christ* (n.d., n.p.). Hereafter cited as Wise, *Pearl and Bryan Church.*
[56]Dean, "Dallas," *Gospel Advocate,* I (June, 1856), p. 190.
[57]*Firm Foundation,* November 2, 1926.

CHURCH GROWTH IN EARLY STATEHOOD PERIOD, 1845-1861   51

house in the village.[58] A devoted member of the church of Christ, he later donated a lot to the congregation which "now numbers seventeen of as respectable men and women as our county affords."[59] However, no significant growth occurred until after the Civil War.

Simultaneously, evangelist Sweet endeavored to plant the cause of Christ firmly in Dallas County. From 1856 to 1859 he devoted his time to "riding and preaching." He vigorously attempted to effect more "scriptural organization" of the churches and awaken the brethren to a "higher degree of Christian morality and true piety . . . thereby enhancing the appeal of Bible religion to the other sects."[60] His report of November, 1858, reveals that he was fairly successful. To that date he had enlisted forty-six additions to the "cause of Bible truth; two from the Cumberland Presbyterians; five from the Methodists; five from the Baptists and thirty-four from the world." One convert was a Methodist preacher, an Englishman of excellent education.[61] By 1859, Sweet had established churches at Pleasant Run, Scyene, and Grapevine Prairie, had strengthened other congregations, and had received 160 converts into the church.[62]

In nearby Tarrant County, J. W. Elliston organized a church of twelve members in Birdville, the first county seat, in February, 1852. The mode of worship

---

[58]George Jackson, *Sixty Years in Texas* (Dallas, 1908), pp. 369-370.
[59]Dean, "News and Notes," *Gospel Advocate*, III (January, 1857), p. 24.
[60]Sweet, "News," *Christian Evangelist*, VIII (February, 1857), pp. 79-80.
[61]L. J. Sweet, "Scyene," *The Evangelist*, X (November, 1859), p. 523.
[62]*Ibid.*

—reading and examining the word of the Lord, breaking the loaf, and contributing money—was evidently a novelty to many preachers and laymen. On one occasion after a service, an old Baptist preacher told Elliston that to him the order of worship was a "bran new thing, having never before, in all this life, seen anything like it."[63]

The first religious organization in Fort Worth was the church of Christ. In 1849, Colonel Ripley Arnold founded Camp Worth near the present Tarrant County Courthouse. At the foot of the hill south of the Trinity River where the first settlements of Fort Worth were located, Colonel Nathaniel Terry settled on a farm. During the harvest season of 1855, A. M. Dean, transient worker and itinerant evangelist, rode up to Terry's fields with a Bible in one saddle bag, a six-shooter in the other. Dean was determined that his services would not be disrupted, even if he had to look at his audience down the barrel of a gun while reading scripture. He harvested wheat by day and souls by night. In August, 1855, he organized a church with nine charter members.[64] During the third week of September, Dean conducted a short meeting and received eighteen new members, five from the Methodists, four from the Baptists, and nine who made a profession of faith. Only seven were baptized as two deferred because of sickness. When the wheat harvest was over, Dean in his parting sermon exhorted the congregation of thirty who had "given themselves

---

[63] J. W. Elliston, "News from the Churches," *Millennial Harbinger* (June, 1852), p. 254.
[64] Polytechnic Church of Christ, *Fort Worth's First Religious Organization* (pamphlet, n.d.), Mr. and Mrs. Berry P. Ayers, Mr. and Mrs. James K. Allen, Mr. and Mrs. W. A. Anderson, Stephen Terry, Mrs. Francis Durrett, and Mrs. Alfred Johnson.

to the Lord and to one another" to stand firm.[65] On December 15, 1858, he returned to Fort Worth, preached a series of sermons, and baptized four women. One, a former Episcopalian dissatisfied with her sprinkling, was immersed at 2:00 P.M. on a Saturday afternoon. The rite so impressed a number of citizens that some were "almost persuaded to become Christians."[66] Dean returned again in November, 1859, and baptized thirteen during a short meeting.[67] The congregation first met in a log house on Belknap Street just west of the square, then for a time in the homes of members, subsequently in a crude concrete structure at the corner of present Belknap and Lamar, and finally in the Masonic building at the Corner of Belknap and Calhoun where it continued to worship until after the Civil War.[68]

Although the church of Christ did not organize the first Sunday School in Fort Worth, it conducted one in conjunction with Sunday worship services in the Masonic building. Howard W. Peak, then a young lad, vividly recalled in 1922 "the hours spent in listening to the explanation of the scriptures and the pleading prayers offered by those patriarchs . . ." Even more clear was his remembrance of the time when he hurriedly brought up the rear of a class procession in "high C" after falling behind. Immediately, Dr. I. L. Van Zandt, his teacher, aptly remarked, "Howard, my boy, you'll have to keep better time or they'll throw

---

[65]Dean, "News and Notes," *Gospel Advocate*, IV (February, 1858), pp. 59-60.
[66]*Ibid.* (May, 1859), p. 156.
[67]Dean, "Report from Texas," *Gospel Advocate*, VI (February, 1860), p. 57.
[68]Polytechnic Church of Christ, *Fort Worth's First Religious Organization*.

you out of the heavenly choir sure, if you even get there."[69]

In the semi-circle area immediately south of the Dallas-Fort Worth vicinity, several small churches were established by itinerant evangelists supported by a few faithful members. B. L. D'Spain preached three sermons in Van Zandt County in May, 1859, and immersed seven, one of whom was a seventy year old lady of the Roman Catholic faith. At her conversion, she "shook as if under the influence of the ague" which profoundly affected the audience, including many of her children and grandchildren. As a result, others were converted and a small church organized.[70] At Red Oak, Ellis County, ministers Polly, Heath and Sweet collaborated in preaching and received thirteen accessions in August, 1855. The following month, Heath and Sweet held a revival, immersed ten, and planted a church of thirty members under "favorable circumstances."[71] In adjoining Navarro County, James H. Addison, a Methodist preacher, declared that the Campbellites were as "thick as hops" in Corsicana in 1852, but no church of Christ was formed until after the Civil War.[72] In the large frontier Johnson County, R. T. Brown moved to Alvarado in October, 1854, and endeavored unsuccessfully for nine months to organize a church. However, upon the arrival of minister John Whitmire in

---

[69] *Fort Worth Star-Telegram*, September 3, 1922. Dr. I. L. Van Zandt, Peter Smith and wife, Mrs. C. W. Peak, Mrs. Dick King, Stephen Terry, and Uncle Jimmy Allen officiated and taught classes.

[70] B. L. D'Spain, "Palestine, Texas," *Gospel Advocate*, V (October, 1859), pp. 310-311.

[71] Sweet, "News," *Christian Evangelist*, VII (January, 1856), p. 45.

[72] T. K. Richardson, *East Texas, Its History and Makers* (Dabney White ed., New York, 1940), II, p. 722.

July, 1855, a church of eleven members was formed.[73] Whitmire, who possessed considerable ability and was esteemed as a "good Christian man," settled at nearby Grandview where he planted a church the next year.[74] At the western tip of Johnson County in Comanche, James Dickson, resident for only a few months, was heartened in 1859 by the addition of four devoted converts to the small group which worshiped together at this frontier outpost.[75]

SOUTH TEXAS

The inverted equilateral triangle area of South Texas with vertices at Huntsville on the northeast, San Saba on the southwest, and Beeville on the south, was the locale of the most fruitful labor of the most numerous and capable evangelists of the church in the pre-Civil War period. Among the more prominent fulltime ministers were Stephen Strickland, Carroll Kendrick, Aaron Newman, John R. McCall, and Henry Thomas. Churches were planted in at least fifteen counties and hundreds of conversions were reported.

In the state capital of Austin, a little village of six hundred inhabitants, a church of Christ was established in 1847 with ten charter members. S. B. Giles and T. A. Rutherford ministered intermittently to the struggling group.[76] During March and April, 1851,

---

[73]R. T. Brown, "News," *Christian Evangelist*, VI (October, 1855), pp. 478-479.

[74]*A Memorial and Biographical History of Johnson and Hill Counties, Texas* (Chicago, 1892), pp. 167-168).

[75]James Dickson, "News from the Churches," *Millennial Harbinger* (August, 1859), pp. 479-480.

[76]*The First One Hundred Years of the Central Christian Church of Austin, Texas 1847-1947* (n.d., n.p.). Hereafter cited as *Central Christian Church of Austin, Texas*. Charter members were: Esther Durham, Elizabeth Smith, Thomas Wood and wife Sarah, James Caulfield, Brother Lawrence, Brother McShan, Sarah D. Welsh, and William Simpson and wife Permelia.

John McCall spoke twenty-two times to the church, which met in a schoolhouse, and received sixteen new members into the fold. Encouraged by the additional disciples, and Giles' promise to preach regularly, the congregation unsuccessfully solicited funds for a building.[77] Nevertheless, under the leadership of Henry Thomas, a successful evangelist of Paris, Missouri, who arrived in Austin in 1853, the assembly of forty increased rapidly. Within two years, forty children were enrolled in the Sunday School and over one hundred attended the Sunday morning worship service. To accommodate the large crowds, the congregation purchased the old Methodist house on Congress Avenue. It served as a meeting place for the next thirty years.[78] W. B. Burditt commended the brethren for meeting "regularly every first day to worship the Great God according to his word," a practice seldom found among the churches of Christ in Texas prior to the Civil War.[79] Further growth occurred when the renowned Carroll Kendrick delivered a series of sermons in 1857. Beginning in August, Kendrick in nineteen days of preaching recruited fifty-six converts. Returning a week later after keeping a previous engagement, he obtained fourteen additions in seven days.[80] Within ten years after its establishment, the Austin church with more than 150 members was one of the largest congregations in Central Texas.

Simultaneously, churches of Christ were planted in

---

[77] John McCall, "From Texas," *Christian Magazine*, IV (June, 1851), p. 188.
[78] John T. Poe, "The Church of Christ in Austin, Texas," *Gospel Advocate*, XXVII (July 15, 1885), p. 444.
[79] W. B. Burditt, "Near Austin, Texas," *ibid.*, II (December, 1856), p. 374.
[80] E. H. Darter, "News and Notes," *ibid.*, III (December, 1847), p. 410.

Robertson, Walker, Madison and Burleson counties. At Bald Prairie, Robertson County, a sparsely settled region, members of the church of Christ and the Baptist Church assembled together in 1847 with the understanding that each group should retain its own doctrine. After two years of fellowship, each body formed its own church, the church of Christ with fifteen charter members.[81] In Lyons, Burleson County, four women members of the church of Christ who desired to unite with the Baptists were denied admission unless rebaptized in accordance with Baptist doctrine.[82] Rebuffed but not dismayed, they wrote Henry Thomas who came eighty miles through rain and cold in January, 1858, preached ten days, immersed fifteen, received seven Baptists, and organized a church of twenty-six devout members. Returning in May, Thomas was astonished to find the congregation worshiping in a commodious new building. Greatly encouraged, he conducted a ten-day revival, received twenty-three new members, and left the church in a flourishing condition.[83] In the same year, Benton Sweeney, after holding a three-day meeting at Madisonville, established a church of nineteen members,[84] and on July 7, 1860, he

---

[81] *Firm Foundation*, May 16, 1893. The members were E. Rains and wife, Levi Bogges and wife, Ryley Donegan, a Brother Phillips and wife, W. A. Bedford and wife, Clinton Owens and wife, Allen Jackson and wife, D. M. Owens, and Metilda Wilson.

[82] Baptists consider baptism administered by an ordained Baptist pastor as the only method of induction into the Baptist Church. Baptism has no connection with salvation which is obtained by faith alone. On the other hand, churches of Christ consider baptism essential to salvation, the one way by which a person can get into Christ (Gal. 3:27). Christ will save all persons who believe in him, and then are baptized, regardless of who administers the baptism.

[83] Henry Thomas, "News from the Churches," *Millennial Harbinger* (September, 1858), pp. 529-530).

[84] T. M. Sweeney, "Good News from Texas," *Gospel Advocate*, V (February, 1859), p. 54.

organized a church of seventeen disciples at Huntsville. Two years later, J. W. Bush and J. H. Bantau were appointed elders of the latter, and under their guidance the Huntsville congregation met weekly throughout the Civil War.[85]

To the west, churches were planted in the Georgetown-Burnet area. John R. McCall, who preached two weeks in Georgetown in April, 1851, organized a church of twenty-eight members. With commendable foresight, he urged the brethren in the "states" to do something for Texas because "I am persuaded it is a fine field and at no distant day will be one of the finest portions of our Union."[86] By 1858, when Stephen Strickland, a hometown minister, conducted one of "the largest tent meetings ever held in Western Texas," the congregation numbered seventy.[87] In the same year at Florence, twenty miles to the north, Kendrick organized a church of twenty members who promised to "meet regularly and keep the ordinances."[88] Twenty-five miles west at Burnet, although plagued by "heat, dust and politics on one hand, the world, the flesh and the devil on the other, and hydra-headed sectarianism in front . . ." Strickland converted eighteen during a revival held in the courthouse.[89]

At the western vertex of the triangle, churches of Christ were organized in Lampasas and San Saba prior to the Civil War. Amid the tents of visitors to the

---

[85]David Lipscomb, "Notes on Texas Travel," *ibid.*, XIV (July 11, 1872), pp. 660-665.
[86]John R. McCall, "From Texas," *Christian Magazine*, IV (June, 1851), p. 188.
[87]Stephen Strickland, "News and Notes," *Gospel Advocate*, IV (August, 1858), p. 248.
[88]Kendrick, "Texas Department," *ibid.*, IV (November, 1858), p. 352.
[89]Strickland, "News and Notes," *ibid.*, II (November, 1856), p. 349.

Sulphur Springs near Lampasas, a nearly continuous series of revivals were conducted in the summer of 1858 by visiting Cumberland Presbyterian, Baptist, Methodist and Christian evangelists. In July, on the final day of the Cumberland Presbyterian meeting, Kendrick announced he would begin a series of sermons on the following day. He could not forego answering the Presbyterian accusation that "Campbellites" were "worse than the devil because they weighed down the merits of the blood of Christ with water." During the revival, a Methodist preacher, who frequently attended, solemnly reprimanded Kendrick for the "impropriety of his assertion that Christ was immersed," and hopefully implored him "not to do so any more, my brother." Nevertheless, he was an interested observer at each of the twenty immersions performed during the meeting. Later, Kendrick banteringly remarked that "I thought of admonishing him for looking on and seeming interested in such horrible wickedness, but did not meet an opportunity." Despite opposition, Kendrick organized a church of twenty-seven.[90] Further west, when the town of San Saba was surveyed in 1856, a town lot was set aside for each religious body. Immediately, two alert disciples obtained the block allotted to the church of Christ. In 1860 it was traded for a corner block on West Wallace, on which was erected a frame building that served the congregation until destroyed by a windstorm in 1890.[91]

About a hundred miles to the southeast within the triangle area, churches were established in Lockhart and San Marcos by hard-working Henry Thomas. He

---

[90] Kendrick, "Texas Department," *ibid.*, IV (September, 1858), pp. 279-280.
[91] Alma Ward Hamrick, *The Call of the San Saba* (San Antonio, 1941), pp. 148-149.

planted a church of ten members at Lockhart in November, 1853, promised to preach for them once a month, and evidently received additions after each service. Within two years, the congregation numbered about one hundred communicants.[92] In January of the same year, Thomas formed a church of two zealous members in San Marcos. By July its membership had climbed to thirty. Evidently Thomas preached a simple but persuasive gospel for a seventy-two year old Methodist lady and a seventy-four year old Presbyterian lady were immersed into Christ. Traveling to a new settlement near Eckert, where a Brother Laremore had gathered fifteen disciples in 1854, Thomas conducted a revival, immersed eighteen, and firmly established the infant church.[93]

To the east and southeast, churches were planted in LaGrange and Hallettsville. The establishment of a church in June, 1858, at LaGrange, located on the Colorado River below Austin in Fayette County, occurred as the result of a truth seeking, non-conforming zealot. The man had asked Reverend Hill, a Baptist pastor in the community, to baptize him but not to consider him a member of the Baptist Church. Hill refused on the basis that baptism was the door into the Baptist Church. Although his wife had been immersed and accepted as a member of the Cumberland Presbyterian Church, the gentleman was likewise unwilling to affiliate with that body. When Aaron Newman arrived, he preached ten days, baptized three others, gathered a number of scattered disciples from the community, and established a small but strong church

---

[92]Burditt, "News and Notes," *Gospel Advocate*, II (January, 1856), p. 31.
[93]Henry Thomas, "News," *Christian Evangelist*, VI (November, 1855), pp. 327-328.

CHURCH GROWTH IN EARLY STATEHOOD PERIOD, 1845-1861   61

of Christ.[94] Thirty miles south, Thomas formed a church of thirty members at Hallettsville, Lavaca County, in March, 1859, after conducting a six-day revival.[95]

Near the southern vertex of the triangle, churches were established in Victoria, Yorktown, Goliad and Beeville. At Victoria, a small congregation under the direction of elder James Lovelady in May, 1860, requested a good preacher to come to this "large and vacant field."[96] Three years later, evangelist A. P. H. Jordan organized a "frontier or border congregation" at Yorktown, thirty miles northwest of Victoria in Dewitt County. The Yorktown church experienced an amazingly rapid growth. Within four years, it numbered about two hundred and far outstripped the "sects of the region."[97] Twenty-five miles south at Goliad, a camp meeting was held in August, 1856, with forty-eight baptisms, but no church was established because many of the converts were visitors from adjoining counties. Two years later, however, minister E. Jones preached ten days, immersed forty-one, and formed a strong church.[98] Among the members was William Hunter, who had miraculously survived the Fannin Massacre of March 27, 1836. Evidently he was left for dead but during the night crawled away, hid in the brush, and eventually escaped. In 1882 Hunter served as a judge in Goliad.[99] Thirty miles to the southwest,

---

[94] Aaron Newman, "News and Notes," *Gospel Advocate*, IV (August, 1858), p. 251.
[95] Thomas, "News from the Churches," *Millennial Harbinger*, (June, 1859), p. 358.
[96] Felix B. Webb, *ibid.* (September, 1850), p. 535.
[97] A. P. H. Jordan, *ibid.* (May, 1857), p. 297.
[98] E. Jones, *ibid.* (November, 1858), p. 657.
[99] Chisholm, "Notes of Travel," *Gospel Advocate*, XXIV (June 8, 1882), p. 353.

sixteen disciples agreed to meet weekly in the home of W. B. Burditt near Beeville in May, 1860.[100]

HOUSTON—SAN ANTONIO—UVALDE

In South Texas outside the triangle area, efforts were made to establish the church in Houston and San Antonio, but without success until several decades after the Civil War. Benton Sweeney, who preached in Houston in July, 1858, received a few accessions but was unable to organize a church.[101] At San Antonio, no church was planted because of the powerful Roman Catholic influence, apathy on the part of resident members, and the seeming exclusion of the Alamo City from the itinerary of evangelists of churches of Christ. In 1858, John Henshaw, who moved to the town because of its beauty and healthful climate, characterized the scattered members as "poor and new beginners." However, he pledged a liberal contribution to any evangelist who would come, feeling that he could be well received since the "sects have large audiences." Endeavoring to arouse some interested preacher, he told of a congregation which met twenty-five miles south of San Antonio at the head of Luros Creek in Atascosa County.[102]

Farther west, on the edge of the vast West Texas frontier, a church was planted in the beautiful, small cattle town of Uvalde. In the spring of 1857, C. C. McKinney arrived and found that neither "preacher nor preaching" was known in the town. Shortly afterward, a Methodist circuit rider stopped and delivered

---

[100] Burditt, "Texas News," *Gospel Advocate*, VI (August, 1860), p. 250.
[101] Benton Sweeney, "News," *Christian Evangelist*, IX (October, 1858), p. 480.
[102] John Henshaw, "San Antonio," *Gospel Advocate*, IV (July, 1858), p. 221.

the first sermon. In October, 1858, James F. Scruggs, a minister of churches of Christ, arrived from Missouri and immediately upon settling in the Nueces River valley began preaching. Within two months he had spoken ten times, baptized fourteen, and organized a church of forty members. Accompanying his report to the *Gospel Advocate* was the exceptionally large list of twenty subscribers to this religious journal, conclusive evidence of the frontiersmen's quest for knowledge concerning events which had occurred in other states.[103]

TIRELESS EVANGELISTS

The establishment of churches of Christ in all sections of Texas in the statehood era before the Civil War was due primarily to toiling, self sacrificing, often unremunerated evangelists. Although a majority of these heroes of the Cross remain unknown, a few have left records of their achievements for posterity. Undoubtedly, the most widely traveled and effective was "indefatigable" Carroll Kendrick. Arriving from Kentucky where he had been editor of the *Ecclesiastical Reformer* in 1851, he first settled near Crockett but soon moved to Salado, Bell County. He vigorously labored in all parts of the state until he moved to California in 1877. Apparently his most productive ministry was in the decade before the Civil War. Preaching hundreds of sermons in widely dispersed places each year, organizing dozens of churches after receiving hundreds of converts, Kendrick literally "evangelized" the state. One year after his arrival, G. W. Banton of Huntsville praised him as a capable

---

[103] C. C. McKinney, "Report from the Border," *ibid.*, V (March, 1859), p. 94.

and esteemed evangelist. Because he had converted so many to Christ, Banton said, "If Tennessee and Kentucky would send us a few 100 such preachers, more could be done here than they could accomplish with their 1000's."[104] In 1858, Benton Sweeney cited him as "doing wonders in the more western counties by way of tent and other big meetings."[105] These evaluations of his ability were not exaggerated as Kendrick reported two hundred additions to the church "since harvest" on November 6, 1858.[106] Two years later, he estimated he had witnessesd about two thousand additions to the church during his nine years in Texas. Of that number, he attributed to himself in his reports to religious journals during the period some 830 accessions.

Kendrick was a wise evangelist who learned when to speak to accomplish the most good and how to overcome obstacles to effective preaching. By 1858, he concluded little could be done by "meetings in winter or during crop time." In many places, he found that Fourth of July or other holiday celebrations, balls, Odd Fellows processions, parades, and other affairs of public interest greatly diminished his audiences. At a camp meeting in Bell County, a lack of spring water and a sudden spring shower prematurely ended a revival. Determined to proclaim the gospel despite many hindrances, Kendrick obtained a large tent which was hauled from place to place, pitched and surrounded by small ones to accommodate the ladies. The tent

---
[104] G. W. Banton, "News," *Christian Magazine*, V (January, 1852), p. 26.
[105] Benton Sweeney, "News," *Christian Evangelist*, IX (October, 1858), p. 480.
[106] Kendrick, "News from the Churches," *Millennial Harbinger* (December, 1858), p. 718.

also served as sleeping quarters for the men and serving of meals during inclement weather.[107] During the summer of 1860, Kendrick conducted revivals in Bell, Milam, Lampasas and Burnet counties with seventy-two additions. The following year he held a successful revival at San Gabriel, Milam County, despite severe and constant rain. To prevent people from leaving to vote at a state election, he influenced officials to open polls on the camp grounds. Moving to Lampasas Springs, his tent comfortably sheltered the audience during a night-long heavy rain; not even the appearance of hostile Indians in the vicinity broke up the services. Some of the men left to drive them away, but others continued to attend services. The adverse conditions helped to make the meeting a success and eleven were immersed. Arriving on one occasion at Sandy Creek, Bastrop County, while many were herding stock, Kendrick persuaded the people to attend a five-day revival and received fifty-one additions to the church, a remarkable achievement.[108] Despite the fact that several other preachers usually assisted Kendrick in each meeting, he was required to speak from two to five times each day, counting the lectures at the water prior to baptisms and at the sunrise prayer services. Justifiably, he said, "I am, therefore, greatly worn down; but having adopted the habit of talking in a plain, easy style rather than preaching, in the popular sense, go on with but little rest."[109] Testifying to the success of his tent meetings was Kendrick's

---

[107]Kendrick, "Progress of Reform," *Millennial Harbinger* (November, 1860), pp. 655-656.

[108]Kendrick, "Texas Department," *Gospel Advocate*, VII (December, 1861), pp. 365-366.

[109]*Ibid.*

report in 1865 which indicated he had received over 1000 additions since 1860.[110]

In addition to his extensive preaching, Kendrick intended to begin "Philanthropia Institute" at Salado in January, 1857. In order to continue his evangelistic work, he planned to secure competent teachers. He proposed to accept only those boys who would submit to strict discipline, be able to pay part or all of their expenses by working at the school, and abide by the same rules and regulations as Kendrick's four sons who would also be enrolled. The course of study was to be elementary at first, designed to prepare the students for college. Kendrick astutely remarked that "many persons cannot send to college—many students should not be sent."[111] However, his plans apparently did not materialize because of the Civil War, as no reports were forthcoming concerning the school and its progress.

Another tireless evangelist of the churches of Christ was "circuit rider" Samuel Henderson. Henderson, who evidently arrived in the 1840's, located at Millville, Rusk County. A devout and enterprising worker, he rode from place to place, preaching the first principles of the gospel with great success. In 1851, after laboring with Kendrick in Rusk County, he reported 242 converts;[112] the next year he gained eighty-nine. At the end of 1855, Henderson summed up his experience as a "circuit rider" in a brief statement: "I have been riding nearly four years in Texas and have im-

---

[110]Kendrick, no title, *Millennial Harbinger* (December, 1865), p. 573.
[111]Kendrick, "Philanthropia Institute," *Gospel Advocaate*, III (January, 1857), p. 31.
[112]Randolph Gugate, "News from the Churches," *Millennial Harbinger* (October, 1851), p. 713.

mersed 398 persons in six counties . . . I would like to say much, but have been sorely afflicted with sore eyes for five months which pain me very much."[113] Nevertheless, his afflictions did not stop him from his work, as available reports attribute to him over eight hundred baptisms by 1860.

Broken in body as he approached the end of the Biblical life-span of three score and ten, Henderson was forgotten by the churches and resorted to farming to earn a living. With justifiable sarcasm, a fellow-preacher denounced the churches for abandoning a good, sensible preacher who had devoted the flower of his life to the defense of the gospel. "Still the brethren say they want preaching."[114] Undaunted in spirit, although destitute and afflicted like Job, Henderson not long before his death was patiently waiting, as the psalmist, for the end: "I wait for the Lord—my soul doth wait, and in his word do I hope . . . of being raised from a state of dishonor to one of everlasting honor."[115] He died in 1867 at Millville.

Other devoted and consecrated evangelists expounding the gospel received hundreds of converts into the church. During a 160-day period in late 1856 and early 1857, Aaron Newman traveled 1200 miles, preached 130 sermons, received 68 additions and "wished he had done more."[116] In the fall of 1858, Henry Thomas toured Dewitt, Goliad, Lavaca, Caldwell and Fayette counties in six weeks, and baptized

---

[113] Samuel Henderson, "Church News from Texas," *Gospel Advocate*, II (February, 1856), p. 63.

[114] Anonymous, "News and Notes" *ibid.*, IX (June 20, 1867), p. 498.

[115] Henderson, "News and Notes," *ibid.*, VIII (May 1, 1866), p. 288.

[116] Aaron Newman, "Texas Department," *ibid.*, III (April, 1857), pp. 124-125.

about seventy, mostly in towns where no churches previously had been founded.[117] Stephen Strickland, in conjunction with several other preachers, received 233 additions from July 1 to December 25, 1858, all in four or five counties.[118] Laboring in the vicinity of Austin from May to November, 1857, S. B. Giles reported over two hundred accessions to the church.[119] During the period August-October, 1860, Thomas Barrett conducted services in the following towns in East Texas despite wind, rain, dust and heat: Antioch, seven days; Sulphur Springs, five days; Antioch again, two days; Mt. Vernon, thirteen days; Mt. Pleasant, thirteen days; Sturgis Mill, three days; Paris, seven days. Thus Barrett spoke fifty times in fifty days and received 156 additions to the church. He triumphantly exclaimed, "This is a time long to be remembered. We thank God and take courage. Praise the Lord, O my soul!"[120]

Spiritual Deficiencies

Despite the rapid numerical growth of the churches of Christ in Texas effected by the vigorous efforts of their dedicated evangelists, no corresponding spiritual development occurred. Some contributing factors were the scarcity of church buildings, a great deficiency of competent church leaders to effectively prosecute local congregational activities, inadequate discipline of delinquent members, a dearth of located preachers, and a membership generally uninformed concerning funda-

---

[117] Thomas, "News from the Churches," *Millennial Harbinger* (December, 1858), p. 718.
[118] Strickland, "Texas Department," *Gospel Advocate*, IV (February, 1858), p. 59.
[119] S. B. Giles, "News from the Churches," *Millennial Harbinger* (March, 1857), pp. 176-177.
[120] Thomas Barrett, "Report from Texas," *Gospel Advocate*, VI (March, 1860), p. 93.

mental doctrine. P. F. Southern, who baptized twenty-five at Shelbyville in the fall of 1856 and planted a church, found "mammon, covetousness, avarice, envy and some drunkenness" in the church the following year. Although he endeavored to reclaim those who had "gone back into the world," many refused to desist from their evil practices. Encouraging Southern to persist in his efforts to purge the church of sin was Carroll Kendrick, who asserted that not all members of the churches of Christ were genuinely converted. He cited a similar situation in Kentucky where he found two stills using church property as operating fixtures. "When we tried to 'exorcise' them, it was found they had many friends—should we say brethren? Truly all are not Israel that are Israel."[121] After traveling through Grimes, Walker, Leon, Limestone, Houston, Freestone and Madison counties, J. A. Clark in 1858 contended the churches needed "good, common sense, practical men . . . who practice what they preach."[122] Supporting Clark's contention was Kendrick who requested evangelists to effect in the members "more piety and good works." Estimating that churches of Christ lost more members than the first century church, he urged ministers to follow the apostolic method and teach the new converts "to observe all things whatsoever I have commanded you . . ." (Matt. 28:20). "Thus, if our evangelists labored properly to teach Christian duties, and set churches in gospel order, would we not have fewer church difficulties, and lose fewer members?"[123] Departing from

---

[121] P. F. Southern, "News and Notes," *ibid.*, III (April, 1857), p. 126.
[122] J. A. Clark, "Texas Department," *ibid.*, III (January, 1857), p. 29.
[123] Kendrick, "Difficulty in Churches," *ibid.*, VI (January, 1860), p. 28.

the generally accepted preacher policy of endeavoring to gain the maximum number of converts, Kendrick stated that "members have not been a primary object with me." Although Kendrick received only eight additions in one meeting in 1860, he felt the results quite encouraging "considering the fact that our constant and leading purpose is the edification of the disciples, and their consequent increase in good works."[124] Seemingly, he felt that a few faithful, devoted Christians wielded more influence for the church than many left at the baptismal water uninstructed as to Christian duty. Although several thousand converts were added to the church through his preaching, he concluded, "I am not so sure that what I did toward these additions has been the most important of my labors."[125]

In order to rectify the spiritual deficiency existing among the churches, an unnamed lady who lived in Circleville urged all disciples to practice strict Bible religion. Although churches of Christ theoretically claimed a "perfect system of Christianity," she candidly asked, "Does she not look exactly like the sects and the world generally?" Specifically, she reprimanded worldly members who wore costly apparel and gold, jested, read novels, sought pleasure, and neglected reading the Bible and doing Christian deeds. Requesting these members to reform in order that they might imitate the "primitive Christians in all things," she exclaimed, "Oh, may I live to see it—that is what I hope to see."[126]

Numerous petty disputes over doctrinal beliefs oc-

---

[124] Kendrick, "Progress of Reform," *Millennial Harbinger* (November, 1860), pp. 655-656.
[125] *Ibid.*
[126] A. L. Hayslip, "Good Thoughts from a Sister," *Gospel Advocate*, VI (January, 1860), p. 25.

curred. One such had to do with the nature of the soul before and after death. In an effort to pacify the extremists on this point, J. L. Thorp of Dallas answered, "What does it matter if the soul be conscious or not between death and the resurrection? Let each have his own private opinion and not bring it as a test of fellowship."[127] At Palestine, the church in 1859 split over the "one man pastor" controversy. After hearing the arguments of both sides for five days, Kendrick succeeded in uniting the two factions, whereupon Tolbert Fanning urged both groups to humble themselves and devote all their energies to serving God.[128]

Some spiritual growth was evidenced, however, by the increasing awareness of churches to the necessity of adequately remunerating their ministers. J. A. Clark commended the disciples in Central Texas for their liberal support.[129] Thus, spiritual progress was forthcoming as the churches became better organized and functioned more efficiently in execution of all their duties.

THE SLAVERY ISSUE

The most pressing issue that confronted all churches during the period was the sectional conflict over slavery. In this controversy the churches of Christ had a unique situation. Most Protestants joined the issue in support of their respective sections. Division within the church on a North-South basis occurred first on May 1, 1845, when the Methodists in a conference held

---

[127] J. L. Thorp, "Fellowship," *Christian Evangelist*, VII (February, 1856), pp. 87-88.
[128] Tolbert Fanning, "Palestine, Texas," *Gospel Advocate*, V (June, 1859), pp. 181-182.
[129] Newman, "Texas Department," *ibid.*, III (April, 1857), p. 124.

in Louisville, Kentucky, formed the Methodist Episcopal Church South. Seven days later, Baptist delegates from eight slaveholding states organized the Southern Baptist Convention in Augusta, Georgia. In 1857, the New School Presbyterians in general assembly overwhelmingly denounced slavery or slaveholding on the part of its bishops or members. Thereupon, delegates from the South withdrew and formed the United Synod of the South.

In contrast with the Methodists, Baptists and Presbyterians, no division occurred among the decentralized churches of Christ over slavery. Although many of its members sanctioned the practice and owned slaves, no ruling body could legislate as to its validity or impropriety and have such a decision binding upon all the congregations. Since each church made its own decision, usually based upon the prevailing view, it actually fell into the realm of opinion, not a matter of faith or doctrine. Just before the Baptist and Methodist divisions over slavery occurred, Alexander Campbell in 1845 clearly asserted that "we are the only body in the world whose principles preserve us from such an unfortunate predicament."[130] His reference was to the absence of any means whereby the opinion of either an individual or group could be made the law of the church and so bring about schism. Nevertheless, members of the churches of Christ reached decided opinions on the issue and seldom hesitated to express them. Many Northern members vigorously contended that slavery was wrong from a scriptural point of view, that it was a moral and political evil. A minority argued that the Bible neither con-

---

[130] Alexander Campbell, "Our Position to American Slavery," *Millennial Harbinger* (February, 1845), p. 51.

doned nor condemned it. On the other hand, many Southern members generally maintained that it was upheld by the Bible, that it was the exercise of one's political and economic freedom. A few moderates agreed with their Northern brethren that the Scriptures were silent on the subject. Although there could be no legal split, actually the unofficial division within the churches of Christ was clear-cut between North and South. The American Missionary Society, organized in 1849, continued to hold its annual national meeting on through the Civil War, but only a minority of churches were represented and they had no power to enforce their doctrinal interpretations upon any church. Thus, only local incidents evidence the position of the church in a particular section.

In Texas, the churches of Christ generally were strongly pro-Southern as evidenced through several incidents. An excellent example is provided by an occurrence just prior to the Civil War. A preacher from Iowa, Solomon McKinney, visited a slave owner by the name of Smith while looking for a suitable place to settle in Texas. While present, he was asked by Brother Smith to preach on the duties of the master and the slave. Although he felt that he used candor, care and discretion, his sermon was distorted and condemned as incendiary, designed to endanger peace and property. Unfortunately, none of his sermon is available. Thereupon, McKinney was seized, cast into jail, barbarously whipped, and driven from town with threats of subsequent severe punishment should he return. The mob even molested some of the members of the church who attempted to assist McKinney. One member was assaulted and thrown into jail, charged with being an accomplice. Upon his return to Bloomfield, Iowa, McKinney's version of the incident was circulated in the North. Alexander Chatterton, editor of *The Evangelist,* begun in Davenport, Iowa, in 1849, urged Texas brethren not to consider McKinney either a "slavery agitator or abolitionist."[131]

During the Civil War, Mansil Matthews suffered a similar experience. Although he had resided in Texas for thirty years, he opposed secession and freed his slaves at the outbreak of war. In 1864, while traveling in a caravan, he was arrested on charges of treason and arraigned before the "high vigilance committee" in Gainesville. E. M. Daggett, an early builder of Fort Worth, who also opposed secession, journeyed to Gainesville and told the court that "Matthews' mind may be with the North, but his heart is with the South." Evidently persuaded, the court commuted the death sentence to three days in jail but did not inform Matthews of its decision. Daggett, who thought the verdict cruel, arranged a visit to the jail in order to tell him of the edict. Upon arrival, Daggett began a lengthy discussion with Matthews about the Bible, causing the bored guard to become inattentive. Daggett then asked Matthews to quote his favorite Bible verse, and Matthews asked Daggett to do the same. " 'Fret not thy gizzard and zizzle not thy whirlagig; thy soul art saved,' Daggett told the preacher. Matthews looked at the floor and trembled, daring not to show more emotion before the guard."[132]

MILITARY SERVICE AND WAR

A secondary issue was precipitated by the outbreak of war. Could members of the churches of Christ en-

---
[131]Alexander Chatterton, "Elder Solomon McKinney," *The Evangelist,* XI (April, 1860), p. 186.
[132]*Fort Worth Star-Telegram,* October 30, 1949.

"*Fret not thy gizzard or zizzle thy whirlagig; thy soul art saved.*"

gage in military service? Again, this was a matter of personal opinion as the churches had never faced the necessity of formulating any doctrinal policy on the question. Editor Chatterton tackled the problem by advocating forthright New Testament answers supporting the negative. He posed some questions to lead his readers to the conclusion desired: "Shall Christians from either of the contending sections go into war?" Without attempting an answer, he then asked, "Will we be justifiable in so doing by that book which is to judge us in the day of eternity?" Citing the life of Christ, Chatterton quoted with unmistakable clarity the compelling words of Jesus to Peter after he had wielded the sword in defense of his beloved master: "Put up thy sword; for they that take the sword shall perish with the sword." He then summoned the apostles to his aid with the following supposition: "If the twelve were here, six in the South, six in the North, would they be urging brethren to mortal combat?" With scathing denunciation, he proceeded to condemn all clergymen fomenting and agitating their brethren to war. "Men who claim to be successors of the apostles, are openly, before heaven and earth, exulting in this impiety. . ."[133] This was a Northern view, little read in Texas.

In the widely circulated *Gospel Advocate*, editor Tolbert Fanning expressed the Southern view by partially concurring with Chatterton that "weapons of Christian warfare are spiritual. . ." He argued that should the laws of God and country be in contradiction, Christians were to obey God.

We notice quite a number of religious writers

---
[133]Alexander Chatterton, "Shall Christians Go to War?", *The Evangelist*, XII (June, 1861), pp. 318-319.

who maintain, that when the state calls, Christians are released from all personal responsibility. This is a shallow conclusion. We should by all means perform our duties to our country unless we are required to violate the laws of Christ's kingdom, and then, at the cost of all earthly, we are required to obey God.

But with apparent inconsistency, Fanning justified the South. "It is honorable religiously to even rebel against oppression, as we conscientiously believe it is for the states South to politically rebel against the assumed authority of the states North."[134] He possibly meant that one could religiously and politically overthrow an existing order by all means short of physical force. Thus, editors, preachers and writers argued their respective views in religious journals that circulated among churches of Christ. In the final analysis, each individual, North or South, allowed his own conscience to be his guide, but in most instances followed the group conscience of the section in which he lived.

In Texas, very little opposition to military service was voiced by members. A few preachers, among whom the best known were J. R. Wilmeth and B. F. Hall, served as chaplains. Hall, who served as chaplain for a regiment of Texas Rangers commanded by Barton Stone, son of the renowned Barton W. Stone, acted more like a soldier than a minister. "He rode a fine mule, had a splendid rifle, and expressly requested of all friends that if a 'Yankee' appeared, please let him get his share." Before the battle of Pea Ridge, Arkansas, William Baxter and Robert Graham, two ministers of the churches of Christ, visited the Confederate army encamped near Fayetteville, Arkan-

---

[134]Tolbert Fanning, "Religious Aspects of the American Revolution of 1861," *Gospel Advocate*, VII (July, 1861), p. 213.

sas, to talk with Hall. Both were shocked by Hall's violent tirades against the North and his apparent intense desire to kill Yankees. When Graham asked Hall how he felt toward his Northern brethren, he replied that he had no brethren in the North; they were all infidels.[135] Among those members who served in the Confederate army and later became leaders among the churches of Christ in Texas were Addison and Randolph Clark, John T. Poe, Austin McGary, and General R. M. Gano. However, no uniform policy emerged. After the war, an anonymous preacher in Williamson County wrote, "The brethren here were generally opposed to war in every form, even during the recent contest, and very few of them engaged in it, few could ever be forced into it."[136]

With outbreak of war in 1861, the Texas churches of Christ became isolated not only from the North but also virtually from contacts with sister congregations in the South, particularly Tennessee and Kentucky where they had traditionally looked for leadership. Thus, the self-governing congregations were left without the unifying forces of religious publications. The *Gospel Advocate,* only organ serving churches of Christ in the South, ceased publication from 1861 to 1866. *The Evangelist* remarked in 1861 that "Our readers miss, no doubt, the spicy productions of Elder J. A. Butler, a Southern writer of Arkansas. There is no mail communication . . . and he can be heard no more, we presume, till the war shall end."[137] After the May, 1861, issue, the paper was not sent to South-

---
[135] William Baxter, *Pea Ridge and Prairie Grove* (Cincinnati, 1864), pp. 113-123.
[136] Anonymous, "Texas Department," *Gospel Advocate,* X (May, 1868), p. 520.
[137] Alexander Chatterton, writing in *The Evangelist,* XII (September, 1861), p. 503.

ern states. Perhaps the first letter to the *Millennial Harbinger* after the war from a Texas minister was written by Kendrick. "It has been a long time since I saw a copy of the *Millennial Harbinger*, 6 or 7 years."[138] Although the *Harbinger* carried numerous Texas reports before the war in each issue, only two appear from the Lone Star state in the period 1861-1869. Such was evidently true in regard to other periodicals published in the North.

Devoid of the opinions of editors, local teaching, and views of the frequent itinerant evangelists, Texas members declined in spirituality throughout the war years. Most did what was right in their own eyes. It was not until the cords of the Union had been forged again that the spiritual ties were resumed. Thus, the Civil War provides an interlude in the history of the churches of Christ. It seems appropriate, therefore, before proceeding with the post-war development to summarize and compare its statistics with several leading denominations in Texas and to evaluate its progress.

CHURCH STATUS IN 1860

The statistics for 1860 indicate the status of the churches of Christ and their growth during the Texas statehood period. Although several authorities on a national level have given estimates, all have been somewhat inaccurate. In 1848, Alexander Hall, editor of the *Gospel Proclamation* published in Lloydsville, Ohio, compiled statistics of Christian (churches of Christ) churches in America and Europe. Apparently based upon reports appearing in his paper, which had a meagre circulation in Texas, Hall listed for the Lone

---

[138]Kendrick, "News from the Churches," *Millennial Harbinger* (October, 1866), p. 573.

CHURCH GROWTH IN EARLY STATEHOOD PERIOD, 1845-1861

Star state 11 churches, 230 members, 4 preachers, and 7 elders or exhorters,[139] obviously a woeful underestimate. In a more accurate approximation, Joseph Belcher computed the total for the United States in 1853 to be 225,000 members of whom 5,000 resided in Texas, 2,700 churches, and 2,250 preachers. He made no estimate of the number of churches or preachers in Texas[140]

The United States Census for 1850 reported for Texas as follows:

	Number of Churches	Value of Buildings	Seating Capacity
Methodist	173	$58,195	34,058
Baptist	70	23,000	10,020
Presbyterian	47	20,070	8,520
Catholic	13	79,700	6,760
Episcopalian	5	15,100	1,025
Christian	5	150	100[141]

Obviously, the statistics for the Christians were too low. Unfortunately, the United States Census religious report for 1860 listed only the number of churches, value of buildings, and their seating capacity. For Texas the statistics are as follows:

Church	Number of Churches	Value of Buildings	Seating Capacity
Methodist	410	$319,934	119,934
Baptist	280	228,030	77,435
Union	96		
Presbyterian	72	120,550	19,567
Christian	53	27,395	15,905

---

[139] *The Christian Register* (compiled and published by Alexander Hall, editor of the Gospel Proclamation, 1848), pp. 45-46.
[140] Joseph Belcher, *The Religious Denominations in the United States* (Indianapolis, 1855), p. 811.
[141] *Statistical View of the United States* (Compendium of the Seventh Census). J. D. B. Debow, Superintendent of the United States Census (Washington, 1854), pp. 134-137.

These figures indicate the average church building owned by the churches of Christ was worth about five hundred dollars and could seat approximately three hundred. Since the churches of Christ had erected only a few buildings, mostly small, the approximate seating capacity seems much too large. An average seating capacity of one hundred would be more nearly correct. The authors of the *Disciples of Christ, A History*, who had access to the 1860 census, apparently used a percentage of the "sittings" to estimate the number of members in Texas as 2,500.[142] No other membership figures for Texas in any previous year are cited.

The only figures directly from Texas were those submitted by Kendrick, itinerant evangelist since 1851, based upon personal observation. In 1856 he listed 160 churches, generally small, with few if any elders or evangelists to serve or direct the work. He numbered about eighty preachers, only ten or twelve of whom were active on a full time basis.[143]

After the Civil War, several additional sets of figures were presented. In 1867, H. P. Dyer of Kentuckytown, Texas, claimed, "We have, I am sure, a membership of at least 6,000 and perhaps 10,000. . ."[144] In the same year, evangelist L. H. Dowling of Indianapolis estimated the national membership at 341,000 of whom 3,500 members were in Texas. Of 1642 preachers in the United States, only fifteen were known to be in the Lone Star state, but he explained that his list was not complete because the South was

---
[142]Garrison and DeGroot, *Disciples of Christ*, p. 329.
[143]Kendrick, "The Cause in Texas," *Gospel Advocate*, II (September, 1856), p. 288.
[144]H. P. Dyer, "Texas Department," *ibid.*, IX (May 23, 1867), p. 419.

"in such a disorganized condition as to render it impossible to obtain a very correct report from that section."[145]

The statistics present a rather confusing array of information. However, a fairly reliable estimate may be obtained by adding all the accessions to the church listed by ministers in their reports to religious periodicals from 1845 to 1861. During this period, 145 reports from ninety-two different preachers in the *Millennial Harbinger, Gospel Advocate, The Evangelist, Christian Evangelist, Christian Review, Christian Magazine, Gospel Proclamation,* and *Christian Record,* listed a total of 4,726 additions to the church. If the approximately one thousand members resident in 1845 are added and allowance is made for immigrant members, those returning to other states, those who died, failure of some evangelists to report additions, and defections of some to different sects, a reasonable estimate of the total members in Texas in 1861 would be in excess of six thousand. Submitted data named 118 churches, most of which were organized. Using Kendrick's on-the-scene estimate of 160 churches in 1856 and making allowance for the fact that many churches were never listed in any periodical, a probable figure of about two hundred with an average membership of about thirty corresponds with the six thousand total estimate and fits his description of "small." The majority of congregations worshiped once each month in school buildings, court houses, lodge halls, or in a church building made available by other religious bodies. Kendrick reported a total of eighty preachers in 1856 and ninety-two are accounted for in religious

---
[145]L. H. Dowling, *The Christian Almanac for the Year of Our Lord and Saviour 1867* (Indianapolis, 1867), p. 32.

journals by 1861. Allowing for those who died, stopped preaching, moved to other states, or were unreported in a religious journal, probably about one hundred of the ministers of the churches of Christ proclaimed the gospel in Texas in 1861. Even though Kendrick indicated only ten or twelve preached every Sunday in 1856, letters carried in the several publications reveal that at least thirty were holding religious services every first day of the week in 1861.

In comparison with other religious bodies in Texas, churches of Christ ranked fifth numerically, behind the Methodists, Baptists, Catholics and Presbyterians in that order; seventh in value of buildings but fifth in seating capacity. The Methodist edifice at Jefferson, valued at thirty thousand dollars, was the most elegant church building in the state.[146] In comparison, churches of Christ probably had no building worth more than two thousand dollars.

Nationwide, churches of Christ in Texas, although still quite young, compared favorably. The lack of fine edifices, or of any building whatever, was not unique with Texas congregations. In 1859, the churches of Christ were the only prominent religious body in the nation which did not have a house of worship in Washington, D. C. A plea for funds was made in order to erect a commodious house in which members might worship "when sojourning in Washington." Answering the call in true Texas fashion were Virginia S. Longscope of Texas with a donation of $2.50; church at Victoria, $4.45; E. W. Dabney, Austin, $5.00.[147] Texas congregations already ranked eighth

---

[146] Thrall, *Methodism in Texas*, p. 149.
[147] Anonymous, "Church in Washington," *Millennial Harbinger* (October, 1859), pp. 594-597.

among the states in total membership, although the Lone Star state had been in the Union only sixteen years. The outbreak of war brought a stalemate in its growth. With the end of the war, vast areas of cheap or free land were made available to enterprising frontiersmen. It was in such an environment that churches of Christ best thrived.

CHAPTER IV

AN ERA OF CONSIDERABLE ADVANCEMENT, 1865-1906

Post-War Conditions

The weary figure of Robert E. Lee surrendering to Ulysses S. Grant at Appomattox Court House on April 9, 1865, signaled the end of the disastrous Civil War, but not the misery, heartache and ruin which plagued the prostrate South. Four years of savage conflict had left deep scars which had not been erased entirely four decades later. Social and economic rehabilitation was desperately needed, but avaricious Northern politicians began a wild orgy of political reconstruction based upon hate and prejudice. Amid the squalor and gloom, deepened by Northern indiscretion, shone the faint glimmer of hope—the church.

Texas, as a part of the Confederacy, although escaping the massive physical destruction visited upon most of the South, nevertheless suffered a serious spiritual decline during the war. Preoccupied with pressing economic, social and political problems, its people tended to postpone spiritual matters until a more propitious time. Churches of Christ suffered along with other religious bodies in the temporary spiritual eclipse.

In 1865, Moses E. Lard, editor of a new religious journal, *Lard's Quarterly,* published at Frankfort, Kentucky, proposed a role for the churches of Christ in the reconstruction of the South. In a similar appeal at the convention of the American Christian Missionary Society in Cincinnati in 1867, which was attended by only a few Southern delegates, Lard with great propriety urged the immediate evangelization of the bleeding South. "No spot on the American continent, perhaps not in the world," he pleaded, "presents as inviting field for missionary labor as the great South over which the late war swept with such destruction." Exercising commendable discretion, Lard judiciously suggested:

> But in order to realize from this field the largest possible results . . . it is necessary to till it with more than common skill. The only men who can do this are the preachers bred on its soil and whose hearts beat in unison with its broken hearted and sensitive citizens . . . while the heart of the South is yet bleeding, let it be seeded with the truth of Him who is the friend of all.[1]

The destitute spiritual condition of the churches of Christ in Texas was the central theme of the several reports submitted by ministers from 1866 to 1869. J. H. Cain, evangelist in Harrison County, lamented in 1866, "Our churches in East Texas, most of them, have come to nothing."[2] The following year William Defee, itinerant preacher in East Texas since 1837, described the churches as "cold." Unable to secure any subscribers for the *Gospel Advocate*, he intoned, "I never saw money so hard to get."[3]

E. C. Chambers of Montgomery County in 1868 aptly characterized the public mind in response to gospel preaching as beset by "bitter sectarianism, in-

---
[1] Moses E. Lard, "The South as a Field," *Lard's Quarterly*, III (October, 1865), p. 43.
[2] J. H. Cain, "Texas Department," *Gospel Advocate*, VIII (September 18, 1866), p. 622.
[3] William Defee, *ibid.*, IX (February 28, 1867), p. 180.

fidelity and general indifference." Some congregations assembled only on Sunday morning to worship; others simply died or melted away in disinterest. Numerous meeting houses, once crowded and brightly lighted for evening services, were now dark and empty, week after week.[4] The following year, after a tour among the churches in Central Texas, Kendrick wrote, "We need labor, labor, labor. Few feel half their responsibility. . . We lack zeal, conscience, faith."[5]

Equally distressing was the decreased activity of many preachers. Because of the perilous economic conditions, most were forced to engage in secular work in order to sustain their families. Chambers, being poor in this world's goods, explained that "our preaching brethren," with few exceptions, labor without compensation, and at their own expense; as a result, there is little labor done except to attend to Lord's day meetings for worship.[6] Evangelist C. H. Appling reasoned that "Christianity was at a low ebb" because the preachers, compelled to work at other jobs to earn a livelihood, had become worldly minded. Such an attitude on the part of the ministers cooled the ardor and weakened the zeal of the members.[7] Noting the lack of full-time preachers, John T. Poe of Huntsville encouraged young single men to come and evangelize the state. To provide incentive for their coming, Poe promised "enough of this world's goods" for a comfortable living.[8]

The climax of the inactivity of the ministry was exemplified in a situation which arose in Seguin, Guada-

---

[4] E. C. Chambers, *ibid.*, X (June 4, 1868), p. 536.
[5] Kendrick, *ibid.*, XI (October 21, 1869), p. 973.
[6] Chambers, *ibid.*, X (June 4, 1868), p. 536.
[7] C. H. Appling, *ibid.*, X (October 8, 1868), pp. 980-981.
[8] John T. Poe, *ibid.*, XI (October 21, 1869), p. 973.

lupe County, in 1867. Sister M. Burrows had taught the gospel to several persons in the town who expressed a desire to be immersed. Since there was no one present to perform the ordinance, she wrote three letters to the *Gospel Advocate* urgently pleading for a preacher to come to Seguin.[9] Whether anyone heeded the call is unknown.[10] In the same year, another report gave credence to the dearth of evangelists in South Texas. William Baxter of Matagorda wrote that "Our whole coast country from the Sabine to the Rio Grande, including Houston and Galveston . . . is almost, if not entirely, unbenefited by Christian preaching." With questionable hope, he asked, "Is there no help for it?"[11]

Despite the rather destitute condition of the churches of Christ immediately after the war, renewed activity by their ministers and members brought about considerable growth before their formal division in 1906. In order to show best this growth, it seems appropriate to consider five major areas of the state: East Texas, east of a line from Paris to Conroe; North Texas, centered around the Dallas-Fort Worth vicinity; Central Texas with focal points at Austin and Waco; the Gulf Coast area from Beaumont to Corpus Christi; and Southwest Texas with San Antonio as a hub.

EFFORTS IN EAST TEXAS

At the southern extremity of East Texas, churches

---

[9] Anonymous, *ibid.*, IX (March 7, 1867), p. 200.
[10] Mary Scott (Dallas), to Stephen Eckstein, interview, December 18, 1952. Should a similar situation arise today, evangelists and elders of the churches of Christ would usually urge the lady to baptize the candidates. Mrs. Scott immersed her invalid mother in a bath tub.
[11] William Baxter, "Texas Department," *Gospel Advocate*, IX (February 28, 1867), p. 178.

of Christ were planted in Montgomery and Walker counties. In 1862, a church of eleven members was formed at Montgomery. Four years later, it numbered sixty and had erected a fine building. Nearby at Conroe, a church of ninety members met each Sunday.[12] Thirty miles north, the Huntsville church, founded in 1860 with seventeen disciples, grew during the war years because two of its original elders carefully disciplined and instructed the members. By 1867, sixty-eight additional disciples had been baptized, but four had been dismissed by letter, fourteen cut off for immoral conduct or for leaving during the war and not returning, leaving a total of sixty-two ". . . good, substantial, orderly members."[13] Four years later, the church had about eighty members and services every Sunday. John T. Poe endeavored to induce members from other states to immigrate to Walker County because land was selling from fifty cents to five dollars an acre and three preachers proclaimed the gospel at some place every Lord's day.[14] In 1878, evangelist J. M. Barnes visited Huntsville and preached in the state penitentiary to a "most attentive and appreciative audience."[15] Although the congregation continued to grow, the greatest increase occurred during a revival, October 20-November 2, 1887, conducted by evangelists T. R. Burnett and James Mulkey. "The large opera house has been crowded day and night and the meeting resulted in about 150 converts. The house was literally packed" to hear Burnett's farewell sermon.[16] Undoubtedly, the Huntsville congrega-

---
[12]W. N. Linton, *ibid.*, VIII (September 18, 1866), p. 616.
[13]J. H. Bautau, *ibid.* IX, (April 18, 1867), p. 220.
[14]Poe, *ibid.*, XIII (August 31, 1871), p. 797.
[15]*Ibid.*, XX (July 18, 1878), p. 444.
[16]*Huntsville Gazette*, November 2, 1887.

tion, with well over two hundred members after 1887, was one of the largest in East Texas.

In nearby Polk and Houston counties, other churches were organized. In the summer of 1867, Samuel Henderson left his home in Rusk, Cherokee County, and journeyed fifty-six miles to a Baptist meeting house in Polk County where he delivered nine sermons. His first discourse dealt with the children of Israel in the wilderness and the erection of the tabernacle. Then he outlined the Jewish dispensation which he contended ended with the words of Jesus, "It is finished," uttered while the Savior hung on the cross just before his death. In his concluding message, he described the establishment of the church on Pentecost; "henceforward, the Holy Spirit has dwelt in and animated the body of Christ." At the close of the final sermon, "nineteen Baptists, nine Methodists, three Presbyterians, two Universalists, and one Hard Shell Baptist came forward and joined the church of Christ." Praising the Almighty, Henderson joyfully exclaimed, "Thou art the God of wonders. Thou hast declared thy strength among the peoples."[17] Two years later, Kendrick and W. T. Fuller conducted a meeting at Moscow, Polk County, organized a church of twelve members, and ordained aged evangelist R. T. Walker as elder.[18] In Houston County, no church was formed until 1899-1900 when a small band of disciples began meeting in the opera house, then in the courthouse under the leadership of Virgil Graves. Within a year, H. H. Hamilton assisted the brethren in erecting a building.[19]

---
[17] D. M. Priest, "Texas Department," *Gospel Advocate*, X (January 2, 1868), p. 17.
[18] Kendrick, *ibid.*, XI (October 21, 1869), p. 973.
[19] A. A. Aldrich, *The History of Houston County, Texas* (San Antonio, 1943), pp. 115-116.

Simultaneously, efforts were made to establish the cause in Shelby, San Augustine, Nacogdoches and Sabine counties. Council Billingsley, who came to Texas in 1858, founded the Pine Grove church (later called Oak Grove) in 1861 about ten miles east of Center, Shelby County, on his land; Willow Grove church in 1866 about twelve miles north of Center; and one in 1872 in the Weaver community five miles west of Timpson. During the next few years, Billingsley and P. F. Southern spoke in private homes, brush arbors, in the open woods, or in whatever place was available. As a result they won many converts, but created considerable prejudice among the Methodists and Baptists.[20] In the Antioch congregation, founded near San Augustine in 1836, a most unusual event occurred in 1880. H. H. Johnson, an Episcopalian, unwilling to allow his child to die unbaptized, summoned W. H. Eaves, an elder and preacher of the Antioch church to baptize it. Eaves administered the rite upon its deathbed. Immediately, N. W. Ware, another elder and minister of the Antioch church, challenged Eaves' right to perform the rite in opposition to the doctrine of the Bible as taught by churches of Christ.[21] Although the outcome of the dispute is not recorded, it reveals a departure from the practice of the majority of members of the church regarding the rite of baptism. In adjoining counties, J. A. Abney, an attorney, assisted by Billingsley, converted seven at Melrose, Nacogdoches County, two at Hemphill, Sabine County,

---

[20] G. L. Crockett, *Two Centuries in East Texas* (Dallas, 1932), pp. 297-298.
[21] *Ibid.*, churches of Christ assert the Bible teaches that children up to the age of accountability are in a state of innocence, therefore, do not need to be baptized (Matt. 18:3). Also, they contend that only believers in Christ are proper candidates for baptism (Mark 16:16).

and one at the church called Philadelphia, Shelby County, in July, 1869. Shortly thereafter, Abney found it necessary to spend several weeks in court practicing law in order to provide sustenance for his family but promised to resume preaching the gospel as soon as possible.[22]

Meanwhile, ministers of churches of Christ evangelized Cherokee, Henderson and Wood counties with some success. While conducting a meeting at Jacksonville, Cherokee County, in 1885, an unknown preacher met a Mrs. Berryman who was born in Nacogdoches in 1804 and was thought to be the oldest native Texan living. "She is hale, hearty, cheerful, and has sent a home-made patch-quilt to the exposition at New Orleans."[23] Apparently stimulated by the revival, the Jacksonville church, assisted by congregations at Troupe, Lone Dove and Larrissa, sent evangelist H. Hamilton to "sound the word" in the surrounding counties. At Athens, Henderson County, A. J. Bush established a church after conducting a revival in the Presbyterian building in 1887. The following organizational creed was adopted:

> We the undersigned immersed believers in Christ, covenant together to keep the ordinances of the Lord Jesus as delivered to the Holy Apostles, for mutual edification and growth in the divine life, and for the furtherance of the cause of the Redeemer in this midst; taking the scriptures of the Old and New Testament as our only book of faith and the New Testament as our rule of life. Said organization to be known as the "Church of Christ" in Athens, Texas.

---

[22] J. A. Abney, "Texas Department," *Gospel Advocate*, XI (September 2, 1869), p. 809.

[23] Anonymous, "Oldest Native," *ibid.*, XXVII (June 3, 1885), p. 340.

Four years later, Granville Jones spoke at a revival in the courthouse with fifty added to the congregation. Shortly thereafter, the church was reorganized and the name changed to "Christian Church,"[24] probably because of the introduction of an organ into the worship services. Thirty miles to the north in Wood County, W. Lyles and wife, who arrived in January, 1866, reported only two other members of the church of Christ could be found in the vicinity.[25] At Mineola, James Dickson preached three times in September, 1875, and baptized a man from Sweden. Evidently encouraged by an inaccurate prophecy of a Primitive Baptist, "The Campbellites will take the town," William Jones purposed to move to the thriving railroad town and establish a church.[26] Apparently, however, he was unsuccessful.

About forty-five miles to the east at Longview, a little railroad town of about twelve hundred population, a few disciples first met in the fall of 1874. After some discussion, two wealthy members agreed to furnish materials for a house of worship while the others consented to erect the building. On June 7, 1875, twenty members dedicated the new edifice.[27]

During the next decade, the church grew rapidly

---

[24] J. J. Faulk, *History of Henderson County, Texas* (Athens, Texas, 1929), pp. 91, 109. Charter members of the Athens church were W. E. and Mrs. J. N. Redding, W. G. and Mrs. Susan Scott, T. J. Eads, G. H. and Mrs. S. A. Roberts, V. I. and Ida Stirman, G. R. Davis, A. H. Sumner, W. M. Gauntt, C. G. Hatch, Jeff C. Davis, Thos. Bradshaw, J. R. Pierson, G. H. Richie, Mary A. and Mary T. Richie, T. B. Spencer, Fannie R. Spencer, Mrs. Mina Miller, Mrs. Annie Chambers and Mrs. A. E. Williamson.
[25] *Firm Foundation*, January 28, 1896.
[26] William Jones, "News," *Gospel Advocate*, XVII (September 30, 1875), p. 935
[27] George Harrison, "Longview," *Apostolic Times* (Lexington, Kentucky), VII (September 9, 1875), p. 405.

An Era of Considerable Advancement, 1865-1906

until the organ question arose. Although the congregation did not use instrumental music in its services in 1884, some members indicated their sentiment for an organ by circulating the following advertisement: "A magic lantern entertainment for the benefit of the Episcopal Church will be given in the Christian Church . . . Admission 25c, children half price . . . proceeds to be applied toward purchasing a new organ for the Episcopal Church." Immediately, minister Poe denounced the advertisement as an endeavor to "court favor with all the Babylonish sects," and cried for an Elijah who might give a "thus saith the Lord."[28] In spite of the resulting controversy, the church increased to about seventy by 1899.[29] However, when L. A. Dale introduced the organ into the church in January, 1895, the inevitable division occurred. The twenty-five anti-organ members, who withdrew under Poe's leadership, termed the majority "heretics and schismatics." Even though the minority group reorganized within a week, the discouraged Poe soon moved away. When he returned in February, 1900, he found only a few still opposed to the organ. Evidencing great tenacity, he gathered seven anti-organ disciples who worshiped together for a year without receiving any additions. When the first convert was added in March, 1901, Poe exclaimed, "Praise the Lord!" Within six months, the church numbered nineteen staunch members.[30]

In nearby Hopkins County, James Dickson successfully proclaimed the gospel in rural areas in the sum-

---
[28]Poe, "Texas Department," *Gospel Advocate*, XXVI (March 5, 1884), p. 148.
[29]*Ibid.*, XXXI (October 23, 1889), p. 677.
[30]John T. Poe, "Longview," *ibid.*, XLIII (October 17, 1901), p. 669.

mer of 1868. After receiving sixteen additions, including a Methodist preacher, during a meeting at Black Jack Grove in August, Dickson established a church of twenty-six members; at a Brother Ward's house he organized a congregation of twenty-seven. Greatly encouraged, Dickson declared, "The good cause is prevailing in this county over all opposition."[31]

In adjacent Harrison and Upshur counties, other churches were established. At Marshall, the church which had wasted away during the Civil War, was re-established in 1890. Two years later, R. F. Carter moved to town because he believed the eight hundred men who worked in the Texas and Pacific Railroad shops would be receptive to the gospel. Apparently his preaching was successful, as he received twenty-four additions to the church within six months. Shortly thereafter, however, he was forced to leave because of his wife's ill health. Nevertheless, Carter envisioned a steady growth for the church.[32] About the same time, William Holloway of Longview arrived in Gilmer and preached in the courthouse. After meeting in the courthouse each Sunday for several years, the small congregation in 1897 erected its own building.[33]

To the north in Titus and Morris counties, T. R. Burnett firmly established the church of Christ during the post-war period. Conducting protracted meetings in the vicinity each summer, Burnett baptized hundreds. In 1900, during a seven-week period, he re-

---

[31] James A. Dickson, "Texas Department," *ibid.*, X (November 12, 1868), p. 1091.

[32] R. F. Carter, "News," *ibid.*, XXXV (October 12, 1893), p. 654.

[33] G. H. Baird, *A Brief History of Upshur County* (Gilmer, Texas, 1946), p. 39. Among the eight original members were Mr. and Mrs. S. T. Richardson, Sheriff J. W. Willeford and wife, Mrs. Douphrate, and Mrs. J. L. Basset.

ceived 170 additions to the church, of whom 81 were added to the Center Grove church, Titus County.[34] Even more productive were his efforts at Rocky Branch, Morris County, six miles north of Daingerfield. At the conclusion of his sixth revival with this church in August, 1901, he received sixty converts, was liberally compensated with sixty dollars for his services, and was requested to return for a seventh meeting the following summer. Joyfully, Burnett remarked, "This is now the largest and best church in the eastern portion of the state. It has a large and elegant meetinghouse . . . four-fifths of the members are my children in the gospel, and they are very dear to me."[35]

In extreme northeast Texas at Texarkana, a church of ten members was established by J. C. Mason in October, 1883. A year later, the small band met in Conductors Hall at 213 Walnut Street. The first house of worship was constructed in 1905 on a lot donated by J. F. Kirby.[36] Previously, in 1900, T. E. Tatum, evidently a member of the congregation, proposed the establishment of an orphans home and industrial school, operated by members of the church of Christ, upon a twelve hundred acre tract of land just west of town which had been donated by S. D. Lary of Texarkana. Although an elaborate plan was formulated for fulfilling the adventurous project, apparently it was never executed.[37]

---

[34]T. R. Burnett, "Church News," *Gospel Advocate*, XLII (September 13, 1900), p. 589.
[35]*Ibid.*
[36]Barbara Overton Chandler and J. Ed. Howe, *History of Texarkana and Bowie and Miller Counties, Texas-Arkansas* (Shreveport, 1939), p. 147.
[37]T. E. Tatum, "Church News," *Gospel Advocate*, XLII (June 14, 1900), p. 384.

At the northern edge of East Texas, some church growth occurred in Red River and Lamar counties. At Detroit, Red River County, the Rose brothers, evangelists of the church of Christ from Mississippi, arrived in 1890 during cotton picking time. Although a church had existed for many years in the community, it had experienced little growth because of prejudice. Seemingly, the prejudice had evolved from the teaching of some disciples who claimed that non-members of the churches of Christ would be consigned to hell on the judgment day. However, during the revival conducted by the Rose brothers crowds increased at each service. Colorful and impressive baptismal services were performed by the two small ministers in nearby pools. Several members of the influential Guest family of Guest Prairie and relatives were baptized. The ministers found it necessary to call for assistance when immersing Joe Wheeler Guest, who weighed well over two hundred pounds. As a result of their preaching, the church was revived and it appeared that the schism had been healed. However, shortly after their departure, the dissension erupted again when an organ was introduced into the church.[38] Seventeen miles to the west, Charles Carlton preached seventeen days in Paris, baptized thirty, restored thirty-five, and organized a church of eighty members in 1869.[39] Twenty-three years later, his minister son D. T. Carlton led the church to erect a new building on Lamar Street.[40] Thus, additional churches of Christ were planted in

---

[38] Emma Guest Bourne, *A Pioneer Farmer's Daughter of Red River Valley* (Northeast Texas) (Dallas, 1950), pp. 122-125.
[39] Charles Carlton, "Church News," *Gospel Advocate*, XI (August 18, 1869), p. 782.
[40] H. F. Williams, "Field Findings," *ibid.*, XXXIV (May 5, 1892), p. 279.

DALLAS

Meanwhile, comparable growth took place in a square area of North Texas bounded by Greenville and Kaufman on the east, Corsicana and Hillsboro on the south, Mineral Wells and Jacksboro on the west, and the Red River on the north. In the forefront were the churches in the Dallas-Fort Worth vicinity. The Dallas congregation, founded in 1856, became one of the strongest churches of Christ in North Texas in the nineteenth century. The small band which met in the upper room of the courthouse for several years was greatly strengthened by the arrival in 1861 of Charles Carlton, teacher, preacher, and graduate of Bethany College. Carlton began teaching school in a log house south of the courthouse. Shortly thereafter, he announced the opening of a Lord's day school in an upstairs room on Main opposite present Sanger Brothers, a blacksmith shop occupying the ground floor. He preached on alternate Sundays, beginning the service at 8:30 A.M. and dismissing at noon.[41] According to Mrs. Sarah Harwood, an early and long-time member, the Collins, Eakin, Smith, Saunders, Barton, Stone, Fletcher, Morrow, Martin, and Dr. Johnston families joined the church in the early 1860's.[42] Dr. I. L. Van Zandt, a physician who arrived in May, 1866, found a few meeting in an "upper chamber" to study the Bible, observe the Lord's supper, and hear an occasional visiting preacher. A month later, H. D. Bantau of White Rock spoke one Sunday and General R. M.

---
[41] *Dallas Morning News*, October 1, 1935.
[42] *Firm Foundation*, November 2, 1926.

Gano, ex-Brigadier General in the Confederate army, held a meeting during the summer.[43]

The story of the first church building in Dallas is contained in a letter written by Van Zandt dated October 14, 1925. In the summer of 1867, Dr. B. F. Hall, who had been preaching in Texas for many years, held a revival and converted Van Zandt's wife. Stirred by Hall's sermons and spurred on by Colby Smith, leader of the "church builder movement," the church erected a one-room frame structure near the Missouri, Kansas and Texas depot, two blocks north and one block east of the courthouse, on what was then known as Carondelet Street (now Ross Avenue), named in honor of Baron Carondelet, a famous colonial governor of Louisiana. Dallas then had a population of about three thousand.[44] On December 4, 1938, the Dallas Christian Churches in cooperation with the Dallas Historical Society placed a bronze plaque on the site of the original building. The appropriate inscription reads, "Site of Christian Church. Built 1867. This was the first church building erected in Dallas."[45]

The growing church continued to meet in the new building until it divided in 1877. General R. M. Gano received thirty-two converts into the church during a revival in the fall of 1872. Three years later, Knowles Shaw, the singing evangelist, introduced an organ into the church while holding a meeting. Shortly after his departure, he was killed in a train wreck near McKinney, and the congregation soon thereafter disagreed, unfortunately, over the use of the organ in the worship services. On August 24, 1877, a minority

---

[43]Wise, *Pearl and Bryan Church*.
[44]*Ibid*.
[45]*Dallas Morning News*, December 5, 1938.

AN ERA OF CONSIDERABLE ADVANCEMENT, 1865-1906   99

group of thirty-six members who favored the use of instrumental music withdrew and formed the Commerce Christian Church.[46] The following year, the city directory listed the services of the two churches as follows:

> Commerce Christian Church—Commerce between St. Paul and Harwood—Pastor Rev. Kirk Baxter—services 11 A.M.-7:30 P.M. Sabbath School 9:30 A.M.
>
> First Christian Church—Carondelet and Austin—Pastor Rev. Green L. Surber 11-7:30. Sabbath School 9:30.[47]

At this time Dallas had twenty-one churches, fifteen white and six colored.[48] Although two colored Christian churches were listed, nothing was reported about them until 1887 when C. M. Wilmeth simply mentioned Negro work without comment.

Despite several reverses after the division, the First Church enjoyed a decade of considerable growth. In 1880 it sold its building and purchased a lot 100 by 215 feet on the corner of Pearl and Bryan. Before erecting a new building, the church invited J. M. F. Smithson of Weatherford, formerly of Tennessee, to hold a tent meeting upon the newly acquired property. Choked by the stifling dust which arose from the inadequately watered rock streets of Dallas and the artesian well drinking water hauled around on wagons selling for "one bit a barrel," Smithson jestingly attempted to make the best of an unpleasant situation by announcing his "chemical recipe" for Texas water as a combination of "one gallon of Tennessee water,

---
[46] Wise, *Pearl and Bryan Church*.
[47] *Directory, City of Dallas*, 1878-1879, pp. 23-24.
[48] Albert Hansfords, *Texas State Register for 1879* (Galveston, 1879), pp. 76-77.

add to it one tablespoon of soda; one tbs. of common salt; 280 grains of chloride of potash; ½ oz. lye soap, leave standing over night, shake well, it is now ready for use." Although he was more than compensated for his discomfort by the hospitality of the brethren, the meeting was abruptly terminated by a sudden windstorm which turned the tent inside out and demolished several buildings, including the Congregational meeting house.[49] Within the following year, the energetic members completed a neat brick edifice.[50]

During the next decade, the Pearl and Bryan church grew spasmodically. O. M. Thurman, who visited it in July, 1882, found only thirteen students and three teachers in attendance at Sunday School, thirty-eight at the morning service, and twenty-eight at night, even though he judged G. L. Surber a minister of "considerable ability."[51] Shortly thereafter, evangelist "Weeping" Joe Harding arrived from Tennessee. Under his vigorous leadership, Sunday School attendance reached two hundred by 1885.[52] The following year, minister Gano spent so much time in protracted meetings that the congregation had little preaching and lapsed into indifference.[53] In 1890, under the able direction of W. H. Wright, the church received 158 new members, of whom seventy were added during a seven week revival conducted by renowned T. B. Larimore.[54]

Simultaneously, influences were exerted which after

---

[49] J. M. F. Smithson, "News," *Gospel Advocate*, XXIII (July 28, 1881), p. 461.
[50] Wise, *Pearl and Bryan Church*.
[51] O. M. Thurman, in the *Gospel Advocate*, XXIV (August 10, 1882), p. 504.
[52] Joe Harding in *ibid.*, XXXIX (November 9, 1887), p. 711.
[53] C. M. Wilmeth, "News," *ibid.*, XXIX (November 9, 1887), p. 711.
[54] W. H. Wright, "Texas," *The Christian Evangelist* (St. Louis), XXVII (January 8, 1891), p. 29.

first widening the breach, tended to promote unity between the Pearl and Bryan and Commerce churches. Unsuccessful efforts were made in 1880 to reconcile the differences. The nature of the controversy was characterized in the will of Jefferson Peak, a charter member of the Pearl and Bryan church, who died in 1885. In his will, Peak, who had made liberal contributions to the church, bequeathed a city lot toward payment of the debt on the new building with a provision that "if any instrument of music be introduced into the worship of the church or Sunday school, the lot should revert to his natural heirs."[55] Two years later, the Commerce church set up a "Christian Church Restaurant" on the Texas State Fair Grounds. The scheme, copied by other religious bodies in Dallas, was designed to replenish depleted church treasuries. Although conservative evangelist C. M. Wilmeth condemned the enterprise as "in accord with the progressive, human society, organ worship idea . . . more after the style of doing evil that good may come of it —patronizing a gambling institution to get money for the Lord,"[56] three years later Wright commended the fine fellowship existing between the congregations, and in 1893, John T. Poe, who visited Pearl and Bryan, found "a longing desire on the part of many of the members to unite with Central (formerly Commerce) and have only one church instead of two."[57] Nevertheless, within a decade the controversy over the organ permanently ended all hope of union.

Notwithstanding the differences of opinion, the **Pearl** and Bryan church, led by elders R. M. Gano, A.

---

[55] Anonymous, "News," *Gospel Advocate*, XXVII (December 2, 1885), p. 754.
[56] C. M. Wilmeth, *ibid.*, XXIX (November 9, 1887), p. 711.
[57] *Firm Foundation*, February 28, 1893.

T. Sitz and William Lipscomb, made excellent progress. Beginning in 1896, A. Alsup served as minister for several years. On July 1, 1899, James S. Dunn began a revival which was marred by the tragic death of Lipscomb, principal of Dallas Central High School. John T. Carlisle, who had been discharged as school janitor, thought Lipscomb responsible for his dismissal. On Monday evening, July 10, as the congregation sang the invitation hymn, "Why Do You Wait, Dear Brother?" Carlisle responded to Satan instead of to Christ; he walked down the aisle and shot Lipscomb, who was standing in the front row. Lipscomb was rushed to the hospital but lived only two days.[58] As a result of the shooting the revival was terminated, but the following year the church purchased a tent and conducted numerous revivals throughout the city and county. Beginning in North Dallas with fourteen additions, the successful series of tent meetings prompted the elders afterward to urge all congregations in large cities to adopt the method.[59] On February 1, 1902, Jesse P. Sewell began his ministry for the church, which numbered at the time about three hundred members, mostly women. The congregation met in a tent while the new building was being constructed. Late in the year, Sewell delivered the dedicatory sermon, "That For Which We Stand."[60] He also commended the elders for their exceptional leadership. On the first Sunday of each month, they met to consider and plan the affairs of the church. At the same time, they spiritually evaluated the entire membership

---

[58] Wise, *Pearl and Bryan Church*.
[59] W. H. Sewell, "News," *Gospel Advocate*, XLII (July 12, 1900), p. 448.
[60] Jesse P. Sewell, "That For Which We Stand," *Gospel Advocate*, XLV (February 26, 1903), p. 131.

"*Responding to Satan's invitation rather than Christ's.*"

alphabetically. Any members found to be delinquent or wayward were promptly admonished, an example of discipline rarely equalled today. One elder, who usually shook hands with nearly all the members after the services, could recite the residence, occupation, financial and spiritual status of each disciple.[61]

Meanwhile the Pearl and Bryan church had initiated missionary efforts west of the Trinity River. Its endeavor led to the establishment of the Western Heights church in 1872. General Gano, assisted by Major B. F. Johnson, a Civil War friend, conducted the first meetings in the old Mt. Airy school house. Since the community was sparsely settled, heralds on horseback advertised the revival to the citizens in the surrounding community. In the ensuing services, over fifty were baptized in nearby Coombs Creek. Shortly thereafter, the new church was augmented by the arrival of "Weeping" Joe Harding's congregation from Tennessee.[62] In 1887, C. M. Wilmeth suggested the Pauline "house to house" method (Acts 20:20) to combat the rapid strides of sectarianism."[63] Apparently no laborers heeded his call. Three years later a frame building with a tall steeple and bell was erected. Mrs. Mattie Hoard Crawford, who donated the building site, spearheaded the building fund drive. Riding in a buckboard, she solicited funds from every business establishment in Dallas. When she asked the proprietor of a tavern for a contribution, he hesitatingly answered, "I am a saloon keeper." Equal to the occasion, she quickly retorted, "The more need for you

---
[61] Jesse P. Sewell, "Pearl and Bryan St., Dallas," *Gospel Advocate*, XLIV (September 18, 1902), p. 596.
[62] *Firm Foundation*, November 14, 1933.
[63] C. M. Wilmeth, "News," *Gospel Advocate*, XXIX (November 9, 1887), p. 711.

to do good with your money." Evidently convinced, he gave one hundred dollars. In order to obtain money from a farmer, not known for his generosity, Mrs. Crawford pursued him up and down corn rows while he was plowing, explaining her need, until he promised a contribution.[64]

Simultaneously, a few churches existed in various stages of development in rural Dallas County. In 1887 the church at Lancaster erected a new building; at Salem, one elder wanted a regular preacher while another felt such was an unnecessary financial burden; at Garland, a faithful few met in a rented hall in 1901.[65] By 1906, the United States Census reports listed over one thousand members in Dallas County, a nucleus around which many new churches developed in the twentieth century.

FORT WORTH

Comparable to the growth of the church in Dallas was that enjoyed in nearby Fort Worth. Begun in 1855, the struggling little church did little until Joseph Addison Clark and his two sons, Addison and Randolph, arrived in 1867. Clark, who became the first postmaster of Fort Worth, was invited by Major K. M. Van Zandt, recent settler and staunch member of the church of Christ, to use a corner of his store as an office. On Sundays, Clark and his sons preached in the surrounding communities.[66]

---

[64]*Firm Foundation*, November 14, 1953. Some of the preachers who labored with the church were L. A. Sweet, A. C. Borden, W. H. Walker, W. P. Barcus, G. Q. Grasty, T. R. Burnett, and C. M. Wilmeth.

[65]Thomas E. Milholland, "News," *Gospel Advocate*, XLIII (September 26, 1901), p. 621.

[66]M. Norvel Young, *A History of Colleges Established and Controlled by Members of the Churches of Christ* (Kansas City, Mo., 1949), pp. 69-70. Hereafter cited Young, *History of Colleges*.

The church took a big step forward in 1870 by beginning construction of a "new commodious house, to be of brick with adequate materials and money on hand to complete it."[67] According to one authority it was the first church edifice in Fort Worth, "a modest unpretentious structure located on the block bounded by Main, Houston, Fourth and Fifth streets."[68] Evidently the building was not completed as David Lipscomb, editor of the *Gospel Advocate* who visited Fort Worth in 1872, recommended that the brethren complete their house in "a neat and comfortable manner."[69]

Since the church was composed largely of "earnest and devoted" young people, Lipscomb stated it was capable of great future development. During his stay, he spoke fifteen times and converted seventeen. Eighteen-year-old George Gavin, a competent young song leader who had arrived recently from Nashville, Tennessee, led the singing. Since song leaders were a rarity among members of churches of Christ in Texas, Gavin served in this capacity throughout the next thirty years in revivals all over the state. Also, Lipscomb praised Clark and his two sons for conducting an excellent Christian school in the church building on week days.[70] Although Fort Worth was described as a village of about seven hundred inhabitants living in hastily but poorly constructed buildings and only two years removed from Indian raids, Lipscomb envisioned rapid and continuous growth of the town.

---

[67]J. A. Clark, "News," *Gospel Advocate*, XII (January 27, 1870), p. 87.

[68]B. B. Paddock (ed.), *Fort Worth and the Texas Northwest* (Chicago, 1922), II, p. 637.

[69]David Lipscomb, "Notes on Texas Travel," *Gospel Advocate*, XIV (September 12, 1872), pp. 847-853. Hereafter cited as Lipscomb, "Notes on Texas Travel."

[70]*Firm Foundation*, April 26, 1938.

The Southern Pacific Railroad had promised to build a repair shop in Fort Worth, which would make it an important point on a route to the Pacific Coast. When a visit by Colonel Tom Scott, president of the railroad, caused a wave of speculation in real estate, Lipscomb warned his listeners that "excitements of a monetary character are the hardest to counteract and are most fatal to all religious influence on others."[71]

During the 1870's the church made notable progress. In July, 1875, Robert Trimble of Mayfield, Kentucky, and H. D. Bantau, the local evangelist, conducted a seven day meeting with twenty-two additions.[72] The shoddy meeting house was condemned and in 1876 the church moved to the corner of Throckmorton and Sixth, site of the present First Christian Church.[73] The following year, highly esteemed Judge G. A. Everts, in his eighty-first year but alert in mind and body, was immersed. A large crowd, many openly crying, witnessed the baptism which evangelist W. Y. Taylor called the most beautiful scene he expected to see this side of the "better world."[74] A massive two-story stone building with a basement for a Sunday School and a large auditorium for worship services was completed in 1879, at a cost of eight thousand dollars. It was the finest edifice of churches of Christ in Texas at the time. J. A. Meng, itinerant evangelist from Missouri, in May delivered the first sermon in the building to begin a revival in which eighteen converts were added to the church. Because the congre-

---

[71] David Lipscomb, "Correction," *Gospel Advocate*, XIV (August 8, 1872), p. 768.
[72] Anonymous, "News," *Apostolic Times* (July 15, 1875), p. 308.
[73] *Firm Foundation*, March 29, 1938.
[74] W. Y. Taylor, "A Baptism," *Gospel Advocate* XIX (July 26, 1877), p. 461.

gation included many prominent business men and was located in a fast growing town, Meng optimistically predicted a bright future for it.[75]

Meng's prophecy came true. By 1890 the church had become one of the strongest in the state. Tennessee evangelist A. L. Johnson, who had arrived in 1882, portrayed Fort Worth as a teeming mass of over ten thousand strangers, many of whom were Christians from other states, but virtually without fellowship. Although most members of the churches of Christ had not presented their letters of commendation from former churches, Johnson hopefully envisioned the rounding up of all the spiritual strays into a compact and properly functioning flock.[76] Evidence of the prevailing spiritual lethargy was the omission in the 1882 city directory of the Sunday School service. It listed "Usual services—11 A.M. and 7:30 P.M. Elder T. W. Caskey, Pastor."[77] However, during the next few years a number of transient members united with the church. Under the leadership of minister R. E. McKnight, the membership had climbed by 1887 to nearly four hundred, and was purported to be the largest in the state.[78] But it experienced its most rapid growth in the decade 1890-1900. In April, 1890, minister J. W. Lowber reported twenty-four additions in one week; by the end of the year, 170 had been added. The rapid growth led the *Fort Worth Gazette* to comment that "the services of this church are awakening a great deal of enthusiasm, and the church is crowded both

---

[75] J. A. Meng, "Fort Worth, Texas," *ibid.*, XXI (June 19, 1879), p. 395.
[76] A. L. Johnson, "News," *ibid.*, XXIV (February 23, 1882), p. 121.
[77] *Fort Worth City Directory*—1882, p. 16.
[78] W. Lipscomb, Jr., "News," *Gospel Advocate*, XXIX (July 20, 1887), p. 460; *Firm Foundation*, March 29, 1938.

morning and evening notwithstanding warm weather. It is like a protracted meeting all the time."[79] The congregation had planned already to establish a mission in the south part of town and a colored church.[80] Within two years, a Christian Endeavor Society and Ladies Aid Auxiliary had been started. After an organ was brought into the Sunday School in June, 1893, an ardent supporter of all these so-called "innovations" by the name of Collings declared that "Since these changes were completed, a marked improvement has manifested itself in all departments of church work."[81]

Although some of the eight hundred members disapproved of these practices,[82] the schism did not occur until 1897 during the ministry of Homer T. Wilson, a persuasive pulpiteer of exceptional ability. Shortly after Wilson's arrival, the following announcement appeared in the *Fort Worth Register*: "First Christian Church—Sunday School—9:30, Christian Endeavor—6:30, Preaching—11. No service in the evening as Homer T. Wilson will preach at the First Baptist Church, the congregations worshiping together."[83] Immediately, the conservative members of the church objected to fellowship with the Baptists who used instrumental music to accompany their congregational singing. Notwithstanding this sentiment, Wilson soon boldly and openly advocated the use of the organ in the worship service. When elders John Randle and K. M. Van Zandt rejected his proposal, he resigned,

---

[79] "Fort Worth Gazette," quoted in the *Gospel Advocate*, XXXIII (June 24, 1891), p. 393.

[80] J. W. Lowber, "Ft. Worth," *The Christian Evangelist*, XXVII (January 22, 1891), p. 61.

[81] ....Collings, "Growth of the Word," *Gospel Advocate*, XXXV (October 12, 1893), p. 641.

[82] Anonymous, "Growth of the Word," *ibid.*, XXXVIII (July 9, 1896), p. 439.

[83] *Fort Worth Register*, January 24, 1897.

and with about 120 members who were favorably disposed to the use of the organ formed the Second Christian Church in an opera house nearby.[84]

Even after the schism, the majority of the First Church seemingly favored the use of the organ but wished to introduce it without causing a division. Within a short time, it called C. E. McPherson, an ardent pro-organ preacher, to succeed Wilson. Shortly after his arrival, McPherson introduced the organ into the First Church but vigorously opposed the efforts of the Second Church to erect a building across the street from the First Church, apparently viewing it as competitive. James Scobey, who visited Fort Worth in 1899, observed the following inscription upon the cornerstone: "The Second Christian Church: Homer T. Wilson, pastor."[85] However, the building was never completed because of the strong opposition of the First Church. Later, it moved to another part of Fort Worth where it became the Magnolia Christian Church.[86]

In the meantime, a small mission known as the South Side Church of Christ had been established in the spring of 1896 at Jennings and Cannon. An advertisement in the paper listed services every Lord's day at 11 A.M. and 7:30 P.M.; Bible School at 9:30 A.M., and S. C. Jackson as opening prayer meeting every Wednesday evening at 7:30 p.m.[87] E. V. Mills of Mineola, who visited Fort Worth in the fall of 1897, described the church as "badly mixed, tangled, and

---

[84]*Firm Foundation*, April 26, 1938.
[85]James E. Scobey, "Church News," *Gospel Advocate*, XLI (June 15, 1899), p. 382. Hereafter cited as Scobey, "Church News."
[86]*Firm Foundation*, April 26, 1938.
[87]*Fort Worth Register*, January 10, 1897.

divided, but a few remain loyal,"[88] meaning that those who had not subscribed to the use of the organ at the First Church had gone to South Side. The next year, Scobey commended it for maintaining "the apostolic work and worship in Fort Worth. The old First Church, which for many years past has been a source of light and strength, has become darkness."[89]

In addition to South Side, two other non-organ churches were organized. A band of ten or twelve brethren, led by John Randle, former elder of the First Church, began meeting in 1900 in a small rented house near the courthouse. The following year, the group moved to the courthouse basement. Within five years, despite "unfavorable comments, unfriendly criticisms, and predictions of failure," the church numbered seventy-five. With daring vision and rare zeal, it asked brethren for financial assistance to build a "substantial, and commodious house of worship, with a seating capacity of not less than four to five hundred . . . The entire cost of the structure, including lot, we estimate at about $8,000." To encourage non-organ churches to make contributions, the Central Church of Christ, as it was now designated, declared it had incorporated under the laws of the state with provisions barring the introduction of all "innovations."[90] Simultaneously, a small church was established at the corner of Rosedale and Alston.[91] Thus, three "conservative"

---

[88]E. V. Mills, "Growth of the Word," *Gospel Advocate*, XXXIX (November 25, 1897), p. 738.

[89]Scobey, "Church News," p. 382.

[90]John A. Randle and William R. Knox, "Letter from Ft. Worth," *Gospel Advocate*, XLVIII (March 15, 1906), p. 172.

[91]A. J. McCarty, "Ft. Worth Meeting," *Gospel Advocate*, XLVIII (January 4, 1906), p. 15.

and three "progressive" churches were established in Fort Worth by 1906.[92]

Concurrently, several congregations experienced growth in rural Tarrant County. At Spring Garden, a small church served by Brother Elkins, a preacher of eloquent speech but corrupt morals, had eighty-one additions in 1868.[93] Four years later, David Lipscomb, who visited in the community, denounced Elkins as an adulterous minister who had left his wife in Tennessee and departed with a prostitute. When the church discharged Elkins because of unfavorable public opinion, Lipscomb sternly rebuked it for failing to do so on the basis of a Biblical precept.[94] At Dunville, evangelists T. Jasper and Satterfield converted sixteen in a brush arbor meeting in 1872. At the same time, a few disciples met in Grapevine.[95] Almost three decades later, in 1900, R. M. Gano conducted a series of services at Bedford. During his first revival, he received twenty additions to the church. Returning two weeks later, he married two couples, preached five nights in succession, and received an additional twenty converts, including a lad who had made the confession at the first revival but had been prohibited by his parents from being baptized. During the second meeting, he chose

---

[92]*Fort Worth City Directory*—1907, p. 7. Conservative churches became known as the churches of Christ after the formal schism in 1906. Progressive churches used the terms church of Christ and Christian church interchangeably. Additional data on conservative and progressive churches will be found in a later chapter.

[93]P. Cheek, "Church News," *Gospel Advocate*, X (August 18, 1868), p. 787.

[94]Lipscomb, "Notes on Texas Travel," *Gospel Advocate*, XIV (September 12, 1872), pp. 847-853. Churches of Christ assert that the Bible commands local congregations to withdraw fellowship from all members who commit adultery (1 Cor. 5:9-13).

[95]*Ibid.*

to "obey God rather than parents," and was immersed.[96]

NORTH TEXAS AND VICINITY

To the north of the Dallas-Fort Worth area the spiritual lethargy of Civil War days gave way to enthusiasm for the gospel during the post-war period, and the fertile black prairies provided bountiful harvests of converts to churches of Christ as well as agricultural crops. In Collin County, the church of Christ grew primarily because of the tireless labor of the Wilmeth family. In 1863, J. B. Wilmeth reported 118 were added during his summer meetings in the vicinity of McKinney.[97] By 1874, J. R. Wilmeth proudly reported that hundreds were obeying the gospel each year.[98]

At the same time, R. C. Horn, destined to be a pillar in the church in North Texas, began his evangelistic labors. Horn came to Grayson County as a young lad in 1858, and was baptized by J. S. Muse four years later. Shortly thereafter, he entered the Confederate army where he faithfully read his ten-cent Testament daily. Upon his discharge he attended Kentucky University, where he received an unfriendly reception at the hands of his fellow-students who decided to preach.[99] Upon returning to Texas, Horn presented a New Testament in place of a ticket to the conductor on the train from Dallas to McKinney. Equal to the occasion, the conductor quickly replied, "That's a

---
[96] R. M. Gano, "Church News," *Gospel Advocate*, XLIII (January 10, 1901), p. 28.
[97] J. B. Wilmeth, "News," *ibid.*, X (October 22, 1868), p. 1019.
[98] J. R. Wilmeth, "Church News," *ibid.*, XVI (September 3, 1874), p. 822.
[99] John Wilson Bowyer and Claude Harrison Thurman (Comps.), *The Annals of Elder Horn* (New York, 1930), p. 64.

mighty fine ticket to one place but it won't lead to where this train is going."[100] Arriving in McKinney, Horn soon preached his first sermon on September 29, 1871.

Shortly after his arrival, Horn launched a vigorous campaign to attract preachers of churches of Christ and immigrant members from other states to North Texas. Through articles in the *Gospel Advocate* and *Apostolic Times* (Lexington, Kentucky), he vividly portrayed Collin County as climatically conducive to health and agriculturally rich in cotton, wheat, corn and vegetable gardens. Land was cheap but becoming increasingly expensive each year as teeming thousands immigrated from other states. He stated that the Baptists, Methodists and Presbyterians were well represented but no known Roman Catholic resided in the county. Among the ten churches of Christ in Collin County, several did not have evangelists or houses of worship.[101] Horn's appeal was apparently not without some success, for by 1875 four of the ten churches had meeting houses (the others met in school houses or in brush arbors in favorable weather), and six preachers labored regularly.[102]

During the next few years, the churches in Collin County experienced marked growth. By 1884 the McKinney congregation numbered nearly two hundred members. Outside of McKinney, twelve ministers, most of whom farmed or taught school through the week, preached to twelve churches with a total mem-

---
[100] *Ibid.*, p. 81.

[101] R. C. Horn, "Success of the Gospel," *Gospel Advocate*, XIII (November 9, 1871), pp. 1041-1042.

[102] R. C. Horn, "McKinney, Texas," *Apostolic Times*, VII (February 4, 1875), pp. 45-50.

bership of about 1500.[103] Some of these churches met at Plano, Weston and Melissa. At Hackberry Grove a camp meeting church, composed of farmers, met from time to time. Horn characterized the children as playing games while the adults listened to the speakers. Although most attendants remained for the picnics, only a few assembled in the afternoon to attend to church business. On one occasion three delinquent members were expelled for swearing and fighting, but one who repented after much admonition, was restored into fellowship.[104] Most of the churches assembled on Sunday to commemorate the Lord's Supper, with or without a preacher. Additional spiritual fellowship was provided by the weekly prayer service which C. M. Wilmeth regarded as a "good omen for the future."[105]

In addition, Horn encouraged preachers to come to Texas because audiences were more attentive and better behaved than in any place where he had spoken. Seeking to allay unfounded fears, he said, "It does not make a man wild to live in Texas." He praised the denominations who "hear us gladly" as gradually drawing nearer the "truth." In McKinney, Jacob Ditzler, a Methodist preacher, argued that "washing of regeneration" (Titus 3:5) did not refer to baptism. "You cannot wash anything by dipping, for you may dip a dirty rag into water and it will come out dirty as ever." T. W. Caskey, evangelist of the church of Christ, countered by stating that 1 Peter 3:21 taught baptism was the answer of a good conscience toward God, not a

---

[103] C. W. Sewell, "Church News," *Gospel Advocate*, XXVI (November 26, 1884), p. 763.

[104] Bowyer and Thurman (Comps.), *The Annals of Elder Horn* (New York, 1930), p. 175.

[105] C. M. Wilmeth, "Notes of Travel in North Texas," *Apostolic Times*, VII (June 17, 1875), pp. 255-256.

washing away of the filth of the flesh. Horn also lectured on baptism, using logical English in deference to an audience unlearned in Greek. Indicating apparent victory, Horn remarked, "It is nothing uncommon to see the Methodists 'go into the water' here. . . They have learned that if they do not 'dip' them, we will have to do it sooner or later."[106]

Although Collin County was described as a "garden spot," its sticky "black mud" in the winter hindered the worshipers from assembling. On one trip to perform a wedding, C. M. Wilmeth was delayed three times by broken harness. One man jokingly told him he was going to fence all his land because it grieved him to see men carrying it off on their feet and their horses' feet." Manifesting splendid initiative, a Presbyterian preacher admonished his flock to "stick to Jesus as tight as black mud stuck to their feet."[107]

In adjacent Denton County, the church, planted in Denton before the Civil War, made little growth until B. F. Hall converted eight in 1867. In 1875, C. M. Wilmeth responded to the call of elders Philip Minor and Providence Mounts to preach once a month because he saw a great potential growth for this church. Evidently Wilmeth so inspired the congregation, among whom were several lawyers, doctors, a chief justice of the county and the sheriff, that it built a nice house for $1500 in 1876 which, unfortunately, was destroyed by fire four years later.[108] Dismayed but not discouraged, a faithful few completed another building by 1883 but needed fire from the pulpit in order to awaken the

---
[106] R. C. Horn, "McKinney, Texas," *Apostolic Times*, VII (February 4, 1875), pp. 45-50.
[107] C. M. Wilmeth, "Notes of Travel in North Texas," *Apostolic Times*, VII (March 4, 1875), p. 77.
[108] T. H. C. Perry, "Church News," *Gospel Advocate*, XIX (June 28, 1877), p. 404.

slumbering majority.[109] Other small bands assembled at Pilot Point, Sanger, and Drum, but had no regular preacher. Approximately one thousand disciples, most of whom were inactive, resided in the county in 1875.[110]

Northward in Cooke County, the church was established first in Gainesville in 1896. Joe Harding, who came at the request of H. C. Pearson, preached first on the courthouse steps, then daily in a rented vacant store building. Soon a church was organized with Pearson and J. W. McKee as elders, J. J. Hawkins and R. L. Milligan as deacons. During the following year, services were conducted in homes of members, in a rented hall, in the R. and W. Hotel, in the Gillis Hotel, and finally in a building on the corner of Broadway and Commerce where E. H. Rogers held a revival. Dissatisfied with constant moving, the church purchased a lot on the corner of Ritchey and Gribble where a 24 by 40 foot house was erected and paid for upon completion. Several revivals were held during the next few years. In 1903, A. B. Barrett conducted a meeting with twenty-six additions. The church thereupon purchased a lot on Commerce Street and erected a larger building.[111]

In adjoining Grayson County, the Sherman church, planted in 1850, was plagued by doctrinal controversies which led to division. After the Civil War a small band, led by "Uncle" Charley Carlton and B. F. Hall, met first in the courthouse and then for several years

---

[109] J. R. Jones, "Trip to Texas," *Apostolic Church*, V (February, 1883), pp. 23-26.
[110] C. M. Wilmeth, "Notes of Travel in North Texas," *Apostolic Times*, VII (July 8, 1875), p. 292.
[111] *Directory of the Commerce Street Church of Christ*, March, 1948. Other charter members were Mrs. H. C. Pearson, Mrs. T. J. Hawkins and daughter Luvy Putman, Mrs. Sarah Williot and daughter Della Strickland, Mrs. R. L. Milligan, and David Johnson.

in the Odd Fellows Hall. In 1874 the congregation of about fifty, known as the Houston Street Church of Christ, constructed a meeting house on the corner of Houston and Montgomery.[112] T. W. Caskey, W. C. Dimmitt and R. B. Hamilton labored successively as its ministers. A small group favoring the missionary society withdrew in 1882 and formed the Central Christian Church on West Mulberry. Nevertheless, the growth of the church continued. In 1894, T. B. Larimore conducted a five-month revival during which over two hundred were added. The following year the church again divided, this time over the organ issue. The anti-organ majority retained the building but agreed to pay the pro-organ minority $2300 for their interest in the church property in order to avoid a threatened law suit when the organ was moved out of the Houston Street Church into the street. The withdrawing group designated itself as the First Christian Church.[113] In December, 1895, a small "gang of rebaptists," as they were called, met in a school house in West Sherman. At the same time, visiting evangelist H. F. Williams preached four or five times to the two or three hundred members of the old Houston Street church. Informed of the divided condition of the church in Sherman, he declared sadly that from the Bible standpoint it was "sinful enough to cause the children of God to weep an ocean of tears."[114] J. D. Tant, after preaching two nights in the Houston

---

[112] J. P. Sewell, "The Church of Christ at Sherman, Texas," *Gospel Advocate*, XLIV (March 6, 1902), p. 154.

[113] *Sherman Democrat*, September 19, 1948.

[114] H. F. Williams, "Growth of the Word," *Gospel Advocate*, XXXVII (December 19, 1895), p. 807. The Re-Baptists were a small group who believed that any person who had not been baptized for the remission of sins must be re-baptized. Additional data on re-baptism will be found in a later chapter.

Street church in 1899, pronounced the greater part of the congregation spiritually dead, evidently on the basis that it had not paid $1300 of the original $2300 owed to the First Christian Church. Obviously disturbed, he asked why a church of three hundred members could not pay off the debt at five hundred dollars a year and still do several hundred dollars of mission work.[115]

After several decades of strife, the churches partially reconciled their differences. The Central and First Christian churches merged as "progressives" while the Re-baptists united with the Houston Street Church of Christ. In 1905 L. S. White, in a five-week revival, obtained eighty-six conversions but was unable to restore fellowship between it and the progressives.[116]

Ten miles north, a small church was planted in Denison in the 1870's. During the next decade it experienced little growth, but in 1891 it was greatly strengthened by seventy additions during a revival conducted by a Brother Smith. Economically, the thriving town of 12,000 was prosperous as a result of the $75,000 monthly payroll of the Missouri, Kansas and Texas railroad.[117] Spiritually, the church soon divided over the use of the organ with the pro-organ faction retaining the meeting house. In 1903, A. B. Barrett conducted a two-week tent meeting for the ten anti-organ members, received forty-eight additions, twenty of whom were from the progressives, and

---
[115] J. D. Tant, "Growth of the Word," *ibid.*, XLI (January 12, 1899), p. 27.
[116] Anonymous, "Church News," *ibid.*, XLVII (December 21, 1905), p. 805.
[117] G. W. Robertson, "Notes from Texas," *Christian Evangelist*, XXVIII (April 30, 1891), p. 287.

established a strong congregation.[118] Elsewhere in the county, churches met in Tioga, Whitesboro, Gunter and Whitewright. In 1875, one lady of the Van Alstyne church paid C. M. Wilmeth with several months wages out of her own pocket on the promise that the church would pay her when it got the money. All preachers probably would have exclaimed with Wilmeth, "Oh, that the church in Texas had a 1000 such women!"[119]

In adjoining Fannin County, during a visit in 1883, J. R. Jones of the editorial staff of the *Apostolic Church* (Louisville, Kentucky), designated Bonham as the "Jerusalem of Texas" because Carlton College, the *Christian Messenger*, and a strong church of Christ were located there. Begun in 1869 by Carlton, the Bonham church of eighty members had grown rapidly. Within five years the congregation of several hundred members had erected a fine, comfortable and well furnished building capable of seating about seven hundred.[120] T. W. Caskey's revival in 1883 was better attended than any other previously held in Bonham.[121] The Bonham and Savoy congregations in 1905 purchased a tent for $125, and secured John T. and R. D. Smith to evangelize Fannin County. During that summer, the Smiths established churches at Windom, Casey, Fairview, Telephone, Moore's Chapel, Chapel Hill, Honey Grove, and Randolph.[122]

---

[118]Gay Jackson, "Good Work at Denison, Texas," *Gospel Advocate*, XLV (May 14, 1903), p. 318.

[119]C. M. Wilmeth, "Notes of Travel in North Texas," *Apostolic Times*, VII (March 18, 1875), pp. 100-101.

[120]Anonymous, "Church News," *Gospel Advocate*, XVI (November 5, 1874), p. 1053.

[121]J. R. Jones, "Trip to Texas," *Apostolic Church* (Louisville, Kentucky), V (February, 1883), pp. 23-26.

[122]R. D. Smith, "Evangelizing Fannin County," *Gospel Advocate*, XLVII (November 9, 1905), p. 718.

To the south in Hunt and Kaufman counties other churches were planted. A small group of five men and five women constituted the church in Greenville in 1882. Two years later, S. R. Ezzell consented to preach for them three Sundays each month and devote the other to the Sulphur Springs church.[123] However, **the organ issue caused considerable trouble in the 1890's.** In 1901, twenty-seven non-organ members were meeting regularly when R. R. Hamlin conducted a meeting for the church.[124]

Fifty miles to the south in Kaufman, V. I. Stirman and family, who arrived in December, 1867, met with three other families to worship. In September of the following year, Ed Stirman, after preaching in the Cumberland Presbyterian house for two weeks, organized a church of forty disciples. The church purchased the Presbyterian building about 1873, but the progressives retained the church property after the division over the organ.[125]

To the southwest, the first concerted effort to establish the cause in Ellis County occurred in the 1870's. Although "Old Father" Sweatt delivered the first sermon by a preacher of the church of Christ as early as 1853, only a few itinerant evangelists spoke in the county for a quarter of a century afterward. The first of significance was Addison Clark who conducted a revival at Waxahachie in August, 1878, baptized

---

[123] S. R. Ezzell, "Texas News," *Apostolic Church*, VI (January, 1884), p. 32.

[124] R. R. Hamlin, "Church News," *Gospel Advocate*, XLIII (June 6, 1901), p. 368.

[125] V. I. Stirman, "Kaufman," *ibid.*, XLIX (May 2, 1907), pp. 284-285. Other families were Mr. and Mrs. R. A. Hindman, Mr. and Mrs. Ephraim Goss, and Captain Harrison Kieser and his wife.

AN ERA OF CONSIDERABLE ADVANCEMENT, 1865-1906

twenty-one, and organized a church of fifty members.[126] Fifteen miles to the southeast at Ennis, Elder Elijah Elgin gathered a small group in the Higginbottom residence for social and Bible classes in 1876. The following year, a small building was erected but soon had to be replaced by a larger, and in 1884 the more than four hundred members constructed still another edifice at a cost of four thousand dollars.[127] Eight miles to the west, A. C. Borden organized a small band in Antioch about 1881. At first the congregation met in a crude, unstripped box-house. W. H. Craig, a visiting minister, testified that the members shivered in subfreezing temperatures while observing the Lord's Supper. Nevertheless, he commended them for worshiping, with three exceptions, every Sunday for three years.[128] Elsewhere in the county, five other churches met regularly, four of which were served by evangelist C. E. McPherson on successive Sundays.[129]

Simultaneously, several churches were established in adjoining Navarro County. In 1878, T. F. Driskill organized a church of thirty-four members in Corsicana, but it made little progress for the next ten years, by which time this bustling town of ten thousand population had two railroads, three public schools, and several factories. John Poe in 1888 conducted a ten-day revival, converted twenty-one, and persuaded the church of sixty-two members to meet regularly in the YMCA hall.[130] Unfortunately the congregation, soon

---

[126] Addison Clark, "Church News," *ibid.*, XX (September 5, 1878), pp. 284-285.
[127] *Ellis County, Texas* (Chicago, 1892), p. 202.
[128] W. H. Craig, "Church News," *Gospel Advocate*, XXV (October 10, 1883), p. 644.
[129] H. G. Orr, "News," *ibid.*, XXI (October 30, 1879), p. 698.
[130] Poe, "Texas Department," *ibid.*, XXX (October 24, 1888), p. 7.

torn by dissension, declined until only a few continued worshiping in an upper room in a rented hall. Beginning in November, 1892, Joe Harding, assisted by evangelists A. G. Graham and C. R. Nichol, preached on the streets during the day and in the hall at night for four months. As a result, 86 were converted and a church of 106 members reorganized. Shortly thereafter, all disciples in Corsicana, free from dissension for the first time in four years, united in a "grand and glorious meeting."[131]

Fifteen miles west at Blooming Grove, a splendid church, organized in 1877, met once a month in a school house. Dissatisfied with this arrangement, the congregation erected a commodious building with a seating capacity of five hundred for $1800. Manifesting great zeal, the 120 members vowed to fill it as rapidly as possible.[132] Nearby at Dawson, thirty-five were baptized, including former Methodists, Catholics, Episcopalians and Presbyterians, during a ten-day meeting in July, 1886. Similarly, ten Baptists, one Presbyterian and one Methodist were among the twenty-two converted at Brazette.[133]

In adjacent Hill County, a church of twelve members was organized in Hillsboro in the home of D. C. Wornell in 1881. Two years later, during a revival conducted by G. A. Faris in the courthouse, the congregation decided to build a meeting house on the corner of Walnut and S. Waco. When this building burned in 1893, the membership met in the Presbyterian house until a new edifice was erected on the corner of N.

---

[131] Anonymous, "Church News," *ibid.*, XXXV (September 28, 1893), p. 620.

[132] J. P. Howard, "Church News," *ibid.*, XXXI (July 10, 1889), p. 447.

[133] Anonymous, "News," *ibid.*, XXVIII (August 11, 1886), p. 510.

Pleasant and Craig. Within a short time, the organ was introduced. As a result, a minority, led by Tom Boswell and Sam Reid, moved a block away, constructed a small frame building on a lot donated by Reid, and added to it periodically commensurate with their numerical increase.[134]

To the northwest in Johnson County, churches were established in Alvarado and Cleburne. At Alvarado the church, previously organized in 1855, became a camp-meeting type congregation. Here Addison Clark and H. D. Bautau conducted many meetings attended by families who came from all over the county in wagons and on horseback to hear the proclaimers. Clark reported in 1874 that devoted "Father and Mother Bills" attended every service of a week-long revival by making a ten-mile round trip by wagon each day.[135] Finally, however, a formally organized church of thirty members, under the leadership of W. R. Bounds and a Brother Worlay, met in the school house on the third Saturday and Sunday of each month.[136] Twelve miles to the west at Cleburne, William M. Ewing, a member of the church of Christ who as a lad had served under General Andrew Jackson in the Battle of New Orleans, arrived in 1870, but was unable to establish a church in the next two decades.[137] However, in 1890 a church of ten members was formed in the home of Mr. and Mrs. R. A. King. Shortly thereafter, through the efforts of George Wilmon, the little band met in a school house until it moved to a

---

[134] *Firm Foundation*, July 29, 1941.
[135] Addison Clark, "Church News," *Gospel Advocate*, XVI (September 10, 1874), p. 850.
[136] *A Memorial and Biographical History of Johnson and Hill Counties, Texas* (Chicago, 1892), p. 189.
[137] *The Lone Star State—Johnson and Hill Counties* (Chicago, 1892), pp. 346-347.

house on English street donated by J. S. Curry.[138] According to Mrs. J. S. Curry, who was present for the first service in the meeting place in 1879, "scriptures were read, songs were sung, the Lord's supper was observed, and a contribution was taken." In 1955 Mrs. Curry, at the age of ninety-six, attended the dedication of a new church building at Cleburne.[139]

Meanwhile, Dr. William Yater, a devout disciple who had moved to Cleburne, greatly strengthened the band of Christians. Although he jokingly referred to the meeting place as a "cockle burr patch," he gave the church a lot on Williams Avenue. Greatly encouraged, the congregation quickly erected a building, but moved it to the corner of E. Wardville and N. Robinson in 1902. Within two years, however, the increase in membership made it necessary to construct a larger building. At the same time, the church obtained G. A. Dunn as its first full time evangelist. Fifty years later, the church numbered over one thousand members.[140]

In adjacent Hood County, churches were planted in Thorp Spring and Granbury. Although S. S. Taylor preached in the county as early as 1854, he had little success because of Indian raids and the sparse population.[141] A church was started in 1873 in conjunction with Add-Ran College, founded by the Clark family at Thorp Spring. During the next two decades the membership, consisting largely of college students, increased until 1893 when an organ was introduced. After that it declined rapidly. At Granbury, three

---

[138] *Firm Foundation*, June 17, 1941.
[139] Otto Foster, Dedication Remarks, October 2, 1955.
[140] *Ibid.*
[141] Joseph C. McConnell, *The West Texas Frontier* (Jacksboro, Texas, 1933), p. 195.

miles away, the church underwent a similar experience with equally disastrous results.[142]

To the west in Erath and Eastland counties, small churches were established in several localities. Evangelist H. North of Stephenville reported in 1885 that he preached at four different places in Erath County each month.[143] At Ranger, Eastland County, disciple Amy Lemley of Arkansas arrived in 1875 but found no church. Three years later, evangelist A. Lawrence preached at Russell Creek, five miles to the east, baptized two ladies, but did not establish a church. Determined that the cause should be planted firmly, Mrs. Lemley wrote J. L. Castleman of Wise County who conducted a meeting at Russell Creek in August, 1880. After a large number were baptized, Mrs. Lemley exclaimed, "My cup runneth over!" On the last Sunday of the meeting, a church was organized in a log school house nearby and the Lord's Supper was served.[144]

Northward in Parker and Palo Pinto Counties, churches of Christ were firmly planted. At Weatherford, nineteen disciples gathered in the home of B. K. Emerson in 1856 to hear H. H. Taylor deliver a sermon. About a year later, the group organized in the courthouse with Taylor as minister and Emerson and Thomas Toler as elders. It was augmented by the arrival of N. B. Hoffman and wife from Carrollton, Missouri. The following year, Hoffman began preaching in the county and served in conjunction with evangelists Dean, Gano, Matthews, Addison Clark, and J. J. Hamilton. During the next few years, church affairs

---

[142]T. H. Dabney (Granbury, Texas) to Stephen Eckstein, interview, June 14, 1953. An account of Add-Ran College will be found in a later chapter.

[143]H. North, "Church News," *Gospel Advocate*, XXVII (June 10, 1885), p. 359.

[144]*Christian Leader*, October 25, 1927.

were neglected because of the Civil War, Indian raids, and political unrest. In spite of these difficulties, one inhabitant said that there was not so much "selfishness and party (denominational) strife as . . . their feelings seemed to have been mellowed by the surrounding trials." The arrest of Matthews and other church members on serious political charges created so much excitement in the community that the church met in the home of Toler "for greater protection in 1864."[145]

After the Civil War, the church entered on a new era of growth. In 1869, the Clark family conducted a revival at which time forty-six were added to the church.[146] The following year, Elder J. D. Beckwith and wife defected to the Missionary Baptists but returned in 1872. Greatly encouraged, the congregation, which met in Milam's Hall, was able to erect a nice building within four years under the leadership of minister H. D. Bantau.[147] J. M. F. Smithson of Tennessee, who visited in 1883, described the church as composed of "earnest, faithful brethren and sisters. They have a magnificent Sunday School." In respect to the town, Smithson praised the water and the climate as the best of any place he had visited in Texas. He portrayed the social strata as extending "from the low-jabbering, rat-eating Chinaman to the most refined and cultivated." A story circulated that a young man who had committed a crime was told by friends to leave

---

[145] H. Smythe, *Historical Sketch of Parker County, Texas* (St. Louis, 1877), pp. 65-69. Matthews and other church members were arrested on charges of treason. Soon, however, Matthews was found not guilty and released.

[146] K. M. Van Zandt, "Weatherford," *Gospel Advocate*, XI (September 30, 1869), p. 902.

[147] John A. Sidner, "Church News," *ibid.*, XVIII (December 21, 1876), p. 1233.

An Era of Considerable Advancement, 1865-1906

before he was arrested by the law. The offender replied, "I don't know where I'll go to, for I'm already in Texas." Smithson insisted that although the story did not fairly represent the Lone Star State, all classes of Weatherford society needed more Christianity.[148]

During the next two decades, the church grew despite hindrances from within and without. The organ controversy, which erupted in the 1890's, was settled by 1900. Shortly thereafter the church, with commendable vision and planning, erected a beautiful stone building. After the so-called "$6,000 extravaganza" was completed in 1904, several churches and editors of religious journals harshly criticized the congregation as "worldly minded." However, evangelist A. W. Young praised the church as doing more "to have the gospel preached in destitute places and assist more poor people than congregations of stingy brethren who are always howling about somebody else 'wasting the Lord's money'."[149]

Ten miles to the west in Millsap, a church of seven members was planted in 1877 by H. D. Bantau. Within six years the congregation numbered 185, had constructed an excellent meeting house, and was worshiping every Sunday. Bantau received about twenty Baptists into the church in 1883 after conducting a six-day debate with W. A. Jarrell, a famous Baptist debater.[150] At Mineral Wells, Palo Pinto County, in 1889, a church of fifty-four members with three elders and three dea-

---

[148] J. M. F. Smithson, "Weatherford," *ibid.*, XXIII (August 4, 1881), p. 485.

[149] A. W. Young, "Texas Field Notes," *ibid.*, XLVII (February 9, 1905), p. 92.

[150] H. D. Bantau, "Weatherford," *ibid.*, XXV (February 1, 1883), p. 75.

cons was organized during a meeting conducted by a preacher whose name has been forgotten.[151]

To the north in Wise, Jack and Young counties, the cause was established in several localities. At Oliver Creek, Wise County, about twelve miles west of Decatur, Jasper Matthews and a Brother Calloway conducted the first meeting ever held by ministers of the church of Christ in the area in September, 1876. During a nine-day period, thirty-four were baptized, "several united from the Methodists, Baptists and Presbyterians," and a church of sixty members was organized.[152] From this modest beginning, the church grew rapidly in Wise County, for in 1902 seventeen congregations which had not "introduced into their worship and work instrumental music and societies," were assembling regularly. R. F. Whitaker did as much as possible in ministering to these scattered rural churches.[153] To the west at Jacksboro, Addison Clark held a seven-day meeting in 1874, baptized ten, and organized a church of twenty members.[154] During the next decade the congregation grew rapidly, and in 1883 erected a commodious frame house 28 by 40 feet, with seating capacity of about 250, at a cost of nine hundred dollars. Mr. and Mrs. J. D. Brown contributed liberally to make the project a reality. On Saturday night, August 5, the new edifice was dedicated.[155] At Graham, twenty-five miles to the west, a church was established in the 1880's but soon divided over the use of the or-

---

[151] Anonymous, "News," *ibid.*, XXXI (May 8, 1889), p. 291.
[152] H. S. Wilson, "Church News," *ibid.*, XVIII (October 12, 1876), p. 985.
[153] Anonymous, "Church News," *ibid.*, XLV (July 30, 1903), p. 485.
[154] Addison Clark, "Church News," *ibid.*, XVI (October 1, 1874), pp. 930-931.
[155] *Jacksboro Gazette*, August 2, 1883.

gan. Although the conservative minority withdrew, no church was organized until evangelist T. H. Phillips conducted a meeting in the courthouse in August, 1902, baptized five, and persuaded twenty-five disciples to worship regularly.[156]

To the north in Clay County, churches were planted in Henrietta and Newport. At Henrietta, evangelist D. V. _____ conducted a one-week meeting in the Methodist building in July, 1884, to very small audiences. Since the people feared tornadoes, and clouds "were in sight every night," only a few left their "dug outs" to attend the services. Although the minister found twenty-five delinquent members of the church of Christ in the vicinity, he was unable to organize a church because they were "too busy gathering cattle and shipping them." Two years later an unknown evangelist conducted a meeting, received twenty-three into the fold and set the church in order.[157] Twenty miles to the south at Newport, J. L. Castleman received ten additions while preaching in May, 1880, and encouraged the brethren to worship God faithfully.[158] Thus, dozens of churches of Christ with a membership of several thousand disciples worshiped regularly in Dallas, Fort Worth and surrounding areas.

CENTRAL TEXAS

Meanwhile, churches of Christ were planted in numerous villages and towns of Central Texas with focal points at Austin and Waco. David Lipscomb, editor of the *Gospel Advocate*, in 1872 made an extensive

---

[156] T. H. Phillips, "Church News," *Gospel Advocate*, XLIV (August 14, 1902), p. 527.

[157] Anonymous, "Church News," *ibid.*, XXVIII (September 22, 1886), p. 606.

[158] J. L. Castleman (Pella, Texas), card to Amy Lemley, May 12, 1880.

tour throughout Central Texas from Austin to the Dallas-Fort Worth vicinity. Although he found a scarcity of church buildings, Lipscomb predicted rapid congregational expansion because there were "more men who sometimes preach, in proportion to population, than in any state in the Union."[159] In Austin, the church of Christ, begun in 1847, grew slowly for several decades. After the Civil War, the congregation met in a log house on Congress Avenue between Fourth and Fifth Streets. A frame building was constructed in 1867 at Eighth and Calhoun but was replaced in 1872 by a two-story house with a basement for a Sunday School. During this period, elder W. H. D. Carrington preached each Sunday morning to about one hundred worshipers. On one occasion, the rector of St. David's Episcopal Church in Austin delivered a sermon on "Baptism" in which he asserted that sprinkling was proved by ancient pictures. Carrington's reply, which some members of the church of Christ termed as "a learned and able discourse" on baptism, contended that the Bible taught only immersion.[160] Soon, however, the congregation apparently divided into two "embittered factions," each of which Carrington believed had about as much love for the other as the "Jews had for the Samaritans in olden times," and within a short time attendance dwindled to a mere handful.[161]

In 1879, W. E. Hall, a talented speaker with a magnetic personality, began a five-year ministry with the church. From the outset in his preaching, he scath-

---

[159] Lipscomb, "Notes on Texas Travel," XIV (July 4, 1872), pp. 630-636.
[160] A. C. Hill, "Sprinkling Proved by Pictures," *Millennial Harbinger* (September, 1868), p. 511.
[161] W. H. D. Carrington, "News," *Gospel Advocate*, XXV (June 20, 1883), p. 394.

An Era of Considerable Advancement, 1865-1906

ingly denounced drinking, gambling, dancing, and theater attendance. On Sunday mornings, he challenged the members to improve their every-day conduct and execute their Christian duties more efficiently. His evening sermons, addressed primarily to youth, were so popular and eloquently delivered that many young people from other Austin churches attended. As a result, the Sunday School enrollment doubled and the membership increased from one hundred to about three hundred. Although Hall seemed very progressive, he removed an organ which had been placed in the Sunday School while he was on vacation in 1882.[162] On the other hand, he attended "Cinderella," a fund raising social, but was severely criticized by aged member E. Hansbrough. Austin McGary, a zealous new convert, disagreed with Hall over the "propriety of certain customs in the congregation." Also, a few members felt his $2500 yearly salary was exorbitant. Addison Clark, while conducting a twelve-day meeting in July, 1883, endeavored to reconcile Hall and the dissatisfied members of the congregation, but apparently failed as Hall soon left amid considerable controversy.[163]

During the next few years, the church separated into two factions which finally became two congregations. In 1885, a visitor found only twenty-nine in Sunday School and thirteen in the morning worship service.[164] Apparently trying to invigorate the apathetic congregation, W. A. Morris and Hardin Welsh, two of the three elders, invited the state meeting of

---
[162]*Ibid.*
[163]Addison Clark, "Church News," *Gospel Advocate*, XXV (August 8, 1883), p. 507.
[164]Anonymous, "Austin," *ibid.*, XXVII (July 15, 1885), p. 444.

disciples to convene in Austin. The following year, the delegates, who met in the church building, formed the Texas Christian Missionary Society. According to one account, sixteen members, who opposed the missionary society and the use of the organ in the worship, soon withdrew and formed another congregation. Shortly thereafter, the group wrote a letter of reconciliation to the elders which evidently was rejected.[165] In 1887, evangelist J. D. Tant was invited by the group which withdrew, now numbering eighty-seven members under the leadership of McGary and J. W. Jackson, to conduct a meeting.[166] The next year the following advertisement appeared in the *Firm Foundation*: "The Church of Christ in Austin, will meet every Lord's day at 1014 E. 7th at their own hired house and all Christians opposed to innovations in the work and worship of the Lord's plan are cordially invited to meet with us when possible."[167] This body formed the nucleus for the University Avenue Church of Christ in the twentieth century. The old church became the Central Christian Church.

Thirty miles to the southwest in San Marcos, the small church which had been planted in 1855 but had dwindled away during the Civil War, was reorganized in 1869 by J. L. Green, S. D. Jackman, I. B. Donalson and William Gosden. Although the original building on Gold Street, constructed of lumber hauled by Jackman and Green from Austin, was renovated several times, it still stood in 1948. Evangelist J. J. William-

---

[165] *Central Christian Church of Austin, Texas.*
[166] *Firm Foundation*, January 21, 1936.
[167] *Firm Foundation*, April 15, 1888.

Grandma Driskill

son assisted by Green and elder J. A. Driskill preached in the church for many years.[168]

After the organ was introduced in 1887, the congregation lapsed into inactivity. Williamson and Green favored the use of the organ but were opposed by Driskill. Rallying to the support of her husband, "Grandma" Driskill went into the meeting house and demolished the organ with a hatchet. The organ faction, nevertheless, retained the building but soon disintegrated.[169] While visiting San Marcos in June, 1889, John Poe found the meeting house door ajar. Upon entering, he was astonished to see the interior covered with dust and cobwebs. Probing through the deserted building, he found a Sunday School roll dated "January, 1888," apparently indicating that the congregation had not met during the past eighteen months. Although there was no organ in the building, Poe candidly remarked, "The Devil is still in the brethren . . . they attend sectarian churches . . . while their own house and own altar is neglected."[170] In 1893, however, the anti-organ group regained possession of the building and began a slow rebuilding campaign.

In the vicinity of Austin, churches were established in several localities. A few miles to the east at Walnut Creek, Travis County, the congregation of fifty members had ten acres of land but no meeting house. Farther east a congregation of thirty-eight disciples met once a month in Bastrop. Nearby at Circleville, the church, established in 1852, was very active twenty years later and had not "failed to meet on Lord's day

---

[168] Dudley R. Dobie, *A Brief History of Hays County and San Marcos, Texas* (San Marcos, 1948), pp. 28-29.
[169] J. D. Tant, "Preaching on the Old Range Again," *Gospel Advocate*, XLV (February 12, 1903), p. 111.
[170] Poe, "News," *ibid.*, XXXI (June 12, 1889), p. 271.

ten times in as many years," a record equalled by few churches of Christ in the state.[171]

About seventy-five miles east of Austin, churches were active in Austin, Washington and Brazos counties. The church at Concord, Austin County, planted in 1854, had been taught from its inception that each member must work and contribute of his means every Sunday. As a result, the congregation erected and paid for a nice meeting house while assembling regularly on Sunday and for Bible study. In addition to local efforts, it supported E. W. Dabney in mission work in surrounding counties. Dabney reported in 1873 that he had traveled 1025 miles by private conveyance and 471 by railroad, had received sixty-four into the fold, and had planted two new churches.[172] To the north at Brenham, disciples began meeting in private homes as early as 1867. Ten years later, evangelist A. J. Bush organized a church of eighteen zealous members who erected a fine building which was destroyed by fire a few years later.[173] Farther north at Bryan, a few brethren who evidently worked on the railroad, organized in 1870. Two years later, about twenty-five to forty of the one hundred members were worshiping each Sunday.[174]

Directly north of Austin in Williamson County, churches of Christ were located in several towns. At Taylor, the church bought lot one, block thirty-two on April 8, 1878, and soon erected a small frame house.

---

[171] Lipscomb, "Notes on Texas Travel," XIV (July 4, 1872), pp. 630-636.

[172] E. W. Dabney, "Church News," *Gospel Advocate*, XV (February 20, 1873), p. 178.

[173] Charles F. Schmidt, *History of Washington County* (San Antonio, 1949), p. 121.

[174] Lipscomb, "Notes on Texas Travel," XIV (July 4, 1872), pp. 630-636.

It was replaced in 1891 by a fine brick edifice which served the congregation well into the next century.[175] About twenty miles to the northwest, the Georgetown church of seventy members divided into two political factions and in 1872, upon a motion by evangelist Stephen Strickland, ceased to assemble because the worship service had been turned into a "political rally." On the other hand, the church at Florence was blessed with three men who actively proclaimed the gospel rather than political views.[176]

Simultaneously, small churches were organized in Milam and Bell counties. At Standpoint, Milam County, George Brown and David Pennington planted a church in 1863. Four years later, the congregation began meeting regularly. By 1872, under the leadership of J. D. Hooker and A. J. Foster, it numbered 104. Nearby at Largeville, Pennington in 1870 gathered a band of forty disciples. During the next few years, Hooker preached occasionally to the congregation, which met irregularly.[177] To the northwest at Temple, L. W. Scott pitched his tent in August, 1883, conducted a revival, baptized four, discovered eighteen other disciples, and organized a small church. In appreciation of his efforts, the ladies of the congregation presented him with a fine suit of homemade clothes.[178] A few miles to the west at Belton, C. W. Sewell established a small congregation, mostly of women who were "willing to work," in 1877.[179]

---

[175] *Taylor Daily Press*, January 12, 1923.
[176] Lipscomb, "Notes on Texas Travel," XIV (July 4, 1872), pp. 630-636.
[177] *Ibid.*
[178] L. W. Scott, "News," *Gospel Advocate*, XXV (September 19, 1883), p. 596.
[179] C. W. Sewell, Jr., "Belton," *ibid.*, XIX (February 29, 1877), p. 115.

To the north, the cause was established in Falls, Leon and Freestone counties. The Marlin church, which was begun in July, 1886, held services in rented places for several years. After Isham J. Pringle and Matthew D. Chilton were appointed elders in 1893, the congregation worshiped regularly in a hall until a building was erected in 1903. Shortly thereafter, J. W. Harper and other conservatives agreed to unite with the church provided the organ, Sunday School literature, and the Ladies Aid were set aside. When a vote was taken, the conservatives received the majority and closed the organ on the next Sunday. When the doorkeeper tried to lock the door after the services, Harper, who had changed the lock, said, "You'd better let me lock it. Your key won't fit." However, after a lawyer, hired by the progressives, told Harper his possession was illegal, the conservatives departed and purchased an old Baptist house.[180] Nearby at Carolina, Falls County, seventy-five members met irregularly. To the east at Leona, Leon County, a band of eight, established in 1864, had grown to thirty within three years. About twenty miles to the northwest in the same county, a church was organized at Marquez during a union camp meeting of the Methodist Church South, Methodist Protestant, Southern Baptists, and Primitive Baptists. Since each preacher from the respective denominations expounded his doctrine, "many interesting and ludicrous things" were presented, according to evangelist A. J. McCarty. Speaking in conjunction with W. H. D. Carrington, McCarty claimed the church of Christ had ten confessions, but only eight baptisms as two deferred to a later date, while

---

[180] Fannie Pringle, "History of Christian Church of Marlin, Texas" (unpublished manuscript, Texas Christian University, Ft. Worth, 1951), p. 2.

the sects had none. Victoriously he exclaimed, "In the midst of the fiercest opposition, and the most vindictive misrepresentation, the truth triumphed greatly."[181]

Meanwhile in Waco, the other focal point for churches of Christ in Central Texas, a church had been organized. In this thriving little town of twelve hundred population, eighteen disciples had begun meeting from house to house in 1867. Three years later, B. F. Hall conducted a revival and established a church of about forty members with Thomas Moore and Joseph Lehman as elders. By 1872, with H. D. Bantau as evangelist, the congregation numbered about seventy with fifty children enrolled in "Bible Class." Lipscomb, who visited Waco in the same year, praised the women as "very zealous" and commended the members for contributing of their means every Lord's day.[182] The sacrificial members in 1875 erected a neat brick building on a lot on South 5th Street. While J. H. Crutcher, W. E. Hall and G. L. Surber served as ministers, the church experienced considerable growth.[183] Unfortunately, however, the church divided about 1880 when the organ was introduced.

During the next few years, the little band of anti-organ disciples, who had withdrawn from the Central church, met in a small hall on the corner of Sixth and Franklin. The congregation was strengthened in 1889 by the arrival of A. B. Darden and his wife who taught from house to house. The following year, the church

---

[181] A. J. McCarty, "News," *Gospel Advocate*, XXVI (October 29, 1884), p. 690.
[182] Lipscomb, "Notes on Texas Travel," XIV (July 4, 1872), pp. 630-636.
[183] Ida Moore Hays, "History of the Central Christian Church, Waco, Texas" (unpublished manuscript, Texas Christian University, Ft. Worth, 1945), pp. 5-8.

rented a place on South Fifteenth between Mary and Jackson Streets, and although they had no preacher, the members were mutually edified by regular Bible classes, singing, prayers, and the weekly observance of the Lord's Supper.[184]

In the next decade, the cause grew in both Waco and East Waco. Manifesting an excellent missionary spirit, the Waco church secured C. W. Sewell to hold a tent meeting in East Waco in May, 1893. As a result, sixty-three were baptized, a church organized, and building 28 by 40 feet was purchased for $450.[185] Encouraged by the success in East Waco, the Waco church launched a building program of its own which culminated in the erection of a nice house in 1902. Since the building had no baptistry, candidates were immersed in a small creek near South 20th Street.[186] The congregation later became known as the Columbus Avenue Church of Christ.

West of Waco, evangelists of the churches of Christ were active in Coryell and Hamilton counties. In the summer of 1871, Bantau held a meeting on the Leon River in Coryell County, baptized twenty-one, and organized a country church of thirty-four members.[187] To the northwest, Addison Clark delivered the first sermon by a minister of the church of Christ in Jonesboro in 1874. Apparently influenced by the story that one hundred Indians pursued by Rangers passed by while he was preaching, he called the place "a wild frontier town." Although six were baptized during his

---

[184] *Firm Foundation*, June 2, 1896.
[185] *Firm Foundation*, July 16, 1940.
[186] *Ibid.*
[187] H. D. Bantau, "Success of the Gospel," *Gospel Advocate*, XIII (August 31, 1871), p. 799.

stay, no church was organized.[188] Fifteen miles farther northwest, the church at Hamilton which had wasted away during the Civil War was reorganized in 1876.[189]

In adjoining Comanche and Mills counties, small churches were founded. In Comanche, a bustling town of four thousand population, only Methodist and Baptist preachers had labored until 1875 when W. E. Pendegrass gathered and organized a small group of disciples. Pendergrass encouraged ministers and members to come to Comanche, not only because of the excellent crops, favorable economic conditions, and the cessation of Indian raids, but also because thieves and other potential converts inhabited the area. About thirty miles to the south, J. D. Tant, denied the use of the Baptist and Methodist buildings, held a meeting in a saloon in 1887 and organized a church. Although he was not converted, the saloon keeper was somewhat influenced by the sermons as he gave Tant one hundred dollars to build a "church house in Goldthwaite where a man was privileged to preach the Gospel."[190] Several years later, a controversy arose in the church between elders J. H. Allen and J. Lockabay. After Allen moved away, Lockabay rebuked the members who attended a Baptist meeting, contributed money to their cause, and sang to the accompaniment of instrumental music. As a result, some disciples who believed that those in other sects would be saved were offended and in 1896 forced Lockabay to resign.[191]

---

[188]Addison Clark, "Church News," *ibid.*, XVI (September 10, 1874), p. 853.
[189]Tant, "Growth of the Word," *ibid.*, XL (December 1, 1898), p. 766.
[190]*Firm Foundation*, June 12, 1934.
[191]*Ibid.*, April 26, 1896.

GULF COAST

Meanwhile, efforts to establish churches of Christ along the Texas Gulf Coast from Beaumont to Corpus Christi were less successful. In 1905, W. W. Stone characterized the churches as small, few in number, far apart, and in need of regular ministers. At Beaumont in October, 1903, W. T. Kidwill held a ten-day meeting, baptized four, and formed a small church.[192] Two years later, minister J. E. Carnes labored with the twenty faithful members but remained only a short time because he had no income other than that earned through secular work.[193]

To the southwest, churches were established in Harris and Chambers counties. Although Benton Sweeney had conducted a revival in Houston in 1858, no church was organized. During the next quarter century, the scattered members who resided in the city and the few preachers who occasionally visited there apparently made no effort to establish one. In 1885, W. J. Jones of Manor, Travis County, consented to preach in Houston for one month, and remain longer if adequate financial support was obtained. Although he received only $3.50, donated by four preachers, Jones went to Houston in March. Aided by a Dr. Throgmorton, an influential city physician, he had formed a church of twenty-six disciples within a month after his arrival.[194] In the meantime an anonymous visionary, desirous of advancing the cause in Houston, made a unique appeal in the *Advocate*. In order to purchase a lot and erect a building in the city, he asked churches of Christ in

---

[192]*Ibid.*, October 27, 1903.
[193]J. E. Carnes, "Beaumont," *Gospel Advocate*, XLVI (April 20, 1905, p. 253.
[194]W. J. Jones, "News," *ibid.*, XXVII (May 27, 1885), p. 324.

Texas and throughout the nation to urge each of their members to contribute a nickel or dime once a month for the Houston fund. Apparently his plea was without success.[195]

During the next few years, the church suffered from controversy over doctrinal matters. After Jones departed, J. C. Mason, a pro-organ and missionary society evangelist, arrived and was able immediately to introduce so-called "innovations," since the opposition had no vigorous leader. Austin McGary, editor of the *Firm Foundation,* after attending a worship service on January 1, 1892, objected to the use of the organ and the omission of a prayer of thanks for the loaf and cup before the Lord's Supper was served. He described the communion service as follows: "Bro. Mason read a chapter and prayed, and then the deacons went around, one with the loaf and the other following after with the cup."[196] Shortly thereafter, the conservative members evidently ceased to attend the services. William Crain, who arrived in Houston in 1899, declared four years later that no "loyal" preacher had spoken during that time in the city.[197] A few disciples, in August, 1903, began meeting in a rented upper room in a building located at Bingham and Houston. Two months later A. A. Lucas commended the twenty-nine members who met faithfully each Sunday and Wednesday as the only congregation in the city of nearly a hundred thousand population that was "trying to work and worship according to apostolic example."[198] The next month, J. D. Tant brought his tent to town,

---

[195] Anonymous, "News," *ibid.,* XXVII (May 5, 1885), p. 276.
[196] *Firm Foundation,* January 19, 1892.
[197] William Crain, "Growth of the Word," *Gospel Advocate,* XLV (August 20, 1903), p. 541.
[198] A. A. Lucas, "Growth of the Word," *ibid.,* XLVI (October 13, 1904), p. 651.

preached fifteen days, baptized nine, and urged the forty members to erect a house of worship.[199] Shortly thereafter, a neat, comfortable chapel was built on Spring Street.[200] From this time on, churches of Christ enjoyed a growth commensurate with that of the city. Meanwhile at Cedar Bayou, Harris County, amid a large Methodist community, A. T. Winfree organized a church of about fifteen members in May, 1892; similarly, a small band met at Mont Belvieu, Chambers County.[201]

Simultaneously, a church was established in Galveston. Jefferson Milam, who had married Eliza McKinney of the devout McKinney family, upon moving to Galveston and finding no church of Christ in that city, persuaded General Gano of Dallas County to hold a series of meetings. Assisted by C. M. Wilmeth of Collin County, Gano organized a church in 1877.[202] The next year, W. R. Gaurlay of Kentucky preached for a short time with little apparent success. Likewise, R. A. Milam, J. B. George and W. L. Mosely appealed unsuccessfully to the brotherhood for funds with which to erect a building.[203] Nevertheless, the faithful few continued to meet regularly. An advertisement in an 1885 issue of the *Galveston Evening Tribune* announced that C. E. Mortimer would preach on "Self Consecration" at the morning service and on "Man" in the evening. Alex McArthur found only ten in attend-

---

[199] F. L. Young, "The Cause of Christ in Houston, Texas," *Gospel Advocate*, XLVIII (July 12, 1906), p. 442.
[200] *Houston Post*, December 31, 1951.
[201] A. T. Winfree, "News," *Gospel Advocate*, XXXIV (June 9, 1882), p. 365.
[202] Matthews, "Historical Sketches," XLVIII (July, 1936), pp. 1-5.
[203] R. A. Milam, J. B. George, and W. L. Moseley, "News," *Gospel Advocate*, XXI (November 20, 1879), p. 741.

ance when he arrived the following year.[204] Energetic evangelist J. W. Lowber, who arrived in 1893, increased the congregation from thirteen to over a hundred within a year.[205] Soon a fine house was built at 20th and Avenue K,[206] and it appeared that the church was off to a successful start. Unfortunately, the hurricane of 1900 destroyed the building and the church entered a period of comparative inactivity.

Some one hundred miles to the southwest, small congregations met in Jackson, Victoria and Goliad counties. At Ganado, Jackson County, L. R. Sewell baptized three in November, 1903, among whom was a former Methodist pastor who began preaching for churches of Christ; a few miles to the southwest he organized a small church at Edna.[207] In adjacent Victoria County, disciples met regularly at Crescent Valley and Mission Valley. In 1882, L. C. Chisholm found small groups in Goliad and at "Bethel," a country church organized in 1856, meeting every Sunday. At Charco, Goliad County, a small group, mostly women whose men folk afforded every facility for the ladies to worship "but took no stock in heavenly things themselves, with a few honorable exceptions," assembled each Sunday. W. S. Dabney made the "circuit" monthly.[208]

In the meantime, efforts had been made to establish the cause in Wilson, Atascosa, De Witt and Karnes counties. An unknown but evidently alert and well

---

[204] Alex McArthur, "Galveston," *Gospel Advocate*, XXVIII (June 30, 1886), p. 403.
[205] J. W. Lowber, "Galveston," *ibid.*, XXXVI (April 5, 1894), p. 214.
[206] *Galveston in 1900* (Clarence Ousley, ed.; Atlanta, 1900), pp. 89-90.
[207] L. R. Sewell, "Southwest Texas Mission," *Gospel Advocate*, XLV (November 19, 1903), p. 749.
[208] L. C. Chisholm, "News," *ibid.*, XXIV (June 8, 1882), p. 355.

educated disciple in 1877 described in glowing terms the economic, climatic, medical and religious benefits to be derived by immigrants who would settle in Stockdale, Wilson County. A vast crop of fruit and vegetables had been harvested; fat, sleek cattle were in abundance, and enough acorns wasted to "fatten a million pounds of pork." Land was selling at two or three dollars an acre but choice lots were increasing gradually in price. Gulf breezes insured pleasant summers and mild winters. Nearby mineral springs of black and white sulphur water provided splendid health baths. No liquor was sold in town and the Baptists, Methodists and Catholics had churches. The church of Christ was erecting a neat house 20 by 40 feet and did not "worship the idol, the organ."[209] At Pleasanton, Atascosa County, a few members met in 1882. Fifteen miles in the country, elders Appling and McMains faithfully led a little flock which served dinner on the ground after each Sunday worship service.[210] At Kenedy, C. W. Sewell and E. W. Bonham in 1899 conducted the first meeting by evangelists of the churches of Christ.[211] About forty miles to the northeast at Cuero, Dewitt County, five members met in 1903. James Harding, who conducted a revival in the Masonic Hall, promised to remain for three months in order to plant the cause firmly in the area.[212]

To the south in Live Oak and San Patricio counties, small churches were established. In 1893, evangelist A.

---

[209] Anonymous, "News," *ibid.*, XIX (October 25, 1877), pp. 661-662.

[210] L. C. Chisholm, "News," *ibid.*, XXIV (May 25, 1882), p. 326.

[211] C. W. Sewell, "Church News," *ibid.*, XLI (July 27, 1889), p. 474.

[212] J. Harding, "Evangelistic Work in Texas," *ibid.*, XLV (December 24, 1903), p. 827.

J. Bush came to the vicinity on a "yellow-sided" pony with a Bible and hymn book in one saddle bag and clean linen in the other. He spoke at Papalote, Bee County, but moved on toward Largarto, Live Oak County, when he heard it needed a preacher. On a Sunday morning when he stopped at the home of a Brother Stillwell, about three miles from town, he was greeted with great joy. Shortly afterward, when Stillwell with a group of men armed with guns and knives arrived in town, Bush became alarmed, but Stillwell allayed his fears by calmly explaining that "we have 3 or 4 Mexicans to hang tonight, and then we will be ready for a meeting."[213] Subsequently, Bush organized a church. A few miles to the southeast, W. R. Sewell, after a three-week revival at Mathis, formed a church of twenty-five members who agreed to "work on the New Testament plan."[214]

To the south, the establishment and maintenance of the church in Corpus Christi were due primarily to the burning zeal and tireless effort of C. W. Sewell. Born in Tennessee, reared in the church of Christ, Sewell moved to the vicinity of Waco in 1876 where he farmed and preached until his health failed in 1898. He thereupon moved to the more salubrious climate of Corpus Christi, where in January, 1899, he prevailed upon ten disciples to meet in his house. With the assistance of E. W. Bonham he conducted a ten-day revival in the spring, but only one was baptized because "the people gave us a complete boycott from the first." During the next six years, the little band of from eight to fifteen members met in Sewell's home. A tent meeting conducted by his brother L. R. Sewell in De-

---

[213] Anonymous, "News," *ibid.*, XXXV (May 4, 1893), p. 274.
[214] Sewell, "Southwest Texas Mission," *ibid.*, XXXV (May 4, 1893), p. 274.

cember, 1903, likewise failed to increase the attendance.

In order to plant the church firmly, Sewell planned a big tent revival, declared impossible by the local Methodist preacher at a Methodist conference.[215] Desiring to obtain more publicity, Sewell in May, 1905, moved the little church from his home to a rented hall, and secured a job as a carpenter for five days a week in order to make more personal contacts. The next month, J. P. Sewell, a brother, held a twenty-one-day meeting with three baptisms. Crowds were good, sometimes nearly filling the tent, but persistent rain during the last two weeks caused the tent to collapse one night, prematurely ending the revival. Nevertheless, a church of thirty dedicated members took new courage for future labor.[216]

Meanwhile, C. W. Sewell had fervently but unsuccessfully endeavored to plant a church in Kingsville. When he arrived in the town in July, 1905, he had found only a sick man and his working wife who were members of the church of Christ. Notwithstanding, he pitched his tent and began a meeting on a Saturday night with a seven year old girl and five year old boy as his entire audience. Dismayed but hopeful, he returned the next morning but this time no one came to hear him. Although disappointed and astonished at the apparent indifference of the inhabitants to his preaching, Sewell tried again that evening and the next with better success. He had about ten present each time. Thoroughly disheartened, he struck his tent, paid his board, bought a railroad ticket to Corpus

---

[215] C. W. Sewell, "The Work in Corpus Christi," *ibid.*, XLVII (May 25, 1905), p. 330.
[216] C. W. Sewell, "The Corpus Christi Meeting," *ibid.*, XLVII (July 13, 1905), p. 443.

Christi, paid $9.80 freight cost on his tent, and candidly asked, "Was that doing missionary work?"[217]

SOUTHWEST TEXAS

Simultaneously in Southwest Texas, with San Antonio as a hub, churches of Christ were gaining a foothold. Although some members had resided in the Alamo city since 1857, seemingly no preacher had braved this Catholic stronghold during the next two decades. In 1883, evangelist J. T. Hawkins, decrying the hit-and-miss efforts in mission work and the resulting waste of time and money, proposed that the church concentrate its efforts upon a few strategic points. Selecting San Antonio as one of the most important, he suggested that one hundred Texas members pledge ten dollars annually for five years in order to send evangelist G. L. Surber to the city. Foreseeing that some might question the "five years," he said, "We mean business—we want to succeed," explaining that it would take that long to build up a congregation, erect a house, and place the church on a self-sustaining basis. With commendable devotion, he volunteered to serve as treasurer without remuneration and promised to send receipts to all who contributed.[218] Unfortunately, Hawkins' logical and workable plan received negligible support.

Meanwhile David Pennington, formerly of Missouri and for several years itinerant evangelist in Milam and Falls counties, arrived in San Antonio in May, 1883. He requested the privilege of speaking in any of the twenty-odd churches, the courthouse, or numer-

---

[217] C. W. Sewell, "Church News," *ibid.*, XLVII (October 12, 1905), p. 564.

[218] J. T. Hawkins, "Mission in San Antonio," *ibid.*, XXV (January 25, 1883), p. 57.

ous school buildings, but was altogether unsuccessful. In desperation, he resorted to the city park, site of a Methodist ice cream social, a Negro emancipation celebration, and a weekly Wednesday evening band concert. As Pennington was preaching, residents near the park complained that he was disturbing the peace and induced the city council to pass an ordinance prohibiting preaching in the park. Bewildered and disheartened, Pennington started preaching in private homes and assembled about twenty disciples to worship regularly. Utilizing all his faculties, he had increased the number to forty-five by November. Although he was disappointed greatly when churches and brethren who had promised seventy-five dollars per month sent only $16.70 in October and nothing in November, he refused to leave.[219]

During the next decade, the church experienced some growth but eventually divided. Under Pennington's zealous leadership, the sixty members erected and paid for a 35 by 57 foot building in July, 1884. As the congregation began to grow, the organ issue arose. Pennington, who opposed the use of an organ in the church, alienated several wealthy members who favored the use of instrumental music and soon abandoned the field in which he had labored so diligently.[220] W. J. Barbee, who began his ministry in November, 1886, characterized the city a nineteenth century Athens—"wholly given to idolatry." Buffeted by strife within the church and almost total indifference on the part of non-members, Barbee left in despair in De-

---

[219] David Pennington, "News," *ibid.*, XXV (November 21, 1883), p. 740.

[220] *Ibid.*, XXVI (October 1, 1884), p. 626.

cember, 1887.[221] Plagued by controversy, the church rented their house to the Presbyterians. In June, 1889, however, evangelist A. C. H._____ conducted a two-week meeting with sixteen converts and reorganized the church. The newly appointed elders vowed, "If we do not live, we deserve to die."[222] The following year, during the ministry of John A. Stevens, J. J. Lockhard held a six-week revival with one hundred additions.[223] However, the organ issue arose anew in 1893 and the church divided, the pro-organ majority retaining the building.

The non-organ church grew rapidly after Joe Harding arrived in 1897. He stimulated the congregation to liquidate their debt, repair their "dilapidated" house, and purchase a tent. Soon Harding was preaching under the tent nightly for two weeks in one place, then in another section of town where the process was repeated. The next year, according to E. W. Herndon of Austin, the predominance of Catholicism, the low spiritual tone of the 70,000 inhabitants—one-third Anglo, one-third Mexican and negro, and one-third Jewish and German combined—and the wholesale desecration of Sunday, all indicated that the only successful way to evangelize the city was through tent meetings.[224] Evidently the method bore fruit, as J. W. Jackson reported that the church had eighty-seven additions from May, 1897, to May, 1898, while the pro-organ church had not added one new convert.[225] Neverthe-

---

[221] W. J. Barbee, "One Year in San Antonio, Texas," *Christian Standard*, XXII (December 24, 1887), p. 410.

[222] A.C.H., "Texas Department," *Gospel Advocate*, XXXI (June 26, 1889), p. 414.

[223] John A. Stevens, "News," *ibid.*, XXXII (May 7, 1890), pp. 303.

[224] E. W. Herndon, "Growth of the Word," *ibid.*, XL (June 23, 1898), p. 398.

[225] *Firm Foundation*, May 10, 1898.

less, rapid growth of the churches of Christ in San Antonio did not occur until well into the twentieth century. In 1903, a visitor to San Antonio stated he had not found a "sound" gospel preacher, meaning a non-organ minister, within fifty miles of the city.[226]

To the northwest of San Antonio, small churches of about twenty members each were meeting regularly in 1904 at Bandera, Medina and Kerrville.[227] Farther to the northwest, a church had been planted by B. F. Gooch in Mason in 1877. He donated a lot and promised to pay for the construction of a building if the other members would place all the materials on the site. After a commodious stone house 55 by 35 feet had been erected at a cost of one thousand dollars, R. Cox asked, "Can the older states furnish a better example of a pure Christian, saying nothing about the frontier of Texas?"[228] Ten years later, J. W. Jackson listed many inducements for people to come to Mason. The church of Christ had an average attendance of thirty to thirty-five; all houses were made of rock; a beautiful school capable of accommodating two hundred students had been built by a special tax; Lutherans, Presbyterians, Episcopalians and "Northern" Methodists had meeting houses. The major drawback seemed to be the failure of many country members to attend the church services because of the difference in dress and etiquette between rural and the city residents. To make it easier for the rural members, Jackson tactfully suggested to the city members that they exercise courtesy and friendliness toward their coun-

---

[226] Letter from S, "Church News," *Gospel Advocate*, XLV (June 18, 1903), p. 298.
[227] J. D. Tant, "Who Can Come?" *ibid.*, XLVI (March 3, 1904), p. 144.
[228] R. Cox, "News," *ibid.*, XIX (December 13, 1877), p. 779.

try brethren rather than cold formal adherence to custom.[229]

Ninety miles west of the Alamo city, C. C. McKinney, who had moved to Uvalde in 1857, held forth with a few disciples after 1866. Hungry for news, he requested all the back issues of the *Advocate* from 1862, not knowing that it had discontinued publication during the Civil War.[230] Twenty years later, L. C. Chisholm found the town of five hundred excited by the arrival of the railroad and the resultant "newcomers." He lamented that the church of Christ was content to meet once a month in the courthouse and hear I. N. Gibson preach while the Baptists, Methodists and Episcopalians had caught the spirit of progress and were erecting new meeting houses. Endeavoring to arouse the congregation to action, Chisholm spoke several times, organized a Sunday School, and secured a promise from a few brethren and several sisters that they would "keep house for the Lord." Moving twenty miles down the Leona River to a large farm owned by a Brother Bates near present Batesville, Uvalde County, he found a church composed primarily of share-croppers who cultivated six or seven hundred acres irrigated from the river and urged the members to meet regularly in the school house on Bates' land.[231]

Farther to the west, a small band began meeting in 1904 at Fort Clark near Brackettville. At Del Rio on the Rio Grande a few members met first in 1900 in the courthouse, then in the Methodist building, and finally from house to house. Joe Harding, who arrived

---
[229]*Firm Foundation*, October 1, 1887.
[230]C. C. McKinney, "Uvalde," *Gospel Advocate*, VIII (February 20, 1866), p. 126.
[231]L. C. Chisholm, "Travel," *ibid.*, XXIV (May 18, 1882), p. 312.

in July, 1901, preached three days, baptized two, and induced the ten members, including deaf sister Lottie Fanning, to meet every Sunday.[232] Five years later, J. A. Cunningham preached for several months but succeeded only in edifying the twenty-four members, as all who were almost persuaded to become Christians waited for a "more convenient season."[233] Thus, by 1906 churches of Christ had been planted in several towns in the vast Edwards Plateau region.

SUMMARY AND COMPARATIVE GROWTH

Throughout the period from the Civil War to its formal division in 1906, churches of Christ experienced considerable growth in Texas. The greatest growth occurred in North Texas centered around Dallas and Fort Worth. By 1906, over five thousand disciples resided in Dallas, Tarrant, Collin and Denton counties. Somewhat less growth occurred in Central Texas, focused around Austin and Waco. A lesser increase took place along the Gulf Coast and in Southwest Texas. In East Texas, the least growth occurred. Long-time minister S. R. Ezzell reported in 1887, "We have comparatively but few brethren in this vast region, and only now and then a preacher of the ancient gospel. The denominations are very popular, prevalent and well established all over this country."[234] According to the United States Census, churches of Christ in Texas between 1860 and 1906 had grown from about 2,500 members and 53 churches to 34,006 and 637 respectively. The Presbyterians had grown

---
[232] *Firm Foundation*, July 30, 1901.
[233] J. A. Cunningham, "Report from Del Rio, Texas," *Gospel Advocate*, XLVIII (November 15, 1906), p. 730.
[234] S. R. Ezzell, "News," *Gospel Advocate*, XXIX (May 25, 1887), p. 329.

An Era of Considerable Advancement, 1865-1906

comparatively, from 2,500 members and 4 presbyteries in 1860 to 23,724 members and 438 churches in 1906. The Methodists with 37,996 members comprised the largest Protestant body in Texas in 1860; in 1906, the Baptists with 247,306 members were the largest. In percentage of population in 1860, the Methodists comprised about 6 per cent, the Baptists about 5 per cent, the Presbyterians and churches of Christ about .4 per cent each. In 1906, the state population was composed of about 7 per cent Baptists, 6 per cent Methodists, 1 per cent churches of Christ, and .7 per cent Presbyterians. Thus in forty-six years, churches of Christ, although far outstripped numerically by the Baptists and Methodists, had over a 1000 per cent increase, as compared to about 900 per cent for the Baptists, 700 per cent for the Methodists, and 900 per cent for the Presbyterians. This increase may be attributed primarily to the flaming spirit of evangelism which characterized most of its preachers, missionaries, editors and educators.

CHAPTER V

BEGINNINGS OF CHURCHES OF CHRIST IN WEST TEXAS

The vast reaches of West Texas, last frontier of the Lone Star state, were settled during the period 1870-1900. Waving grassy plains, previously traversed by wandering bands of Indians and herds of fat cattle, were rapidly homesteaded by an ever-increasing tide of land-hungry pioneers. The Indian menace was removed with the successful termination of the Red River War in 1875; the Texas Pacific and Southern Pacific Railroads completed transcontinental routes through Texas in 1882, and the Fort Worth and Denver Railroad traversed the Panhandle by 1888. Thus, one of the last and most beautiful grasslands of the great American frontier was engulfed by an avalanche of tillers of the soil. These settlers were unaware that within a few decades the seemingly limitless treasure of oil would gush from the dusty plains, motivating the construction of new cities in the midst of the West Texas prairie.

Amid the settling of West Texas, several religious bodies made strong efforts to promulgate the gospel. In the forefront were the Baptists, Methodists, and churches of Christ. Preaching under arbors, in school houses, courthouses, in rented halls, and on ranches, their ministers succeeded in establishing churches in nearly every community. As a result, prior to World War II, a Baptist Church, a Methodist Church and a church of Christ were located in most communities.

ABILENE AND VICINITY

Ministers of churches of Christ in the greater part of the area were relatively successful. At Abilene in 1883, W. L. Gibbs, a teacher and printer by trade, began preaching because no other members of the church of Christ in the town would. Within four years, a church of sixty members had been organized and a neat chapel erected. Although the nearest minister of the church of Christ was over one hundred miles away, the congregation promised to pay six hundred dollars to any evangelist who would labor in the area for one year.[1] In 1891, controversy arose over the use of the organ in the church. The pro-organ majority gained possession of the building, and within two years minister W. B. Carnes reported that the "house was full at every service."[2] Although Gibbs made a plea for funds with which to purchase a lot and erect a meeting house for the conservatives in this bustling town of five thousand inhabitants, his plea went unheeded.[3]

Meanwhile, itinerant evangelists proclaimed the gospel in the vicinity. Albert and Cornelia McDonald, who moved in 1890 from East Texas to Tuscola, about twenty miles south of Abilene, began meeting with a few disciples in a blacksmith shop in Buffalo Gap, eight miles to the north. Shortly thereafter, evangelists Walker and MaCarock held meetings in the vicinity, baptized a few, organized a church at Buffalo Gap, and appointed McDonald and a Brother Deaver as

---

[1] H. C. Dimmitt. "Texas State Meeting," *Christian Standard*, XXII (July 23, 1887), p. 235.
[2] W. B. Carnes, "News," *Gospel Advocate*, XXXV (February 23, 1893), p. 128.
[3] W. L. Gibbs, "Come Over in the Spirit and Help Us," *Orthographic Review*, XXXIV (August 27, 1891), p. 2.

elders.[4] A few years later evangelist Jesse P. Sewell, who conducted revivals at Eula and Potosi, Callahan County, and at Nubia, Taylor County, described the country as beautiful and healthful but destitute of "gospel preaching."[5]

During the next few years, the church of Christ was established permanently in Abilene. After moving to Abilene about 1900 to be near "good schools," McDonald and his family began worshiping wth the progressives but soon became dissatisfied.[6] Shortly thereafter, McDonald secured a house in which conservative evangelist Price Billingsley conducted a meeting in September, 1903, and organized an active church of forty members. Returning in June of the following year, Billingsley held a tent revival, baptized twenty-six, reclaimed eleven members, and left a strong congregation of 101.[7] After meeting in the courthouse for a while, the church purchased a small building at Sixth and Chestnut streets, which was used until the congregation moved in 1906 to the auditorium of Childers Classical Institute. The school, later renamed Abilene Christian College, permitted the "college church" to assemble in its auditorium until the congregation erected its own building in 1952.[8]

The city of Coleman is about fifty miles south of Abilene. Disciple V. R. Stapp of Indiana, who arrived in 1879, described it as a "big tent city," and reported that half of the settlers in what was then Runnels

---
[4] Don H. Morris and Max Leach, *Like Stars Shining Brightly* (Abilene, 1953), p. 8. Hereafter cited as Morris and Leach, *Like Stars Shining*.
[5] J. P. Sewell, "Church News," *Gospel Advocate*, XLI (August 10, 1899), p. 507.
[6] Morris and Leach, *Like Stars Shining*, p. 9.
[7] *Firm Foundation*, July 5, 1904.
[8] *College Church of Christ Annual*—1954, p. 1.

County lived in camps. In 1886 a church of Christ was organized, primarily through the efforts of itinerant evangelist W. E. Hawkins. Hawkins also labored in the surrounding area endeavoring to instruct "Christians in their various duties." After preaching for several months, Hawkins declared that the country churches could not prosper permanently unless the members approached the "divine standard" in conduct.[9] Minister G. W. Bonham, who arrived in Coleman in 1890, depicted the area as economically productive, the climate healthful, and the schools and society "good." He encouraged members of the church of Christ who wished to settle in the vicinity to send for a "descriptive circular" of Coleman. Bonham reported that twenty-nine had been added to the growing church in the preceding nine months.[10]

Thirty miles to the southeast at Brownwood, evangelist J. R. Wilmeth conducted the first service of the church of Christ in 1876 but made no effort to organize a church because of the transient populace.[11] During the next few decades, disciples apparently met from house to house but, in November, 1905, minister J. R. Jones secured a hall in which he began preaching. When promised three dollars a month by the Pontotoc Church of Christ in Mason County, Jones refused to consider the offer until he had organized a church and erected a meeting house in Brownwood.[12]

Meanwhile, about one hundred miles north of Abilene, Hilary G. Bedford, a cattleman and preacher of

---

[9] W. E. Hawkins, "Coleman City, Texas," *Gospel Advocate*, XXIX (March 16, 1887), p. 168.
[10] G. W. Bonham, "News," *Gospel Advocate*, XXXIII (May 27, 1891), p. 335.
[11] Matthews, "Historical Sketches," XLVIII (November, 1936), pp. 1-2.
[12] *Firm Foundation*, November 14, 1905.

the church of Christ, had founded in August, 1885, the town of Benjamin named for his deceased son. Shortly thereafter he organized a church of twenty members. Evidently through Bedford's influence, the county judge, sheriff, trustee, tax collector, treasurer and justice of the peace became members. By January, 1890, when minister J. M. Barnes arrived, the town had almost nine hundred population. After attending the services of the church and talking to members of the congregation, Barnes characterized Bedford as the "Abraham of the West," because he possessed large herds of cattle and was a devoted man of faith.[13] In November of the same year, evangelist E. Milwee arrived and began preaching in the vicinity. Supported by the local church which he termed "God's institution for the furtherance of the gospel," Milwee established several nearby rural churches.[14]

About twenty-five miles to the east at Seymour, Tant successfully planted the cause despite considerable opposition from the Baptists. After holding a meeting in May, 1896, and receiving several Baptists into the church of Christ, Tant returned and conducted another two-week revival in September. At the third evening service, an Elder Jones and several Baptists were present and voiced strong opposition to Tant's preaching. At the conclusion of the ensuing debate, Jones requested that all Baptists who were present kneel and pray that Tant "not have a single convert." Contending that the "Baptist prayers did no good," Tant continued the revival and claimed three confessions, two of whom were young girls from a Baptist

---

[13] J. M. Barnes, "News," *Gospel Advocate*, XXXII (January 29, 1890), p. 75.

[14] E. Milwee, "Benjamin," *ibid.*, XXXII (December 3, 1890), p. 771.

family. After one was baptized, Tant asserted that the other girl was forced to return home and "not allowed to obey the Scriptures," but claiming she would run away and "be baptized if she cannot otherwise."[15] As a result, a small band of disciples was planted in Seymour amid much rancor and religious bitterness.

To the north, small churches were founded in Wilbarger and Hardeman counties. At Vernon, a body of disciples in 1889 began meeting in the county courthouse. Three years later a group began assembling at Chillicothe, Hardeman County.[16] Fourteen miles to the west at Quanah in 1905, J. D. Tant organized a small group in the courthouse. The congregation shortly rented a school house in which to worship each Sunday.[17]

Seventy miles west of Abilene, several efforts were made to plant the cause in Scurry and Mitchell counties. In August, 1900, minister J. H. Lawson of Denton made a twelve-day evangelistic tour of the area. While preaching to the friendly and receptive ranchers who lived in "dugouts," Lawson received thirty-one adidtions to the church of Christ. Although Lawson made no effort to organize a church because the members were too scattered, he prayed that they might be "gathered up" in the future.[18] Six years later, John Poe of Longview termed his revival at Loraine, Mitchell County, the first by a church of Christ minister, as a "splendid failure." Despite high winds which blew "almost unceasingly," Poe reported

---

[15]Tant, "Church News," *ibid.*, XXXVIII (October 15, 1896), p. 663.
[16]*Amarillo Sunday News-Globe*, October 5, 1958.
[17]Tant, "Church News," *Gospel Advocate*, XLVII (March 2, 1905), p. 143.
[18]J. H. Lawson, "Church News," *ibid.*, XLII (September 27, 1900), p. 662.

large, attentive audiences, but no one responded to the gospel.[19] Eight miles to the west at Colorado City early in 1906, a few families who were assembling each Sunday in the courthouse, planned to construct a building in the near future.[20]

San Angelo and Westward

Seventy miles southwest of Abilene lay Tom Green County. In 1880 it extended to the New Mexico line and was larger than several states. The following year, Tennessee evangelist J. M. F. Smithson arrived at a camp ground on the South Concho River about fifteen miles from the county seat of Ben Ficklin, where he found disciples R. W. Landrum and Frank Lerch conducting a revival. Lerch, a former Lutheran from Germany who had become a member of the church of Christ shortly after his arrival in America, spoke four modern and two ancient languages. Landrum was a local farmer. After attending several services, Smithson characterized Landrum and Lerch as "harmonious co-workers" who "mean to possess the land for the Lord."[21]

Moving about ten miles up the river to the small settlement of Dove Creek, Smithson found a small congregation of disciples worshiping regularly. The church, which was established by Landrum in 1880, was the only religious organization in the county.[22]

Greatly encouraged by what he had found, Smithson went to Ben Ficklin, a town of a few hundred inhabi-

---

[19] Poe, "From Northwest Texas," *ibid.*, XLVIII (October 18, 1906), p. 670.

[20] George Klingman, "Church News," *ibid.*, XLIX (May 20, 1907), p. 341.

[21] J. M. F. Smithson, "Preaching on the Frontier," *ibid.*, XXIII (November 10, 1881), p. 710.

[22] *Ibid.*

BEGINNINGS OF CHURCHES OF CHRIST IN WEST TEXAS 161

tants for the purpose of establishing a church of Christ. Upon his arrival he found disciple Mrs. Fannie Metcalfe, a recent immigrant from Tennessee, conducting a Sunday School in her home. Thereupon, Smithson held a two-week revival in the new stone courthouse, baptized eighteeen, and organized a church. Since these were the first baptisms enacted there, Smithson explained the ordinance to the crowd which assembled on the banks of the Concho and convinced others they should be immersed. These baptisms performed on the frontier were made more impressive because four young ladies dressed in white robes prepared by Mrs. Metcalfe were among those who were immersed. Landrum and Lerch promised to preach for the new congregation.[23]

Shortly afterward, Smithson went to "San Angela." After delivering his first sermon in Mrs. Tankersley's hotel, he baptized the town constable, the first convert to the church of Christ in the new town.[24] From this small beginning, the cause grew slowly. In 1884 a few disciples began meeting intermittently in the school house, and later in the Methodist Church, occasionally to hear itinerant evangelist R. O. Charles. Little growth was made, however, until evangelist J. A. Sidenar performed several baptisms during revivals in 1894 and 1898.[25] Two years later during a protracted revival, minister A. J. McCarty persuaded the congregation to hold regular services. Then, three years later, he returned, preached for a month in the courthouse, baptized five, and induced the congrega-

---

[23] *Ibid.*
[24] *Ibid.*
[25] *Firm Foundation*, March 30, 1937.

tion to purchase a lot for a building site.[26] When the building was erected in 1905, Jesse P. Sewell was called to be the regular minister for this church of one hundred "loyal and zealous" members.[27]

Thirty-five miles northeast of San Angelo, the conservatives and progressives began efforts simultaneously in Ballinger. In January, 1891, conservative minister A. W. Moss of Paris spoke in the home of "Weeping Joe" Harding as the conservatives' new church building was not yet completed. In the north part of town Baxter Golightly, who arrived in March, ministered to some sixty-five progressives who were without a meeting house. After the anti-organ congregation had completed its new building, Golightly, manifesting an unusual attitude, prayed for its success; but despite this friendly spirit, no reconciliation was effected.[28] At the conclusion of a meeting two years later in South Ballinger, Moss baptized two on one side of the Colorado River while at the same time a progressive minister was immersing six on the opposite bank. Moss reported that "we kneeled on the shore and prayed, they stood."[29] When minister T. W. Phillips of Fort Worth in 1902 visited the "loyal brethren" in the south part of town, he found that they had been named "sticktights" by the progressives. Phillips in an effort to turn the intended ridi-

---

[26]A. J. McCarty, "Church News," *Gospel Advocate*, XLV (April 9, 1903), p. 236. McCarty claimed San Angelo at this time had a population of approximately three thousand persons.

[27]*Firm Foundation*, September 5, 1905.

[28]Baxter Golightly, "My Bow," *Christian Courier*, IV (March 11, 1891), p. 220.

[29]A. W. Moss, "News," *Gospel Advocate*, XXXV (April 6, 1893), p. 220.

cule into an advantage remarked: "May the Lord help them to ever stick tight to the word of God."[30]

To the southeast of San Angelo, the cause was established in Kimble and Edwards counties. A congregation of sixteen members was organized by A. J. Bush at Junction in 1880 with James D. Armstrong and Robert Phillips as elders. The next year, itinerant evangelist R. O. Charles baptized a large number during a revival. Among the new members was W. R. McKee, who later served as an elder and assisted the church to a great extent with his wealth and influence.[31] Through the energy of evangelist John S. Durst, a son of Major John Durst who settled in Junction in 1883, the congregation by 1900 had become one of the largest and most active in West Texas.[32] Durst, who preached throughout the surrounding area without eliciting much response, established a church of Christ in 1891 at Rock Springs, Edwards County, where he was more successful with those who came to town for supplies and "religion." Some came twenty miles to be baptized in the Nueces River.[33]

In the vast area to the southwest of San Angelo, scattered missionary efforts were made. Evangelist W. P. Skaggs of San Angelo in the spring of 1905 made an extended itinerary covering five counties. At Fort McKavett, Menard County, he held a ten-day revival in April, baptized one, and organized a church of seven members. Later in the month he conducted a meeting at Juno, Val Verde County, about one hundred miles

---
[30] T. W. Phillips, "Church News," *ibid.*, XLV (January 1, 1903), p. 16.
[31] *Firm Foundation*, October 9, 1934.
[32] *Preachers Who Blazed the Trail*.
[33] *Firm Foundation*, November 3, 1891.

to the southwest where he baptized one and planted a church of six members. A few days later at Ozona, Crockett County, Skaggs assisted evangelist W. A. Schultz in a meeting in which eleven were added to the small church. About thirty miles to the east at Sonora, Skaggs, after being denied the use of the school house by the trustees, conducted a nine-day revival in a barn that resulted in two baptisms. Twenty-two miles to the north at Eldorado, Schleicher County, Skaggs had even less results for he baptized only one.[34] In June of the same year, Early Arceneaux of Uvalde had seven additions to the small church during a meeting at Sanderson, Terrell County. Arceneaux commended the brethren for their influence for good and for their earnest intention to build a house of worship.[35]

To the northwest of San Angelo, only minor efforts were made to establish churches of Christ. Evangelist G. C. McCraw of Erath County arrived in 1901 in Coke County, and during the next four years labored in the area "accomplishing much good."[36] In 1905 Skaggs baptized only one person after preaching three days in Sterling City.[37]

Meanwhile, preachers of the church of Christ made intermittent efforts to plant the cause in far West Texas. A few small isolated towns were located along the railroad to El Paso. At Pecos from March 7 to 15, 1898, in the Baptist meeting house, evangelist A. J.

---

[34] W. P. Skaggs, "Church News," *Gospel Advocate*, XLVII (July 13, 1905), p. 448.
[35] Early Arceneaux, "Church News," *ibid.*, XLVII (July 13, 1905), p. 448.
[36] *Gospel Preachers Who Blazed the Trail.*
[37] Skaggs, "Church News," *Gospel Advocate*, XLVII (July 13, 1905), p. 448.

McCarty conducted the first service of the church of Christ and gathered a few disciples together. Informed that no church of Christ existed in Barstow, Odessa or Midland, McCarty promised to include these towns in his fall itinerary.[38]

The overall condition of the churches of Christ in far West Texas was depicted by minister W. L. Swinney in 1901. Judge Bailey Anderson was the only member in Stanton. The nearest disciple was John Ray, ten miles away. Although some of the "best gospel preachers in Texas" had done "spasmodic preaching along the railroad," only a few scattered members could be found. Pointing to the future, Swinney suggested that "much patient teaching" was essential to the "permanent establishment" of the church of Christ.[39]

At El Paso in the westernmost tip of Texas, the church of Christ was one of the last religious groups to be established. Even the Episcopal Church, with only one missionary to minister to the vast diocese of 110,000 square miles west of the Pecos River, had sent Bishop Gonzales there in the early 1890's.[40] About the same time, Professor E. R. Bruner, a teacher at Eureka College in Illinois, moved to El Paso because of his health. Three years later Bruner was preaching to a small congregation fairly regularly.[41] In 1894. minister F. S. Young arrived in this "wicked place" to serve as the first full-time minister. During the following January, B. B. Sanders of Austin conducted a three-week revival, baptized ten, reclaimed nineteen

---

[38]*Firm Foundation*, March 29, 1898.
[39]*Ibid.*, September 17, 1901.
[40]A. W. S. Garden, *The Story of West Texas* (Hartford, Connecticut, 1915), p. 3.
[41]Earl West, *The Search for the Ancient Order* (Indianapolis, 1950), II, p. 420.

who had been "cold and indifferent," and warmed the congregation to "new zeal and activity."[42]

Lubbock and the South Plains

Meanwhile, numerous efforts were being made to establish the cause on the South Plains. The first sermon to be delivered in that vast region by a minister of the church of Christ was by itinerant evangelist H. M. Bandy, a graduate of Add-Ran College, on the fourth Sunday in May, 1890, in the old Singer Store in Lubbock. Bandy continued to preach in the vicinity, sometimes to cowboys on isolated ranches.[43]

In the fall of 1890, a caravan of settlers from Thorp Spring set out for the high plains. The group, which included minister S. W. Smith, one of the founders of Lockney Christian College, J. B. Green, W. R. Green and wife, later known as "Aunt Mary," stopped enroute each Sunday to conduct divine worship. In November the band of pioneers arrived at the intersection of the trails from Ft. Griffin and Ft. Stockton, about six miles northeast of present day Lubbock. Mrs. Green depicted the site as a "crossing of cowtrails decorated with rolling tumbleweeds." Here the "church on wheels" halted to attend a service conducted by Bandy in a blacksmith shop.[44] The group then proceeded to Lubbock where Smith and J. B. and W. N. Green with their families settled on November 12. Minister S. W. Smith delivered his first Lubbock sermon in the dining room of the Nicolett Hotel which

---

[42]F. S. Young, "El Paso," *Gospel Advocate*, XXXVII (February 28, 1895), p. 141.
[43]*Story of a Church* (undated pamphlet printed by the Broadway Church of Christ, Lubbock), n.p.
[44]Mary Green (Lubbock) to Stephen Eckstein, interview, December 14, 1950.

stood at the present southwest corner of Broadway and Avenue H. A dozen members met regularly on Sundays for services conducted by Smith.[45] For a short time the worshipers met in a blacksmith shop on the north side of the square, and then in a jail.[46] After a number of members moved into the country, services were held in the old Canyon school house about six miles out of town until 1900 when the meeting place was changed back to town, first in the county courthouse for three years, and then in the newly erected Baptist building.[47]

After the arrival of Liff Sanders, a "cowboy preacher," the Lubbock church experienced a constant growth. Sanders was born in Jacksboro March 19, 1872, the son of a pioneer who settled in 1855 in Jack County. After attending Nashville Bible School for a year, he was baptized by Joe Warlick in 1890, began preaching three years later, and shortly afterward moved to Lockney. While visiting relatives in Lubbock in 1898, he was urged to become the minister of the Lubbock church. The invitation was made more attractive when merchant J. D. Caldwell offered to assist in building Sanders a house. Sanders returned two years later with his bride, the former Lucy Wood. He delivered his first Lubbock sermon in the courthouse and was the first preacher to make his home in Lubbock. To augment his preaching pay of fifteen to twenty dollars per month, he clerked in the Clark, Acuff and Graves Store. Under the leadership of

---

[45]*Lubbock Avalanche Journal*, October 15, 1950. Among the charter members were the Smith, J. B. and W. N. Green families, W. S. Clark, A. J. Clark and D. M. Ayley families.

[46]*Story of a Church.*

[47]*Lubbock Avalanche Journal*, October 15, 1950.

Sanders, the congregation increased to about forty by 1901.[48]

The church grew rapidly during the next few years. After the Baptists erected a new house, some disciples circulated a petition for and proceeded to raise funds for a building of their own. Ranchmen Frank Bowles and T. A. Acuff gave one hundred dollars each; J. D. Caldwell, F. E. Wheelock and Rollie Burns, other well known citizens, also contributed. After the sum of one thousand dollars had been subscribed, Sanders went to Colorado City, purchased the lumber, and had it freighted by wagon to Lubbock. Zealous members quickly erected in 1906 a 36 by 56 foot structure with a belfry and tower. It was the tallest building in Lubbock and seated about three hundred. The congregation numbered about one hundred.[49] This house at 603 Main Street, across from the present Santa Fe Railroad station, was later moved to Tenth and Avenue L because the trains made so much noise.[50]

During the next few years, Sanders proclaimed the gospel to other Plains communities. Speaking on ranches, under arbors and in school houses, he baptized hundreds into the church. When caught on the prairie at night, he curled up in his bed roll near his faithful pony and slept beneath the starry heavens. Due to his unceasing efforts, churches of Christ were established at Tahoka, Post, Littlefield, Slaton, Lamesa and Brownfield.[51]

About fifty miles to the southwest at Seminole, Gaines County, near the Texas-New Mexico state line,

---

[48]Liff Sanders (Lubbock) to Stephen Eckstein, interview, December 14, 1950.
[49]*Ibid.*, December 17, 1950.
[50]*Lubbock Avalanche Journal*, October 15, 1950.
[51]Sanders to Eckstein, interview, December 17, 1950.

G. W. Austin made initial efforts to establish the cause. Arriving in 1904 before Gaines County was organized to do some building for W. B. Austin, a distant relative, Austin found only a few shacks occupied by "four section" men. Shortly thereafter, he helped his relative put in a small business and build a "comfortable residence." On Thursday and Friday, November 4-5, 1904, W. B. Austin celebrated the completion of the two buildings with a barbecue-dance which was attended by some people from Midland and Stanton, seventy-five miles to the southeast. At the conclusion of the dance on Friday night, C. H. Eubank, a member of the church of Christ, obtained the attention of the crowd by pounding on the floor with his cane and surprisingly announced there would be preaching the following Sunday. In response to the announcement, ten persons were present to hear G. W. Austin deliver the first sermon of any kind in the county on November 7. Austin soon left but returned in 1908 as principal of the county seat school, and began preaching to a few faithful members who met in the Seminole courthouse.[52]

Forty-five miles to the north of Lubbock at Plainview, evangelist Thomas Nance organized a band of disciples on September 9, 1889, in a little sod school house. Little growth was experienced, however, until minister E. C. Dimmitt conducted a short meeting in February, 1891, baptized two, and ordained elders and deacons in the church. He reported that "Plain View" was a village of four hundred inhabitants with a Methodist, Baptist, and church of Christ.[53] By 1897 the

---

[52] G. W. Austin (Truth or Consequences, New Mexico), letter to Stephen Eckstein, August 3, 1961.
[53] E. C. Dimmitt, "News," *Gospel Advocate*, XXXIII (March 4, 1891), p. 131.

congregation was sufficiently strong to purchase the Methodist house, but it soon thereafter divided into the "progressives and non-progressives." The progressives met in a school house while the conservatives remained in the old Methodist building. Because of the division, the two assemblies soon disbanded and the building was sold. In 1909, both reorganized to from the First Christian Church and the church of Christ.[54]

Churches were planted in the southern part of Hale County near the turn of the century. Nance received the plaudits of small churches outside of Plainview for his "devotion and sacrifice" in preaching the gospel in rural communities. A small band began meeting in 1898 at Petersburg,[55] and seven years later evangelist J. T. Showalter of Virginia conducted a successful revival with thirty-three additions. Small congregations worshiped at Sand Hill and Lakeview.[56]

Floyd County became an important center during the 1890's for the church of Christ. Minister C. W. Smith, who first began preaching in 1890 at Lockney, and his brother S. W. Smith,[57] who had been preaching in Floydada without any apparent success, teamed up in 1894 to establish a church of twelve members and found Lockney Christian College.[58] The church, augmented by an increasing number of college student members, grew rapidly. Evangelist N. L. Clark reported in 1903 that it held three services each Sunday

---

[54] Mary L. Cox, *History of Hale County, Texas* (Plainview, 1937), p. 130.
[55] *Firm Foundation*, October 4, 1898.
[56] J. T. Showalter, "On the Plains," *Gospel Advocate*, XLVII (September 21, 1905), p. 608.
[57] Claude V. Hall, *The Early History of Floyd County* (Canyon, Texas, 1947), pp. 126-127.
[58] *Amarillo Sunday News-Globe*, October 5, 1958.

and a prayer meeting each Wednesday night. He characterized the congregation as composed of "moral, intelligent and enterprising" members who wielded considerable influence in the community.[59] Evangelist J. T. Showalter, who obtained fifteen additions during a revival two years later, described the three hundred members as "truly a model church." Showalter was agreeably surprised to find more preachers in the church than in any other he had visited in many years.[60]

In nearby Crosby County, the church of Christ was not established until after the turn of the century. Joe Day and C. W. Smith often traveled from Lockney on horseback or in a buggy to preach in the Emma school house. About 1904 a church of six members was organized, and shortly thereafter Smith baptized Mrs. J. W. Milwee, the first Crosby County convert, in a horse tank. When a new school was erected, the young congregation purchased the old building for five hundred dollars for use of the church exclusively.[61]

Churches were established slowly in Hall, Briscoe and Swisher counties. At Turkey, Mrs. Alice Yowell, a widow, assisted by her sixteen year old son, began conducting services in 1897 in her home. Shortly afterward, upon her invitation evangelist Joe Baumann of Era, Texas, held a revival in Turkey and organized a small church.[62] When minister R. W. Officer of Paris

---

[59]N. L. Clark, "Lockney," *Gospel Review*, I (March, 1903), pp. 37-38.
[60]J. T. Showalter, "From Virginia to Texas," *Gospel Advocate*, XLVII (August 24, 1905), p. 543.
[61]Nellie Witt Spikes and Temple Anna Spikes, *A History of Crosby County, Texas* (San Antonio, 1952), pp. 162-163. The charter members were Mr. and Mrs. J. A. Bedingfield, Mr. and Mrs. J. J. Hammack, Mrs. J. W. Carter, and Mrs. E. Luce.
[62]R. W. Officer, "Turkey, Texas," *Gospel Advocate*, XLIII (August 1, 1901), p 493.

arrived on July 7, 1901, and found that there were no regular services in the community, he decided to remedy the unsatisfactory situation. Seven disciples and twenty visitors sat under a brush arbor with walls of "pure, good air" to listen to Officer's first sermon. Upon learning, however, that some members lived forty-five miles away and that distances were too great "to walk," Officer decided to hunt for "greener pastures." Shortly afterward he was endeavoring to induce members of the church of Christ to settle in Hall County by depicting its favorable environment. He portrayed the area as a series of large barbed wire enclosures secured by stock companies for cattle grazing. Settlers had formed permanent "neighborhoods" on the ranch land, generally about fifteen miles apart. Twelve families in his neighborhood used a brush arbor for school and church assemblies. Although the nearest cotton gin was thirty-five miles distant, Officer declared that the land was plentiful, cheap and fertile. He reported that the climate was invigorating, the people friendly, and the area free from crime for the jail doors were ajar and the courthouse yard was sown in turnips.[63]

Since he was the only preacher of the church of Christ in Hall and Briscoe counties, minister Officer felt that it was his duty to serve the isolated communities to the best of his ability. After three members moved away in 1902, the Turkey congregation numbered only four. Occasionally, Officer visited the small congregations in Memphis, Estelline, Lakeview, and one meeting in a farm house at Jago. A church organized at Silverton in 1902 experienced some growth, but failed to gain the next year when a Professor

---

[63]*Ibid.*, XLIV (February 20, 1902), p. 128.

Thomas conducted a fifteen-day vocal singing school for it.[64] Twelve miles north at Grimsley's school house a few faithful disciples gathered from time to time, a loyal band of five worshiped regularly in a farm house twelve miles west of Silverton, and a few brave souls in Tulia began holding services in their homes in 1906.[65] Officer soon became obsessed with the typical West Texas spirit of optimism, predicting that with the certain development of the area some of these small churches would become large and wealthy.[66]

AMARILLO AND THE PANHANDLE

Amarillo in the Panhandle had no preacher of any denomination as late as 1888. Saloons were crowded both day and night. Sunday was a work day. When someone was killed, Judge H. H. Wallace read a burial service from the Episcopal Prayer Book. Early the next year, Isaac Mills of the Childress Methodist circuit preached the first sermon. During the service, Mills took up a collection for foreign missions, to the amusement of his listeners who fully realized the irony of the act as few places needed the gospel more than Amarillo. Whether he obtained any donations is not recorded, but he must have received some encouragement or eventually realized the need on the home front for the gospel, for shortly he had established a Methodist Church in that God-forsaken frontier cow-town.[67]

Before the end of the summer, a church of Christ had been established. When evangelist Nance of

---

[64]*Ibid.*
[65]*Amarillo Sunday News-Globe*, October 5, 1958.
[66]Officer, "Letter from West Texas," *Gospel Advocate* (November 20, 1905), p. 763.
[67]G. A. F. Parker, "Incipient Trade and Religion in Amarillo," *Panhandle Plains Historical Review* (Canyon, Texas, 1929), II, pp. 141-144.

Plainview arrived in a freighter wagon with a suitcase of "preacher clothes," disciple Mrs. Jennie Wetzel went from house to house inviting people to attend his first service in town in the home of Mr. and Mrs. William Harrell. Apparently Nance aroused considerable inetrest, for in August he conducted a meeting in the "box house" which served as courthouse, school building and dance hall. At the close of the meeting a church was organized, and Nance agreed to come from Plainview once a month for five dollars per trip. Within a year the church had obtained S. K. Hallam as a regular minister. Hallam was a success. The church grew steadily under his leadership, and in 1894 he began holding prayer meetings each Thursday evening in the Red Flat saloon. Cowboys and hard-bitten sinners joined in with the godly in singing lustily without manifesting any disrespect.[68] J. D. Tant in April of the next year conducted a revival attended by large and attentive audiences in advance "intellectually and educationally," he believed, of Easterners because the "more enterprising class . . . push further west."[69] Unfortunately, the church soon was plagued by controversy over the introduction of the organ. The conservative minority withdrew but did not organize a church until October, 1908.

In the eastern part of the Panhandle, only a few scattered congregations were organized. At Claude, Armstrong County, Mr. and Mrs. C. Wolf and Mr. and Mrs. W. W. Hood in 1900 invited their neighbors to meet with them, but six years elapsed before a church was organized, and then it was compelled for lack of

---

[68]*Amarillo Sunday News and Globe, Golden Anniversary Edition*, 1938.
[69]Tant, "Church News," *Gospel Advocate*, XXXVII (May 18, 1895), p. 307.

finances to use the courthouse for its meeting place. Farther to the east at McLean, Gray County, the first service of the church of Christ was held in 1903 in the home of Mrs. L. E. Cunningham. The next year, James W. Barrows met J. H. Chambers in the Green Drug Store and in the ensuing discussion discovered that each was a member of the church of Christ. Thereupon, they began conducting services in their respective homes on alternate Sundays. When T. A. Cooke and family of Ellis County arrived in 1905, the little band organized and within a short time had made plans to erect a meeting house.[70] Twenty miles to the east at Shamrock in 1903, evangelist W. C. Scruggs from Oklahoma pioneered the cause, and during the next few years succeeded in planting several churches in the vicinity.[71] At Higgins, Lipscomb County, W. L. Swinney conducted a revival in the Baptist building in 1899 without success, but reported that at Lipscomb, about twenty miles to the northwest, there were a few scattered members over the community. Apparently Swinney was more impressed with the fishing in the vicinity, as attested by the response to his preaching and his comment that in the region "numerous streams of clear, limpid water abound in fine specimens of bass, perch, and speckled trout."[72]

In the northwestern Panhandle, a church was organized at Dalhart in 1903 in a 24 by 26 foot box house located at 1100 Lincoln street. D. L. Hutcheson, who found it necessary to devote most of his time to supporting his family, ministered to the nine members as well as he could. Fully aware of his own limitations and convinced that the country would develop rapidly,

---
[70] *Amarillo Sunday News-Globe*, October 5, 1958.
[71] *Preachers Who Blazed the Trail.*
[72] *Firm Foundation*, August 15, 1899.

Hutcheson urged evangelists of the church of Christ to come while the "harvest is white and the laborers are few."[73]

Finally, to the southwest of Amarillo, a church of Christ was first established at Hereford. In 1902, a Mr. Johnson and a Mr. Falwell during the course of their conversation discovered that their wives were members of the church of Christ. Shortly thereafter, Mrs. Anna Johnson contacted Mrs. Falwell with the exclamation: "Thank God for another member of the church of Christ in Hereford!" The two women soon had arranged for worship services from house to house. In 1905, visiting minister A. S. Higgins held a revival and organized a church of fifteen members with a Brother Megert and a Brother Cypret as elders. Two years later the congregation erected a "small house with a large belfry."[74]

The churches of Christ experienced considerable development in West Texas from 1865 to their formal division in 1906. At the end of the period, church strength lay primarily in Abilene, San Angelo, Lockney and Lubbock. Compared to the denominations, churches of Christ were third numerically, ranking behind the Baptists and Methodists. From these modest beginnings, churches of Christ grew more rapidly during the first half of the twentieth century in West Texas than in any other part of the state.

---

[73] D. L. Hutcheson, "Preaching Needed in the Panhandle," *Gospel Advocate*, XLVI (March 3, 1904), p. 143.
[74] A. S. Higgins (Texline, Texas), letter to Stephen Eckstein, September 4, 1956.

CHAPTER VI

EVANGELISM

The vital motivating force of most Protestant bodies in the United States since about 1795 has been an energetic evangelistic program. Early in the nineteenth century, most denominations discarded the deterministic doctrine that salvation was for only a few elect for the more democratic doctrine of individual free will. Even the staunch Calvinist Presbyterians relented somewhat in 1837. Having accepted the new interpretation, several sects, led by the Baptists, Methodists, Presbyterians and churches of Christ, launched vigorous efforts on the American frontier to move men to exercise their freedom to accept salvation. Although various methods were used to proclaim the good news to the populace, public preaching was the most effective and widely employed means.

The evangelistic fervor of the churches of Christ may be attributed primarily to the burning zeal of its ministers to fulfill the commission Christ delivered to the apostles before his ascension: "Go into all the world and preach the gospel to every creature. He that believeth and is baptized shall be saved; he that believeth not shall be condemned."[1] In Texas, its preachers were impelled to obey this command of Jesus in two ways: by declaring the gospel in all sections of the state, and by exposing the so-called "erroneous teaching" of other sects. Each of these may be illustrated by an example.

---
[1] Mark 16:16.

J. D. Tant, itinerant evangelist at the beginning of the twentieth century, vividly portrayed the spiritual destitution of a vast area of Southwest Texas. In nineteen counties south and west of San Marcos, with a population from one to eight thousand each, Tant did not find a minister of the church of Christ who devoted full time to preaching. Appalled but not dismayed by the immensity of the task, he called upon churches to send a man with a tent into the area to conduct meetings for ten months of each year for three years. To effect realistic action, Tant offered to preach one month in the area and donate ten dollars or give fifty dollars a year to a volunteer. Simultaneously, evangelist A. Driskill promised twenty-five dollars toward the purchase of a tent.[2] In response to the call, L. R. and C. W. Sewell held tent meetings in 1904-05 in the area between San Marcos and Corpus Christi.[3]

The second example is taken from an experience of Carroll Kendrick in 1869 while attending a revival conducted by the Rev. James Bond of another denomination near his home town of Salado. After Bond had finished his sermon, about one hundred persons fell on their knees in response to his call for mourners. Several songs, interspersed with prayers for mercy on the penitents, then followed. Suddenly, "a stalwart, unlettered, pure Texan . . . in his shirt sleeves . . ." rose as if electrified with a shout that he had found Christ and immediately began a series of loud "Hallelujahs." The rejoicing convert was joined at once by a chorus of others, seemingly irrefutable evidence of

---

[2] J. D. Tant, "A Tent Wanted in Texas," *Gospel Advocate*, XLV (March 12, 1903), p. 171.
[3] C. W. Sewell, "Church News," *ibid.*, XLVII (October 12, 1905), p. 654.

a "perfect pentecostal blessing poured out upon the people." Using these so-called "false conversions" as an incentive to stir the churches of Christ to missionary activity, Kendrick sounded the "loudest call" for qualified missionaries. He wanted churches and schools to send men able to refute the teaching of other sects with Bible quotations. Kendrick concluded, "Labor is not in vain here. If it does not pay well in time, it will in eternity."[4]

Devoted Evangelists

Many unsung evangelists and homespun preachers responded to these and other "Macedonian" like calls. Usually they complied with the commission by preaching as the opportunity afforded. Benton P. Sweeney reported in 1873 that he had traveled fifteen hundred miles, preached two hundred sermons, and received sixty additions to the church during a twelve-month period.[5] In 1879, he spoke three hundred nights and had two hundred accessions in Freestone, Limestone, Hill and Robertson counties.[6] In the summer of 1881, he spoke 106 nights with only five exceptions for travel.[7] More energetic and more concentrated was the labor of S. R. Ezzell in 1885 in Northeast Texas. During a ninety-two-day period from June 6 to September 6, he traveled 1700 miles, spoke at 19 different places, delivered 136 discourses, and received 164 converts into the church.[8] From the hundreds of reports

---

[4] Carroll Kendrick, "Loud Call from Texas," *Millennial Harbinger* (November, 1869), p. 651.
[5] B. P. Sweeney, "Church News," *Gospel Advocate*, XV (April 3, 1873), p. 331.
[6] *Ibid.*, XXII (January 15, 1880), p. 43.
[7] *Ibid.*, XXIII (October 6, 1881), p. 630.
[8] S. R. Ezzell, "News," *Gospel Advocate*, XXVII (September 23, 1885), p. 593.

submitted to religious papers, it is evident that the majority of preaching was executed in this manner.

Other evangelists contributed to the growth of the churches of Christ in Texas. R. M. Gano, the son of a minister, was born in Kentucky in 1830. He was baptized at an early age into the church of Christ and subsequently determined to become a physician. After graduating from Louisville Medical School, he practiced medicine in several states before entering the Confederate Army. Serving first under General John H. Morgan, he rose later to the rank of Brigadier General. After Gano began to preach in 1867, he moved to Texas where he labored for forty years, baptized an estimated seven thousand, and endeared himself to many.[9]

Simultaneously, V. I. Stirman, who was born in Kentucky in 1830, arrived in Bonham in 1845. He served in numerous federal and state offices, often riding a horse with two coin-filled bags from city to city where banks were located. Stirman and his sons Rollin and Thomas proclaimed the gospel in every part of the state after 1866 and baptized thousands.[10]

T. M. Sweeney, who was born in Kentucky in 1834, attended Franklin College where he studied under learned Tolbert Fanning. After his conversion at the age of twenty-four, Sweeney preached for forty-six years and baptized about three thousand people. He served twenty-five years of his ministry in Texas. At the age of seventy, he remarked that if he could live his life over, "I would sow more gospel coupled with some honey and but little vinegar."[11]

---

[9] *Preachers Who Blazed the Trail.*
[10] *Ibid.*
[11] *Ibid.*

Although he did not baptize thousands, Lawrence W. Scott edified the saints and refuted infidelity. Born in Virginia in 1846, Scott arrived at Mt. Pleasant in 1863 where he became a bartender. After hearing Thomas Barrett preach, he read the Bible entirely through. When he had reread the New Testament, he quit his job, walked fifteen miles to Mt. Vernon, and asked Barrett to baptize him. It was necessary to break the ice on a pond nearby in order to perform the baptism. Shortly afterward, while attending Kentucky University, Scott began preaching, primarily to church members. Returning to Texas, he wrote the popular and readable *Handbook on Christian Evidences,* and preached throughout the state for many years.[12]

In point of service to Texas churches of Christ, John S. Durst was probably foremost. He was born in Nacogdoches in 1841, son of Major John Durst who had arrived in Texas in 1812. Although his father had embraced the Catholic faith, he turned against it just before his death at Galveston in 1851 because the priest asked him to renounce Masonry before extreme unction was given. After the priest left, John heard his father say, "When you go home, tell your mother and brothers and sisters what you have witnessed and for your father's sake have nothing more to do with Catholicism."[13] In subsequent years, John heeded his father's advice and was baptized by Benton Sweeney while a soldier in 1864. He began preaching after the Civil War at Leona, Texas, and subsequently baptized thousands. Moving to Junction in 1885, Durst remained there and continued preaching until shortly

---

[12] H. Leo Boles, *Biographical Sketches of Gospel Preachers* (Nashville, 1932), pp. 359-363. Hereafter cited as *Sketches of Preachers.*
[13] *Firm Foundation,* February 11, 1908.

before his death in 1924. After proclaiming the gospel for sixty years, he wrote in 1924, "If I have been of any service to my fellow citizens, and to the cause of my Master, it has been no more than my duty and in my humble way have fulfilled my mission."[14]

Another long-time minister was J. A. Clark. Born in 1815 in Tennessee, he came to Austin in 1839. In conjunction with his preaching in the next fifty years, he served as a surveyor, editor of a newspaper, practiced law, and founded Add-Ran College. In his seventy-ninth year, the consecrated evangelist was still enthusiastic about his work. "I can still preach . . . I would like to travel over Texas on a preaching tour once more before I go home."[15]

Probably the most colorful evangelist in Texas was Johnson "Weeping Joe" Harding. Harding was born in Tennessee in 1832. After an illustrious preaching career in many states and some of the chief cities of the nation, he arrived at West Dallas in the 1870's accompanied by a large portion of his home congregation from Gallatin, Tennessee.[16] The group purchased a plot of land and built their own homes. Many of the streets still retain the names of the Harding family and other members of the group. Shortly thereafter, Harding began a vigorous evangelistic program in the area.

Harding, whose services were always well attended, conducted his revivals with considerable fanfare. Assisted by a co-worker, "Harding's Timothy," he rode in a phaeton which headed a cavalcade of wagons transporting his whole congregation. Next came a

---
[14]*Frontier Times*, October, 1924.
[15]J. A. Clark, "News," *Gospel Advocate*, XXXVI (December 13, 1894), p. 790.
[16]*Preachers Who Blazed the Trail.*

"Stop singing that song; you are singing a lie!"

EVANGELISM

long wagon, directed by a uniformed driver, with seats on each side on which his singers were seated. Harding, who was an excellent singer, took great pride in his chorus.[17]

His powerful presentation of the gospel, forcefully aided by dramatic gestures, led thousands to be baptized during his ministry. In the heat of his fiery denunciation of sin, often he removed first his coat, then his vest, collar and tie. His favorite hymn was "Oh, How I Love Jesus." At one revival, as the song was being sung with great fervor, Harding spied a man who appeared "unsaintly." Immediately he rushed to the man, pointed a cane in his face, and cried out, "Stop singing that song; you are singing a lie!" This strapping six-foot evangelist with a magnetic personality left his imprint upon Texas for all time.[18]

No story of evangelists of the churches of Christ in Texas is complete unless Knowles Shaw, nationally renowned revivalist and musician, is included. Shaw, who probably had no peer as a religious showman in his day, was killed in a train wreck near McKinney in 1875 after holding a meeting in Dallas. In nineteen years, he had preached in nearly all states and had baptized eleven thousand. C. M. Wilmeth, editor of the *Christian Preacher* (Dallas), described Shaw as "tall and well proportioned, has a searching eye, cheerful countenance, and luxuriant whiskers, and is past the meridian of life." After listening to some of Shaw's sermons and viewing his mannerisms, Wilmeth gave the following vivid first-hand impression of the evangelist:

> He reasons like Paul; is as bold as Peter; and as tender as John. He is natural like Shake-

---
[17] *Firm Foundation*, November 14, 1933.
[18] *Ibid.*

speare; witty like Swift; pathetic like Burns. He is as independent as Beecher; as idiosyncratic as Talmage; and as indefatigable as Moody. He sings with the energy of Sankey; and plays with the action of Blind Tom. He can support the character, in the same scene, of clergyman and clown, actor and dope, nightingale and parrot. During his discourse, you may see him pacing the platform singing some thrilling song of Zion, or seated by the organ, playing some touching sentimental ballad. You may behold him on bended knee, before some cruel king, in tender tones imploring mercy; or perched upon the end of a bench, off in the amen corner, stiff as a poker and cold as a midnight spook, burlesquing the lukewarm Christian to the tune of "How tedious and tasteless the hours." You may behold the audience baptized in tears, while he stands in memory by the bedside of a beautiful dying daughter, who says, "I'm going home dear father, and after a few more years of toil and tears you'll follow me"; or you may see them convulsed with laughter, as he portrays, in pantomime, with walled eyes and distorted countenance, gestures and grips, grimaces and grins, as balky horse or bad boy. He is true to his mottos, "Much go-aheaditiveness and never-let-go-itiveness."[19]

Evangelists experienced considerable success by use of the protracted meeting which regained its popularity toward the close of the nineteenth century. Often it was conducted by the larger and stronger city congregations. Usually, a so-called "big" preacher was called and given "big" wages, comparatively speaking, for holding the meeting. The "big name" evangelist, often imported from another state, usually attracted larger crowds and succeeded in winning more souls.

---

[19]"Christian Preacher," quoted in William Baxter, *The Singing Evangelist—Life of Knowles Shaw* (Cincinnati, 1879), pp. 151-155.

In August, 1884, a Brother Black from Illinois held a one-month meeting in Ennis. Excellent interest was manifest from the beginning. Some came from twenty miles to attend. After a service one night, 1135 were counted who passed out the gate, although some in a hurry leaped over the fence. Since the crowds were too large for the house, an opening was cut opposite the pulpit, a large canvas was stretched over the yard outside the building, and hundreds of seats placed under the improvised tent. No frenzy or wild emotion characteristic of many religious revivals interrupted the services, but "earnest, thoughtful interest pervades every mind." As a result, 120 were converted which one observer attributed to Black's loving deportment, his well seasoned teaching, and "his heart melting appeals."[20] In an abbreviated seventeen-day revival at Dublin in 1886, Joe Harding received ninety-five additions. In reporting the meeting to the *Advocate*, Harding apologetically lamented that "if I had not taken sick, I believe we might have gained as many more."[21] At Birdville in 1900, R. M. Gano held such a soul-stirring revival that after the first week, the *Fort Worth Register* commented that "considerable interest is being taken in the effort to save souls."[22] Some evangelists, like F. W. Smith of McMinnville, Tennessee, held a series of revivals while visiting in Texas. In 1903, Smith conducted protracted meetings at Dallas, Denton, Corsicana, Bonham, Weatherford, Midlothian and Mt. Pleasant.[23]

---

[20] N. B. Gibbons, "News," *Gospel Advocate*, XXVI (September 14, 1884), p. 596.
[21] J. Harding, "News," *ibid.*, XXVIII (November 24, 1886), p. 739.
[22] *Fort Worth Register*, September 9, 1900.
[23] F. W. Smith, "News," *Gospel Review* (Dallas), I (May, 1903), p. 31.

T. B. Larimore—The Sherman Revivals

The longest, most widely publicized, and fruitful protracted meeting among churches of Christ in Texas was conducted by the inimitable T. B. Larimore in Sherman from January 3 to June 7, 1894. Born in East Tennessee in 1843 and reared on a farm, Larimore was able to attend school only ten or twelve weeks each year. He studied diligently at night, however, and entered Mossy Creek Baptist College at the age of sixteen. After receiving his diploma from that institution, he joined the Confederate army and remained in service until the end of the Civil War. In 1864 he became a member of the church of Christ, began preaching two years later, and shortly afterward enrolled at Franklin College near Nashville. Upon graduation in 1867 he delivered the valedictory address. After preaching for four years in Alabama and Tennessee, he opened "Mars Hill Academy" at Florence, Alabama, in 1871. Students were taught all the subjects then commonly included in the curricula, but Larimore emphasized the study of the Bible and Webster's Dictionary.

Leaving Mars Hill in 1887, Larimore devoted the remainder of his life entirely to preaching. He traveled extensively, filling pulpits "from Maine to Mexico and from Canada to Cuba." He usually spoke three times on Sunday and according to one authority, "Perhaps he preached more sermons to more hearers and baptized more people than any other preacher of his day." He spoke in a clear, earnest, straightforward manner, clothing his thoughts with a superb and well chosen vocabulary. One eyewitness portrayed his face as manifesting a "settled expression of goodness and melancholy which touched the hearts of the people with a feeling of sympathy and love." When he spoke, it seemed that he displayed an "indescrabable and irresistible pathos in his voice, manner, and general appearance which melted audiences to tears and moved hearts long hardened by sin to repentance at the appeal of the gospel.[24] Prior to his meeting in Sherman, Larimore had conducted a two-month revival at the Pearl and Bryan church in Dallas in 1890 with seventy-three additions to the church. According to minister W. H. Wright, the entire membership had been reconsecrated to the work of Christ.[25]

Larimore announced his monumental effort in Sherman on January 4, 1894, by distributing cards advertising "Preaching in this city by T. B. Larimore at 3:30 P.M. and 7:30 P.M. every day and at 11 A.M., 3:30 P.M. and 7:30 P.M. every Sunday." He would continue, the card read, "the good work indefinitely, as long at least, as it may seem best for this community and the cause of Christ."

Periodic reports on the progress of the meeting clearly evidenced its magnitude. During the first month, sixty-two were added to the church. After nine weeks, 188 discourses and 153 conversions, one observer characterized the meeting as "steadily and constantly increasing in interest." In March, elder W. C. Dimmitt reported the house was filled for every service and many were turned away for lack of chairs. "The spirit of the man is so kind and gentle that little children throng around him in swarms, just for a smile and a warm shake of the hand . . . our congregation

---

[24] Boles, *Sketches of Preachers*, pp. 332-335.
[25] W. H. Wright, "News," *Gospel Advocate*, XXXIII (January 7, 1891), p. 3.

is revolutionized. The Spirit of Christ is manifest everywhere among us."[26]

Simultaneously, editor David Lipscomb became so interested in the meeting that he sent a questionnaire to Larimore. In his candid reply, printed in full in the *Advocate*, the tireless evangelist revealed his personality.

> We are just beginning to get things loosened up at the roots. The interest is increasing every day. You are anxious to know how I am holding up. I am well. Nothing can be better for me than to preach twice every day and three times on Sun.—unless it is to preach three times "every day and Sun. too." My voice? It's all right. Length of sermons? Fifty minutes—entire service, seventy minutes. When is the meeting to close? No mortal knows. Subjects and materials for sermons? The Bible is full of them. Its treasures simply inexhaustible. Study? That I do. I am not only studying, but learning—learning rapidly every day. I see new beauties in the Bible every day, and am simply astonished at the sweet, sublime, simplicity of God's eternal truth. Exhaust the Bible themes and thoughts, and truth, at this rate, after a while? Yes, when the swallows drink the ocean dry. What books do I consult? The Bible, Webster's Dict., and the Bible—these three, and no more. How long do I propose to fight on this line? Till mustered out of service. This is a glorious country. Sherman is a good, growing town. Young and old are standing by me bravely in this fight. May the Lord bless them all. We are having a pleasant meeting—not wild, bewildering excitement, but a genuine revival, the effects of which will last till time shall be no more—a sacred school, where a thousand pupils are learning the work,

---

[26]W. C. Dimmitt, "Sherman," *ibid.*, XXXVI (March 22, 1894), p. 185.

the will, and the way of the Lord. I have a perfect home, where every wish is gratified.[27]

The success of the revival alarmed the editor of the *Baptist Observer* who attempted to counteract its influence. He was not in agreement with those who argued, "Oh just let Campbellism alone; it will die of itself." Comparing the argument to a farmer who let Johnson grass and burrs alone, the editor reminded Baptist readers that Larimore had received over one hundred additions at Sherman and issued a plea for them to "awake, awake and buckle on your armor; the enemy is upon us!"[28]

There was still considerable interest after the revival had been in progress four months. Elder Dimmitt again wrote of the unabated interest and reaffirmed Larimore's intention to continue indefinitely. Although 222 had been added to the church, accessions were becoming increasingly less frequent because "material from our own families is about exhausted. We are now among our neighbors, blessing them and their children who are 'afar off'." Some of the congregation who had attended every service hoped Larimore would continue for a year.[29] The *Sherman Daily Register* reported in April, "Unusual interest, great enthusiasm and several conversions at the Christian revival . . . Baptismal services as usual after the sermon tonight." Catching the spirit, the *Register* remarked that even though the meeting had continued for fifteen weeks, "yet the enthusiastic and persistent

---

[27] T. B. Larimore, in *ibid.*, XXXVI (March 22, 1894), p. 172.
[28] *The Baptist Observer*, quoted in *ibid.*, XXVI (March 29, 1894), p. 188.
[29] Dimmitt, "Sherman," *ibid.*, XXXVI (May 10, 1894), p. 291.

demand for indefinite continuance has never been stronger than now."[30]

Despite the expressed enthusiasm the great meeting concluded on June 7. In 154 consecutive days Larimore had delivered 333 sermons and 254 had been added to the Sherman church. Although the church in gratitude unanimously invited Larimore to become its regular minister, he declined. He preferred to spend his remaining years in nationwide evangelism.[31] Eight years later, he returned to Sherman and conducted a revival for a month. Baptist minister S. W. Stewart, who attended the meeting, left his impression of the preaching of the talented evangelist.

> T. B. Larimore, one of the most scholarly Campbellite preachers in the South . . . clings so close to the exact wording of the Scriptures, and makes such profound impression against partyism, that many may be led by him. Here is a sample: "The Bible says baptism is for the remission of sins; it nowhere says it is for anything else." This is the only statement in four long sermons that I heard him make that I could not accept as true, both as to purpose and meaning. The statement is difficult to prove false, but evidently teaches baptismal generation . . . I am told he never debates. Like Dr. Gambrell, it is beneath his dignity. No man visits Texas who elevates Campbellite doctrine more than T. B. Larimore. There is no use for Baptists to make sport of him or his doctrine.

In conclusion, Stewart predicted that "any town where he has preached a month will have Campbellism spreading like Johnson grass, and like Johnson grass,

---

[30]*Sherman Daily Register*, quoted in *ibid.*, XXXVI (April 26, 1894), p. 258.
[31]A. A. Andrews, "Church News," *ibid.*, XXXVI (September 6, 1894), p. 556.

it can never be destroyed, except by digging it up and growing something else in its place."[32]

CAMP MEETINGS

Churches of Christ also held numerous successful old-fashioned camp meetings characteristic of the frontier. In the summer of 1886, a great camp meeting was conducted at Bartlett, twenty miles south of Temple. Carroll Kendrick, who Tant claimed had baptized ten thousand in Texas and started fifty young men preaching in twenty years of labor, was summoned from California to hold the meeting. He directed activities each day in a systematic fashion. Rising with the sun, he walked around ringing a bell until all the campers awoke. Everyone who could leave the camp assembled near an improvised pulpit where the "social meeting," an hour of prayers, songs, short talks by both men and women, was conducted. After breakfast, everyone carrying their Bibles, gathered at ten to discuss a portion of scripture for one hour. At three in the afternoon, the morning exercises were duplicated after which all went to the river to watch Tant baptize the candidates. The evening service, which began at seven, consisted of thirty minutes of singing, thirty minutes of prayer and Bible study, and one hour of preaching. In reminiscing, Tant estimated that attendance varied between fifteen hundred and four thousand and that a large number were baptized.[33]

Over a hundred miles to the west at Fredonia, Mason County, in August, 1887, a seven-day camp meeting

---

[32]*American Baptist Flag*, March 8, 1902, quoted in *ibid.*, XLIV (May 29, 1902), p. 393.
[33]*Firm Foundation*, March 23, 1909.

which attracted visitors from nearby counties was held under an arbor about fifty feet square, well seated and provided with a shingle roof. Attendance at evening services reached 1500 but day crowds dwindled to 350 because of a scarcity of stock food on the camp ground. Evangelists E. Hansbrough, E. P. Baize, J. J. Larimore and R. W. Floyd delivered the sermons. "Daily exercises were prayer and investigation at 9:00 A.M., preaching at 11:00 A.M., 3:30 P.M. and at night." Evidently the social benefits outweighed the spiritual, as only two were baptized.[34]

Nine years later, the eminent T. R. Burnett conducted a two-week camp meeting at Summers Mills, Bell County. In his fluent and descriptive manner, Burnett vividly depicted the camp grounds as "an open grove of pecan trees and oaks, on the bank of the sparkling Salado River." A lemonade stand in the midst of the camp dispensed iced drinks to the people. Since Burnett had held a debate in the locality the previous summer, he feared there would be partisans who would not attend. His fears were unfounded, for he reported that "I have never had larger audiences or more attentive interest in a meeting. I preached twice a day, frequently three times a day, and answered hundreds of questions through the query box." After preaching primarily about faith, repentance and baptism, Burnett immersed "a large number of believing penitents while the multitude stood on the pebbly beach beneath the shade of the big sycamore trees and sang the songs of Zion."[35]

---

[34]*Ibid.*, October 1, 1887.
[35]T. R. Burnett, "Church News," *Gospel Advocate*, XXXVIII (August 20, 1896), p. 531.

Immersing believing penitents

Debates and Debaters

Next to preachers, the public debaters were the most effective agents for evangelism. They served primarily in strengthening the new converts in church doctrine and exposing the so-called erroneous teachings of the denominations. Although all debaters were evangelists, only a few evangelists possessed the ability to debate successfully. Since the manner of presentation was usually more effective than the argument, debating devolved upon the most adept and astute preachers. Fortunately, churches of Christ in Texas had a few such preachers.

Two evangelists of the church of Christ who apparently conducted debates with some success, primarily with the Baptists, were J. D. Tant and T. R. Burnett. Tant, who began preaching in 1881, scheduled his first debate with Dr. W. A. Jarrell, the renowned Baptist debater, in Coryell County in 1886. Tant was overjoyed when Jarrell had to cancel the debate because of illness, since he realized that he was no match for his distinguished opponent. Nevertheless, the Baptists secured minister W. N. Leak, who arrived with a large trunk of books, to debate Tant. Leak evidently affirmed and Tant denied that "faith only was necessary to salvation." After the debate, Tant claimed the victory on the basis that he had persuaded nine Baptists to unite with the church of Christ. In the next three years, Tant conducted fourteen debates and claimed numerous conversions.[36] Simultaneously, Burnett, who was converted from the Methodist Church in 1874, began debating. During the next twenty years, he engaged in thirteen public debates with the Methodists

---
[36]*Firm Foundation*, August 13, 1935.

and even more with the Baptists;[37] with what results, unfortunately, it is not known.

T. W. CASKEY

The outstanding debater of the churches of Christ in Texas was T. W. Caskey. Caskey was born about 1817 in Mississippi. He began his career as a blacksmith but in 1855 began preaching in Jackson. The next year, spiritualism took the town by storm, intellectuals and all. After studying the spiritualist text book for one week, Caskey lectured on it to overflowing crowds for three nights. He ridiculed the seances and jokingly described a so-called medium as a "sable daughter of Africa, as black as a crow, and as stupid as a donkey." As a result, the "humbug" was rendered inoperative, the town regained its equilibrium, and Caskey obtained his initial fame and experience.[38]

Caskey arrived in Texas in 1874 where he began twenty-two years of preaching, practicing law, and debating. He spoke first at Dallas and then ten days at Fort Worth. At the latter place, Addison Clark characterized his lecture on "Temperance" as "rich in anecdote, fertile in imagery and so perfect in mimicry that a drunkard would have been put to shame." After Caskey closed his lecture by singing "Am I a Soldier of the Cross," several veteran drunkards responded to the call for mourners. When he asked all in the audience to sign a paper advocating temperance, "eyes of scorn and indignation" were focused on all the dram sellers and church members who refused.[39]

---

[37] *Preachers Who Blazed the Trail.*
[38] Thomas W. Caskey, *Caskey's Last Book* (B. G. Manire, ed.; Nashville, 1896), pp. 65-78.
[39] Addison Clark, "Church News," *Gospel Advocate,* XVI (April 23, 1874), pp. 403-404.

At the close of his first ten-day meeting at Fort Worth, the Baptists arranged a debate between Caskey and Methodist Pastor W. M. Price, the "Campbellite killer of Texas." Clark, who attended the debate, described Caskey as fifty-seven years of age, six feet three and one-half inches tall, dry and humorous in conversation, and as having never "shed a tear since his mother whipped him, and I doubt much whether he did then."[40] During another debate at Cleburne between the two men, the *Cleburne Chronicle* characterized Caskey in appearance and decorum.

> He is rather awkward and uncouth in manner, but withal having such a spire of originality about him as makes this defect of grace becoming. His head is small and narrow across the forehead, his eyes keen, piercing, flashing about the room like vivid streams of electricity. His manner on the stand is that of a surgeon who picks and lays bare to the eye the muscles and veins and sinews and ligaments of the dissecting room.[41]

Afterward, Caskey debated Price at Dallas, and Baptists Sledge and Jarrell at Woodbury and Alvarado.[42]

Caskey began a three year ministry at the Sherman church in 1874. Shortly after his arrival, however, seven Protestant ministers of Terrell summoned him to debate a Mr. Kilgore, a Seventh-Day Adventist preacher from Michigan, who was defecting some of their members. Caskey accepted, debated Kilgore five days, ably arguing that Christians were under the law of Christ rather than the Mosaic law so effectively

---

[40]Clark, "The Caskey and Price Debate," *ibid.*, XVI (April 7, 1874), p. 443.

[41]*The Lone Star State—Johnson and Hill Counties* (Chicago, 1892), pp. 168-169.

[42]Caskey, *Caskey's Last Book*, p. 65.

that his opponent struck his tent and moved to Rockwall. The ministers, well pleased at the outcome, paid Caskey seventy-five dollars and urged him to "follow him to Rockwall, stick to him, drive him and his ism out of Texas, and we will foot the bill." Caskey accepted the offer. At Rockwall, he critically analyzed one of Kilgore's sermons and challenged him to a debate. Kilgore, however, refused to debate, and moved to Plano. Caskey thereupon returned to Sherman, but not for long, for his fame as a debater was known in Plano. He accepted the invitation of six Plano pastors to debate Kilgore in their town and afterward claimed he killed "the pestiferous thing." To Kilgore's announcement that he would debate no more, Caskey retorted: "That is the only sensible thing you have said since you have been in the state. . . I advise you to take your ism and all your inferior brethren whom you boss, with you to some other latitude."

When Caskey returned to Sherman, he found Rabbi Brown of Atlanta, Georgia, assailing Christianity in a series of lectures delivered in the Cumberland Presbyterian house. After he reviewed Brown's lectures at the request of the Presbyterian pastor, Brown went to McKinney and Dallas followed by Caskey. As a result of the ensuing debates, Brown accepted Caskey's suggestion to return to Atlanta.

Probably Caskey's most famous and amusing debate took place in Sherman in the spring of 1877 with a Mr. Wilson, a leader of Spiritualism. Wilson, whom Caskey praised as a true gentleman if he would desist from propagating his diabolical doctrine, attracted large audiences to his lectures even though he charged fifty cents admission. In the local paper, Wilson boldly challenged the clergy to a debate affirming that Spir-

EVANGELISM

itualism parallels the Bible. Gripped with fear, leading citizens pleaded for Caskey to meet him in a debate which was arranged to be held in the uncompleted courthouse.

On the first night the building was packed, without standing room left. All the Spiritualists from their hotbed in Denison arrived by chartered express car to witness the demise of Christianity and the Bible. Wilson began with a dignified and masterly speech of one hour. Caskey's reply surprised both Wilson and the audience. Instead of assuming his opponent was honest and sincere as he had done in all previous debates, he scathingly denounced Wilson as the prince of humbugs, and his ism, senseless and soulless, begotten of Satan. Although he was often interrupted by laughter and cheering, Caskey sarcastically ridiculed Wilson and his doctrine for one hour. Thus, without using one reason or argument, Caskey easily vanquished his adversary the first night.

The next evening, Wilson began by calling Caskey a fool, a buffoon, and clown. Caskey laughingly replied that one must deal with a fool in such a manner. Wilson, losing his composure for the first time, angrily damned the clergy as morally corrupt and cited several ministers who had fallen through loose women. Seizing the opportunity, Caskey clinched his victory by showing how Wilson could retire to a hotel room, summon a beautiful woman spirit, clothe her in shimmering garments, and thence withdraw for the night as bride and groom. The next morning, Wilson could cause her to disappear while an orthodox preacher had to feed and clothe the female with whom he had spent the night, unable to "spirit" her away. If this fearful power existed, Caskey forcefully concluded, "It is devil begotten and sinborn, the vilest spawn of hell. If it does not exist, then he and all his lecturing crew are the greatest knaves, biggest liars and vilest imposters, that ever cursed the church or world, and filled their pockets with hard earned money of credulous people." As a result, the debate ended, Wilson departed for Nebraska, and Spiritualism waned in Texas.[43]

The next day the editor of the *Denison News*, an ardent Spiritualist, began a year-long slander of Caskey by word and charcoal sketches. In obvious displeasure, S. R. Haywood, editor of the *Fort Worth Daily Standard*, denounced the doctrine of Wilson as so horrible that "we would not believe it if lightnings of heaven should brand it on our bodies." Haywood accused the editor of the *News* of prejudice and affirmed that Caskey had vanquished Wilson fairly and with "fervid eloquence."[44]

Despite his popularity and service to the church, Caskey resorted to the practice of law after 1878 because the Sherman church would not pay him sufficient wages.[45] However, he returned to ministerial labor at Fort Worth in 1884.

While passing through Sherman in 1890, Caskey attended a Christian Science lecture. At the conclusion of the lecture, designed primarily for women, the clever but "effeminate man" asked if there were any questions which did not involve any controversy. The audience was silent until Caskey said, "Professor, if you will tell me what question I can ask that will not involve controversy, I will ask it. I see through your trick." Thereupon, Caskey announced he would ex-

---

[43] *Ibid.*, pp. 65-78.
[44] *Fort Worth Daily Standard*, May 12, 1877.
[45] Thomas W. Caskey, *Caskey's Book* (C. G. Mullins ed.; St. Louis, 1884), p. 19.

pose the "mind cure" at the Sherman church and offered the professor an equal chance to reply. The Christian Science practitioner refused and went to Denison where he was arrested. Upon his release, he left Texas "wiser if not happier."[46]

When Caskey closed his debating career in 1896, he declared that he felt Texas was indebted to him for driving from her fair land "the host of false teachers who have her borders filled, as the locusts filled the land of Egypt."[47] Although Caskey may not have baptized thousands into the church of Christ, he most certainly kept many of the baptized from embracing new dogmas of which they knew little or nothing.

EVANGELISM AMONG NEGROES

Although a large number of preachers and a lesser number of debaters spearheaded evangelism of churches of Christ in Texas, missionary minded ministers made sporadic efforts to establish the cause among the Negroes, the Indians, and in Mexico. Prior to 1900, only a few dedicated men were willing to make attempts to declare the gospel in these neglected fields. Colored evangelists N. Howe and T. Kuykendall conducted the first known meeting for Negroes in Texas in September, 1867, in the white church of Christ building at Circleville with four baptisms.[48] Five years later, Lipscomb reported that two Negro ministers labored with 125 Negro members in East Waco but the origin of the church is unknown.

Most efforts among the Negroes were made by itinerant evangelists. In 1894, G. P. Burnett reported

---
[46]Caskey, *Caskey's Last Book*, pp. 65-78.
[47]*Ibid.*
[48]J. N. McFadin, "Circleville, Texas," *Gospel Advocate*, X (January 2, 1868), p. 15.

338 baptisms among the Negroes in Houston and Trinity counties. He asserted that he could baptize twice as many in the following year if white brethren would send him travel money.[49] Pat Willis of Harrison County, who many thought excelled most white preachers of the church of Christ, was characterized as so eloquently "logical and truthful in his preaching, that many whites hear him at every appointment." D. E. Allen conducted successful tent meetings among the Negroes in 1895 in Austin and Galveston. In order to bolster Negro evangelism, white minister J. W. Jackson of Austin urged all disciples to support it with prayers and liberal contributions.[50]

The most successful missionary work among the Negroes was at Texarkana. In September, 1898, evangelist A. W. Davis held an extended tent meeting and organized a church of 140 members. The new congregation then purchased a lot 74 by 204 feet and paid two-thirds of the five hundred dollars purchase price down. After a building 44 by 44 feet was erected, white minister John K. Smith said, "The congregation is poor, like all Negro congregations, but very earnest and eager for the word."[51]

Missionary Efforts in Mexico

Evangelist C. M. Wilmeth of Dallas in 1897 launched the first missionary effort by Texas churches of Christ in Mexico. Since he had done no prior work among Mexicans, he selected Monterrey as his first mission station because of its locality, railroad connections, and apparently favorable religious conditions. The

---

[49] *Firm Foundation*, April 2, 1895.
[50] *Ibid.*, August 27, 1895.
[51] John K. Smith, "Church News," *Gospel Advocate*, XLI (August 10, 1889), p. 511.

EVANGELISM 201

Baptists, who had about two hundred Mexican members in that city, had their mission headquarters in Monterrey. The Methodists had sixty members, a two-story house purported to be the best Protestant house of worship in Mexico, and a small college. A small number of Presbyterians were meeting in a little house. When Wilmeth arrived in the city, he found a lady who was a member of the church of Christ and conducted the first service in April, 1897, in the Baptist building. The Protestant groups, however, told Wilmeth that the only successful way to convert Mexicans was to go from "house to house." Discouraged and without funds to rent a house where he could preach, Wilmeth moved to Tampico.[52]

In the new field, the work was exceedingly difficult and the results negligible. Wilmeth was denied permission to preach in the one Protestant building. No public halls were available. Finally, he was allowed to speak in a barber shop. Further inquiry revealed that a room could be rented for five dollars a month, but his plea for five brethren or churches to send a dollar a month went unheeded. In desperation, Wilmeth tried to preach on the streets but was prohibited by the government from speaking anywhere outdoors.[53] As a result, the Mexican mission was limited to Wilmeth's home where he and his family worshiped alone as the few American members in Tampico did not attend the services. Wilmeth died suddenly on October 12, 1898, at the age of fifty-one.[54]

The Methodists proved that a successful program

---
[52] *Firm Foundation*, May 4, 1897.
[53] C. W. Wilmeth, "Tampico, Mexico," *Gospel Advocate*, XL (July 7, 1898), p. 435.
[54] Matthews, "Historical Sketches," XLVIII (November, 1936), pp. 1-2.

could be executed provided sufficient money, personnel and energy were used. In 1900, Bishop C. C. McCabe of Houston reported that ten thousand people were attended by the Methodist ministry and about four thousand children were enrolled in their day schools in Mexico.[55] Nevertheless, it was several decades before Texas churches of Christ again attempted to send missionaries south of the Rio Grande.

INDIAN MISSIONS

Only a few preachers of Texas churches of Christ endeavored to establish missions among the Indians. As early as 1860, J. J. Trott proposed the establishment of a mission in Indian Territory and accurately predicted that this "great area on the road to Texas will be a great state of the union . . ."[56] However, the first known attempt was not made until April, 1874, when a Brother Ellis crossed the Red River near Gainesville, preached to a group of Chickasaw Indians, and baptized about twenty. C. M. Wilmeth of Dallas viewed this initial success as an indication that the Indians would welcome missionaries and urged North Texas churches of Christ to sponsor the work.[57] His plea went unheeded.

Two denominations began successful missionary efforts among the Indians. In 1874, Thomas C. Battey, a Quaker school teacher, established a Sabbath school among the Kiowas. Four years later John McIntosh, a Baptist preacher, began working among the

---

[55] *Houston Post*, February 16, 1900.
[56] J. J. Trott, "News from the Churches," *Millennial Harbinger* (September, 1860), p. 505.
[57] C. M. Wilmeth, "Church News," *Gospel Advocate*, XVI (May 7, 1874), p. 453.

Wichitas north of the Wichita River and founded a church by 1880.[58]

Minister R. W. Officer of Gainesville in 1880 began successful missionary work among the Indians for churches of Christ. He devoted all his time to preaching and distributing tracts and books in Indian Territory among those who could read. The Chickasaws manifested such an interest in the gospel that Officer sent to Alabama for evangelist M. Askew of Indian descent. Subsequently, Askew converted a considerable number of Chickasaws to the church of Christ. In September, 1883, Officer attended the Indian council at Tishimingo, Chickasaw Nation, for the purpose of obtaining permission to plant a mission and establish an industrial school. When permission was granted, Officer requested some church to sponsor the project.[59]

The missionary minded Paris, Texas, Church of Christ, directed by elders E. L. Dohoney and W. L. Sluder, heeded the call. It requested that churches contribute one Sunday's collection toward the erection of a meeting house in the Chickasaw nation.[60] Unfortunately, no funds were received. Early in 1884 Askew suddenly died, leaving the entire work to Officer. Discouraged but still determined to do his best, Officer conducted four revivals among the Chickasaws during the summer. He praised the Indians as less prejudiced than the whites.[61]

---

[58] Ernest Wallace, "The Comanches on the White Man's Road," The West Texas Historical Association *Year Book*, XXIX (October, 1953), p. 27.

[59] R. W. Officer, in the *Gospel Advocate*, XXVI (August 24, 1884), p. 546.

[60] E. L. Dohoney and W. H. Sluder, "News," *ibid.*, XXV (November 7, 1883), p. 708.

[61] Officer, "Paris, Texas," *ibid.*, XXVIII (April 28, 1886), p. 259.

Two new developments temporarily bolstered the hope for an Indian mission. Texas disciples Thomas Goode and William Norther promised to give all profits from the sale of a patented quilt-frame in Indian Territory for a mission. Officer lauded the charitable gesture. In reading in 1886 the laws of the Choctaw nation of 1869, Officer discovered a provision which allowed 640 acres to any religious body which would build and conduct a mission or school on said property. When Texas churches again failed to heed his plea for funds, Officer left the Indian work and went to West Texas.[62]

Religious Periodicals

Supplementing evangelism by churches of Christ in Texas were religious papers published by members. These papers were begun primarily by preachers and educators to promulgate their beliefs. On the whole, these journalistic ventures were limited in duration, as only two papers begun prior to 1906 have continued to the present.

During the pre-Civil War period, other denominations preceded the churches of Christ in publishing religious papers in Texas. The Methodists published the *Texas Wesleyan Banner* in 1847 in Brenham but renamed it the *Texas Christian Advocate* in 1855.[63] In the same year, the Presbyterians began publication of the *Texas Presbyterian*.[64] The first paper published by a member of the church of Christ in Texas was the *Christian Philanthropist* (Salado), early in 1856. Evangelist Carroll Kendrick served as editor. It was short-lived, however, and merged with the *Gospel Ad-*

---

[62]*Ibid.*, XXVI (April 2, 1884), p. 212.
[63]Thrall, *Methodism in Texas*, p. 114.
[64]Red, *Presbyterian Church in Texas*, p. 127.

EVANGELISM 205

vocate in September. Since the *Advocate* already had a large number of Texas subscribers, editor Fanning transferred all subscribers of the *Philanthropist* to the *Advocate* and asked Kendrick to edit a "Texas Department" for their benefit.[65] In *The Evangelist* (Ft. Madison, Iowa), February, 1861, the following advertisement appeared: "The Christian Messenger, a new monthly, is about to be issued from Austin, Texas. Price per annum $1." Whether the first issue was published is unknown but the outbreak of the Civil War eliminated any possibility of continued publication.

After the war, Kendrick again attempted to publish the *Christian Philanthropist*. The *Advocate* praised the first issue, published in August, 1866, as sound in the faith and worth reading. The difficulties, however, of printing in a time of scarce money and few subscribers made it necessary for Kendrick again to consolidate his paper with the *Advocate* in January, 1867. Although Kendrick strongly asserted that a monthly could be sustained in Texas, he admitted the labor and expense would more than offset the good accomplished. He accepted an offer again to edit a "Texas Department" in the *Advocate*.[66] In May, 1869, however, Kendrick and several other preachers proposed to combine "means and energies" in order to "bring into the service of the church in Texas, as far as possible, the full force and power of the printing press."[67] Their intentions did not materialize.

The *Christian Messenger* (Bonham 1875-89 and Dal-

---
[65] Tolbert Fanning, in the *Gospel Advocate*. II (September, 1856), p. 286.
[66] Kendrick, "Texas Department," *ibid.*, IX (January 17, 1867), p. 58.
[67] *Ibid.*, XII (January 27, 1870), p. 84.

las 1889-95) was the first successful paper published by a member of the church of Christ in Texas. In 1869, evangelist T. R. Burnett purchased the *Bonham News* and edited it with W. T. Goss until 1889.[68] Using the *News* press, he began the *Messenger* with evangelists E. Elgan, A. Clark, R. C. Horn, J. M. Baird, and Kendrick as staff writers. Burnett, known for his straightforward, sarcastic and forceful manner of expression, energetically denounced the missionary society, instrumental music in the churches, and rebaptism. The editor of the *Apostolic Church* described the *Messenger* as "lively . . . full of racy paragraphs and sharp, humorous criticisms."[69] Because of limited circulation, Burnett moved the *Messenger* to Dallas in 1889. But failing health and a lack of funds caused Burnett to sell the paper to the *Advocate* in 1895, and become an associate editor on its staff.[70]

Other Texas evangelists endeavored to spread the gospel through religious papers. Minister J. I. Dyches of Circleville, Williamson County, edited the short-lived *Texas Christian Reformer* (1872) (Lockhart). It was a semi-monthly containing twenty-four neatly printed pages on good paper, but ceased after a few issues.[71] On March 25, 1875, evangelists C. M. and J. R. Wilmeth advertised that they would publish the *Christian Monthly* in McKinney. After the first issue appeared in September, editor Lipscomb of the *Advocate* commended it as "pleasing in variety of matter, original, and selected." Shortly afterward, the name was changed to *Texas Christian Monthly*. But con-

---

[68] *Bonham News*, July 12, 1909.
[69] B., "Texas News," *Apostolic Church*, VI (February, 1884), p. 30.
[70] *Preachers Who Blazed the Trail*.
[71] J. I. Dyches, "Texas Christian Reformer," *Gospel Advocate*, XIV (April 4, 1872), p. 334.

fronted by financial difficulties, the Wilmeths proposed a merger with the *Christian Messenger* under the new name *Texas Christian*. When editor Burnett of the *Messenger* rejected their offer, the Wilmeths, with the financial support of several other preachers, began the *Texas Christian* on September 1, 1876. Lipscomb congratulated the brothers on their new weekly crowded with "twenty-eight columns of religious matter. Terms, $2 per annum."[72] Nevertheless, poor reception among the churches caused the Wilmeths to combine the *Texas Christian* with evangelist W. H. Hall's *Iron Preacher* to form the *Christian Preacher* in August, 1877, to be published jointly by Hall and the Wilmeths in Dallas. Two years later, minister A. P. Aten joined the staff as "editor at large."[73] The new paper, which attacked the missionary society, had a small subscription list. Because of financial difficulties, the *Christian Preacher* merged with the *Christian Student*, a paper published by Add-Ran College, Thorp Spring, by editor "Uncle Mac" Wilmeth. The following year the short-lived *Texas Christian* merged with the *Advocate*.[74]

Evangelist Austin McGary of Austin next entered into religious journalism. On August 6, 1884, McGary, ardent advocate of rebaptism and a rabid enemy of the missionary society and instrumental music, advertised in the *Advocate* that he would begin the *Firm Foundation* "devoted exclusively to the dissemination of religious thought." He promised to allot space in each issue to those affirming a different position from

---
[72]Lipscomb, "Texas," *ibid.*, XVIII (October 5, 1876), pp. 970-971.
[73]"Texas Department," *ibid.*, XVI (May 22, 1879), p. 331.
[74]*Texas Christian*, quoted in *ibid.*, XXVII (September 30, 1885), p. 618.

his. He challenged all disciples to read what several "old soldiers" have to say about the inconsistencies between "our practices" and "our plea."

McGary dedicated the initial issue, published at Austin in September, 1884, to that group of brethren who regarded the New Testament as an "infallible guide through this wilderness of sin to the promised haven of safety beyond." He assured his readers that he would not "pipe the popular airs of the day with pedantic or sophomoric swell to get dancers" but rather would try to "sing the song of Moses and the lamb by the notes of eighteen hundred years ago." McGary vowed that no individual or principle would be spared in wrestling against "spiritual wickedness in high places," a vow which he kept with unusual ardor. The remainder of the first issue was given to the propagation of McGary's rebaptism views and a martyr type attack upon all opponents.[75]

The *Firm Foundation* progressed steadily despite the "radical" label placed upon it by some progressives. Evangelist A. J. McCarty, a close friend of McGary, firmly asserted that the *Firm Foundation* "has come to stay, and with all the opposition it has . . . will continue to expose error, cry aloud and spare not, and earnestly contend for every item of the faith once for all delivered to the saints."[76] Evidently its appeal to Texas churches of Christ in some degree counteracted the long-held monopoly of the *Advocate* is it became a bi-weekly February 1, 1887, a weekly on March 7, 1889, and has continued uninterrupted

---

[75] *Firm Foundation*, September, 1884.

[76] A. J. McCarty, "In Defense of an Innocent Man," *American Christian Review*, XXIX (June 24, 1886), p. 202.

EVANGELISM

publication on that basis to the present. By 1900 it had over nine thousand subscribers.[77]

To offset the influence of the *Firm Foundation* in Texas, several progressive preachers soon began a paper. Evangelist J. A. Clark, editor of the *Texas Christian* (Thorp Spring, 1885-1888), gave his subscription list in 1888 to progressive preachers W. K. Homan and Chalmers McPherson. Homan had agreed to edit the proposed *Christian Courier*. In the final issue of the *Texas Christian*, Clark assured his readers that the *Courier* would supply them with "a larger and better paper."[78] In July, 1888, the first issue of the *Courier* was published in Dallas. It strongly supported the missionary society and the use of instrumental music in the churches and bitterly renounced rebaptism. The *Foundation* took issue at once. As a result, the two papers engaged in written controversy until the formal schism of the church in 1906. The *Courier* has continued to the present as a publication of the Disciples of Christ (progressives or Christian Church) in Texas.

Several other short-lived papers were published by preachers intent on propagating their respective views. The *Gospel Missionary* (1898-1908?) was edited by W. J. Rice of Corpus Christi. This weekly strongly advocated the "order of worship" (Acts 2:42), upheld rebaptism, and condemned the Sunday School. The *Bible Student* (Lockney, 1899-?) was edited by G. H. P. Showalter, president of Lockney Christian College, and minister S. W. Smith, one of the founders of the college.[79] *Burnett's Budgett* (Dallas, 1899-1909)

---

[77]*Firm Foundation*, October 29, 1901.
[78]*Texas Christian*, April 28, 1899.
[79]*Firm Foundation*, September 26, 1899.

was edited by evangelist T. R. Burnett, former editor of the *Christian Messenger*. Burnett attacked those who used the organ, condemned the missionary societies, ridiculed rebaptism, and opposed the Sunday School as an organization separate and apart from the church.[80] The *Gospel Review* (1903-1904), edited by evangelists Joe S. Warlick, Jesse P. Sewell and R. H. Boll, was published monthly at Dallas. Lipscomb commended the paper as "pure, and clean, instructive and Christian," and as "worthy of a place in any home." The editors stated that their purpose was to "give our readers the very best work of our very best writers," thus preserving their teachings in permanent form for generations yet unborn.[81] It was supplanted soon by the *Gospel Guide* (1905-1909?), a monthly from Dallas edited by Joe Warlick. Endeavoring to escape the financial difficulties connected with the ill-fated *Gospel Review*, Warlick stipulated a subscription price of fifty cents per annum, in advance. In 1905, evangelists A. C. Huff, J. S. Dunn, G. A. Dunn and J. B. Nelson proposed the *Bible Student*, probably in no way connected with the paper of the same name begun at Lockney in 1899. It was to be a twelve page monthly, 9 by 12 inches, fifty cents per year. To induce subscriptions, persons were invited to send ten cents to Meridian, Texas, in order to receive the first three copies. "Try it three months, and we are satisfied you will keep it coming."[82] Whether it was published is not known. The *Eye-Opener* (Celeste, 1904-1909), edited by W. F. Lemmons, strongly supported

---

[80]*Preachers Who Blazed the Trail.*

[81]"Gospel Review," quoted in *Gospel Advocate*, XLV (April 23, 1903), p. 257.

[82]A. C. Huff, "Church News," *ibid.*, XLVII (July 13, 1905), p. 437.

the Sunday School and upheld rebaptism. After the paper was moved to Tyler in 1909, the editor of the *Tyler Courier* termed the first issue he had read as "red hot," and one in which Lemmons "peels the hide" of anyone who does not agree with his religious convictions.[83] Thus, church of Christ evangelists, zealous of spreading their particular teachings through religious papers, found their circulation limited primarily to sympathetic churches, preachers and members.

As a supplement to religious papers, minister Washington Lyles of Quitman, Wood County, proposed the establishment in 1873 of a publishing house. He wanted to make "more books, better books and much cheaper books" available to the churches. In addition, Lyles purported that a publishing house could fulfill the following urgent needs of the churches of Christ: the publication of a correct translation of the Bible which would give the exact English word synonymous with the original Hebrew and Greek words, the publication of a complete commentary of the New Testament, the printing of a small Christian hymn book in harmony with New Testament teachings in simple form with shaped notes to enable the training of nonprofessional singers.[84] His proposal did not become reality until the twentieth century.

EDUCATIONAL INSTITUTIONS

Evangelism was promoted also by educational institutions where young men were systematically trained in the Bible before entering the evangelistic field. As early as March, 1855, Mt. Enterprise Male

---

[83]*Tyler Courier*, January 7, 1909.
[84]Washington Lyles, "A Christian Publishing House," *Gospel Advocate*, XV (July 24, 1873), pp. 690-691.

and Female Academy in Rusk County was advertised in the *Millennial Harbinger*. Charles Vinzent financed the school and T. P. Campbell, a graduate of Bethany College, was its president. The school operated on strictly an academy or pre-college level, failed to attract much attention, and soon closed its doors. At Salado, Bell County, Kendrick's proposed Philanthropia Institute, scheduled to open in January, 1857, apparently never materialized as no subsequent report of its activity is extant.

After the Civil War, Kentuckytown Male and Female Academy was established in 1865 by Charles Carlton, graduate of Bethany College, at Kentuckytown, Collin County.[85] About three years later, Carlton moved the school to Bonham and renamed it Carlton College. J. P. Saunders moved from Dallas to Bonham to attend what he termed a "very excellent school . . . and satisfactory to the brethren generally."[86] Addison and Randolph Clark, later president and vice-president respectively of Add-Ran College, attended for two years. In 1869 the school enrolled 160 students, but for unknown reasons soon became a girls' school.

Add-Ran College was founded by evangelist J. A. Clark and his two sons, Randolph and Addison, in Fort Worth in 1869. According to one authority, it was the first full-fledged college operated and controlled by members of the churches of Christ west of the Mississippi.[87] Clark intended to instruct young men in the Bible and related subjects and send them out as

---

[85]Charles Carlton, "Texas Department," *ibid.*, IX (June 20, 1867), p. 499.
[86]J. P. Saunders, "Bonham, Texas," *ibid.*, XI (December 16, 1869), p. 1146.
[87]Young, *History of Colleges*, p. 69.

evangelists. Church members responded to Clark's plea for books, sending copies of the *Gospel Preacher, Living Pulpit, Orchard's History,* Bibles, hymn books and tracts to the college library.[88]

Because of "evil influences" in Fort Worth, Clark moved the school in 1873 to Thorp Spring, Hood County. Here he felt was an ideal environment in which to train church of Christ evangelists. Clark proudly announced that Thorp Spring was "free from the vices, evils, and dangers incident to railroad and river towns." The legislature had passed a law prohibiting the sale of spiritous liquors within two miles of the town. In order to control the "general character of the school," Clark asked the brotherhood to adopt the college and to appoint trustees if they thought best.[89] Shortly thereafter, leaders of Texas churches of Christ met at Plano and adopted the following resolution: "The college building and grounds are, as yet, individual property; but is none the less a Christian College, and the brethren are earnestly solicited to examine strictly its merits."[90]

From a small beginning in 1873 with seventy-five students, Add-Ran grew until enrollment reached 416 in the 1886-87 school session. In 1890, the name was changed to Add-Ran University, a board of trustees was appointed, and a new charter obtained. Addison Clark became president and his brother Randolph vice-president. The school enjoyed its best year in 1890-91 with 462 students enrolled from 82 Texas counties and six other states.[91]

---
[88]"Books," *Gospel Advocate,* XI (December 16, 1869), p. 1144.
[89]J. A. Clark, "Add-Ran Male and Female College," *ibid.,* XV (December 11, 1873), pp. 1188-1189.
[90]Young, *History of Colleges,* pp. 70-71.
[91]*Ibid.,* p. 72.

A few years later, the "organ incident" occurred during a revival on the campus. According to Dr. T. H. Dabney, an eyewitness, the incident occurred in the fall of 1893 while B. B. Sanders was conducting the revival in the college chapel. When an organ was played during the first service, J. A. Clark went forward and asked his son Addison not to allow it. Addison, after a short consultation with his brother Randolph, told the organist to proceed. Thereupon, a relatively large portion of the audience, led by J. A. Clark, walked out.[92] Evidence by eyewitnesses as to the exact date and percentage of the audience that left the service is contradictory. T. H. Dabney, as he recalled after more than half a century, thinks that it must have been two-thirds of the audience. Plez Taylor, another eyewitness, in a report of the incident published in the *Firm Foundation*, April 10, 1894, corroborates Dabney on both facts. Colby Hall, in the *History of TCU*, lists the date as 1893 and claims that about half the congregation left. On the other hand, Mrs. J. H. Fuller, *nee* Miss Bertha Mason, who was the organist, wrote a "Memorandum of the Organ Incident at Thorp Spring" from memory while attending Texas Christian University in 1951-53. She gave the date as the fall of 1895, declared that 140 walked out while 425 remained in their seats, and that the meeting then continued successfully. According to the remembrance of eyewitness Sister Betty Taylor, published in the *Firm Foundation* December 3, 1940, the revival was conducted in the fall of 1895 by W. M. Davis (rather than Sanders), and that a majority walked out. When it appeared that the meeting was

---

[92] T. H. Dabney (Granbury) to Stephen Eckstein, interview, June 14, 1953.

"bogged in failure," word was passed around that if those opposed to the organ would return, it would not be used. The organ remained silent for the remainder of the revival, but the preacher denounced persons who "read their Bibles through a keyhole." The available data indicates that the incident occurred in 1893, and that a majority of the audience departed when the organ was played.

As a result of the organ incident Add-Ran College began to decline, and in 1895 J. D. Tant reported that it was "gradually going progressive."[93] In the fall of the same year some progressive members of the faculty moved to Waco, where they occupied the plant of the deceased Waco Female College. Founder J. A. Clark tried to minimize the loss of the progressive faculty members. In January, 1896, he declared that the "progressive cyclone has passed over Thorp Spring, spent its fury, and is now lying exhausted at Waco." With hopeful optimism, Clark asserted that the college no longer has any "religious foolishness in it" and thus was destined to be the "largest and best Christian school in the state."[94] However, the few remaining conservative faculty members soon left and the school closed. When the Waco plant burned in 1910, the progressive school moved to Fort Worth where it became Texas Christian University.[95]

Meanwhile, several other schools had been established throughout the state. In 1880, five years after its beginning, Holt's School, located at Italy, Ellis County, boasted that it possessed "facilities for educational, moral, and religious training equalled by few

---

[93]Tant, "Learn Your Business," *Gospel Advocate*, XXXVII (October 10, 1895), p. 651.
[94]*Firm Foundation*, January 28, 1896.
[95]Young, *History of Colleges*, p. 72.

institutions in the land and perhaps surpassed by none."[96] Nevertheless, it failed to fulfill this glowing appraisal and closed shortly thereafter. At Thornton, Limestone County, in 1883, evangelist C. W. Sewell recommended highly Thornton Institute under President E. C. Chambers and Professor T. F. Driskill, both ministers, because most of its students became members of the church of Christ.[97] At Woodville, Tyler County, D. A. Leak and R. H. Bonham, graduates of Add-Ran College, conducted Huntington Institute in 1887. They advertised it as the school which would prepare ministers of the churches of Christ for service in eastern Texas.[98] When this school failed they went to Patroon, Shelby County, where they founded Patroon College in 1893. Although this school enrolled as many as three hundred students, it was too far removed from the majority of the churches and closed in 1897. Meanwhile Leak, who had left in 1895, joined the short-lived Allen Academy at Madisonville, and thence moved to Venus, Johnson County, to help establish Burnetta College in 1896 in conjunction with A. P. Thomas, also a graduate of Add-Ran. The school advertised in the *Firm Foundation* that it offered degrees, was well equipped, upheld good morals and discipline, and that the town was free of saloons. Board and tuition for nine and one-half months was $125 to $135.[99] Many years later, Thomas stated that during the eight years he was connected with the school, the largest enrollment was five boarders and 325 day stu-

---

[96] Anonymous, "Holt's School," *Gospel Advocate*, XXV (October 10, 1883), p. 399.
[97] C. W. Sewell, "Mooresville, Texas," *ibid.*, XXV (October 10, 1883), p. 644.
[98] D. A. Leak and R. H. Bonham, "Woodville, Texas," *ibid.*, XXIX (October 26, 1887), p. 684.
[99] *Firm Foundation*, July 28, 1896.

EVANGELISM

dents. Also, he claimed a competent staff of eight or ten teachers were paid fifty dollars per month, the highest salary then paid in any school in the state.[100] In west Dallas, C. M. Wilmeth, a former teacher at Add-Ran, founded Nazareth University in August, 1886. W. R. Fisher donated the land and considerable money for the buildings, and R. M. Gano, N. W. Lewis and J. W. Fevar served as trustees. Dormitories were available for both men and women. Instruction was given in Bible, ancient and modern languages, mathematics, science, printing, music, and art.[101] Four years later, however, Wilmeth moved to Corinth, Arkansas, where he conducted the school for the next few years.[102] At Lockney, Lockney Christian College (1894-1918) was founded by C. W. and S. W. Smith with J. D. Burleson as president. It was advertised as situated in the "heart of the plains and in one of the most natural wonders of Texas."[103] Twenty students enrolled for the first term. Although the Bible was the text book, "other branches are studied that assist in a proper understanding of the Bible."[104] The school attained college level under the presidency of G. H. P. Showalter (1897-1906), and enjoyed its highest enrollment of 425 in 1899. Three years later, it was incorporated and renamed Lockney College and Bible School. In 1910-11, the school officials and leaders of the local church disagreed over the propriety of "Bible classes on Sunday in the church." Thereafter the school slowly declined, and in 1918 was a World

---

[100]*Dallas News*, July 5, 1931.
[101]*Firm Foundation*, November 14, 1933.
[102]Matthews, "Historical Sketches" (November, 1936), pp. 1-2.
[103]*Firm Foundation*, October 2, 1894.
[104]*Ibid.*, August 30, 1898.

War I fatality during the presidency of J. W. Lowber.[105]

A few colleges were established after 1900 before the formal schism in the church. At Lingleville, Erath County, D. S. Ligon began Lingleville Christian College in October, 1901. It was "chartered by the laws of the state and owned by loyal brethren," meaning those who did not use the organ or subscribe to missionary societies. Although the third session opened in 1903, evidently the school closed shortly thereafter.[106] At Gunter, Grayson County, Gunter Bible College (1903-1928) was organized under auspicious circumstances. Colonel Jot Gunter, who owned 16,000 acres in the vicinity, gave the school five acres and five hundred dollars. Shortly afterward the school was promised additional funds by an anonymous donor provided that the Bible only be used in public services, no "Sunday school" be attached to the church, and no women teach in a public way in the church services.[107] Since President N. L. Clark supported these views, the board agreed to accede to the stipulations. Nevertheless, the school never gained favor with the vast majority of the churches and had a precarious doctrinal and financial existence until its demise in 1928.[108] Nearby at Denton a group of business men formed a stock company in 1901 and organized John B. Denton College, but were unable to get it in operation. Three years later the stockholders offered the property to the church of Christ if they would open a school. Since the church had about three hundred

---

[105] Young, *History of Colleges*, pp. 151-152.
[106] *Firm Foundation*, October 6, 1903.
[107] A small minority of members of the church of Christ believed that a Sunday School, the use of literature in the church, and women teachers were unscriptural.
[108] Young, *History of Colleges*, pp. 152-158.

EVANGELISM

members, several of whom were quite prominent, the offer was accepted and Southwestern Christian College opened on October 4, 1904.[109] The college offered a curriculum of Bible, music, expression, physical culture, and art. Despite the opposition of some church members, the study of the Bible was not compulsory. Nevertheless, a surprising 60 per cent of the students enrolled in a Bible course.[110] Financial difficulties led in 1908 to a reorganization of the school under the new name of Southland University. When a proposed drive for funds the following year failed because of dissension between the board and faculty, the school closed and the property was sold to the city of Denton.[111]

While many preachers were endeavoring actively to establish Christian schools, a minority opposed the movement. In 1888, evangelist E. Hansbrough of Austin cited the founding of Bethany College, Bethany, Virginia, in 1841 as the greatest mistake made by Alexander Campbell. Turning to Texas, he attributed most of the ills plaguing churches of Christ to "salaried pastors, manufactured mostly in our Bible colleges."[112] The next year, editor Austin McGary of the *Firm Foundation* denounced the Bible colleges because of their "fruits," obviously referring to the preachers graduated. He further stated that he would oppose all religious papers which produced a kindred fruit "but there is not the same danger in a paper that there is in a Bible College because the teaching of the paper is open to public criticism, while that of a Bible

---

[109] Jesse P. Sewell, "Southwestern Christian College," *Christian Leader and the Way* (Indianapolis), XVIII (August 2, 1904), p. 5.
[110] *Firm Foundation*, October 18, 1904.
[111] Young, *History of Colleges*, p. 164.
[112] *Firm Foundation*, February 1, 1888.

college is not."[113]   Minister John S. Durst of Junction scathingly rebuked the colleges for training "professional preachers . . . place hunters . . . popular pastors . . . salaried ministers . . . stereotyped preachers . . . graduates with skeleton sermons dictated by the learned professors." He felt that the churches which called graduates of Bible colleges instead of sending them out, violated the principle of the commission of Christ, "Go into all the world and preach the gospel to the whole creation."[114]   Nationally, the *American Christian Review* (Indianapolis, 1856-   ) (name has varied since founding but presently as indicated), published by conservative members of the church of Christ, consistently opposed Bible colleges as unscriptural, but it had little circulation or influence in Texas. The majority of Texas churches of Christ have supported Christian education, but not directly from the church treasury. Members have been urged to give liberally as individuals rather than in the name of the church.

A few ministers endeavored to proclaim the gospel in lectureships. In 1884, Chalmers McPherson of Waxahachie and several other preachers invited J. W. McGarvey, professor of Bible at Transylvania College in Kentucky and a recent traveler in Palestine, to present in Texas an "institute," to consist of a series of lectures illustrated by stereoptic slides of the Holy Land. At Add-Ran College from December 6-8, 1893, J. B. Briney, a minister and debater of Tennessee, lectured on "Geology and Evolution in the Realm of Christian Evidence, Faith and Conscience, and Faith and Expediency."[115]

---

[113] *Ibid.*, March 21, 1889.
[114] *Ibid.*, June 7, 1898.
[115] *Ibid.*, January 3, 1893.

Weaknesses of the Evangelistic Method

The results of several decades of evangelistic labor by ministers of the churches of Christ augmented by its debaters, editors and educators, may be characterized as numerical rather than spiritual. Although the Lone Star state had been crossed and criss-crossed by scores of evangelists and thousands had been added to the churches, few were functioning according to New Testament principles.

The primary reason for the spiritual ineptness among the churches of Christ was the failure of their ministers to teach the new converts the duties attendant to membership. Doctrinally and morally, the majority of members were in dire need of competent and continuous instruction. L. C. Chisholm noted in his rather extensive travel throughout the state in 1882 that the members were well informed relative to faith, repentance and baptism, but seemed to attach so much importance to these "first steps into Christ's kingdom . . . that one would really be led to conclude that many believed that faith, repentance and baptism would finally save them in heaven at last." Chisholm stated that if the preachers would fulfill the last half of the commission, that is, "Teach them to observe all things whatsoever I have commanded you," the cause would prosper as never before.[116] Evangelist A. G. Huckaba, who made a short tour through the state in 1902, found trouble in nearly every congregation which he ascribed to the failure of the evangelists to preach "all things" as required in Matthew 28:20. With forthrightness, he accused preachers of teaching first principles only and then leaving the new converts to "starve for want

---

[116]L. C. Chisholm, "Notes of Travel," *Gospel Advocate*, XXIV (June 1, 1882), p. 345.

of milk to drink." He classified the most newly appointed elders as incompetent. "As a consequence of such lamb growing as this, you need not think it very strange when you see the wolves so plenteous and fat."[117] I. C. Vickery lamented the sight of so many congregations "starving for the lack of spiritual food." After lauding the evangelists for their spirit of self-sacrifice, Vickery then reprimanded them for neglecting their duties, "letting new born babes in Christ dwindle and die for lack of nurture and admonition."[118]

A major weakness of this type of evangelism was the omission of instruction on the importance of "giving." While concentrating on salvation, little or no attention was placed on the pocketbook. T. W. Caskey, who practiced law for six years because his salary as a minister was inadequate, believed that the majority of the churches were able to pay a preacher but were "laboring under the pleasing delusion—the dream of avarice, while sleeping in the cradle, rocked by a hand of some of our earlier preaching brethren—A FREE GOSPEL."[119] J. D. Tant, who began preaching in 1876, claimed that he had preached for three years without remuneration. After receiving only $9.75 for his labor in 1880, he interrupted his preaching to break horses for $5 a head.[120] Shortly he was preaching again, but found it necessary in 1901 to spend three years in secular work to liquidate a $4,500 debt and "make a living" for his family.[121] Tant, like many

---

[117] *Firm Foundation*, September 9, 1902.

[118] I. C. Vickery, "Starving Congregations," *Gospel Advocate*, XLVIII (October 4, 1906), p. 634.

[119] Caskey, *Caskey's Book*, p. 314.

[120] *Firm Foundation*, January 30, 1934.

[121] Tant, "Church News," *Gospel Advocate*, XLIII (October 31, 1901), p. 703.

EVANGELISM 223

other preachers, reaped in a large measure what he had sown.

Another weakness of church of Christ evangelism was the concentration upon the annual "big" summer meeting. J. H. Lawson of Denton stated in 1900 that nearly all meetings were held in July or August. Two years later at Whitewright, he asked if the churches in Texas had only a "hot-weather" religion since evidently most had gone into so-called "winter quarters."[122] T. B. Wilkinson, who moved to Pine Mills near Mineola in 1905, found Texas brethren like those in other states—hibernating spiritually from one summer meeting to the next. He declared that it would be a blessing to many brethren if they could die in summer time for their religion "freezes when cold weather comes."[123] However, Wilkinson may have been unduly critical because some members often had to travel several miles in freezing weather in open wagons to worship, and heavy rains often turned the roads into virtual quagmires. In the same year, minister Price Billingsley of Abilene observed that many congregations' "losses in winter wipe out summer gains."[124]

Preachers often failed to create in members a genuine interest in their religion. One devout Methodist, who moved into an area without a Methodist Church, visited the church of Christ. Upon entering the building, he was shocked to hear a discussion of the "Grange," which ceased only for the worship service.

---
[122] J. H. Lawson, "Field Gleaning," *ibid.*, XLIV (January 10, 1902), p. 78.
[123] T. B. Wilkinson, "Church News," *ibid.*, XLVII (January 26, 1905), p. 58.
[124] Price Billingsley, "Need to Grow in Winter," *ibid.*, XLVII (December 21, 1905), p. 801.

He never returned.[125] At Terrell in 1889, less than half the church attended a revival because the Georgia Minstrels followed by the Sells Brothers Mammoth Shows were in town. Others claimed they had to pick cotton and take it to town.[126]

Evangelists who preached "first principles"[127] created in many members an attitude of self-righteousness. Disciples who had believed, repented and had been baptized, often condemned those in other sects who had not subscribed to this formula of salvation. Disciples who tried to teach members of other sects by recognizing their good points were too often severely criticized. James L. Thornberry, a long time preacher in Texas who was baptized by Barton W. Stone in 1833, reflected from his home in Scyene in 1884 on the state of the church. For trying to be courteous and friendly with good people in all sects, he was reprimanded as compromising the truth, particularly because he wrote for Baptist papers. In defense Thornberry admonished his critics, "Some of us are too distant and unkind to our own brethren whom we esteem in error and too harsh toward the good among the sects. Standing firm on the Bible, let us try to win and not drive. We need more of that charity that covers little errors."[128] More teaching,

---

[125] Anonymous, "Church News," *ibid.*, XVII (November 11, 1875), p. 1072.

[126] A. C. Henry, "News," *ibid.*, XXXI (December 4, 1889), p. 771.

[127] First principles were according to preachers of the churches of Christ the four steps to salvation. First, the hearer must have faith in Christ as the Son of God; he must then repent of his sins, confess with the mouth Jesus Christ as the Saviour, and be immersed.

[128] James L. Thornberry, "Fifty Years Ago," *Apostolic Church*, VI (September, 1884), pp. 20-21.

particularly by editors, that love was the basic tenet of Christianity was needed.

A paramount weakness in evangelistic preaching was the failure to stress the importance of assuming responsibility. One anonymous brother suggested in 1885 that the prevalent "one man rule" be supplanted by a plurality of elders who would teach, preach, and rule for the betterment of the whole body. "Such an eldership we have seldom seen in any of our churches."[129] In 1900, B. B. Sanders requested that a small church near Dallas properly publicize his forthcoming revival. Upon his arrival, Sanders was amazed to find that no announcement had been made and that the meeting house was locked. The member who rang the bell and opened the building had left town without delegating the responsibility. Dismayed but hopeful, Sanders climbed in the window and unlocked the door. After about an hour's wait, he preached to seven people. Next morning, he left the "dead church."[130] In Caldwell County, Nat F. Gray attended the services of the sects because there was no church of Christ in the vicinity. He wrote Lipscomb asking if he should move to a place where a "church of the living God" was located. Lipscomb replied that no disciple should live in a community six months without making a diligent effort to form a church. "The solemn responsibility then rests on every Christian . . . if he fails to make an effort God will hold him accountable."[131]

Another weakness was the failure of evangelists to

---

[129] Anonymous, "News," *Gospel Advocate*, XXVII (May 20, 1885), p. 308.
[130] B. B. Sanders, "A Dead Church," *Christian Courier*, XII (October 25, 1900), p. 1.
[131] Nat F. Gray, "Church News," *Gospel Advocate*, XI (May 20, 1869), p. 271.

instruct members in regard to church discipline. J. L. Sewell, who held a meeting in 1883 at Troy, Bell County, found many members addicted to whiskey. When the few sober members arraigned a disciple before the church for drunkenness, the meeting broke up in disagreement over "how much must a man drink before he is considered drunk?" Sewell soon began preaching again to about forty who pledged themselves to have nothing to do with whiskey, horse racing, or dancing.[132] At Mantua, Collin County, the church split over the failure of the elders to discipline a preacher accused of adultery. Minister B. F. Hall's attempt to unite with the church by letter in May, 1870, was rebuffed by elder J. B. Wilmeth on the basis that Hall had a living wife while married to another woman. When efforts to have him desist failed because some of the members including elder Ashley McKinney were friendly, Wilmeth and more than thirty other members in March of the following year withdrew their letters.[133] A Sherman farmer was acquitted for baling hay on a Sunday in 1898 after he insisted that the hay would have been ruined by rain. Evangelist T. R. Burnett remarked, "The Texas Sunday law is very lenient," inferring that the church was even more so.[134]

On the other hand, a few churches which practiced discipline reaped a beneficial harvest. At Concord, Leon County, the church membership book from 1854 to 1885 has after a relatively large number of names the notation "Withdrawn" for dancing, drunkenness,

---

[132] J. L. Sewell, "News," *ibid.*, XXV (October 16, 1883), p. 664.

[133] J. B. Wilmeth, "Church at Mantau," *ibid.*, XIV (January 4, 1872), pp. 13-16.

[134] T. R. Burnett, "Growth of the Word," *ibid.*, XL (December 29, 1898), p. 827.

bad conduct, or neglecting the assembly of the saints. In most instances, however, an additional notation "Restored" appeared under a later date. Apparently the forthright discipline had been effective.[135] Although C. M. Wilmeth observed in his travels about North Texas in 1875 that many churches which had shrunk from the duty of discipline had become "incurably diseased," the Hackberry Grove church in Collin County was cited as an exception. For many years it had endeavored to practice the principle outlined in Galatians 6:1 ("If a brother be overtaken in a fault, ye which are spiritual restore such a one in the spirit of meekness . . ."). As a result, the guilty parties usually repented when confronted with their offense. Thus, Wilmeth recommended this procedure rather than one of procrastination or disregard.[136]

Evangelistic efforts by preachers of churches of Christ in Texas prior to division ushered thousands into the church, but left most at the baptismal water, uninformed as to Christian duties and responsibilities. Incompetent leaders, often appointed on the spur of the moment, administered little discipline or instruction relative to the practical application of the sermon on the mount in daily life. Editors, bent upon teaching a particular personal doctrine, neglected to write articles about the development of Christian character. Educators primarily indoctrinated the young ministers with the "first principles" of church doctrine. As a result, many members, entirely ignorant of church doctrine, lapsed into indifference. Others vehemently asserted that their narrow interpretation of scripture

---
[135] Anonymous, "News," *ibid.*, XXVII (July 8, 1885), p. 524.
[136] C. M. Wilmeth, "Notes of Travel in North Texas," *Apostolic Times*, VII (March 11, 1875), p. 88.

was the only correct interpretation. It is not surprising, therefore, that churches of Christ suffered from numerous internal controversies which ultimately terminated in division.

CHAPTER VII

CONTROVERSY AND DIVISION

During the post-Civil War period, churches of Christ became involved in numerous doctrinal conflicts which led to bitter discussion and after 1880 evolved into outright schism. The controversy significantly affected churches of Christ in Texas. Formal and official recognition of division came in 1906. Two major issues confronted the church. The first was in regard to the American Missionary Society and resultant state societies. The second was concerning the introduction of instrumental music into the worship services of the church. In addition to the two major issues, several lesser, but highly controversial, problems were debated. These were in regard to the use of one cup in the Lord's Supper, the propriety of the Sunday School as an integral part of the church, and the use of literature other than the Bible in the church. Limited primarily to Texas were the disputes concerning rebaptism and the order of worship services.

THE AMERICAN MISSIONARY SOCIETY

The American Christian Missionary Society was founded in 1849 in Cincinnati under the aegis of Alexander Campbell. For a decade Campbell had published without any apparent success in the *Millennial Harbinger* appeals from members of churches of Christ in numerous communities for missionaries. Eventually, concluding that some other means of recruitment were necessary, he called a meeting of brethren in 1849 in

Cincinnati, the "primary object being to devise some scheme for a more effectual proclamation of the gospel in destitute places, both at home and abroad."[1] A few members from scattered churches, mostly in the Ohio valley, responded. No representatives from Texas attended, probably because the meeting had not been publicized there or because of the great distance. Campbell, for fear of being called a "dictator," did not attend. Nevertheless, those present organized the American Christian Missionary Society for the purpose stated in the call and elected Campbell its first president. This was the first attempt by churches of Christ to establish a national organization.

The new organization immediately became controversial. Shortly after the 1849 meeting, ardent advocates organized state societies in Indiana and Kentucky. In 1850, minister B. F. Hall of Collin County expressed his hearty approval of the formation of the missionary society. Citing the great need for missionaries in Texas, he asked, "Will not the society send two or more to that rich, beautiful and growing state!"[2] The following year, John R. McCall of Austin urged the society to send "one or two good laborers into this great field."[3] Others strongly opposed, drawing upon the Bible as authority for their objections. In 1857, William Rawlins of Pleasant Run, Dallas County, condemned all "religious convocations, conventions, co-operations, confederations, conferences, and councils for business purposes outside of one Christian assembly as utterly unauthorized by the

---

[1] W. K. Pendleton, "The Convention of Christian Churches," *Millennial Harbinger* (December, 1849), pp. 689-690.
[2] B. F. Hall, "Things in Texas," *Millennial Harbinger* (December 5, 1849), pp. 103-104.
[3] John R. McCall, "From Texas," *Christian Magazine* (May, 1851), pp. 156-157.

law of liberty or practice of the early Christians."[4] Tolbert Fanning, editor of the *Gospel Advocate*, emphatically objected because "we see no necessity for creeds, human platforms, constitutions, 'resolves,' president, vice-president or officers unknown in the scriptures." Although he believed congregations "may cooperate" in any good work for spreading the gospel, "we hope to see the saints freed from sectarian machinery."[5] Similar opinion was voiced in *The Evangelist*, published in Iowa: "It is not necessary to make any new machinery, societies, or organizations. There is one organization or body divinely appointed and authorized and but one—the congregation."[6] Moses E. Lard, one of the most influential men in the church after the Civil War, summarized the views of the opponents in 1865:

> These societies are not divine but human institutions. They can never claim not even a constructive sanction from the Word of God for their existence. . . The sole business of a missionary society is to cause the gospel to be preached in places where it could not or would not be preached without its aid. This business imposes upon the society two duties and only two, namely, to employ preachers and to pay them. . . The church of God should do the former; the liberality of the brethren the latter. . . Beyond this a missionary society can be of no service to Christ.[7]

The primary point of contention was the definition of the terms "cooperation" and "organization." No

---

[4] W. H. Rawlins, "Problem in Texas," *Millennial Harbinger* (June, 1858), pp. 323-332.

[5] Fanning, "American Christian Missionary Society," *Gospel Advocate*, V (November, 1859), p. 331.

[6] A. H., "Co-operation," *The Evangelist*, XIII (May, 1862), pp. 209-210.

[7] Moses E. Lard, "Missionary Societies," *Lard's Quarterly*, II (July, 1865), p. 443.

one questioned the right of several churches cooperatively to finance an evangelist to preach the gospel in communities where there was no church of Christ, but a society with officers designated as president, vice-president, and secretary (as opposed to the New Testament elders and evangelists), opponents condemned as unscriptural. They argued that the church with its duly appointed officers could transact all necessary affairs. In 1866, minister Jeremiah Smith asserted that "All divisions that have been among Christians since the day of Pentecost, were brought about by, and on account of things not revealed in the will of God." He insisted that missionary societies "are things not revealed in the will of God," and asked if a portion of the church by sustaining and insisting upon missionary societies would divide the church.[8]

In spite of the attacks the society grew. The largest number of delegates in its eighteen years attended the 1867 convention in Cincinnati. California churches were represented for the first time, making the conclave national in scope. Thirteen thousand dollars for the support of the missionary society were collected. The delegates, however, were not official representatives of their respective churches and were not clothed with any ecclesiastical power.

Although relatively isolated from the national activity of the church, Texas disciples had been actively meeting their local problem of evangelism. For several years congregations had been cooperating in mission work. Church delegates held numerous meetings, but no formal organizations were effected. In 1867, William Baxter of Matagorda wrote that in Texas

---

[8]Jeremiah Smith, "Church News," *Gospel Advocate*, VIII (December 4, 1866), p. 781.

"the Church of God is his missionary society and ours. . . . We have kept up, for some ten years, regular annual meetings, and have raised some funds to support evangelists."[9] At a Shelby County cooperative meeting on April 7, 1867, Center church contributed $12.00, Antioch $10.00, Fruit $10.00, Philadelphia $11.50, Oak Grove $5.80, and Christian Union $3.75.[10]

TEXAS STATE MEETINGS

Eventually an effort was made to organize a missionary society in Texas. The first attempt took place in Bryan in June, 1872, when the elders of the local church invited fellow elders and all evangelists to meet. David Lipscomb, editor of the *Advocate,* who was touring Texas at the time, influenced the group when he declared at the meeting "that all Christian labor should be through the Church of God, and that we should do nothing without divine authority." T. M. Sweeney of Leona afterward reported that some in attendance earnestly desired to organize a society, but that no "human plan" for spreading the gospel was adopted. He warmly commended brethren Dabney, Poe, Dyches and others for their firm opposition.[11]

Another attempt was made on July 4 of the following year at the state meeting in Waco. The *Bremond Visitor* observed that since neither "the scripturality nor expediency" of a separate organization could be shown, it fell short of supporters. Apparently the

---

[9] William Baxter, "Church News," *ibid.,* IX (February 28, 1867), p. 178.
[10] "Delegates and Donations to Meeting of Co-operation April 7th, 1867, Shelby County, Texas," *ibid.,* IX (July 4, 1867), p. 536.
[11] T. M. Sweeney, "State Meeting," *ibid.,* XIV (August 8, 1872), p. 765.

majority were averse to supporting a plan which was likely to meet with opposition and create confusion.[12]

The movement for state missionary societies received a setback as a result of action taken by the national convention. It its 1869 meeting in Louisville the convention adopted the complicated "Louisville Plan" by which states were to be divided into suitable districts. Churches were urged to contribute annually to the district treasurer, who would forward half to the state treasurer, and the state treasurer in turn would forward half of what he received to the general board.[13] The resulting confusion and chaos caused the plan to be dropped in 1875. Simultaneously, minister R. C. Horn of McKinney thanked God that the church in Texas had been virtually free of dissension in regard to the missionary society. He fervently prayed that it would be spared the bitter controversy then raging in Kentucky, Ohio, Indiana and Missouri where that "whispered in the closet is told on the house top."[14] But Horn prayed in vain.

During the next few state meetings, all attempts to form a state society were thwarted. At the 1876 meeting in Dallas, Kendrick suggested the adoption of a plan similar to the defunct "Louisville Plan." Subsequently, a committee recommended Kendrick's proposal to the delegates. In the ensuing debate T. W. Caskey, orator, debater, evangelist and lawyer, eloquently headed the opposition. Caskey asserted that the proposed plan was in essence the Louisville Plan "whitewashed." Admitting that he had helped formu-

---

[12]"Bremond Visitor," quoted in *ibid.*, XV (August 7, 1873), pp. 730-731.
[13]Garrison and DeGroot, *Disciples of Christ*, p. 354.
[14]R. C. Horn, "Letters to G. W. Elley—No. 2," *Apostolic Times*, VII (February 28, 1875), p. 64.

CONTROVERSY AND DIVISION 235

late the plan in 1869, Caskey regretted his action and explained that he wanted to bury it out of sight and would not "drop a tear over its resting place." Evidently convinced, the delegates tabled the proposal with the suggestion that each congregation do its own mission work.[15] In 1878, only twenty-four delegates assembled at the state meeting in Austin and little was accomplished.[16]

On July 2-3 of the following year, the convention met at Add-Ran College. About sixty preachers and several hundred members were in attendance. The business consisted mainly of reports by preachers concerning progress of church work. Although J. A. Poyner stated that "a few axes were offered but none were ground," and that most of the delegates went away happy, he did not realize that society adherents were neither silent nor pleased with the proceedings.[17] The tumultuous gathering at the 1880 meeting proved how wrong he had been.

The meeting convened at 11:00 A.M. on June 30 in Waxahachie. The discussion was as hot as the summer Texas sun. A motion was made and seconded that preachers take up quarterly collections for mission work in their churches. The proposal specified that the fund was to be placed in the hands of a committee which in turn was to employ an evangelist. When C. M. Wilmeth objected that the proposition was out of order but was overruled by the chair, he addressed to convention directly in opposition to the resolutions. Caskey and Carlton joined Wilmeth in de-

---
[15]B. A. O'Brien, "State Meeting," *Gospel Advocate*, XVIII (August 10, 1875), p. 736.
[16]*Christian Messenger*, quoted in *ibid.*, XX (August 22, 1878), p. 736.
[17]J. A. Poyner, "State Meeting," *ibid.*, XXI (July 17, 1879), p. 455.

nouncing the proposition, but evangelists J. Lampton, W. E. Hall and Chalmers McPherson spoke vehemently favoring adoption. In an effort to calm tempers, W. H. Moore of Waco moved that the resolutions be tabled indefinitely. His motion carried by a large majority.[18]

The next few state meetings followed essentially the pattern of 1880. No agreement could be reached in 1881 at Bonham, in 1882 at Fort Worth, or in 1883 at Ennis. Prior to the Ennis convention, minister G. A. Faris asked, "For what shall we meet? To re-enact the work (?) of the past?—i.e., debate about plans and methods? If so, let's invite some of the experienced ecclesiastical pugilists to attend."[19] At the 1884 conclave at Bryan, the motion to form a Christian Women's Board of Missions as an auxiliary to the national board was voted down.* Just prior to the close of the convention, Caskey withdrew a resolution to dissolve the meeting and organize one composed of pro-society members. With a clear eye to the future, he accurately predicted that it would come sooner or later and the sooner the better, and that it would finally be made a test of fellowship.[20] At the 1885 meeting in Sherman, pro-society delegates desisted from attempting to form a society in deference to the wishes of older brethren.

An unsuccessful attempt was made to form a society outside the state meeting. Ministers A. J. Bush and W. K. Homan tried to organize the "Texas Christian

---

[18]James Scobey, "Texas State Meeting," *ibid.*, XXII (July 22, 1880), p. 474.

[19]G. A. Faris, "Waxahachie," *ibid.*, XXV (March 1, 1883), p. 135.

*The national board had been formed in 1874. An Auxiliary was formed at Ennis on March 3, 1885.

[20]T. W. Caskey, in the *Gospel Advocate*, XXVIII (June 16, 1886), p. 371.

Missionary Society" during the Bible Institute held December 28, 1885, at Add-Ran College. According to A. L. D'Spain of Thorp Spring, however, the scheme never materialized because the majority of the Thorp Spring church and college faculty opposed such an organization.[21]

Pro-society adherents continued their efforts to organize a missionary society. Prior to the next state meeting, elders W. T. Morris and D. H. Walsh of the Austin church requested churches to send delegates who favored organized mission work. John Poe of Longview accused Chalmers McPherson of Waxahachie of sending out a note several months in advance of the meeting urging all society opponents to stay away from Austin.[22] Carroll Kendrick, a former Texas minister who had been in California for nine years, hastened to Austin when he learned through the brotherhood papers that a strong attempt would be made to form a society. "My objects," he explained, "were to prevent a division . . . encourage union, and all the right ways of the Lord."[23]

THE TEXAS SOCIETY

On July 8-9, 1886, about eighty delegates from twenty-five churches gathered in Austin for the historic state meeting. W. K. Homan of Dallas, a leading pro-society advocate, was appointed chairman and immediately filled committees with pro-society adherents. The committee on Ways and Means brought in

---

[21]*Texas Christian*, December 3, 1885, quoted in *ibid.*, XXVIII (January 6, 1886), p. 8.
[22]Poe, "Texas Items," *ibid.*, XXVIII (June 15, 1886), p. 371.
[23]Kendrick, "Our Missionary Machinery, No. III Former and Present State Meetings, Etc.," *Christian Leader*, II (October 16, 1888), p. 1. Hereafter cited as Kendrick, "Missicnary Machinery."

a detailed plan for the formation of a missionary society. "It was what we would, in other days, have called a constitution," Kendrick explained. Several conservatives plainly stated that they could not operate under it without being hypocritical and that division would result from its adoption. The ensuing tie vote was broken by the chairman in favor of the plan.

Immediately, several conservatives unsuccessfully tried to voice their opposition. Kendrick contended that the progressives had forced the issue in order to eliminate their opponents.[24] Poe exclaimed, "True and tried brethren were driven forth and allowed no voice in the meeting unless they would agree to fall down and worship the calf set up." He later claimed that he, R. M. Gano, J. A. Clark, Kendrick, C. M. Wilmeth, W. H. D. Carrington and others were ruled out of order by the chairman and not allowed a voice on the floor unless it was to cry "Great is Diana of the Ephesians."[25] John Durst reported that from the beginning it was evident that the progressives intended to organize a flull fledged missionary society with all its attachments."[26] Minister John T. Brown indicated that organized mission work was regarded by most churches as an innovation "not authorized by God's word," but there were a few who saw a need and were determined to organize.[27]

After the debate subsided, the two groups continued the session separately. The progressives organized the Texas Christian Missionary Society, raised about $1250 in pledges, and adjourned.[28] The conservatives,

---
[24] *Ibid.*
[25] Poe, "Texas Department," *Gospel Advocate*, XXVIII (September 7, 1896), p. 563.
[26] *Firm Foundation*, August, 1886.
[27] Brown, *Churches of Christ*, pp. 286-287.
[28] *Firm Foundation*, August, 1886.

with Carrington as chairman, in a short meeting in the basement of the church building, raised only a few dollars to support an evangelist.

The reaction of Texas conservatives to the apparent division was one of sorrow and bitterness. C. M. Wilmeth of Dallas expressed the general sentiment that "while we deplore division, the Austin meeting served as a crucible to separate the dross from the gold. This dross figuratively speaking, was gathered into a human society with constitution, and by-laws, permanent officers, prescribed membership, etc." He suggested that brethren who wished to do mission work on a scriptural basis meet in July, 1887, at the Pearl and Bryan church with the elders presiding.[29] In a broadside condemning missionary society preachers, editor McGary warned the brethren against A. J. Bush, Alexander Holt, Chalmers McPherson, or any other man or set of men "who are causing divisions or offenses contrary to the doctrine which ye learned. They are planning a systematic canvass of our state in the interest of their human plans."[30]

During the next few years, one unsuccessful effort was made to reconcile the progressives and the conservatives. In 1889, aged J. A. Clark claimed that after a year of failure under their new plan the society had restored basically the original plan. Therefore, he urged both factions to work in harmony.[31] Clark's plea went unnoticed.

The conservatives continued to hold and attend the old type district cooperative meetings. At a meeting

---
[29] C. M. Wilmeth, "Dallas," *Gospel Advocate*, XXVIII (October 27, 1886), p. 681.
[30] *Firm Foundation*, November, 1886.
[31] J. A. Clark, in the *Gospel Advocate*, XXXI (December 18, 1889), p. 803.

in November, 1888, at Willis, Montgomery County, an evangelist was chosen to labor in the surrounding seven counties.[32] In July, 1905, in Gainesville, delegates selected H. F. Oliver to evangelize Cooke County and in two hours raised $450 for his support.[33]

The Texas Christian Missionary Society was beset by several weaknesses. In 1890 A. J. Bush, ardent society advocate, reported that six of its evangelists were laboring in large towns where the church already was established rather than in mission areas.[34] Granville Jones, a progressive minister, frankly acknowledged that many destitute places were neglected because the society preachers went where they would receive an adequate salary. Jones attributed the lack of missionary zeal on the part of many congregations to the improper functioning of the society. "We go on from year to year, begging, dragging, failing."[35] When the state missionary society convention assembled in 1896 in Austin, the *Austin Evening News* reported that many of the delegates did not go within five blocks of the convention hall. "They just wanted to visit the city and sponge on the good facilities of Austin."[36] Conservative minister J. W. Jackson ascribed the indifference to the fact that the convention had passed a resolution which limited the privilege of speaking to "official" convention delegates and those invited by the committee to participate in its deliberations.[37] Conservative J. D. Tant reported that

---

[32]*Firm Foundation*, November 1, 1888.
[33]*Ibid.*, July 18, 1905.
[34]A. J. Bush, "Texas Mission Notes," *The Christian Evangelist*, XXVIII (December 4, 1890), p. 777.
[35]"Granville Jones Tract," quoted in *Gospel Advocate*, XXXVI (May 10, 1894), p. 183.
[36]*Austin Evening News*, quoted in *ibid.*, XXXVI (May 10, 1894), p. 183.
[37]*Firm Foundation*, June 23, 1896.

Bush and Wright had retired, Sanders and Bowen would not work under the State Board any longer as they received all they collected when independent. As further evidence of its weakness, Tant claimed the society had sent out only one evangelist in 1895.[38]

Despite its early weaknesses, the Texas Christian Missionary Society during the next few years became more efficient. When it became an integral part of the national organization, the breach between progressive and conservative factions became irreparable.

INSTRUMENTAL MUSIC

The controversy over the use of instrumental music in the worship service was no less serious. Congregational singing had been a primary part of the worship service of the church from the beginning because the scriptures recorded that the church in the first century praised God in "psalms, hymns, and spiritual songs." Although the singing was not always harmonious, no instruments of music were used in the churches of Christ during the first half of the nineteenth century. The failure to use musical instruments was due partially to the fact that the church was a frontier institution and organs were not available in the West prior to the Civil War. The first recorded use of a musical instrument by a church of Christ was in 1860 at Midway, Kentucky. Although minister L. J. Pinkerton did not introduce the melodeon into the church, he publicly encouraged its use because the singing had degenerated into a "screeching and brawling" utterly lacking in harmony which, Pinkerton jestingly re-

---

[38]Tant, in the *Gospel Advocate*, XXXVIII (March 19, 1896), p. 182.

ported, "would scare even the rats from the worship."[39]

As instrumental music was introduced into more and more churches, particularly in the large cities, the opposition became outspoken in their condemnation. They contended that it was an "innovation," an addition to the worship prescribed in the New Testament, and since it was not divinely sanctioned, it was sinful. The argument most frequently used was the explanation given in 1851 by Alexander Campbell. Alluding to other denominations, Campbell had asserted that to all worshipers "whose animal nature flags under oppression of church service . . . instrumental music would be . . . an essential pre-requisite to fire up their souls to even animal devotion," but that to all spiritually minded Christians such aids would be as a "cow bell in a concert."[40]

Moses E. Lard, editor of *Lard's Quarterly*, contended vehemently that only the doctrine found in the New Testament should be practiced.

> What defense can be argued for the introduction into some of our congregations of instrumental music? The answer which thunders into my ear from every page of the New Testament is none. Did Christ ever appoint it? Did the apostles ever sanction it, or did anyone of the primitive churches ever use it? Never.

Lard proposed three alternatives for anti-organ disciples: all preachers should refrain from speaking in a church where an instrument was used, no person should place his membership in a church which used

---

[39] L. L. Pinkerton, "Instrumental Music in Churches," *American Christian Review*, III (February 28, 1860), p. 34.

[40] Alexander Campbell, "Instrumental Music," *Millennial Harbinger* (October, 1851), pp. 581-582.

an instrument, and finally, members in opposition should withdraw from the church if an organ was introduced in disregard to their fervent pleas to the contrary.[41]

Lard was not the only editor opposing the use of instrumental music in the worship service. An editorial in the *Advocate* contended that instrumental music was not scriptural. It asserted that scripture can authorize a religious practice in only three ways: by express precept or command, by apostolic example, or by furnishing a basis for necessary inference. The editor declared that instrumental music could not be substantiated by either of the first two principles or as a necessary aid to congregational singing.

Despite these apparent scriptural denunciations, the proponents gained ground. They countered the arguments of the opposition by citing Old Testament examples as proof that it was divinely sanctioned. More often, however, they designated it as an "expedient" since the churches of Christ generally deny the authority of the Old Testament rituals as applicable to New Testament practices.

The conservatives, as the opponents came to be known, capitalized on its misuse. In 1879, the church of Christ in Minerva, Kentucky, sponsored a "Moonlight Fete" which consisted of dancing and refreshments. Funds collected from the festival were used to purchase an organ. Horrified conservatives denounced both the fete and its purpose, implying that pro-organ disciples would go to any extreme to pro-

---

[41]Lard, "Instrumental Music," *Lard's Quarterly*, I (March, 1864), pp. 330-332.

cure an organ.[42] The progressives furnished the conservatives with another argument the following year when the pro-organ *Christian Standard* sternly rebuked some churches for abuse of the use of organs and choirs. The *Standard* admitted that without strong church control there was a tendency on the part of choirs or organists to drift into a style of music that is not only destructive of congregational singing but "deadening to all devotional feeling."[43] The conservatives also utilized the arguments of other denominations to support their position. The *Baptist Reflector* felt that the introduction of instrumental music into the "worship of God's house has been harmful to congregational singing." As evidence, it reported that a visitor who attended the First Baptist Church in Nashville was so enthralled by the choral numbers, "so perfect, and so divinely sweet," that he and many others decided to listen rather than disturb the harmony with their "grating voices."[44] In 1883, the *Arkansas Methodist* placed its approval upon choirs and organs only when used in "their proper place." After explaining that the desire for organ and trained choirs "has always accompanied the increasing formalism of our churches," the editor concluded that "we need a revival of the spirit . . . let the whole congregation sing." If the people would try praising God for themselves, they would find their number increased, the joy of the service greatly enhanced, and their spirituality intensified.[45]

---

[42]*Apostolic Times*, quoted in *Gospel Advocate*, XXI (December 11, 1879), p. 788.

[43]*Christian Standard*, quoted in *Old Path Guide*, II (August, 1880), p. 306.

[44]*Baptist Reflector*, quoted in *Gospel Advocate*, XXI (September 4, 1879), p. 557.

[45]*Arkansas Methodist*, quoted in *ibid.*, XXV (May 16, 1883), p. 309.

Conservatives likewise condemned the use of a multiplicity of instruments. They maintained that such use was proof that the music was primarily for entertainment rather than an aid to the singing. A spectacular example of such use occurred at Ennis in 1906 when a piano, cornet, and as many as seven fiddles at once were played during a four-week tent revival.[46] Some pro-organ supporters could not condone such a practice. Progressive L. R. Norton felt that "we ought to be satisfied with one instrument—a good organ for instance, without the fiddle and the horn."[47]

Prior to the formation of the missionary society in 1886, only a few Texas churches of Christ used instrumental music. In 1880, only Waco, Palestine, and Commerce church in Dallas had organs. Six years later, widely traveled evangelist J. D. Tant reported only a dozen churches of Christ in the state used instrumental music.[48] Regardless of the views of members, the cost of organs was prohibitive for most churches. An advertisement in the *Christian Courier* priced them from three hundred dollars up. Even though it was not opposed to instrumental music, the Presbyterian Church in Fort Worth did not procure an organ until April 7, 1877. Joyfully, it was announced that "the choir can now sing praises to the most high accompanied by instrumental music in its most sacred form."[49]

Most pro-missionary society preachers were also pro-organ advocates. The usual method they employed to introduce an instrument into a church was to con-

---

[46] V. L. Stirman, "The Harlow Tent Meeting at Ennis, Texas," *ibid.*, XLVIII (September 20, 1906), p. 605
[47] L. R. Norton, "Worship," *The Christian Evangelist*, XXVII (December 18, 1890), p. 805.
[48] *Gospel Advocate*, March 19, 1896.
[49] *Fort Worth Daily Standard*, April 9, 1877.

vince a majority of the members that it would aid their singing. At Waxahachie in 1885, minister Chalmers McPherson, who solicited funds for and purchased an organ, began private promotion for its introduction into the Sunday School. After several weeks, an organ was placed in the building on Sunday, October 4, before the worship service. Despite the protests of the elders and some members, it was played by a Brother Rosecrans. After it had been played on the next Sunday by the minister's wife, elder Isaac Fuston endeavored to ascertain congregational sentiment as to its use. When conflicting opinions were presented and the congregation became disorderly, Fuston requested all anti-organ members to return at 3:00 P.M. In the ensuing discussion, the majority pro-organ group, led by the minister, offered to compromise by playing the organ only in the Sunday School and in the opening worship service, but two of the three elders rejected the offer. The minority anti-organ group thereupon withdrew and began worshiping in private homes.[50] The schism over the use of the organ in worship services had finally erupted into a division of the congregation into separate church bodies.

Other divisions soon occurred. The next was in the Paris Church of Christ. On July 24, 1890, the majority of the Paris congregation passed a resolution to use an organ. On June 1 of the following year, three elders and minister R. H. Fife, in an effort to pacify the dissidents, stipulated that the organ would remain in the house as "an aid to singing, and not as a part of the worship." Two weeks later, however,

---

[50]Isaac Fuston, "Waxahachie," *Gospel Advocate*, XXVIII (February 3, 1886), p. 66.

fifty-three members signed a letter of withdrawal, protesting the action of the majority against the conscience of the minority. The secessionists gave up all claim to the church property "for the sake of peace, and we hereby declare ourselves severed from your body in the fullest sense of that term."[51] Within three months, they had erected their own meeting house.[52]

Other churches divided in similar fashion. At Denton in January, 1894, W. L. Thurman, a strong organ advocate, called a meeting of all pro-organ members who voted to withdraw from the anti-organ minority. When conservative minister A. Alsup was prohibited from delivering his sermon on the following Sunday, the anti-organ group withdrew.[53] At Kaufman when the progressive majority introduced the organ in 1895, the conservatives withdrew. The pro-organ group thereupon promised not to play the organ at Sunday morning worship services and Wednesday night prayer meetings if the majority would return. The offer was rejected because it was like "a man saying he would not swear and drink on two days of the week if you would let him swear and drink all the rest of the time."[54]

In some instances, at least, the conservatives were able to retain the church building or obtain financial settlement for a proportionate share of its value. At Sherman in 1894, shortly after the great Larimore revival when the church divided over the organ issue, the conservative majority continued to meet at eleven

---

[51]"Petition," *ibid.*, XXXIII (July 22, 1891), p. 454.
[52]James D. Elliott, "Paris," *ibid.*, XXXIII (September 9, 1891), p. 574.
[53]P. B. Hall, "Denton, Texas," *ibid.*, XXVII (November 14, 1895), p. 723.
[54]Anonymous, "Growth of the Word," *ibid.*, XXIX (September 16, 1897), p. 591.

on Sunday morning and the progressives held their services at three in the afternoon. When this arrangement proved unsatisfactory the following year, the progressives withdrew when paid $2300 for their share of the church property.[55] At Holland, Bell County, in 1897, the organ faction withdrew to the Methodist house after failing, primarily due to the vigilance of the conservative elders, to secure the meeting house.[56] At Dawson, Navarro County, John T. Poe, who began a meeting in the strife-torn church on January 21, 1899, declared that the New Testament did not sanction the use of instrumental music. When the progressives removed the organ, Poe lauded the action as a "noble stand."[57]

Meanwhile, the actions of some conservative preachers complicated the issue in the minds of the members. Nationally renowned evangelist T. B. Larimore conducted revivals "with or without the organ, just as the church chooses."[58] Ardent anti-organ preacher Tant reported in 1894 that some brethren were disturbed because he had spoken where an organ was used. He affirmed that he had conducted four revivals in Texas in the previous six years where the organ was used but had never failed to expose the thing when the surroundings demanded.[59] Evangelist H. C. Booth, who asked for the privilege of preaching at the pro-organ Commerce church in 1896 in order to denounce instrumental music, was denied permission on the basis that he was "anti-progressive."[60] Similarly, David

---
[55] *Firm Foundation*, April 9, 1935.
[56] Burnett, "Growth of the World," *Gospel Advocate*, XXXIX (September 16, 1897), p. 591.
[57] Poe, "Dawson, Texas," *ibid.*, XLI (February 9, 1899), p. 93.
[58] *Firm Foundation*, April 17, 1894.
[59] *Ibid.*, June 12, 1894.
[60] H. C. Booth, "Growth of the Word," *Gospel Advocate*, XXXVIII (July 23, 1896), p. 478.

Lipscomb declared he would preach where the virgin Mary was worshiped but would endeavor to show that it was unscriptural. If the church used an instrument, he insisted that it should desist from the practice, not because he opposed it but because God did not command it.[61] On the other hand, Austin McGary, who would not preach where an organ was used, branded Lipscomb as "most inconsistent and unreliable."[62] Minister D. T. Carlton, who was scheduled to conduct a three-week revival in 1899 at Granbury, closed the meeting after delivering two sermons because the church refused to silence the organ and used "crackers" for the Lord's Supper.[63] Such inconsistency on the part of conservative preachers created uncertainty in the minds of some members. Following the most consistent course, minister J. M. Barnes urged the conservatives to properly train their members in vocal music. At a singing school which he conducted in 1896 at the Pearl and Bryan church in Dallas, Barnes observed that the singing improved markedly after the students grasped the idea of singing in harmony and following the leader. Barnes was of the opinion that "if the men at Pearl and Bryan would spend as much money and time to learn to sing to the Lord as they do to have their daughters learn to play the organ, there would be no trouble."[64]

The continued division of churches evidenced two opposing and uncompromising group attitudes in regard to the use of instrumental music in the worship service. Explaining the pro-organ view, minister A. I. Hobbs contended that the progressives evaluated

[61] *Firm Foundation*, April 17, 1894.
[62] *Ibid.*, April 12, 1894.
[63] D. T. Carlton, "Church News," *Gospel Advocate*, XLI (September 14, 1899), p. 587.
[64] *Firm Foundation*, November 10, 1896.

Christian doctrine as a body of great constitutional principles while the conservatives characterized it as a dogma of specific statutes. Hobbs pointed out that anti-organ members regarded worship as specifically prescribed, not only the acts in which it shall consist, but also all their accessories. Hence any innovation, even in regard to accessories, "is denounced as though it were as sinful as the burning of incense to a false deity in the temple of Jehovah."[65] J. W. McGarvey, a renowned conservative scholar in Kentucky, argued that a group which introduced a musical instrument over the conscientious scruples of a minority was "disorderly and schismatical, not only because it stirs up strife, but because it is for the sake of a sinful innovation upon the divinely authorized worship of the church." He urged the loyal element to withdraw from the "heretics" until they repented.[66] Likewise, John Poe declared that the organ controversy was being used by the progressive element as a lever to pry out solid Bible Christians in order to get possession of all church property. He urged the conservatives to withdraw from "those heretics, as they are commanded to do by the word and civil law will give them control of the church property."[67]

As a result of the bitter controversy over instrumental music, Texas churches of Christ split into two irreconcilable religious bodies. In 1896, J. D. Tant reported that the opposing groups in over one hundred churches had gone their respective ways because they could not agree on the question. Editor W. K. Homan

---

[65] A. I. Hobbs, "Principles," *Christian Courier*, IV (April 1, 1891), p. 1.
[66] J. W. McGarvey, in the *Gospel Advocate*, XXIII (April 28, 1881), p. 261.
[67] Poe, "Texas Department," *Gospel Advocate*, XXXV (October 15, 1893), p. 633.

of the *Christian Courier* at first felt that little harm had resulted as long as the organ had been classed as an expedient, an aid to singing, but when the anti-organ brethren asserted that those favoring the use of an instrument were not Christians and should be excluded from all fellowship in the churches, Homan declared this to be the "narrowest sectarianism extant."[68] Thus it was evident that a gulf existed between the two factions which could not be bridged.

REBAPTISM

The third most significant controversy to plague the church of Christ was that of rebaptism. This issue, limited to anti-organ and anti-missionary society churches, attracted public attention about 1884 when Austin McGary, editor of the *Firm Foundation,* vigorously defended the doctrine of rebaptism, and his editorial colleague, David Lipscomb of the *Gospel Advocate,* hotly denied the doctrine. When McGary resigned as editor in 1900, the controversy waned and ceased within a few years.

Rebaptism was defined as baptizing again a candidate who previously had been baptized. Churches of Christ did not accept all forms of baptism used by the numerous sects. According to one authority, ministers of churches of Christ defined the Greek word *baptizo* "to immerse, dip, plunge beneath, submerge."[69] Contending that the English Bible also taught immersion as baptism, one anonymous preacher cited the case of a lady in Texas in 1884 who after studying the scriptures asked a Methodist preacher to baptize her.

---
[68] W. K. Homan, "Music," *Christian Courier*, XIX (November 8, 1906), p. 8.
[69] *Analytical Greek Lexicon* (New York, 1942), p. 42.

When they arrived at the lake for the baptism, the lady walked out into the water but the preacher placed a bench in the lake on which he kneeled and prepared to administer the ordinance. Suddenly, the lady "reached up and caught him by the neck, while he kneeled and quoting the passage Acts 8:38, 'And they both went down, both Philip and the eunuch, into the water,' she gave him a quick jerk and sent him over his head into the liquid Jordan." Then the lady walked out of the water and postponed her baptism until she could find a minister who would administer it in the "scriptural manner."[70] Therefore, anyone who had been sprinkled (*rantizo*) or poured upon (*katexo*) was not considered as scripturally baptized.

The crux of the issue centered primarily around the Baptists and immersed Methodists and Presbyterians, who sought membership in the church of Christ on the basis of their first immersion. Before McGary raised the issue, churches of Christ generally had accepted all immersed believers into their membership without requiring rebaptism although there may have been a fundamental difference of opinion regarding the purpose of baptism. During a meeting near Belton in 1856, Thomas Armstrong had twenty-two additions to the church, seven of whom were from the Baptists without rebaptism.[71] At Brenham in 1859, W. F. Bush received twenty-one accessions to the church, one of whom was a Baptist without rebaptism.[72] The next year S. B. Giles had twenty-two additions during a meeting in Williamson County, one of

---

[70] Anonymous, in the *Gospel Advocate*, XXVI (April 30, 1884), p. 283.

[71] Thomas Armstrong, "Salado, Bell County, Texas," *ibid.*, II (December, 1856), p. 274.

[72] W. F. Bush, "Brenham, Texas," *ibid.*, V (October, 1859), p. 311.

"Into means into"

whom was a Baptist without rebaptism.[73] At Fort Worth, A. M. Dean reported thirteen additions, "six immersions, two from the Baptists, three reclaimed and two by letter."[74] About the same time near Dallas, L. J. Sweet accepted one immersed Presbyterian, and three Baptists without reperforming the baptismal service.[75] Terrell Jasper of Denton County reported in 1861 that one of his eight additions was from the Baptists, one from the Methodists, and two by letter, but that only the four others who confessed the Savior "were buried with their Lord in baptism."[76] In 1871, W. T. Bush and J. L. Dyches during a camp meeting in Bell County obtained seventy-eight additions to the church of whom eight were from the Baptists, seven from the Methodists, and one from the Presbyterians. Only five of the sixteen from other denominations were immersed;[77] eleven were accepted on the basis of their former immersion. Two years later, E. W. Dabney did not rebaptize the six Baptists among his twenty-three accessions during a revival in Austin County.[78] Cass Floyd and Charley Groves, who preached along the Trinity River near Hutchins, Dallas County, in 1878, reported that they did not rebaptize the seven Baptists among their twenty-three additions to the church,[79] nor did J. M. Barnes rebaptize two Baptist

---

[73] Giles, "Texas," *Millennial Harbinger* (February, 1860), p. 114.

[74] A. M. Dean, "Report from Texas," *Gospel Advocate* (February, 1860), p. 57.

[75] Sweet, "Scyene, Texas," *The Evangelist*, XII (September, 1860), p. 422.

[76] Terrell Jasper, "News," *Gospel Advocate*, VII (December, 1861), p. 375.

[77] W. T. Bush, "Church News," *ibid.*, XIII (October 19, 1871), p. 975.

[78] E. W. Dabney, "Church News," *ibid.*, XV (June 26, 1873), p. 618.

[79] E. E., "Hutchins, Texas," *ibid.*, XX (April 11, 1878), p. 229.

additions.[80] In 1883, John S. Durst of Leona received into the fold twenty-seven immersed Methodists and seven Baptists without rebaptism.[81] An analysis of the above cases reveals that over a twenty-seven-year period eleven different preachers of the churches of Christ accepted forty-seven candidates on the basis of their former immersion.

Editor David Lipscomb decried the action of a few preachers who argued the necessity of rebaptism, particularly those baptized by the denominations. He contended that when a man had believed in Christ, repented of his sins, and had been baptized in order to obey God, he was then a Christian. Lipscomb strongly affirmed that any preacher who would require such a person to be rebaptized would be "very presumptuous in the sight of God."[82]

The extremist advocate of rebaptism was Austin McGary. McGary was born on February 6, 1846, in Huntsville. Reared a Methodist and educated in the McKenzie Institute in Clarksville, he joined the Huntsville "Grays" in 1862 and served throughout the remainder of the war along the Texas-Louisiana coasts without seeing any action. After the war, McGary returned to Madison County where he served as sheriff. Later he publicly denounced the Ku Klux Klan at Willis, and served as conveying agent for the state penitentiary. In 1880 he turned to a serious study of religion. Encouraged by his sister, Mrs. J. W. Gillespie, McGary continued his study and was baptized by

---

[80]Poe, "Texas Department," *ibid.*, XX (July 18, 1878), p. 445.
[81]*Ibid.*, XXV (March 1, 1883), p. 136.
[82]Lipscomb, "Re-Baptism," *Gospel Advocate*, XX (September 26, 1878), p. 615.

Harry Hamilton on December 24, 1881. Two years later, he moved to Austin and began preaching.[83]

McGary's first conflict over the rebaptism question was with Methodist evangelist J. Philpot. One Sunday morning McGary went by buggy to a nearby town to preach. Arriving late and finding Philpot conducting a meeting, he took a seat and listened as Philpot, not knowing of his presence, told the congregation that McGary taught that people must be baptized in running water. When Philpot concluded his sermon, McGary stepped to the pulpit and made himself known: "I am a stranger in your town. . . I am Austin McGary from Austin, Texas. I baptized the doctor that Mr. Philpot referred to, but I did not baptize in running water." When the owner of the tabernacle granted McGary permission to speak that afternoon, Philpot evidently became angry and closed his meeting. McGary then preached for several days in the tabernacle.[84]

Shortly thereafter, McGary concluded that baptism "for the remission of sins" was the only valid baptism. In June, 1884, shortly before he began publishing the *Firm Foundation*, he expressed this opinion in an article in the *Gospel Advocate*. He was challenged immediately by editor Lipscomb of the *Advocate* who posed two questions relative to baptism: Does a man sin if he obeys what he understands even if his understanding is incomplete? If a candidate knew enough to obey the command of baptism, did he sin? He then

---

[83]West, *Search for the Ancient Order*, II, pp. 401-403.
[84]*Ibid.*

concluded that "if they do not sin, they would sin to repeat that baptism."[85]

McGary now became deeply concerned over the church's practice of "shaking in the Baptists." Particularly offensive was the teaching of T. R. Burnett, editor of the *Christian Messenger* (Dallas), who asserted that "Christ never authorized the baptism of saved persons, and no saved person was ever baptized. Some persons are baptized who think they are saved, but their think so is only fancy, and they receive the results of baptism despite their fancy." Applying this principle to many Baptists, Burnett contended that the "kingdom of Christ was never a Baptist Church but many Baptists are in the kingdom of Christ." He urged all who had been born of the water and the spirit to "come out of their party enclosure and be one with all baptized believers."[86] To condemn this action, McGary established in September, 1884, the *Firm Foundation,* a monthly. In the initial issue, McGary stated that the journal was directed to brethren who "are willing to turn their steps away from all human systems, plans and directions into the one mapped out by the apostles of our Lord."[87] After reading the first issue of the *Foundation,* Lipscomb aptly characterized it as being devoted to enforcing the idea that those not baptized for the "remission of

---

[85] Lipscomb, "Re-Baptism," *Gospel Advocate*, XXVI (June 18, 1884), p. 390.

McGary quoted the Bible verse, Acts 2:38, "Repent and be baptized every one of you in the name of Jesus Christ for the remission of your sins . . ." as a basis for his contention. The majority of preachers, on the other hand, viewed baptism as an act of obedience to God without any specific meaning or interpretation to the exclusion of all other meanings. Therefore, all candidates who had been immersed, were accepted as scripturally baptized.

[86] *Firm Foundation*, September, 1884.
[87] *Ibid.*

sins" are not scripturally baptized and should be rebaptized.[88] This verbal exchange touched off a spirited and sometimes bitter debate between the two rival editors through the columns of their respective journals for the next sixteen years.

At the outset, Lipscomb explained that he did not defend any baptism other than that ordained by Christ. In a sarcastic vain he prodded McGary to deny that A. Campbell, T. Fanning, and "that host of heroes" were Christians even though they were not baptized for the remission of sins.[89] McGary boldly answered that if Campbell was not baptized for the remission of sins, his baptism was null and void, "because God never authorized such a baptism."[90] Apparently McGary assumed Campbell was baptized properly, as he called him "brother." However, Campbell was baptized in 1811 by a Baptist preacher and did not understand that it was for the remission of sins until his debate with Presbyterian minister W. L. Maccalla in 1823 at Washington, Kentucky.

McGary retorted that Lipscomb and others who defended Baptist baptism were Campbellites. He sarcastically asserted that such men as J. W. McGarvey, F. W. Allen, Isaac Errett, J. A. Harding and J. M. Barnes of other states, Wilmeth and Rawlins, the Clarks, Carlton, McPherson, Homan and others taught that Baptists are "in Christ" and when they die, "strict Baptists, they go to rest in Jesus."[91] Lipscomb capitalized on this assertion by showing that McGary, who accepted no baptisms as valid except those administered by preachers in the church of Christ, was thus

---
[88]*Ibid.*, October, 1884.
[89]*Ibid.*, November, 1884.
[90]*Ibid.*, February, 1885.
[91]*Ibid.*, November, 1885.

"the most complete Campbellite I know." Neither Baptist nor McGary baptism was valid, he continued, but only that ordained by Christ.[92] Thus, to make the administrator important in addition to the design evidenced the uncertainty in McGary's own mind. Although baptized by Harry Hamilton in 1881, McGary later questioned the validity of the rite and asked W. H. D. Carrington to rebaptize him. However, it was purported that he had lost faith in Carrington by 1884 and the question was asked, "What will he do next? Will he get Bro. Poe to re-baptize him?"[93]

Shortly after the dispute arose, articles in several religious papers asserted that McGary's teaching was harmful to the church. The *Christian Messenger* declared that rebaptism "is so preposterous that it seems no man or woman with intellect to be accountable could be deceived by it. Yet this is the delusion that is leading away hundreds of disciples in Texas at the present time."[94] In 1890, staff-writer J. M. Barnes of Dallas stated that if persons had been baptized in the name of Jesus, "were I to baptize them again, I would not know in whose name to do it, for Jesus had not ordered it twice." Contending that only about one in ten of those whom McGary had baptized could define repentance and its design as stated in Acts 2:38, Barnes concluded that rebaptism for the remission of sins was causing confusion in the churches.[95] The *Christian Courier* asserted that the church was suffering from the "rebaptism hobby that is being furiously ridden" by a faction among the Disciples of Christ.

---

[92] *Ibid.*, November, 1884.
[93] Quien Sabe, "News," *Gospel Advocate*, XXIX (February 16, 1887), p. 110.
[94] *Firm Foundation*, February 1, 1888.
[95] J. M. Barnes, "Re-Baptism," *Christian Messenger*, XVI (November 12, 1890), p. 1.

"None are Christian," it argued, "except such as obeyed God in baptism with one design in mind." The *Courier* feared the harmful effects of a doctrine whose advocates would declare non-fellowship with their brethren who disagreed and formed separate organizations.[96] Minister W. H. Bagby of Bryan declared in the *Christian Standard* that he knew of no departure from the faith in modern times so hurtful to the cause of New Testament Christianity as "this hobby" which the *Firm Foundation* had been established to advocate.[97]

The harm to the church is exemplified in the McGregor court case of 1897-1899. The church at McGregor was organized about 1883 and a meeting house was erected the following year. Elders R. W. Pease, G. A. Trott and J. J. Jackson were strong advocates of rebaptism. In 1897, they evidently excluded all members who did not agree with their view. The ousted members thereupon filed suit for the church property. In the ensuing trial plaintiff C. B. Hall, a deacon, contended that baptism for the "remission of sins" was not part of the doctrine when the McGregor church was founded. After hearing testimony from both sides, Judge Marshall Surratt of the nineteenth judicial district determined that the defendants were upholding a doctrine widely variant from those when the church was established and that the doctrines and practices of the two factions of the McGregor church were "radical and unreconcilable." The plaintiffs therefore, were entitled to their rightful property. The Court of Appeals upheld Judge Surratt's decision on

---
[96] Anonymous, "Re-Baptism," *Christian Courier*, III (March 11, 1891), p. 4.
[97] W. H. Bagby, "Texas Tidings," *Christian Standard*, XXI (February 20, 1886), p. 61.

December 21, 1898, and the Supreme Court of Texas on April 27, 1899, refused to review the case.[98]

The dispute reached its bitter climax when McGary vindictively lashed out at Lipscomb and other opponents in a wild tirade of condemnation.

> If they the opponents of rebaptism will not come up to the fair investigation of the question . . . we intend to uncover them and let the world behold their naked double-dealing and hypocrisy in their ghastly deformity and deep depravity. When a man becomes too self-willed, stubborn, sulky, or perverse, to see the error of his way, when it is as palpable as Bro. Lipscomb's, his usefulness as a teacher is gone and he is gone, too, down the way to certain destruction. Such incorrigible deafness to truth and consistency in and religious teacher renders him wholly unfit to teach others the way of salvation, or to reprove or rebuke others for departing from the faith at any point. If all such men do not empty themselves of the demoniacal spirit that impels them in the course that they know is contrary to revealed truth, hell will be their inevitable doom, and the doom of those who blindly follow them. These men of corrupt minds, reprobate concerning the faith, shall proceed no further, if we can help it . . .[99]

The controversy over rebaptism declined after 1900. McGary, chief proponent of the doctrine, resigned as editor of the *Firm Foundation* in 1900 and ceased to write for the paper. Only a few other rebaptist advocates continued to defend the practice. In 1904 G. A. Trott, an elder in the McGregor church, affirmed rebaptism and David Lipscomb denied, in a short debate

---

[98] W. K. Homan, *The Church on Trial* (Dallas, 1900), pp. 123-124.

[99] Lipscomb, in the *Gospel Advocate*, XXXV (November 30, 1893), p. 756.

CONTROVERSY AND DIVISION 261

printed in the *Firm Foundation*.[100] The following year, the short-lived *Gospel Missionary* criticized Lipscomb for his periodic attacks on rebaptism. Staff writer A. M. George affirmed that baptism for the remission of sins was a "stench in the nostrils of the whole sectarian world."[101] Minister T. R. Burnett, who supported Lipscomb, replied that rebaptist preachers subjected candidates to their catechism and rebaptized them "on the faith of the preacher."[102]

Although a few preachers and churches were troubled by the controversy, the majority continued to accept immersed members from the denominations into the churches of Christ without rebaptism. In 1879, W. A. Lyles preached in Wood County and received fourteen additions, one of whom was an immersed Methodist.[103] In 1884 at Irene, Hill County, J. A. Kelton reported fifty-six additions, one a Baptist without rebaptism,[104] and S. F. Castleman of New Hope in 1894 received 152 accessions into the church of Christ of whom fifty were immersed Baptists.[105] In 1896, General R. M. Gano reported a meeting at Elm, Denton County, with 112 additions, of whom six were from the Baptists and one from the Methodists without rebaptism.[106]

Despite the heated controversy over rebaptism, it

---

[100] *Firm Foundation*, December 24, 1907.

[101] A. M. George, "Which Motive Fear or Love," *The Gospel Missionary*, X (July 22, 1908), pp. 1-4.

[102] T. R. Burnett, "Re-Baptism," *Burnett's Budgett*, IX (July 15, 1909), p. 4.

[103] W. A. Lyles, "What Have I Done?" *Gospel Advocate*, XXI (January 9, 1879), p. 19.

[104] J. R. Kelton, "Texas Department," *ibid.*, XXIX (August 24, 1887), p. 531.

[105] S. F. Castleman, "Growth of the Word," *ibid.*, XXXVI (October 11, 1894), p. 637.

[106] Gano, "Growth of the Word," *ibid.*, XXXVIII (September 10, 1896), p. 589.

had little lasting effect upon churches of Christ. This was due primarily to the fact that Baptist churches had become better organized. Through their annual conventions, manuals, improved teaching and local programs, the Baptists became more clearly separated from the churches of Christ. Thus, the number of Baptists who applied for membership in churches of Christ decreased rapidly. In respect to the immersed of the other denominations, the same tendency prevailed.

Minor Issues

Meanwhile, churches of Christ were confronted with a number of minor problems. These involved debate over the Sunday School, the order of worship, and the use of "one" cup in serving the Lord's supper. The controversy was limited to the churches which opposed the missionary society and the use of instrumental music in the worship service.

The Sunday School movement with the Bible as the text was inaugurated in 1780 by Robert Raikes in England. Subsequently, Benjamin Rush and others spearheaded the "First-Day School" in 1790 in Philadelphia. As churches expanded, erected permanent buildings, and enrolled less transient members, they adopted the Sunday School primarily for teaching children. Some disciples, however, opposed it because it was not mentioned specifically in the Bible. As early as February, 1855, the *Christian Evangelist* editorially remarked that it was "strange that the utility of an institution so obviously good as the Sunday School . . . so simple and practicable, should ever have been questioned." In answer to the request for a New Testament precept to authorize its practice, the editor cited the command to parents to bring their children up in the nurture and admonition of the Lord as "the only precept with no exact formula for execution prescribed." Asserting that the Sunday School was an "honorable means—right in the sight of Heaven and Earth," he declared that maps, books on geography, history, and customs of Palestine and the Near East were necessary adjuncts for the proper understanding of the Bible, and insisted that the Sunday School was a means for steady, rational progress. Ministers William Ledlow and Joe Warlick wrote pamphlets explaining how to use the Sunday School properly. *Gospel Advocate* staff writer E. G. Sewell declared that any method of teaching was scriptural because the apostles taught in upper rooms, synagogues, on boats, in jails, by a river, in a chariot, or at any place or time that was available or convenient. Thus, he logically concluded that no specific or unchangeable method was employed in the primitive church nor should be now.[107]

As proof of the value of the Sunday School, Alexander Campbell cited the testimony of the French philosopher Alexis De Tocqueville. Upon his visit to the United States, De Tocqueville was astounded to find that nearly every child in a "Sabbath School" had a Bible. Eagerly, he asked, "Is this common? What a mighty influence it must have on the nation! What a salutary influence, too!" Significantly, Campbell added the Biblical quotation, "The wise shall inherit glory, but shame shall be the promotion of fools."[108] The *Millennial Harbinger* declared forthrightly that the "Bible class . . . for regular systematic study of the 'Word' is absolutely the work of the church through

---

[107] E. G. Sewell, "Sunday School," *ibid.*, XLIV (March 6, 1902), p. 152.
[108] Alexander Campbell, "Foreign Observation," *Millennial Harbinger* (June, 1859), p. 332.

which the seed of the kingdom may be more minutely, carefully and abundantly grown."

In Texas, the first dispute over the Sunday School occurred in 1875. Minister G. W. Harvey of the Concord church, Austin County, labeled the Sunday School as a device to "attract little children, keep them from the prairie on Lord's day running mule eared rabbits, riding jacks and doing mischief generally. In reply to Harvey's question for "a catechism" with which to raise children in the nurture and admonition of the Lord, Lipscomb thoughtfully suggested that a well conducted Sunday School for both old and young is a "true method" of teaching on Lord's day.[109] But McGary retorted that the admonition for parents to teach the Bible to their children laid no foundation for a Sunday School. "Away with Sunday Schools, even if Bro. Lipscomb had memorized the whole New Testament at Sunday School." If the apostles did not have Sunday Schools, he continued, we do not need them and should not have them.[110] Later, however, McGary evidently had changed his mind as he contended that literature prepared "in the light of God's truth and in harmony with it, adapted to unfolding the tender mind of children, cannot be condemned."[111]

Opposition to the Sunday School among Texas churches of Christ was strong at Gunter. Gunter Bible College, begun in 1903, was hampered severely in its teaching program by anti-school stipulations imposed by the local anti-Sunday School church. N. L. Clark, school president, was also a leader in the church. In 1907 Clark admitted that he was opposed to the

---

[109]G. W. Harvey, "Church News," *Gospel Advocate*, XVII (June 3, 1875), pp. 535-537.
[110]*Firm Foundation*, January 15, 1888.
[111]*Ibid.*, May 23, 1899.

name "Sunday School," the division of the congregation into classes, the use of women teachers in the church, and Sunday School literature.[112]

Some churches divided because of the controversy. When minister J. E. Dunn arrived in Peoria in 1898, he found the church divided over the organ and Sunday School issues. Members spoke evil of one another and could not conduct a service on the Lord's day in harmony, peace, and love.[113] About the same time, a lady with several children wrote Lipscomb asking whether she should attend a progressive church which had an organ and conducted a Sunday School, or a "loyal" church which did not have a Sunday School. Not wishing to endorse the pro-organ church nor condone the anti-Sunday School group, Lipscomb replied that there may be occasions in which it is best to forego these rights, meaning the right to choose where one could worship and the parent teach the children at home.[114]

The vast majority of Texas churches of Christ adopted the use of Sunday Schools. Although the anti-Sunday School controversy was widespread, only a few conservative churches, mostly in rural areas, opposed the Sunday School after 1900, and they have steadily declined in number. By 1947, only 54 out of the 2195 churches of Christ in Texas did not have Sunday Schools.[115]

Another minor issue which attracted considerable attention near the turn of the century had to do with

---

[112]*Ibid.*, January 15, 1907.

[113]J. E. Dunn, "Peoria, Texas," *Gospel Advocate*, XL (November 24, 1898), p. 742.

[114]Lipscomb, "Church News," *ibid.*, XLV (July 23, 1903), p. 472.

[115]*1946-1947 Yearbook of Churches of Christ* (Olan L. Hicks, ed.; Abilene, Texas, 1947), pp. 133-165.

the order of worship. A number of preachers became troubled over whether all worship must be performed in the same order as stated in Acts 2:42 ("And they continued steadfastly in the apostles' doctrine and fellowship, and in breaking of bread, and in prayers). The three leading proponents were W. J. Rice, editor of the *Gospel Missionary*, and A. M. George and G. W. Phillips, staff writers and preachers.

Several ministers refuted this teaching. W. T. Kidwill contended that the only order in Acts 2:42 was the "order of words," about the most concise answer possible.[116] R. L. Shirey declared that all Texas churches practice and teach the four items mentioned in Acts 2:42 but not necessarily in the same order as enumerated. He urged all disciples to conduct the worship in a decent manner rather than in a specific order.[117] In 1909, R. L. Whiteside rejoiced that those who went off with Rice on the "order-of-worship hobby" were returning.[118]

Another minor dispute arose over the use of one cup in the Lord's supper. The controversy was limited primarily to rural churches. The churches following the one-cup practice contended that Jesus took "a cup" when he instituted the rite. The use of more than one cup, therefore, was unscriptural. Usually these churches were composed of older members who had used one cup all their lives. As churches grew, it became increasingly more desirable to use individual cups. Although a small minority of rural churches re-

---

[116] G. W. Phillips and W. T. Kidwill, "The Cause and Remedy," *Gospel Missionary*, X (November 1, 1908), p. 1.
[117] R. L. Shirey, "Critic Criticized," *Gospel Missionary*, X (July 15, 1908), p. 2.
[118] R. L. Whiteside, "Texas Notes," *Gospel Advocate*, LI (June 17, 1909), p. 761.

tain the custom, the number is decreasing. Strangely, some so-called "one-cup" churches use two or more cups for practical reasons, depending upon the number of seats in the building. In 1943, a church in Brownwood was using two cups; a larger church in Kansas City, Missouri, currently is using four.

After 1900, the large majority of churches of Christ in Texas adopted common practices. As churches progressed, meeting houses were erected, full-time preachers were secured, classes were arranged on an age basis, women were delegated to teach classes, and various types of literature and teaching aids were introduced. Thus, with few exceptions, the churches outgrew their minor problems. Although churches of Christ were plagued by many doctrinal differences, each congregation, being autonomous, ultimately decided what doctrines and practices it would follow. Certain fundamental doctrines and principles, however, have been instrumental in preventing wide variations among congregations.

Authority—The Role of Religious Periodicals

Churches of Christ are predicated on the fundamental doctrine that the Bible alone is their guide and authority. All church dogma and practice, therefore, must be confirmed by a "Thus saith the Lord." Nevertheless, the Bible was not the sole criterion used in making decisions. Some members did not have Bibles and the majority were uninformed as to its contents except for a few fundamental facts such as faith, repentance, baptism, and the Lord's supper. Most members were baptized by itinerant evangelists and left uninstructed. Consequently, they usually followed the leadership of a few who often gave erroneous or narrow interpretations to scripture based upon their own limited experiences.

Religious papers most effectively influenced the local churches to become either "progressive" or "conservative." The *American Christian Review,* begun in Indianapolis in 1856, propagated its anti-organ and society views throughout the Ohio Valley. On the other hand, the *Christian Standard,* begun in Cincinnati in 1866, and the *Christian Evangelist,* begun in St. Louis in 1884, as pro-organ and society papers, largely offset the influence of the *Review*. As a result, the majority of churches from Missouri through the entire Midwest and into Kentucky adopted the missionary society and organ.

From its beginning in 1855 in Nashville until the formal schism of the church in 1906, the *Gospel Advocate* exerted the greatest influence in molding church opinion in the Lone Star State against the missionary society and organ. Many members and preachers who migrated to Texas from Tennessee continued their subscriptions to the paper. Most Texas preachers reported their work and discussed their views through the columns of the *Advocate*. In November, 1855, T. M. Sweeney of Bell County, who lauded the publication of the *Advocate,* declared that it was welcomed by all and "will prove a very instructive companion."[119] Two years later, the managers of the Shelby, San Augustine and Nacogdoches Co-operation commended the "circulation and reading of the *Gospel Advocate*."[120] J. B. Wilmeth of Pleasant Grove believed that its readers were favorably impressed because it discussed all

---
[119] T. M. Sweeney, "News," *ibid.,* I (December, 1855), p. 190.
[120] A. Oliver, "Co-operation in Texas," *ibid.,* III (April, 1857), pp. 123-124.

important subjects.[121] In 1859, J. J. Boyter of Carolina, Texas, wrote that he was well pleased with the *Advocate,* and Mrs. E. A. Brister of Burleson County who had been a constant reader from the first issue, asserted that she had "made strong efforts to get subscribers."[122]

Although the *Advocate* ceased publication from 1861-1866 because of the war, it resumed after the conflict with an even wider circulation in Texas. In 1869, Charles Carlton of Bonham wrote "to inform the brethren in Texas, where the *Advocate* circulates."[123] Three years later, editor David Lipscomb made an extended tour in the state and secured many subscribers by assuring them of adequate coverage of Texas church news.[124] Evangelist Addison Clark characterized the paper in 1873 as "an intellectual treasure, a literary companion for yourselves and your children— the *Gospel Advocate* every week for four cents a week."[125]

When the argument over instrumental music and the missionary society began, the *Advocate* took a firm stand against both. Addison Clark, president of Add-Ran College, in 1879 praised the *Advocate* as one of the most powerful instruments in the hands of God for the preservation of unity of his church. It had been uniformly and consistently sound from its first issue. Clark felt that no one could charge the paper

---

[121] J. B. Wilmeth, "Texas Department," *ibid.,* III (November, 1857), p. 360.
[122] J. J. Boyter, "Carolina, Texas," *ibid.,* V (February, 1859), pp. 59-60.
[123] Charles Carlton, "Bonham, Texas," *ibid.,* XI (October 28, 1869), pp. 1002-1003.
[124] Addison Clark, "Church News," *ibid.,* XV (December 11, 1873), pp. 1192-1193.
[125] Addison Clark, "Pen of the President," *ibid.,* XXI (March 27, 1879), p. 203.

with being otherwise on any of the prominent issues. The following year, B. P. Sweeney of Bald Prairie, a preacher for over twenty years, asserted that outside of the Bible the *Advocate* "has done more to hold in check those disposed to be wise above what is written and to guard the brotherhood against innovations." Sweeney cited the conservative churches in Central Texas where the paper had a wide circulation as speaking "volumes" for the *Advocate*.[126]

Concerted efforts were made by John T. Poe, editor of the "Texas Department," to increase its circulation. He asked for agents in 1883 who would assist for a commission in putting the *Advocate* in the home of every family in Texas.[127] Two years later, a vigorous endeavor was made to double the approximately two thousand subscribers in Texas. Premiums, including machines and watches, were offered to agents.[128] As a result, probably more Texans read the *Advocate* than those of any other state except Tennessee. The potent influence of the *Advocate* caused progressive preachers to oppose it. Poe termed their efforts as a sly and underhanded attempt to put down the paper in Texas because it pointed out their evil ways in unmistakable language. The *Advocate*, he claimed, had never courted favor with anyone by compromising principle or truth.[129]

The *Christian Messenger* (1875-95) and the *Firm Foundation* which began publication in 1884 in Austin reinforced the conservative stand. The Texas Mis-

---

[126] B. P. Sweeney, "Bald Prairie, Texas," *ibid.*, XXII (October 28, 1880), p. 695.
[127] Poe, "Texas Department," *ibid.*, XXV (April 4, 1883), p. 219.
[128] *Ibid.*, XXVII (May 5, 1885), p. 276.
[129] Poe, "Enemies," *Gospel Advocate*, XXV (August 29, 1883), p. 551.

sionary Society, which was organized in 1886, was attacked vigorously by the *Advocate, Messenger,* and the *Foundation*. The next year, J. D. Tant, itinerant evangelist, reported that these papers were read considerably where he had preached and were a drawback to the progress of the "unscriptural societies" and other innovations held by many of the progressives.[130] In 1903, Tant declared that "had it not been for the *Gospel Advocate* and *Firm Foundation* constantly fighting the human plans, there would be few left on the Lord's side today."[131] The progressives, therefore, felt impelled to establish a journal to propagate their views and "fairly" represent the Texas brotherhood, even though editor McGary contended that his *Foundation,* which published the "whole truth," "fairly" represented the brotherhood.[132]

The progressives' answer was the *Christian Courier,* begun in Dallas in 1888. An anonymous writer in 1890, apparently a Southern conservative, charged the *Courier* with advocating a policy that would lead to strife, contention and divisions among Texas churches. The writer was confident that a mere handful of preachers never could ignore and override the preachers and churches of a "great, independent, self-respecting" religious body in any community by the help of foreign capital and imported, transient pulpit talent. The reference evidently was to northern progressive evangelists who had been brought by the *Courier* to conduct revivals in Texas, but whose "ideas

---

[130] Tant, "News," *ibid.,* XXIX (May 18, 1887), p. 307.
[131] Tant, "Preaching on the Old Range Again," *ibid.,* XLV (February 12, 1903), p. 111.
[132] *Firm Foundation,* February 15, 1888.

and customs" were "wholly extraneous to Christianity."[133]

As the controversy between the conservatives and progressives grew more intense, preachers found it necessary to side with the editor to get their articles published. In 1888, C. M. Wilmeth praised all the conservative preachers who pledged their allegiance to the *Christian Messenger* and *Firm Foundation*.[134] When conservative minister U. M. Browder of Gainesville was prohibited from advancing his view in the *Courier* by editor W. K. Homan, he presented it in the *Advocate*.[135] In 1898, the *Courier* designated Tennessee evangelist John E. Dunn as of the *Advocate* faction, and claimed that he had turned the Peoria and Hamilton churches over to "anti" adherents. The *Courier* advised the progressive congregations to allow Dunn to operate exclusively among conservative churches.[136] On the other hand, minister A. W. Young of Sunset charged that at least one dozen progressive preachers posing as conservatives were reporting their work in the "loyal" papers.[137]

The power of the religious papers over ministers was exemplified in the case of "Weeping Joe" Harding. Harding, who established the church at Ballinger, left when it turned progressive and soon was blackballed by the *Courier*. Later, he held a meeting in Tyler and received some Baptists without rebaptism into the

---

[133] Anonymous, in the *Gospel Advocate*, XXXII (December 17, 1890), p. 806.

[134] C. M. Wilmeth, "News," *ibid.*, XXXI (July 24, 1889), pp. 465-466.

[135] U. M. Browder, in *ibid.*, XXXV (October 26, 1893), p. 675.

[136] *Christian Courier*, quoted in *Gospel Advocate*, XI (October 13, 1898), p. 651.

[137] A. W. Young, "Church News," *ibid.*, XLVII (January 19, 1905), p. 44.

church. Immediately the *Foundation* exclaimed, "As to Weeping Joe Harding, the cause of Christ will be better maintained in any locality by his absence [rather] than by his presence." David Lipscomb of the *Advocate* quickly retorted that papers were to cite facts, not serve as juries on preachers. He decried the arbitrary efforts of editors to force churches and preachers into "menial submission." With needed frankness, Lipscomb averred that the bulls of excommunication were altogether too numerous in Texas, that "this turning out business" should be taken out of the hands of the newspapers and turned over to the churches, where it properly belongs.[138] The principle was correct but seldom practiced.

Editors and preachers admitted the evils wrought by the church papers. In 1896 on the twelfth anniversary of the *Firm Foundation*, editor McGary expressed serious doubt whether the religious papers among the disciples were accomplishing enough good to counter the evil they cause. He feared that the papers were promoting the growth of hostile factions—the *Advocate* family, *Leader* family, *Courier* family, and the *Standard* family.[139] Ten years later, T. W. Phillips of Fort Worth declared that the party line was "drawn tight" for there were three or four factions in Texas that "seem to run wild after papers and editors."[140] Tant made an appeal in 1896 through the columns of the "loyal" papers for evangelists to re-establish the "ancient order" of things by conducting revivals where the conservatives had been driven from their houses

---

[138] Lipscomb, in *ibid.*, XXXV (July 27, 1893), p. 465.

[139] *Firm Foundation*, January 9, 1894.

[140] T. W. Phillips, "Notes from Fort Worth, Texas," *Gospel Advocate*, XLVI (March 31, 1904), p. 206.

of worship.[141] The evidence at hand appears conclusive that the papers interpreted the Bible, expressed opinions, decreed law, and compelled preachers, churches and members either to comply with the new dogma or withdraw from the group. Thus the Bible, although the only accepted authority among churches of Christ, was subordinated to the opinions of editors and of contributors to religious papers.

RECONCILIATION EFFORTS

A few brethren proposed their ideas for reconciliation. On the whole, they met with little permanent success. As early as 1881, evangelist J. A. Meng of Missouri suggested that the organ be eliminated and that the elders be restored to ruling the congregations rather than allowing all spiritual problems to be settled by popular vote. Such he felt would restore peace and unite divided churches.[142] J. A. Clark, a preacher since 1839, implored his brethren to substitute love for fault finding and hate. He recommended that conservatives endeavor to "save" the progressives rather than condemn them.[143] In 1888, W. B. Carnes of Lancaster pleaded for an end of the war between the editors and contributors.[144] Five years later, progressive minister Chalmers McPherson lectured at Thorp Spring on the subject, "The Progressive and the Anti-Progressive Wings of the Disciples—The Demands of the Hour." He complained that the progressives

---

[141] Tant, "Growth of the Word," *ibid.*, XXXVIII (October 29, 1896), p. 702.

[142] J. A. Meng, "Let Us Have Peace," *Old Path Guide*, III (May, 1881), pp. 273-276.

[143] J. A. Clark, "Texas Department," *Gospel Advocate*, XXXI (December 18, 1889), p. 803.

[144] W. B. Carnes, "Texas Department," *ibid.*, XXX (March 21, 1888), p. 1.

usually had ignored, ridiculed or manifest a spirit of antagonism toward conservatives and warned that by such action "we may erect into a test of Christian fellowship the fellowship in our organized work."[145] J. M. Ratliffe, another progressive, lamented that some on both sides had gone to the extreme. Although he was aware that many would regard him as "too broad gauged," Ratliffe declared his love for all disciples whatever their opinions.[146] At Vineland, Collin County, the elders of the church convened a meeting of men from the *Messenger, Foundation* and *Courier* on Saturday, May 29, 1892, to discuss the issues dividing brethren. Unfortunately, no progress toward reconciliation was forthcoming.[147] In 1897, McGary and J. W. Jackson of the *Foundation* and W. K. Homan of the *Courier* published in their respective papers joint statements retracting all unchristian things they had written about each other. Although he commended their action, John Poe revealed the uncompromising attitude of the conservatives at the same time by calling upon the progressives to lay aside their hobbies of the organ and missionary society.[148] Each writer soon forgot his retraction statement.

Another hopeful but unsuccessful idea of reconciliation was suggested by McGary. In July, 1892, he proposed a mass meeting of Texas brethren with representatives from the *Courier, Foundation,* and *Messenger* to discuss the differences. Evangelist W. L. Swinney of Florence immediately suggested the Friday

---

[145] *Firm Foundation*, January 17, 1893.
[146] J. M. Ratliffe, "We Are Brethren," *Christian Courier* IV (March 11, 1891), p. 3.
[147] *Firm Foundation*, June 14, 1892.
[148] Poe, "Texas Department," *Gospel Advocate*, XXXIX (September 9, 1897), p. 562.

and Saturday before the fifth Sunday in November.[149] John Poe again intervened. He declared it was unscriptural on the basis that all decisions must be made on a congregational level. It was just as well. The split between conservatives and progressives had reached an impasse.

Successful efforts at reconciliation occurred in only a few scattered churches. At Sherman in 1895, the churches agreed to disagree after J. P. Loving for the progressives and J. D. Tant for the conservatives had canvassed the nearly five hundred members for three weeks. All parties consented to meet, confess their wrongs, and depart in peace.[150] At Seymour, peace and fellowship were restored temporarily by not using instrumental music during the communion service. Evidently its use in the song service was left to the discretion of the song leaders, according to J. W. Holsapple in his *Autobiography of an Octogenarian*. After several years of schism, the Kaufman congregation united in 1896 without the organ. The Vernon church did likewise a year later. At Terrell in 1901, conservative evangelist G. A. Dunn conducted a revival in the progressives' building without the organ being played.[151] At Mount Vernon, a number of brethren who believed in instrumental music and missionary societies deferred efforts to introduce them in order to maintain peace in the church.[152]

---

[149] *Firm Foundation*, July 12, 1892.

[150] J. D. Tant, "Sherman Church Trouble Settled," *Gospel Aavocate*, XXXVII (February 7, 1895), p. 85.

[151] G. A. Dunn, "Church News," *ibid.*, XLIII (August 1, 1901), p. 493.

[152] J. P. Sewell, "The Church," *ibid.*, XLIV (October 9, 1902), p. 644.

Basic Divergent Attitudes

Despite some sincere efforts to effect reconciliation between the two factions, basic differences in the progressives and conservatives made permanent division inevitable. Preachers and churches in such northern cities as Chicago, Cleveland, Cincinnati and St. Louis, where the industrial revolution following the Civil War had a tremendous impact, were in the forefront of the progressive movement. Progressivism was characterized by liberalism toward denominations and viewed supernatural Biblical teaching as a group of broad principles rather than as a specific body of statutes to be obeyed ritualistically. In 1901, minister J. D. Smith contended that to be consistent with "our position" all the pious unimmersed should be received into formal membership in our congregations. In support of his view, he cited two preachers in large cities, one leading college professor, and several churches as already accepting unimmersed persons.[153] Although the vast majority of churches and preachers throughout the United States considered only immersed persons as Christians, a few dissented. Evidently he referred to Professor J. W. McGarvey of the College of the Bible, Lexington, Kentucky, who in a letter to Hugh B. Todd on January 19, 1895, stated his view of the pious unimmersed:

> Lexington, Kentucky
> January 19, 1895
>
> Dear Bro.:
> Replying to yours of the 15th, I have no doubt there are pious persons who have never been immersed. It would be absurd and ridiculous to

---

[153] J. D. Smith, "Receiving the Unimmersed," *ibid.*, XLIII (September 12, 1901), p. 585.

deny it in the face of what we see and know of thousands of persons living and dead who have exhibited self-sacrificing love of God and man, which puts to shame all common disciples. I have as little doubt that many unimmersed persons will be saved in the final day. It is not necessary, in order to contend for scripture teaching on the subject of baptism, to take the ground that God has tied his hands and put it out of his own power to grant mercy to any who have been misled in regard to that ordinance. He has bound us, but he has not bound himself, except that he is bound to do what he has promised. He has not bound himself to do no more than he has promised. Don't injure the cause of truth by taking positions which rob God of the power to be merciful.

Yours fraternally,
J. W. McGarvey[154]

In Chicago, the Monroe St. Church of Disciples on December 5, 1906, adopted formally the practice of accepting "all whom we admit to be children of God, irrespective of their views on the ordinance of baptism."[155] The *Christian Evangelist*, published in St. Louis, directed by its broad-minded editor J. H. Garrison, seems to have been out front in expounding the liberal interpretation. The *Christian Standard* followed its lead but in a somewhat modified form.

The South, recovering from the ravages of war, was primarily agricultural and rural. Vast Texas, on the western fringe, was being settled by successive waves of immigrants from the economically prostrate South. These people were religiously conservative, viewed change as evil, and without knowing why adhered rigidly to the Bible in theory even though often they did

---

[154] J. W. McGarvey in *ibid.*, XXXVII (December 12, 1895), p. 790.

[155] The Scroll, in *ibid.*, XLIX (January 31, 1907), p. 65.

not practice its precepts in daily life. The *Gospel Advocate* was the principal spokesman for the Southern churches. Directed by its venerable editor David Lipscomb for fifty years, it adhered to the more literal interpretation of the Bible. The majority of Texas preachers and members, with their close connection with Tennessee, were in accord with Lipscomb. Although progressives Addison Clark and W. K. Homan concluded that the two thousand persons who had "pledged themselves to live the Christian life" during the Sam Jones revival in Dallas in 1893 was sufficient evidence to prove it was God's doing, evangelist John S. Durst voiced the sentiment of all conservatives and a large majority of progressives in Texas—these people could not live as Christians since they had not been immersed as the scriptures taught, hence were not Christians.[156]

The two divergent attitudes were expressed by preachers and papers. Evangelist J. P. Longan declared in the *Texas Christian Monthly* (Dallas) that the preachers and members who "dare to disfellowship" their brethren, who use the organ or cooperate in missionary work, will "become a sect in the most offensive New Testament sense." The *Apostolic Times* (Lexington, Kentucky) challenged this assertion with the question, "How can this be apostasy when they oppose to the point of disfellowship a practice unknown to the New Testament?"[157] John Poe stated in 1884 that there was talk of divisions among the disciples. He termed, however, any "sloughing off" as the

---

[156] John S. Durst, in *ibid.*, XXXV (July 6, 1893), pp. 418-419.
[157] *Texas Christian Monthly*, quoted in *Apostolic Times*, VII (August 12, 1875), p. 357.

"worldly" Christians leaving the "true" Christians.[158]

After the formation of the missionary society in Texas in 1886, the lines of division formed clearly. Minister F. D. Srygley stated in 1891 that he regarded the society as an "expedient" rather than as a sinful innovation. But Srygley immediately contradicted himself by declaring that a majority of "brethren in Texas and other southern states will not—they cannot, work through boards, conventions, and societies."[159] Thus, in reality, Srygley held the missionary society unlawful rather than inexpedient.

Other preachers and editors already averred that the conservatives and progressives were in reality two separate bodies. C. M. Wilmeth of Dallas described the two factions as separate as "night and day . . . one winks at the organ, the other condemns it . . . one favors the missionary societies, the other characterizes them as unscriptural."[160] In like manner, Austin McGary declared that the progressives have left us and we should acknowledge it.[161] The progressive *Courier* was of the opinion that even a superficial observer could see two schools of thought among the disciples. Decrying their zealous regard for unity of opinion, the *Courier* likened the conservatives to a group of legalists who viewed the New Testament as applying to Christians in the same manner as the Old Testament did to the Jews. It concluded that the progressives were staunch adherents of true Christian liberty be-

---

[158] Poe, "Texas Department," *Gospel Advocate*, XXVI (February 13, 1884), p. 100.

[159] F. D. Srygley, "Bro. Burnett," *Christian Messenger*, XVII (March 18, 1891), p. 1.

[160] C. M. Wilmeth, "News," *Gospel Advocate*, XXXI (July 24, 1889), pp. 465-466.

[161] *Firm Foundation*, August 29, 1889.

cause they viewed the New Testament as a group of broad principles.[162]

The uncompromising attitudes were manifest vividly in church schisms. In 1899, the two churches in Sherman each selected a preacher to attempt a reconciliation. Minister J. H. Lawson insisted that unity could be restored if the unscriptural organ was removed. Minister J. W. Holsapple refused to comply, whereupon Lawson charged that "selfishness" was at the root of Holsapple's thinking.[163] Had Holsapple been consulted, he probably would have replied in kind. In August, 1900, R. G. Scott, a roadmaster on the Cotton Belt Railroad, and his zealous wife Loula, moved to Commerce and began meeting with the anti-organ disciples in the home of H. C. Booth. Soon Mrs. Scott prevailed upon Booth to secure the use of the progressive house for Sunday afternoon services. After an announcement was made in April, 1901, that conservative evangelist R. M. Gano would conduct a meeting in June, the progressives locked the door so that the conservatives could not use the building on Sundays, April 28 and May 5. Not to be outdone, the conservatives, under Scott's leadership, assembled with the progressives on May 12 and remained in the building for their own worship service after the progressives left. The conservatives then changed the lock and gave a key to an obliging progressive deacon. When they returned in the afternoon of May 19 and found the lock had been changed again, they broke into the building. Lock breaking occurred until the fourth Sunday in June when the conservatives began a re-

---
[162]"Christian Liberty vs. Judaistic Legalism," *Christian Courier*, IV (January 14, 1891), p. 4.
[163]J. H. Lawson, "Church News," *Gospel Advocate*, XLI (May 11, 1899), p. 302.

vival. On Tuesday following, two progressive elders closed the doors with locks and nails. While conservative minister W. A. Sewell was arguing with the elders, a noise was heard at the back door. When the group arrived at the rear entrance, a zealous conservative sister with an ax in hand demanded a key. When refused, she chopped down the door. After inviting the elders to the service, the aggressive conservatives entered and conducted a revival daily for the next four weeks. Subsequently, a strong eldership was appointed and Sewell promised to preach monthly. Booth untruthfully boasted that "we are now in our house; and, by the grace of God and the protection guaranteed to us by the laws of our State, we are here to stay."[164] Evidently the progressives allowed them to take the building by default.

Another disgraceful incident occurred at Myrtle Springs in 1904. The church had been organized in 1891, but divided after a progressive preacher arrived in 1901. Three years later, elder B. Blowers invited T. W. Phillips of Fort Worth to conduct a revival. Although locked out, Flowers opened the door and Phillips began preaching. After the service, Phillips was "rotten egged" by some of the progressives. The magistrate told Phillips that someone had asked him how much the fine would be for throwing rotten eggs at a preacher, and that he had replied twenty-five dollars. Before the revival closed, thirty-three persons renounced their unchristian acts.[165]

The harmful results of the divergent attitudes were manifest in churches throughout the state. Evange-

---
[164]H. C. Booth, "The Church of God at Commerce, Texas," *ibid.*, XLIII (November 21, 1901), p. 739.
[165]T. W. Phillips, "Church News," *ibid.*, XLVI (December 15, 1904), pp. 786-787.

list H. F. Williams, who traveled in 1894 from San Antonio to Gilmer, was received with "kindness and fellowship" by conservative churches but with "downright objection" by progressive congregations.[166] After visiting Texas again in 1904, David Lipscomb sorrowfully reported that no more fatal and fearful results of the effort to form societies and to introduce into the service "things not taught by God" are found than in the churches in the towns and cities of Texas. He observed that in most towns, two small churches warred against each other. Although he found the country churches not so divided, apparently they were discouraged and inactive.[167]

DIVISION AND NAMES

Acknowledging the division was a reality, it was necessary to designate the two bodies with appropriate names. For over a half century, no specific or exclusive name had been adopted. Many preachers and editors now urged that each group adopt a name upon which all could unite. The crux of the problem revolved around the scriptural meaning of the Greek word *ekklesia*, generally translated "church," "assembly," or congregation" in most New Testament translations. Editor Joseph Franklin attacked the problem with forthrightness. He pointed out that many people charged that the reformers were attempting to fashion a new sect, but that the reformers denied the accusation and insisted that they simply hoped for a union of all Christians. There were, nevertheless, a large number who still felt that " 'we' are one of many de-

---

[166] H. F. Williams, "Field Findings," *ibid.*, XXXVI (February 22, 1894), p. 118.
[167] Lipscomb, "A Trip to Texas," *ibid.*, XLVI (July 21, 1904), p. 456.

nominations." Franklin said that the term "Christian Church" seemed to be more in vogue than "Reform Church, Disciple Church or Church of Christ." His reasoning was based upon the fact that thousands of immersed "Christians" were attached to other sects all over America. When they withdrew from a denomination, Franklin affirmed that they did not "join another sect" but lived henceforth simply as Christians. When these Christians met to worship God, he reasoned, they constituted the only "ecclesiastical relationship" described in the New Testament.[168]

Retired minister James Thornberry of Scyene, Texas, expressed another view. He opposed the designation "The Disciples" because it was "partial and inexpressive" and had led to "Disciple Churches" and "Disciples preachers." With respect to those who preferred "Church of Christ," he predicted that "sensible people will call us 'Church of Christians' and 'Church of Christ preachers'." He favored the terms Christian Church and Christians.[169]

Endeavoring to set forth a Biblical concept relative to names, the *Christian Courier* in 1892 stated what all who perceived the restoration movement properly wanted to say. It deemed the terms Christian Church, Church of Christ, and Church of God as "proper when properly applied." The *Courier* further argued that the terms must apply to the whole family of God, some of whom were in heaven, some in the churches, and some among the various denominations. Any name designating any company less than the whole is a de-

---

[168] Joseph Franklin, "Sectarianism in the Reformation," *ibid.,* XXII (August 26, 1880), p. 549.
[169] James L. Thornberry, "Fifty Years Ago," *Apostolic Church,* VI (September, 1884), pp. 20-21.

nominational name, it argued, though expressed in the words of scripture.[170]

As longtime editor of the *Advocate,* David Lipscomb made several observations in regard to names. Although admitting the general use of the term "Christian Church" in 1855, he stated in 1905 that he had refrained from using the designation for thirty years primarily to avoid "profitless controversy," concerning a name not specifically mentioned in scripture. Lipscomb informed his readers that the term "Churches of Christ" in the plural form was used once in the Bible, but "Church of God" appeared many times. Although he saw no impropriety in calling a "Church of Christians" a "Christian Church," he did not use the term or encourage others to use it.[171] Lipscomb argued that God gave no distinctive name to his church. He listed "Saints," "Disciples of Christ," "Christians," "churches," "Churches of Gentiles," "Churches of the Saints," "Churches of Judea," "Churches of Galatia," and "Churches of God" as Bible terms. None, he thought, seemed to be given as a name for universal application. Lipscomb emphatically declared that the expression "church of Christ" is not in the Bible; "churches of Christ" is once used there—but as a descriptive name.[172]

Evangelist J. P. Updike contended that both "Disciples Church" and "Christian Church" were unscriptural. He accepted the term "Church of Jesus Christ" because Jesus designated it as "my church." Updike

---
[170]*Christian Courier,* quoted in *Gospel Advocate,* XXXIV (October 27, 1892), p. 673.
[171]Lipscomb, "The Christian Church," *ibid.,* XLVII (August 10, 1905), p. 503.
[172]Lipscomb, "Distinctive Names," *ibid.,* XLVIII (February 22, 1905), p. 121.

also affirmed the use of "Church of Christ" and "Church of God" as scriptural.[173]

The confusion about names puzzled many members of the church. As early as 1886 a disciple in Corsicana, in a letter to James A. Harding, an *Advocate* staff writer, suggested a mass meeting of "sound brethren" to adopt a name. All who refused to accept it would be termed "Progressive." In 1903 a member who wrote G. W. Savage, editor of the *Foundation*, asked if the "Christian Church" and "Church of Christ" were separate organizations. Savage replied that the progressives and conservatives used the names interchangeably. Although he labeled the term "Christian Church" as one of "construction," Savage felt it did not violate a Biblical principle because the church was composed of Christians.[174]

Lipscomb gave a similar reply to J. M. Cohron of Ronda, Texas, in 1906. He said that he never used the terms to distinguish between the two factions, so could not explain the difference. He explained that some members had designated all churches which favored the so-called "innovations" as "Christian Churches" and all which opposed the organ and missionary society as "Churches of Christ"; however, Lipscomb felt this endeavor had failed because the progressive churches were using "Church of Christ" extensively and many old conservative members still favored the term "Christian Church." Lipscomb thought it wise not to adopt any distinctive name, "as God gave none,"

---

[173] J. P. Updike, "On the Church," *Christian Standard*, XLII (February 2, 1907), p. 97.
[174] *Firm Foundation*, March 24, 1903.

and if done, it would likely be made a sectarian name.[175]

1906 RELIGIOUS CENSUS

The 1906 census was limited strictly to religious bodies. The last religious census had been taken in 1890. Because the census had become so complex, the religious section was omitted in 1900. On March 6, 1902, Congress charged the Bureau of the Census with the duty of collecting statistics for the religious bodies of the United States in 1906. The census reports, however, were not published until 1910.

When the data were in, S. N. D. North, director of the United States Census Bureau, was unable to determine from it whether the several groups, hitherto constituting the Disciples of Christ, Christian Church and churches of Christ, were one, two, or more religious bodies. For assistance in clarifying the confused statistics, North began reading the religious papers published by members of the groups. After reading the *Advocate*, he was unable to determine whether it was identified with the Disciples of Christ or with a distinct body. As North was about to write Lipscomb for clarification, he received a letter from minister William J. Campbell of Marshalltown, Iowa, who claimed that there were "over three thousand 'churches of Christ,' not now connected with the Disciples of Christ, though formerly belonging to that body." Campbell included a list of preachers of the "churches of Christ" published by the McQuiddy Company in Nashville. When North compared the list with the one in the *American Home Missionary*, published by the missionary society, he found duplications. Fur-

---

[175]Lipscomb, "Distinguishing Names," *Gospel Advocate*, XLVIII (February 8, 1906), p. 88.

ther confused, North wrote Lipscomb a lengthy letter on June 17, 1907, and asked four questions: First, was there a body called the "church of Christ," not identified with the Disciples of Christ or any other Baptist body? Second, if such a body existed, did it have headquarters, officers, synods, or conferences? Third, how did it originate and what are its distinctive principles? Fourth, what is the best manner for securing "a complete list of churches"?

Lipscomb, quite surprised, forthrightly answered the questions but somewhat colored by his own personal beliefs. In answer to the first, he replied that there was a group "taking the word of God as their only and sufficient rule of faith, calling their churches 'churches of Christ,' or 'Churches of God,' distinct and separate in name, work, and rule of faith from all other bodies or peoples." They were, he continued in response to the second question, purely congregational, independent in polity and work, and had no general meetings or organizations of any kind. This answer indicates that Lipscomb omitted the churches, regardless of what name they used, which sent delegates to the missionary society conventions. In answer to the third question, he said that their aim was to unite all professed Christians for the sole purpose of "promoting simple, evangelical Christianity as God reveals it in the Scriptures, free from all human opinions and inventions of men." Lipscomb found the last question extremely difficult to answer. The differences still at work among the churches made it difficult to determine to which group certain churches would more nearly belong. Obviously, this was an admission that some churches were in the process of dividing, and others might yet do so. Lipscomb knew of no way to obtain the statistics desired other than to address a circular to each church.[176] North evidently interpreted Lipscomb's and Campbell's replies, which substantiated census data, as sufficient evidence to warrant a separate calculation of the progressives and conservatives. Conservative J. W. Shepherd, *Advocate* staff member of Nashville, was appointed as a special agent to procure the desired data. Evangelist R. L. Whiteside of Corsicana assisted in compiling the Texas data. Religious papers urged each church to send the address of a responsible member of the congregation to Whiteside, who in turn would send a census blank to the designated member.[177]

The lack of church organization resulted in ensuing confusion and incomplete statistics. The communication failed to elicit a maximum response. Both progressives and conservatives reported under several names. In 1908, Whiteside explained in the *Firm Foundation* that many conservative churches had sent reports by mistake to progressive agent G. A. Hoffman and that the "innovators" would get credit. Therefore, he urged such churches to fill out another blank and send it to Shepherd in order to correct the error.[178] Shepherd, also greatly confused, appealed in the *Advocate* for assistance in classifying the churches properly.[179]

The effectiveness of these appeals is hard to estimate. Many rural churches had no regular preacher or elders; thus, no one was in a responsible position to comply with either request. Furthermore, some who

---
[176]Lipscomb, "The Church of Christ and the Disciples of Christ," *ibid.*, XLIX (July 18, 1907), p. 457.
[177]*Firm Foundation*, September 24, 1907.
[178]*Ibid.*, March 24, 1908.
[179]J. W. Shepherd, "United States Church Statistics," *Gospel Advocate*, L (February 23, 1908), p. 53.

complied by mistake the first time apparently did not correct the error. There is conclusive proof of the inaccuracy of the census. After looking over the Texas list in September, 1908, J. D. Tant, who had been preaching in Texas for nearly thirty years, claimed that about 230 conservative churches with over 15,000 members were missing from the census rolls.[180]

The 1906 census lists the two bodies under different names. North apparently designated the conservatives as the "Churches of Christ" because Lipscomb cited the term in his letter. The progressives were listed as "Disciples of Christ" (Christian). Although the appellations seem to clearly distinguish the two bodies, some difficulty remains. The organ and missionary society churches use the names "Church of Christ" and "Christian Church" interchangeably throughout the nation, particularly north of the Ohio River where their strength is great. A few churches use the name "Church of Disciples of Christ." On the other hand, the non-organ and non-missionary society churches have used the term "Church of Christ" exclusively since about 1915. In no case do they carry the lettering "Christian Church" over a meeting house or on their publications. The term "Church of God" or "Church of Jesus Christ" is not used because it might be construed as a Pentecostal sect.

The 1906 census figures give some insight into the relative strength of the two bodies. The Disciples of Christ (Christian) was credited with 39,550 members in Texas; the church of Christ with 34,006. The total for both churches was considerably short of B. B. Sanders' estimate of 90,000 in 1903. However, if the 15,000 claimed by Tant as having been overlooked were

---

[180]*Firm Foundation*, September 15, 1908.

added, less than two thousand would remain unaccounted.

Compared to other religious bodies in Texas, the Disciples of Christ (Christian) ranked fourth in total membership and the churches of Christ sixth. The number of churches and the total membership of the major denominations as revealed in the 1906 census are as follows:

	Churches	Membership
Roman Catholic	225	362,772
Baptist (Southern)	3,098	247,306
Methodist Episcopal (South)	2,341	225,431
Disciples of Christ (Christian)	502	39,550
Methodist Episcopal	561	36,223
Churches of Christ	627	34,006
Presbyterian (US)	393	23,934
Presbyterian (USA)	58	4,118

According to the above statistics, Protestant congregations in Texas averaged less than one hundred members. The numerical superiority of the Roman Catholic over some of the Protestants, including the churches of Christ and the Disciples of Christ, is explained by the fact that the Catholics, unlike the Protestants, included all baptized infants.

Other comparative statistics for the churches of Christ and Disciples of Christ show the number of churches, Sunday Schools, and church membership.

	Churches of Christ	Disciples of Christ
Church edifices	383	360
Halls, etc.	236	19
Seating Capacity	126,983	116,115
Churches (congregations)	627	503
Sunday Schools	229	375
Sunday School		

(scholars)	11,336	25,294
Membership	34,006	39,550[181]

These figures reveal that churches of Christ had smaller congregations but were very strong in rural areas since the Disciples of Christ worshiped in only nineteen school buildings, lodge halls, courthouses or other rented buildings. If Tant's estimate of 230 additional churches of Christ with 15,000 members is included, the difference becomes even more pronounced. The Sunday School statistics indicate the concentration of progressive strength in cities and towns.

County statistics tend to verify the state figures. In the four most populous counties of the state the Disciples of Christ (Christian) had a membership more than three times as large as the churches of Christ.

	Churches of Christ	Disciples of Christ
Bexar	98	524
Dallas	1269	2784
Harris	138	724
Tarrant	354	1640
Totals	1863	5672

On the other hand, in counties where there were no large cities the churches of Christ had the larger membership. A sampling of five representative counties containing fair sized towns shows that churches of Christ had nearly three times as many members as the Disciples of Christ.

---

[181] Department of Commerce and Labor, Bureau of the Census. E. Dana Durand, Director. Special Reports: *Religious Bodies*: 1906 Part II (Washington: Government Printing Office, 1910), p. 272. Hereafter cited as Census, Religious Bodies, 1906.

	Churches of Christ	Disciples of Christ
Denton	1186	689
Johnson	1154	424
Jones	359	52
Nacogdoches	387	36
Parker	898	280
Totals	3984	1481[182]

One oddity of the census was the Bell County report which listed the Disciples of Christ with 173 members and churches of Christ none.[183] Obviously, the conservatives either were ignorant of the census or ignored the requests for data. Conservative preachers had conducted many meetings in the county since 1850. Churches were meeting at Troy, Oenaville, Temple, Belton, Holland, Bartlett, Salado and Rogers, of which nearly all were conservative.

Nationally, the census figures of the two bodies evidence a similar trend.

	Churches of Christ	Disciples of Christ
Churches	2,649	8,293
Members	159,658	982,701
Sunday School Scholars	56,086	578,718[184]

The Sunday School figures show that the progressive churches with better organization and finances were stronger in the urban, industrial North. On the other hand, the poorly organized conservative churches were unable to sustain large Sunday Schools in the rural, agricultural South. Churches of Christ were unable to rectify this weakness to any large degree

---
[182] Census, *Religious Bodies*, 1906, pp. 357-360.
[183] *Ibid.*, pp. 148-149.
[184] *Ibid.*, pp. 357-360.

until the beginning of the latter half of the twentieth century.

As a result of the census, the separation of the two bodies became complete. Churches began reporting to "loyal" papers and placing the proper "name" above the meeting house door. Preachers aligned themselves with the churches of their convictions, and members were henceforth able to chose between the Disciples of Christ or Christian Church and churches of Christ with less confusion.

Another result of the census was that a considerable number of conservative churches placed "restrictive clauses" in the church deeds. Such clauses usually prohibited the introduction of the organ, missionary society, or other innovations. Evangelist C. E. Holt expressed displeasure that the Sunday School was excluded by a few churches. Less than two per cent of all the conservatives contended that it was sinful to teach the Bible to children in separate classes. Holt lamented that such a restriction influenced many youths to attend other churches or none at all.[185]

Controversy among the conservatives over the restrictive clauses was brief. Dr. George Klingman, educator and minister, contended that the restrictive clause was legislating where God had not. He felt that any brother who objected on the ground that it was legislating in the "realm of faith" was loyal to the New Testament teaching. G. H. P. Showalter, editor of the *Firm Foundation*, disagreed on the assumption that many troublesome lawsuits could have been avoided by restrictive clauses.[186] Although

---

[185] C. E. Holt, "Gone Beyond Jerusalem," *Gospel Advocate*, XLVII (September 21, 1905), p. 607.
[186] *Firm Foundation*, December 1, 1914.

preachers and members generally perceived restrictive clauses as a "creed in the deed," some churches retained them, thereby nullifying the New Testament as the sole authority in the church.

After 1906 the churches of Christ, minus those churches which had introduced the organ and missionary society, entered a new era of growth. By the midpoint of the twentieth century, it was the fourth largest religious body in Texas.

CHAPTER VIII

THE CHURCHES OF CHRIST BECOME A MAJOR RELIGIOUS BODY

CHURCH GROWTH

Sunday, October 15, 1950, was a memorable day for Texas churches of Christ. On that day, the Broadway church in Lubbock opened its new six hundred thousand dollar edifice. The structure includes a 2200-seat auditorium, Sunday School facilities for 2000, a chapel with 300 seats, and a nursery with a private bath. An overflow crowd of 2600 heard the first sermon, "We Dedicate Ourselves," by minister Dr. M. Norvel Young. Young described the building as an "instrument to help us in our worship" rather than as a "monument to be worshiped." During the first week, over one thousand visitors from several states attended a series of lectures given by thirty-one preachers. The Broadway congregation at the halfway point of the twentieth century symbolized the growth of the churches of Christ in Texas.

After the formal division in 1906, churches of Christ in Texas embarked upon extensive programs of growth and development. Hundreds of new churches were established, large, well equipped buildings were erected, and the gospel was proclaimed over the radio, in tracts, and in pamphlets. Increased efforts were made to educate the youth on both the secondary and college levels, home mission work was initiated among the Jews, limited efforts were made among the Negroes and Mexicans, foreign missions were supported in India, Japan, Germany and Italy, and benevolent work among the orphans increased.

Rapid growth occurred in Dallas. The Pearl and Bryan church began conducting tent meetings in 1907 throughout the city and successfully planted several new churches. Minister L. S. White during a tent revival on Forney Avenue in 1909 obtained twenty-two baptisms and organized a church of thirty which for a time held services in a school building.[1] By 1916, Dallas had eight churches of Christ with 997 members;[2] nine years later there were twenty churches with over 3,000 members.[3] During the able ministry of Flavil L. Colley from 1931-1933, the Trinity Heights church had 225 additions.[4] The active Sunset church, organized in 1925 with a few dozen disciples, had five hundred in Sunday School and almost one thousand at Sunday morning worship services within nine years.[5] The Oak Cliff church, founded in 1907 with 27 members, grew under the leadership of minister John S. Dunn to 230 in 1916, and by 1927 was the largest church of Christ in Dallas. In the same year, the 800-member congregation erected a beautiful $140,000 building at Tenth and Van Buren which included an auditorium seating 1,500 and modern Sunday School facilities for 1000 pupils.[6] Under the leadership of energetic minister W. L. Oliphant, the church proposed in 1947 a $75,000 building with a gym, educational department and nursery, a bold step for traditionally

---

[1] L. S. White, "News," *Gospel Advocate*, LI (July 18, 1909), p. 849.
[2] *Religious Bodies*, 1916, p. 360.
[3] John H. Cochran, *Dallas County* (Dallas, 1928), p. 262.
[4] *Firm Foundation*, August 15, 1933.
[5] *Ibid.*, October 23, 1934.
[6] *Dallas Morning News*, May 1, 1927.

conservative churches of Christ. Oliphant stated that the gym was for "church athletics."[7] At mid-century 56 white and 4 colored churches of Christ in Dallas boasted a total membership of 11,262.[8]

Nearby at Fort Worth evangelist Horace W. Busby vigorously promoted the cause. Born in Tennessee in 1884, Busby came to Ellis County with his parents eight years later. After attending North Texas State College, he taught school until his baptism in 1904, when shortly afterward he began devoting full time to proclaiming the gospel.[9] In his sermons he repeatedly stressed the theme "faith, repentance and baptism." During his seven years as minister of the Vickery Boulevard church in Fort Worth beginning in 1911 a total of 587 new members were enrolled, a rather remarkable growth. Busby became a full-time evangelist in 1920, conducted fifty-seven revivals in the cowtown in the next eighteen years, and established several congregations. During a protracted meeting at the vacant corner of Avenue I and Little Street, he obtained over one hundred baptisms and organized the Polytechnic Church with 130 charter members.[10] Two years later in a revival at the Glenwood church, Busby proclaimed his appealing message to an estimated two thousand earnest listeners on Sunday nights. Weekday services at 10:00 A.M. had an average attendance of two hundred. "Dozens" were baptized, and the enlarged congregation established a new church in another section of town.[11]

---

[7]*Ibid.*, June 29, 1947.
[8]*Churches of Christ in Dallas and Dallas County* (compiled by Sears and Summitt Church of Christ, January, 1951), n.p.
[9]*Preachers Who Blazed the Trail.*
[10]*Firm Foundation*, July 21, 1936.
[11]*The Living Message* (Morrilton, Arkansas), September 11, 1924.

CHURCHES OF CHRIST BECOME A MAJOR RELIGIOUS BODY 299

The Meadowbrook church, founded in 1951, symbollized the vision manifested by Fort Worth churches of Christ. The congregation on November 2 of the same year moved into a centrally heated and air conditioned concrete building that had a capacity of four hundred. Anticipating continued growth, the elders had the building designed so that the auditorium could be changed easily into classrooms when a larger sanctuary was needed.[12]

At the Sherman church, scene of the great Larimore revival, the popularity of protracted meetings continued undiminished. L. S. White of Dallas during a five-week revival in 1911 delivered eighty sermons and received fifty-one additions.[13] Nine years later, the congregation entered a commodious new three-story $85,000 edifice equipped with eight hundred opera chairs. Evangelist G. A. Dunn, who gained 123 additions during a three-week meeting in the new church, asserted that the building was the "best" owned by churches of Christ in Texas.[14] Evidently inspired by the successful revival, the church began conducting evangelistic tent meetings in the city and sent its minister, George Stephenson, to preach in rural Grayson County in the summer. Stephenson visited small churches of Christ in the winter in order to train their leaders.[15]

Central church best illustrates the growth of the churches of Christ in Houston. Although founded in 1903, it had thirty years later only two hundred members and an average weekly contribution of $180. After World War II, however, the congregation grew

---
[12]*Fort Worth Star-Telegram*, November 3, 1951.
[13]*Firm Foundation*, February 28, 1911.
[14]*Ibid.*, July 27, 1920.
[15]*Ibid.*, May 2, 1939.

rapidly, and erected in 1946 a magnificent brick building with seating for 1010. Special features include walls up to 42 inches thick for insulation from outside noises, educational building with kitchen containing two Sunday School rooms easily convertible to a fellowship hall, fully equipped library, small chapel, complete public address system, and unique, modern facilities for mothers with babies. At each service two nurses attended the fifty numbered beds in the nursery. If a mother saw the number of her baby's bed flashed on a lighted panel at the front of the nave, she retired to the nursery to attend to her infant.[16] The 1000-member congregation, largest of the forty-five churches of Christ in Houston,[17] liberally contributed $103,000 within the first year after the opening of the new building and supported mission work in New England, Mexico and Australia.[18]

Less progress was made amid difficult circumstances at San Antonio. Saloons were opened on Sunday in 1907 and minister Walter Charlton reported that few other than devout members would attend worship services because of the noise from passing trains. The following year, however, under the leadership of Joe Harding, the congregation erected a small house on Flores Street in a more favorable location.[19] A few other churches were established in various parts of the city during the next quarter century. In 1935, a revival held by President J. N. Armstrong of Harding College, Searcy, Arkansas, in the Grove Avenue church

---

[16] Burton Coffman, "Central Church of Christ, Houston" (unpublished manuscript).
[17] *Houston Post*, December 31, 1951.
[18] J. M. F. Smithson (Houston) to Stephen Eckstein, interview, August 24, 1958.
[19] Walter Charlton, "News," *Gospel Advocate*, XLIX (January 3, 1907), p. 12.

provided the spark that led to a period of growth of the church in the city. Minister J. P. Sewell characterized Armstrong's preaching as the "most perfectly balanced presentation of the entire content of Christianity I have ever heard in one week."[20] Inspired by Armstrong's enthusiasm, the Grove Avenue church spearheaded the establishment of five new churches in the next five years.[21]

On the South Plains, Lubbock became a center of churches of Christ. A church membership which reached 250 by 1919 liberally supported minister Liff Sanders in evangelistic work in the surrounding area. In 1922 the congregation moved into the basement of a new building at Broadway and Avenue N, where services were conducted until the 750-seat auditorium was completed two years later. Membership increased from 350 to 1,500 in the next twenty-five years, even though several hundred members joined the eight additional churches of Christ founded in the city during the period. Under the able leadership of Dr. Norvel Young, the congregation outgrew its premises. Young at first attempted to solve the problem by holding two Sunday morning services beginning in 1944, but when it became evident that even then facilities would soon be overtaxed, it was decided to build a new plant. The congregation moved into its magnificent $600,000 edifice at Broadway and Avenue T in 1950. By that date the nine Lubbock congregations had a combined membership of four thousand.[22]

Amarillo was the focal point for Panhandle churches of Christ. The Central church conducted rather suc-

---
[20]*Firm Foundation*, December 10, 1935.
[21]E. N. Glenn (comp.), *Church Directory of Churches of Christ in USA and Canada* (Cincinnati, 1932), n.p.
[22]*Lubbock Avalanche Journal*, October 15, 1950.

cessful tent meetings in various parts of the city from 1911 to 1916. The 500-seat auditorium erected at Tenth and Fillmore in 1916 was inadequate five years later. The new building, erected at Fourteenth and Monroe in 1930, had a unique feature. To bring the audience as close to the pulpit as possible, its sanctuary, which seated 1280, was partly arranged in a quarter-circle.[23] The congregation, not content with promoting its own welfare, supported successful missionary efforts throughout the city and in Vega, Gruver, Panhandle and Higgins. Although many of its members aligned with the four other churches of Christ in Amarillo, the membership of Central church exceeded one thousand in 1950.[24]

Churches of Christ in smaller towns kept pace with the rapid development of West Texas. Many congregations were fortunate to have members who had substantial income from oil wells, ranches, or large irrigated farms. It is not surprising, therefore, that numerous large building programs were launched. On Sunday, October 3, 1948, the Northside church in Abilene dedicated a modern new $55,000 auditorium with a seating capacity of 840.[25] In the same year at Hale Center, Hale County, a building seating 450, equipped with two overflow rooms, loud speakers, two nurseries and ten classrooms was completed.[26] The congregation at Idalou, Lubbock County, composed largely of farmers, on May 29, 1949, dedicated a contemporary American brick structure furnished with oak pews to seat up to five hundred and with ten classrooms.[27] In

---

[23] *Firm Foundation*, October 1, 1940.
[24] *Amarillo Sunday News-Globe*, October 5, 1958.
[25] *Christian Chronicle* (Abilene), September 29, 1948.
[26] *Ibid.*, October 13, 1948.
[27] *Ibid.*, June 1, 1949.

April of the same year, the 280-member congregation at Tulia opened with no outstanding indebtedness a $75,000 building that seated four hundred and had ten classrooms.[28] At Odessa, the Northside church erected the new $55,000 Parkview church with a seating capacity of 435 in another part of the city and then furnished 150 of the charter members to form the new church in September, 1949.[29]

Simultaneously with church growth, initial efforts were made to plant the cause in the lower Rio Grande Valley. Although a few members resided in the area, no churches were established permanently until after World War I. In 1920, evangelist W. A. Schultz established the cause in McAllen,[30] and in November Foy E. Wallace, Sr., conducted a three-week meeting at Harlingen and organized a congregation of thirty-two.[31] The following year, churches were meeting at San Benito, Brownsville, Raymondville, New Mercedes and Mission.[32] Two decades later, a Valley-wide meeting held in the Harlingen Municipal Auditorium with evangelist N. B. Hardeman of Tennessee preaching, concluded on Wednesday evening, February 28, 1940, with about one thousand in attendance. Minister Ira Y. Rice, Jr., reported the "positive preaching . . . greatly strengthened the morale of the Valley Christians . . ." and predicted the churches would renew efforts to evangelize the area.[33]

EDUCATIONAL MEDIA

Churches of Christ supplemented their expanded

---
[28]*Ibid.*, September 28, 1949.
[29]*Ibid.*, October 19, 1949.
[30]*Firm Foundation*, December 14, 1920.
[31]*Ibid.*, January 5, 1943.
[32]*Ibid.*, February 22, 1921.
[33]*Ibid.*, March 19, 1940.

programs by a greater utilization of the printing press. G. H. P. Showalter, editor of the *Firm Foundation,* stressed the power of the press in the religious field. He claimed that every great successful movement had been supported by a strong "propaganda literature." Characterizing the first part of the twentieth century as an age of "writing and reading," Showalter urged churches of Christ to publicize the gospel extensively, and suggested as one means that each congregation spend at least ten dollars a year for the purchase of gospel tracts for free distribution.[34]

Some churches responded to Showalter's suggestions. In 1934 the church in Electra contacted hundreds of townspeople each week by placing one hundred copies of the *Firm Foundation* in as many homes. To stimulate increased interest in the Sunday worship services, six hundred circulars announcing the sermon topics for the morning and evening services were distributed each week. Minister Tillit S. Teddlie felt that a larger number of non-members attended services as a result of the publicity.[35] In the same year at Wink, Winkler County, evangelist J. L. Dabney likened his preaching to "farming in sand. The seed sown sprouted but was soon blown away." To supplement his pulpit efforts, Dabney began mimeographing his sermons each week and distributing hundreds of copies to the transients.[36] At Dallas the Peak and East Side church, supported by twenty-nine other congregations, August, 1943, began publishing each Saturday in the *Daily Times Herald* an advertisement entitled "Gospel of Christ." The articles explained teaching on such subjects as the Bible Faith, Bible Baptism, the

---

[34] *Ibid.,* January 11, 1916.
[35] *Ibid.,* December 11, 1934.
[36] *Ibid.,* May 29, 1934.

Lord's Supper, and New Testament Conversion, and invited readers to request a free map showing the locations of churches of Christ in Dallas. At the end of the first year, all the advertisement articles with comments from various churches were published in a special digest called *The Christian News Service*. A number of reports mentioned that a majority of those who were baptized during the publicity campaign explained that the articles had inspired them to begin attending the church of Christ.[37] Unfortunately, this method of advertising was shortly interrupted by World War II.

Mission work of churches of Christ was favorably publicized by a private newspaper. In 1940 Edgar L. Furr of Goldthwaite described the vast unexploited mission field in Texas. He reported that out of the 254 county seat towns, 120 had congregations and full-time preachers, 66 had congregations but no full-time ministers, and 68, with a combined population of 120,000, mostly in East Texas, were without a church of Christ, and made an urgent plea for missionary efforts to be inaugurated in these towns.[38] Within the next few years, servicemen who were members of the church of Christ sent in reports to their home congregations of the opportunities for mission work in other states and foreign countries. Responding to these pleas, minister Olan L. Hicks of Dallas began publishing the weekly *Christian Chronicle* (Dallas) in June, 1943, for the purpose of arousing missionary interest and zeal among the churches. Pleas for preachers in "destitute" communities in Texas, elsewhere in the United States, and in foreign countries were given banner headlines. Such articles as "Arley Moore Plans

---

[37]*The Christian News Service* (Dallas), August 21, 1944.
[38]*Firm Foundation*, April 2, 1940.

to Preach in Seward, Alaska" and "Natick, Mass. Workers Seek Building to House Work in Pivotal Position," kept churches thoroughly informed of mission work. Within six months the weekly circulation of the new paper had reached two thousand.[39] It continued to grow after Hicks moved to Abilene in 1944, and currently it is the most effective missionary medium among Texas churches of Christ.

The radio has been another effective publicity medium. The first radio sermon broadcast by a church of Christ in Texas was over station WRR on March 7, 1926, by the Pearl and Bryan church in Dallas. Over two hundred cards and letters of appreciation were received from listeners in ten states and Canada. Heartened by the response, the church contracted with WRR for the first Sunday of each month and with WFAA for all fifth Sundays. Programs over both stations were broadcast from 8:00 to 9:30 P.M. Minister James Jackson declared that radio broadcasting was the "most effective missionary work which the church has ever done."[40] In 1939, the Denver Heights church in San Antonio broadcast on station WOAI which, according to published statistics, reached every state in the Union.[41] In the same year, evangelist Eugene S. Smith of Dallas spoke daily for twenty weeks over XERA, Del Rio. At the end of the period, he reported that as a result of his talks twenty had been baptized, one congregation started, and that forty thousand tracts had been sent upon request to listeners in forty states.[42] Stimulated by the success of these pioneer

---
[39] *Christian Chronicle*, February 2, 1944.
[40] *Firm Foundation*, March 30, 1926.
[41] *Ibid.*, April 4, 1949.
[42] *Ibid.*, October 24, 1939.

broadcasting efforts, ministers of churches of Christ were preaching about two hundred sermons per week over an estimated one hundred radio stations in Texas at the middle of the century.

New educational systems and methods likewise were employed to facilitate church growth. In the forefront of this movement were members connected with public and private education. Aware that better qualfied teachers were imperative to improve the efficiency of Biblical instruction, the Walnut Street church in Sherman in 1933 began a teacher training class that met once a week using the theme, "The Church and Her Ideal Educational Situation." Instructor R. L. Speer, an elder and high school principal, declared that its purpose was to "increase the efficiency of the church as a worshiping and serving institution."[43] Two years later the Sears and Summitt church in Dallas sponsored a "Teacher Training School" with Professors James F. Cox and G. C. Morlan of Abilene Christian College as instructors.[44] In a strong effort to bolster its educational program, the Central church in Houston conducted in successive weeks a Visual Aids Workshop, a Vacation Bible School, and a Vacation Bible Music School.[45]

A few churches in cooperation with the public schools educated their youth. Minister John Dunn of Waxahachie reported in 1922 that on the first hour of every Friday, students with parental permission were attending the church of their choice for Bible study. Six graded classes at the church of Christ were studying the Life of Christ. High school students who suc-

---

[43]*Ibid.*, November .14, 1933.
[44]*Ibid.*, June 11, 1935.
[45]*Central Church of Christ Yearbook*, 1954.

cessfully completed the four-year course received one unit of credit.[46] Five years later at Dallas thirty churches, including four churches of Christ, under the supervision of the Board of Education, conducted a similar program each Sunday morning. Students were required to attend eighty forty-five-minute class sessions and submit eighty lesson preparations to obtain high school credit for the course. When the first course had been completed, the nine students at the Pearl and Bryan Church of Christ had the highest average in the city with a score just over 90.[47] At Quanah in 1940, minister Earl Craig directed a released-time Bible study class for one-half unit of high school credit.[48]

The Bible Chair is an important church medium reaching youth in state colleges. It is an arrangement whereby a church selects a qualified instructor to teach for credit Bible courses approved by the college administration. Bible Chair work is usually conducted in a Student Center building adjacent to the college campus. In 1911, minister G. H. P. Showalter reported that only 12 of the 153 members of the church of Christ enrolled in the University of Texas were attending regularly the worship services of the Austin congregation. He urged, therefore, that a Bible Chair be established as an effective means of "reaching a larger number of college students."[49] Under Showalter's able leadership, the congregation in May, 1918, erected a new building at Nineteenth and University Avenue, and at the beginning of the fall semester established a Bible Chair in the church basement.

---
[46]*Firm Foundation*, April 11, 1922.
[47]*Ibid.*, August 14, 1928.
[48]*Ibid.*, October 22, 1940.
[49]*Ibid.*, January 17, 1911.

Minister T. W. Phillips of Fort Worth promised to give one hundred dollars annually to maintain the Bible Chair in Austin and called upon his fellow churchmen in Texas to contribute liberally.[50] Courses for college credit were offered in Old Testament, New Testament, and Evidences of Christianity. Instructor C. H. Roberson, a former teacher at Abilene Christian College, reported in 1926 that 316 had been enrolled during the preceding eight years, and that over twenty thousand pieces of literature had been distributed.[51] Although enrollment in the Bible Chair had been relatively good, inadequate finances forced it to close in 1928.

After World War II, churches of Christ established several Bible Chairs in Texas. Many church leaders recognized that colleges, crowded by an ever-increasing number of students, provided an excellent field for the religious training of youth. In 1947 the Broadway church in Lubbock rented a house at 2411 Main, one-half block off the campus of Texas Technological College, and opened a Bible Chair with Carl Spain as instructor. One hundred ten students, a rather surprising number, enrolled in the first year. Two years later the church purchased a building at 2406 Broadway and enlarged its facilities.[52] At College Station in 1949, minister James Fowler began teaching two Bible courses each semester for college credit in the church of Christ building adjacent to Texas Agricultural and Mechanical College. In the same year, the church of Christ in Canyon established a Bible Chair in a house across from West Texas State College.[53] Recently,

---
[50]*Ibid.*, September 10, 1918.
[51]*Ibid.*, November 5, 1926.
[52]*Ibid.*, June 7, 1955.
[53]*Ibid.*

churches of Christ have erected several Student Center buildings adjacent to state colleges indicating their Bible Chair efforts may expand in the future.

Abilene Christian College is the pride and joy of Texas churches of Christ. It is the only senior college in the Lone Star state owned and operated by members of the church of Christ. Hundreds of its graduates serve as ministers, elders, deacons and Sunday School teachers in congregations. A goodly number are public school teachers. In 1905 several members of the Abilene Church of Christ, led by elder Albert McDonald, began an active campaign to establish a "Christian college" in the bustling little West Texas town of five thousand inhabitants. A board of trustees was appointed, and shortly afterward selected an "oldstyle mansion located on a five-acre tract at the west edge of town as an "ideal site" for the school. Property owner W. H. Childers stipulated an initial purchase price in excess of that which the board was willing to pay, but reduced the price when the board promised to name the school in his honor.[54] On September 11, 1906, Childers Classical Institute, a combination high school and junior college, opened with twenty-five students. President A. B. Barret declared that the school was designed to "teach Bible and build character."[55] During the next few years, enrollment increased slowly but only a few additional facilities were added because of the lack of funds. In 1913, G. H. P. Showalter, past president of Lockney Christian College, asserted that the Roman Catholics had one thousand and the Baptists one hundred times more money invested in schools in Texas than the churches of

---

[54] Morris and Leach, *Like Stars Shining*, pp. 15-18.
[55] *Ibid.*

Christ, and urged members to give liberally to the school at Abilene.[56] Apparently the plea was effective, for within six years annual contributions were averaging in excess of $30,000.[57] In 1919 the board of trustees designated the school as a senior college, and the following year changed the name to Abilene Christian College after local business men had made donations to the school.[58] During the next decade the enrollment increased rapidly, and in 1929 the school moved to a larger campus at the northeast edge of the city.[59] The depression, however, curtailed the growth for a decade.

Abilene Christian College has experienced its greatest development since 1945. Within three years the enrollment had reached an all-time high of 1,688, and a modern science building and fireproof girls' dormitory had been erected. By 1950 the endowment funds, swollen by large gifts from wealthy alumni and church members, reached one million dollars.[60] Its outstanding graduate, Don H. Morris, president of the college since 1939, is currently (1959) directing a large expansion program.

Closely connected with the college was its annual lectureship. The idea evidently had its inception during a series of lectures delivered by Dr. George A. Klingman, a prominent minister of the church of Christ, in January, 1907. However, it was not until 1918 that it was formally designated Bible Lecture Week.[61] Twenty years later, interested people from

---

[56] *Firm Foundation*, December 9, 1913.
[57] *Ibid.*, July 6, 1920.
[58] Morris and Leach, *Like Stars Shining*, pp. 101-105.
[59] *Ibid.*, p. 149.
[60] *Ibid.*, pp. 213-215.
[61] *Ibid.*, pp. 23-24.

ninety-eight Texas communities and twelve other states were among 1,450 who attended one lecture in Sewell auditorium.[62] By 1950, visitors from many states and several foreign countries swelled attendance to over two thousand and made the lectureship the largest annual gathering of educators, preachers, elders and members of the churches of Christ in the United States.

WORK AMONG NEGROES AND MEXICANS

Meanwhile, efforts to proclaim the gospel to Negroes were conducted on a small scale. Only a few white congregations were inclined to support the work. At Houston in 1926, evangelist E. Webster reported that eight zealous colored members of the church of Christ had tried unsuccessfully to purchase a lot on installments.[63] Four years later, Negro evangelist R. N. Hogan held a revival with eighty-six additions, but the majority did not remain faithful.[64] Realizing that the permanency of the Negro work depended upon strong outside support, the white Houston Heights church rallied to the aid of the faithful remnant. It first obtained Marshall Keeble of Nashville, a nationally renowned colored church of Christ evangelist, to conduct a meeting in 1932. After Keeble baptized thirty-two and organized a church, the Heights congregation purchased a building and secured a local minister for their colored brethren. Keeble lauded the members of the church for their support. The major weakness in the missionary program among members of his own race was that the sponsoring white church was withdrawing its support too soon. He must have

---

[62] *Firm Foundation*, March 19, 1935.
[63] *Ibid.*, May 18, 1926.
[64] *The Christian Echo* (Louisville), June 20, 1930.

argued convincingly, for when the Houston Negro congregation outgrew its building, the Heights congregation purchased another for it.[65] At Corsicana the white congregation, encouraged by minister J. L. Hines, established a Negro church in 1927. Seven years later, a strong and active congregation of three hundred was engaged in proclaiming the gospel to the colored people of the community.[66]

The Walnut Street church in Sherman followed the example in Houston. In 1937, minister J. S. Winston began laboring with a small group of Negroes and two years later organized a strong congregation of ninety. The white brethren then erected a neat building for the colored church and supervised an expanded program of work. Walnut Street minister A. R. Holton assisted Winston in instructing six Negroes who wished to become preachers. Mrs. Holton taught a Negro ladies Bible class once each week.[67]

It is not unusual for Negro members of the church of Christ to manifest unusual zeal. Fifty members of the church at Midway, Madison County, chartered two busses and attended for ten consecutive nights a colored revival at Bryan, fifty miles away. Greatly impressed, white minister J. L. Pummill of Bryan declared that if every white congregation were as earnest as these colored members, the church of Christ would "take the world for the Lord."[68] But whether their efforts were stimulated by sincere devoutness or, as is quite likely, by the normal Negro social inclinations is not certain.

The emotional instability of the Negro made mis-

---

[65] *Firm Foundation*, April 25, 1939.
[66] *Ibid.*, December 4, 1934.
[67] *Ibid.*, September 12, 1939.
[68] *Ibid.*, April 25, 1939.

sionary work among them uncertain. Since most of the colored were uneducated, persuasive preachers delivering emotional sermons often effected quick changes in Negro allegiance. At the conclusion of evangelist R. N. Hogan's third sermon during a revival in the Christian Church at Longview in 1936, seventy Negro members renounced the use of instrumental music and joined the church of Christ. The next evening, Hogan joyfully reported that twenty-five more promised to lay aside the "evil" practice.[69] Other church of Christ ministers, however, were not as excited about the results of the revival as Hogan, for they recalled similar experiences having previously happened in several denominations and predicted that most of the group would be "converts" again when a Christian church preacher held a revival.

Misbehavior, seemingly characteristic of the uneducated Negro, greatly hampered the permanency of colored congregations. A San Antonio preacher, who was accused of immorality, reportedly was not respected by those of his own race. Negro editor W. P. Bowser of the *Christian Echo* (Louisville) warned churches to beware of a preacher from Palestine, Texas, who beat his wife and ran away.[70] When minister Luke Miller arrived at Orange in 1939, he found several members of the church were serving jail sentences for theft, gambling and drunkenness.[71]

The work among the Negroes grew slowly in the first half of the twentieth century. The *Christian Echo,* a Negro paper owned by members of the church of Christ, reported in 1927 that there were twenty-six

---
[69]*Ibid.,* April 4, 1936.
[70]*The Christian Echo,* November 20, 1931.
[71]*Firm Foundation,* April 25, 1939.

Negro congregations with a total membership of 1165, most of whom were without a regular minister.[72] Twenty years later, Olan L. Hicks, editor of the *Christian Chronicle,* listed only fifty-four churches in the state.[73] There was one hopeful development, however, for on November 21, 1949, white and Negro members of the church of Christ from eleven states gathered in Fort Worth, and three days later purchased the $500,000 plant of the Texas Military College, Terrell, Texas, for $60,000. The name was changed to Southern Bible Institute, a board of trustees selected, and Otto Foster of Cleburne was named president of the first junior college for Negroes in the United States established by churches of Christ.[74] The college opened the following year with thirty-two students but, unfortunately, it has been faced with continual financial problems. Its success or failure apparently will in a large measure determine the future growth of the colored work in Texas.

Even less missionary work has been attempted among the Mexicans. Many churches of Christ were apathetic to this type of work because of the widespread feeling among members that most Mexicans, traditionally of the Roman Catholic faith, presented a difficult and unfruitful mission field. Nevertheless, a few dedicated men reaped a small harvest. When evangelist E. N. Glenn arrived in El Paso in 1911, he found a Brother Martinez, a Mexican church of Christ minister, peddling fruit because of a lack of support. Martinez faithfully conducted a study group in his home at night. Glenn attended one meeting and baptized

---

[72] *The Christian Echo,* January 20, 1927.
[73] *1946-1947 Yearbook of the Churches of Christ,* pp. 133-165.
[74] *The Christian Echo,* December 20, 1949.

three. Unable to obtain financial assistance for Martinez from the El Paso churches of Christ, Glenn departed, commending Martinez and the little band to God and his grace. Seven years later, Glenn returned and found Martinez working on a ranch nearby. Although Glenn made a new plea for funds, it again went unheeded.[75] A decade later, John F. Wolfe, a Spanish-speaking preacher, arrived in El Paso and within a few years had successfully established a small mission.[76]

Greater progress was forthcoming in San Antonio. On September 6, 1933, minister Jesse G. Gill and wife arrived to labor with six faithful members. Gill initiated a house-to-house visitation program, and within four years had baptized over one hundred Mexicans. Inspired by the success and devotion of Gill, five white San Antonio churches of Christ purchased a lot and erected a building.[77] By 1947, the two hundred member congregation was the largest of the fourteen Mexican churches of Christ in Texas.[78] Wolfe and other Spanish-speaking preachers believe the future of the work is dependent upon training of Mexican ministers to labor among their own people.

A Jewish Mission

A novel feature of mission work was launched among the Jews by S. D. Eckstein, Sr. Born in 1893 in Sassmach, Latvia, Eckstein was reared as an Orthodox Jew and received training in a rabbinical school.

---

[75] *Firm Foundation*, December 14, 1920.
[76] H. L. Schug, "A Brief History of the Spanish Speaking Churches of Christ in the U. S. A.," *Cherokee Courier* (Cherokee, Texas, January, 1957), p. 3.
[77] *Firm Foundation*, October 19, 1937.
[78] *1946-1947 Yearbook of the Churches of Christ*, pp. 133-165.

CHURCHES OF CHRIST BECOME A MAJOR RELIGIOUS BODY 317

Because of ill health, he left the school and came to America in 1914. After his conversion to Christ in 1920 in Denver, Colorado, Eckstein began preaching among his kinsmen. Two years later he was invited to Dallas, and opened a Jewish mission at 111 South Harwood with the assistance of the Garrett Avenue church and Dr. E. V. Wood.[79]

The Jewish mission remained open for twelve years. Worship services in Yiddish were conducted on Sunday afternoon. During the week, Eckstein instructed Jews who came into the mission, and frequently visited them in their places of business. His method of teaching was first to prove that the Old Testament was a revelation from God rather than traditional Jewish literature. Then he showed how the Messianic prophecies in the Old Testament were fulfilled by Christ as recorded in the New Testament. Since many Jews had never seen a New Testament, it was a difficult task, but some were persuaded and baptized. Ministers G. C. Brewer and John Dunn of Dallas and Professors R. C. Bell, Charles Brewer and George Klingman of Abilene Christian College supplemented Eckstein's teaching by speaking on the Christian view of Christ as the fulfillment of Old Testament Jewish prophecies. Of a reported seventeen thousand Jews in Dallas, eleven was the largest number to attend a single mission service. At the end of four years Eckstein had baptized only eleven Jews into Christ, but he was still optimistic for he predicted that Dallas would become the center of a "great missionary enterprise in Israel's behalf."[80] In support of his contention, he printed a Hebrew tract entitled *Jesus Christ, Israel's Messiah,*

---
[79]Stephen D. Eckstein, Sr. (Kansas City) to his son Stephen Eckstein, interview, June 2, 1955.
[80]*Firm Foundation*, February 9, 1925.

and distributed hundreds of copies in twenty-two states, but without any response from Jews.[81] Although twenty-four Jews had been baptized by 1934, the mission closed because of inadequate finances and opposition of a major segment of the sponsoring churches. Eckstein then moved to Kansas City, Missouri, where he began a similar work.[82]

Foreign Missions

Little foreign mission work was attempted before 1945. Apparently this was because most members were isolated from world affairs and were too concerned with trying to make a living. The few missionaries who went abroad were given little financial support. The Pearl and Bryan church in Dallas in August, 1908, sent C. C. Klingman and family to Tokyo, Japan. Klingman estimated that it would require ten years of hard work before a successful mission could be established.[83] Although a few congregations contributed small sums to supplement the finances of the Pearl and Bryan church, insufficient funds eventually caused Klingman to despair and return home. J. M. McCaleb of Louisville, a successful church of Christ missionary in Japan since 1898, who traveled extensively in Texas while on furlough in 1920, pleaded for each of the estimated 150,000 members of the church in the Lone Star state to contribute one dollar to the Japanese work. His plea was virtually unheeded.[84]

A few congregations made regular contributions to

---

[81]*Ibid.*, February 24, 1926.
[82]Stephen D. Eckstein Sr. (Kansas City) to his son Stephen Eckstein, interview, June 2, 1955.
[83]L. S. White, "Brother Klingman and His Work in Japan," *Gospel Guide*, IV (October, 1908), pp. 13-14.
[84]*Firm Foundation*, June 30, 1920.

CHURCHES OF CHRIST BECOME A MAJOR RELIGIOUS BODY 319

mission work. The Thorp Spring church in 1913 began donating annually one hundred dollars for use in India and sixty for Japan.[85] In cooperation with the Thorp Spring church, churches in Dallas, Cleburne and Albany sent small monthly offerings to the same countries.[86] In 1923 the Brownwood church agreed to support Miss Lillie Cypert, a long-time church of Christ missionary, in founding a girls' school in Japan.[87] Miss Cypert, who had been in Japan for many years, opened her school with contributions from Brownwood. The funds, however, shortly stopped coming. Miss Cypert continued to operate her school until 1931 when, deep in debt and broken in spirit, she was forced to close it.

After World War II, the churches of Christ adopted a missionary program that soon placed them in the forefront in this particular activity. Many members who had served in the armed forces returned home feeling that foreign missions were desirable and imperative. They informed their church brethren of the need to fulfill Christ's commission to "Go into all the world and preach the gospel to every creature." In June, 1946, the Broadway church in Lubbock sent minister Otis Gatewood of Salt Lake City and Paul Sherrod, an elder, to Europe on a two-month fact-finding tour. When they returned, a four-day lectureship was held at the Broadway church in August when Gatewood and Sherrod enthusiastically informed the two hundred visitors that Europe was a ripe field ready for harvest.[88] The following year, Gatewood established in Frankfurt, Germany, what was evidently the

---

[85]*Ibid.*, March 31, 1914.
[86]*Ibid.*, June 23, 1914.
[87]*Ibid.*, September 25, 1923.
[88]Broadway Church of Christ, *Lubbock Lectures on Mission Work* (Lubbock, 1946), p. 5.

first church of Christ on the European continent in the twentieth century. From funds donated primarily by the Broadway church, the Frankfurt congregation in 1950 erected across from the University of Frankfurt a beautiful auditorium that had a seating capacity of 800.[89] Twenty-four other missionaries, financed primary by Texas congregations, joined Gatewood in Germany. The most recent reports claim that the missionaries have organized twenty churches in Germany.[90]

Missionary activity in Italy has been more difficult. In March, 1948, the Crescent Hill church in Brownfield sponsored a lectureship on behalf of a proposed Italian mission. Over one thousand visitors from six states and thirty-five preachers attended,[91] and $10,000 for the Italian mission fund was obtained in two months.[92] In November the Brownfield church purchased property at Frascati, twelve miles from Rome, and in January, 1949, missionaries Cline Paden and William Hatcher arrived at the mission post. Paden and Hatcher were soon in trouble with the government. They opened a boys' orphan home and school in connection with the church. Within a few months, the government threatened to close both the church and school. Immediately, church leaders in Brownfield appealed to Congress, charging that the Roman Catholic Church was responsible for the threats. Although other missionaries entered Italy, continued friction resulted in numerous court actions and threats to all missionaries. Despite the opposition of the government, the missionaries continued their efforts. Sev-

---
[89]*Story of a Church.*
[90]*Christian Chronicle*, July 23, 1955.
[91]*Firm Foundation*, April 6, 1948.
[92]*Christian Chronicle*, November 10, 1948.

eral churches have been organized and over one hundred Italians baptized. The resulting publicity benefited the Italian mission, as contributions increased to over three thousand dollars a month. Although the outcome is still uncertain, additional progress has been realized.[93]

BENEVOLENT WORK

Benevolent work was limited to the founding of two orphan homes and one home for the aged prior to 1950. In December, 1923, Mr. and Mrs. W. F. Boles of Greenville, both of whom had been reared as orphans, donated 436 acres near Quinlan, Hunt County, as a site for an orphan home. The Pearl and Bryan church in Dallas was designated as trustee of the property.[94] In response to pleas for money, churches in Texas contributed over seven thousand dollars in the next three months. As a result, ground was broken on March 31 following for the first unit of Boles Orphan Home,[95] and by December a ten thousand dollar plant had been erected and the first orphans admitted. Within the next twenty-five years, the facilities of the home were expanded to care for one hundred orphans. Churches of Christ in many states now donate liberally to the home each month. Near San Benito, the Sunny Glenn Home began in a two-story residence in 1936 with six children. Because of inadequate facilities, the home soon was moved to near San Juan, but was poorly financed. In 1945 an eighty-acre tract near San Benito was obtained and construction began on a modern plant, but soon ceased because of a lack of funds. Construction was resumed in 1948, and within

---

[93]*Ibid.*, February 22, 1949.
[94]*Firm Foundation*, January 22, 1924.
[95]Flavil L. Colley, "Notes," *Christian Messenger* (Dallas), I (October, 1924), pp. 1-3.

eight years available facilities were able to accommodate 112 children. Texas churches of Christ provide most of the financial support.[96] At Gunter, a home for the aged was established on the campus of the defunct Gunter Bible College in February, 1947. Three years later, five elderly men and fifteen aged ladies resided comfortably in five newly constructed fireproof cottages. Plans were formulated for further expansion and churches were encouraged to make liberal contributions.[97]

Premillennialism and Cooperation

Although churches of Christ in Texas experienced considerable growth during the first half of the twentieth century, controversy arose over two doctrinal issues—"premillennialism" and "cooperation"—resulting in two minor schisms. The first issue was in regard to the meaning of the twentieth chapter of Revelation. A minority of preachers and members interpreted the teaching as literal—Christ would reign one thousand years upon the earth at his second coming. A number of fundamentalist bodies, including many Baptists, also promulgated this doctrine. A majority of preachers and members in churches of Christ contended the meaning was spiritual—Christ had been reigning in heaven since his ascension (Acts 1:6-11). The leading advocate of the literal view was R. H. Boll, a preacher in Louisville, Kentucky, and editor of the *Word and Work* (1906-   ). During the 1920's and early 1930's, Boll conducted a number of revivals in Texas and gained a small following. As a result, some contro-

---

[96]*Christian Chronicle*, December 2, 1960 (This was a special issue concerning all children's homes supervised and supported by churches of Christ in the United States).
[97]*Firm Foundation*, October 10, 1950.

versy over the millennium arose, and evidently reached a climax in 1934. On September 6, 7 and 8, a debate was held in the First Baptist Church in Fort Worth in which Dr. J. Frank Norris, renowned Baptist preacher, affirmed the literal interpretation and minister Foy E. Wallace Jr. of the church of Christ denied. During the debate, a few ministers of churches of Christ appeared on the platform with Norris and championed his remarks.[98] Shortly afterward, many preachers wrote articles in the *Foundation* and *Advocate*, condemning "premillennialism" and all who propagated it. Minister J. B. Nelson of Dallas rejoiced that the premillennialists were "coming out in the open where they could be exposed."[99] Evangelist C. M. Stubblefield commended G. H. P. Showalter, editor of the *Firm Foundation*, for standing "four-square against premillennialism," and recommended that all who were "tinctured with premillennialism" should subscribe to the paper in order to be saved from the "destructive error."[100] Within a year about a dozen churches in Texas, primarily in the Dallas-Fort Worth area, were designated as "unsound" from the pulpit, over the radio and in "loyal" religious periodicals. As a result, the majority of churches in Texas, although not necessarily making any formal declaration, severed fellowship with the premillennial congregations. Unfortunately, the issue has not been resolved at present.

The second issue was over the cooperation of churches in financing and directing mission and benevolent work. As more missionaries were sent to foreign countries after World War II, the home or "sponsoring" churches solicited financial assistance from

---
[98] *Ibid.*, November 27, 1934.
[99] *Ibid.*
[100] *Ibid.*

other churches to support the ever-expanding programs. In like manner, sponsoring congregations of homes for orphans and the aged appealed to sister congregations for funds to operate and expand their benevolent work. On the whole, most editors, church leaders and members supported these efforts. However, a few preachers and elders questioned the "scripturalness" of both the institutions and methods of financing the enterprises. The dissent reached a crucial point when Fanning Yater Tant as editor and Foy E. Wallace, Jr., as co-editor, began publishing again the defunct *Gospel Guardian* in 1949 at Lufkin, Texas. In the initial issue, Tant declared the policy of the paper was to guard the gospel from error.

> . . . we shall be vigilant and careful in our "guarding" against what many may consider as small and insignificant departures from the truth. And once an error, or tendency toward error, is detected, we shall oppose it with all the strength we can muster. The best defense against error always is to wage an all-out offensive against it before it gains a foot-hold. Let those who will call this "heresy-hunting"; we call it guarding the gospel of Christ.[101]

In another article, Wallace contended that certain issues "constitute a threat to the future of New Testament Christianity just as clear cut as premillennialism did two decades ago and as digression did two generations ago. These issues shall be met. The *Gospel Guardian*, like her predecessors in this valiant fight for the faith, is set for the 'defense of the church against all errors and innovations'."[102] Issues listed

---
[101] Fanning Yater Tant, "Concerning Our Policy," *Gospel Guardian*, I (May 5, 1949), pp. 2-5.
[102] Foy E. Wallace Jr., "The Issues Before Us," *Gospel Guardian*, I (May 5, 1949), p. 3.

were the so-called subordination of the church to such human institutions as an orphan home or college, one eldership of a church taking over the work of many churches, and the programs for raising money to support missionaries and orphanages. Wallace concluded that "the fight against societies, organizations, centralization of authority, and all that belongs to digression in general, so valiantly made in Tennessee and Texas fifty and sixty years ago, shall be fought all over again."[103]

Unfortunately, considerable controversy over cooperation soon evolved. Although editor Showalter of the *Firm Foundation* initially commended Tant and Wallace on their endeavor,[104] he and many other preachers soon opposed the teaching promulgated in the *Guardian*. Within a year the issues were hotly contested in churches, colleges supervised by members of the churches of Christ, and religious periodicals. Numerous oral and written debates occurred throughout the Lone Star state. The *Firm Foundation* and *Gospel Advocate*, which consistently supported the cooperative efforts of the churches, were bitterly attacked in the columns of the *Guardian*. As a result, preachers and elders with strong convictions on both sides aligned themselves with the papers of their persuasion and often effected division within churches. At present, about 150 churches in Texas are in sympathy with views expounded in the *Guardian* and for practical purposes are no longer in fellowship with the remaining approximately 2450 churches of Christ in the state. Although the intensity of controversy

---
[103]*Ibid.*
[104]*Firm Foundation*, May 17, 1949.

has abated somewhat, no reconciliation is evidently possible in the near future.

COMPARATIVE STATISTICS

As the church of Christ liberalized its program, it became one of the major religious bodies in Texas. United States Religious Census figures show that it outgrew the Disciples of Christ (Christian) during the first part of the twentieth century. From 1906 to 1926, the membership of Texas churches of Christ almost tripled while that of the Disciples of Christ doubled. Likewise, the number of churches of Christ doubled but those of the Disciples of Christ decreased slightly. In 1926, the average membership of churches of Christ was about 80 compared to 160 for Disciples of Christ.[105] These figures seem to indicate that the churches of Christ were more active in rural areas while the Disciples of Christ tended to restrict their efforts primarily to the larger towns.

Compared to major Protestant denominations in Texas, churches of Christ ranked third according to United States Census reports in 1926. Only the Baptist and Methodist among Protestant churches had a larger membership or more churches.[106]

[105]

	Churches of Christ		Disciples of Christ (Christian)	
Year	Churches	Membership	Churches	Membership
1906	627	34,006	502	39,550
1916	1240	71,542	544	54,836
1926	1280	98,909	489	77,150

[106]

	Membership	Churches
Baptist (Southern)	465,274	3,038
Methodist Episcopal Church (South)	380,453	2,569
Churches of Christ	98,909	1,286
Disciples of Christ (Christian)	77,150	489
Presbyterian (USA)	33,318	310

CHURCHES OF CHRIST BECOME A MAJOR RELIGIOUS BODY

It is difficult to determine church growth after 1926. Because of the lack of cooperation by ministers in all denominations, the United States Religious Census of 1936 was incomplete. According to it, all denominations showed sharp declines from 1926, an obvious inaccuracy. Minister Leslie Thomas of Corsicana, census agent for churches of Christ in Texas, reported that the response from ministers was very unsatisfactory. In an effort to obtain better cooperation, Thomas cited the Biblical injunction that Christians should obey the civil government.[107] The delinquent ministers either failed to see his appeal or else did not take that part of the scripture seriously. As a result, the government ceased taking a religious census after 1936.[108]

Independent efforts to compile statistics of churches of Christ likewise were incomplete and conflicting. Preachers and editors, without any channel for contacting all churches, frequently made inaccurate estimates. In 1932, minister E. N. Glenn of Los Angeles compiled a church directory, admittedly inaccurate, of churches of Christ in the United States and Canada. In it, Texas was listed as having 1,351 churches,[109] apparently a little low. Editor Olan Hicks of the *Christian Chronicle* compiled a 1946-1947 yearbook for churches of Christ. Admitting that the work contained duplications and omissions, Hicks listed Texas as having 2,195 churches of Christ out of an estimated total of ten thousand in the United States.[110] In 1949 the *Firm Foundation* published a church directory

---

[107] Romans 13:1, 2.
[108] *Firm Foundation*, June 3, 1941.
[109] E. N. Glenn (comp.), *Church Directory of Churches of Christ in USA and Canada* (Cincinnati, 1932), n.p.
[110] *1946-1947 Yearbook of Churches of Christ*, pp. 133-165.

which listed only 1,865 churches of Christ in the Lone Star state.[111] Apparently the *Foundation* listing was not all-inclusive, for in addition to omitting a number of churches named in Hicks' directory, it failed to list a great many that had been organized after Hicks' directory was published.[112] Although the correct count possibly may have been still less than Hicks' estimated 2,195, it obviously was more than the *Foundation's* 1,865 estimate and could well have exceeded the Hicks figure.

Reliable figures for religious bodies in Texas at the middle of the twentieth century are not available. Estimates indicate that the Baptists had 2,000,000 members, the Methodists 1,500,000 and the churches of Christ 450,000. Even without accurate data to use in evaluating their past, churches of Christ, the third largest Protestant body in Texas at the mid-point of the twentieth century, could look back over a century and a quarter of growth and development with some satisfaction.

SUMMARY

The church of Christ in the United States originated in the upper reaches of the Ohio valley at the beginning of the nineteenth century in conjunction with the tide of frontiersmen, moving ever westward to possess the seemingly limitless expanse of virgin land. It evolved from the cooperative labors of reform preachers Barton Stone, Alexander Campbell and Walter Scott, who united on the precept that the Bible alone is authoritative in determining all religious practices and beliefs. A

---

[111] G. H. P. Showalter and Leslie G. Thomas (comps.), *Church Directory and List of Preachers of Churches of Christ 1949* (Austin, 1949), pp. 179-202.

[112] Weekly reports appearing in the *Chronicle* and *Foundation* provide abundant evidence of this.

few of its members were among the doughty pioneers who crossed the Mississippi and entered Spanish Texas, and in 1836 wrested this vast domain from Mexican jurisdiction. During the republic era, a dozen of its homespun preachers "broke the bread of life" to a few hundred faithful disciples, and energetically proclaimed their gospel to the immigrants who entered the "promised land." Augmented by a goodly number of Tennessee disciples who arrived in the early statehood period, churches of Christ increased rapidly and numbered about six thousand members at the outbreak of the Civil War.

Churches of Christ entered a new phase of development in the post-war period. Churches in the North, situated amid a rapidly expanding industrial economy, became more progressive in the practice of their religion. An increasing number of ministers declared that the Bible contained a group of broad principles rather than a body of strict laws. Many churches introduced instrumental music into the worship services and sent official delegates to state and national missionary society conventions. Southern churches, on the other hand, generally remained conservative in their thinking. The horrible aftermath caused most Southerners to cling to traditional beliefs and practices. The *Gospel Advocate,* the spokesman for the churches of Christ in the South and widely read in Texas, urged all disciples to return to the "old landmarks." As a result of the conflicting attitudes held by the "progressives" and "conservatives," heated controversy between the two factions terminated in irreconcilable and formal division in 1906. Simultaneously, tireless itinerant evangelists were preaching the word in all sections of the Lone Star state, particularly in the towns and communities on the western plains.

After separating from the progressive Disciples of Christ (Christian) group, Texas churches of Christ experienced great growth and development. Led by aggressive and more liberally inclined West Texas brethren, the churches of Christ in Texas have far outstripped sister churches east of the Mississippi. Recently extensive building, educational and missionary programs have been launched and new methods in teaching employed without creating new schisms, since all the autonomous congregations have adhered to the fundamental doctrines—the weekly observance of the Lord's Supper, the preaching of the "plan" (faith, repentance, and baptism), and congregational singing without the aid of instrumental music.

At the halfway point of the twentieth century, Texas has become the center of churches of Christ. Approximately thirty-five per cent of the total membership and twenty-five per cent of all congregations are within its borders. Within shortly more than a century, the church of Christ has grown from very humble beginnings to third place among Protestant churches in Texas. If the current trend continues, it is possible that, within the foreseeable future, a majority of its members will reside in the Lone Star state.

BIBLIOGRAPHY

Manuscripts, Official Documents, Correspondence and Interviews

Austin, C. W. (Truth or Consequences, New Mexico), letter to Stephen Eckstein, August 3, 1961.

Blanchard, Kate Priestly. "History of La Iglesia de Cristo in El Paso and Juarez. Manuscript in possession of its author, El Paso, 1951. (typed)

──────. "History of the Montana Street Church of Christ, El Paso, Texas." Manuscript in possession of its author, El Paso, 1951. (typed)

Castleman, J. L. (Pella, Texas), card to Amy Lemley, May 12, 1880.

Coffman, Burton. "Central Church of Christ." Undated manuscript, Central Church of Christ, Houston, Texas. (typed)

Dabney, T. H. (Granbury, Texas), interview, June 14, 1953.

Eckstein, Stephen D., Sr. (Kansas City, Missouri), interview, June 2, 1955.

"First One Hundred Years of the Central Christian Church of Austin, Texas 1847-1947." Undated manuscript, Texas Christian University, Fort Worth, Texas. (typed)

Foster, Otto. "Dedication Remarks at the Opening of the Central Church of Christ, Cleburne, Texas, October 2, 1955." Manuscript in possession of its author, Washington, D. C. (typed)

Green, Mary (Lubbock, Texas), interview, December 14, 1950.

Hays, Ida Moore. "History of the Central Christian Church, Waco, Texas." Unpublished manuscript, Texas Christian University, Fort Worth, Texas, 1945. (typed)

Higgins, A. S. (Texline, Texas), letter to Stephen Eckstein, September 4, 1956.

Hufstedler, Virginia. "A Study of the Activities of the Church of Christ in Lubbock County from 1890 to 1905." Unpublished Master's thesis, Texas Technological College, Lubbock, Texas, 1933. (typed)

Pringle, Fannie. "History of Christian Church of Marlin, Texas." Unpublished manuscript, Texas Christian University, Fort Worth, 1951. (typed)

Sanders, Liff (Lubbock), interview, December 17, 1950.

Smithson, J. M. F. (Houston), interview, August 24, 1958.

Texas. *Constitution of the Republic of Texas*, Article I, Section VI.

United States. *Constitution of the United States of America*, Amendment I.

United States Department of Commerce and Labor, Bureau of the Census. *Special Reports: Religious Bodies: 1906*, Pt. II. Washington, 1910. Pt. II, 1916. Special religious census reports were made by the United States Government in 1906, 1916, 1926 and 1936.

NEWSPAPERS AND PERIODICALS

Amarillo Sunday News and Globe, Golden Anniversary Edition (Amarillo)

Amarillo Sunday Globe-News (Amarillo)

Bonham News (Bonham)

Christian Chronicle (Abilene)

Christian Echo (Louisville)

Christian Leader

BIBLIOGRAPHY

Christian News Service (Dallas)

Dallas Morning News (Dallas)

Firm Foundation (Austin). This periodical began publication in 1884 and has continued to the present. A complete file of this religious paper is in the office of the Firm Foundation Publishing House, Austin, Texas.

Fort Worth Daily Standard (Fort Worth)

Fort Worth Register (Fort Worth)

Fort Worth Star-Telegram (Fort Worth)

Frontier Times (Bandera, Texas)

Gospel Advocate (Nashville). This periodical was published from 1855 to 1861, and from 1866 to the present. A complete file of this religious paper is in the private library of C. E. W. Dorris, Nashville, Tennessee; a partial file in the office of the Gospel Advocate Company, Nashville. David Lipscomb, editor from 1867 to 1917, quoted from many current newspapers and religious periodicals in his editorial column.

Houston Post (Houston)

Huntsville Gazette (Huntsville)

Jacksboro Gazette (Jacksboro)

Living Message (Morrilton, Arkansas)

Lubbock Avalanche Journal (Lubbock)

Sherman Democrat (Sherman)

Taylor Daily Press (Taylor)

Telegraph and Texas Register (Houston)

Texas Christian (Thorp Spring)

Tyler Courier (Tyler)

Church Directories and Pamphlets

Central Church of Christ Yearbook, 1954. Central Church of Christ, Houston, Texas, 1954. (printed)

Churches of Christ in Dallas and Dallas County. Compiled by the Sears and Summit Church of Christ, Dallas, Texas, January, 1951. (printed)

College Church of Christ Annual, 1954. College Church of Christ, Abilene, Texas. (printed)

Directory of the Commerce Street Church of Christ. Commerce Street Church of Christ, Gainesville, Texas, March, 1948. (printed)

Ft. Worth's First Religious Organization. Polytechnic Church of Christ, Fort Worth, Texas, n.d. (printed)

Glenn, E. N. (comp.), *Church Directory of Churches of Christ in USA and Canada.* F. L. Rowe, Cincinnati, 1932. (printed)

Hicks, Olan. *1946-1947 Yearbook of Churches of Christ.* Chronicle Pub. Co., Abilene, Texas, 1947. (printed)

Membership Directory of the University Avenue Church of Christ. University Avenue Church of Christ, Austin, Texas, December, 1954. (printed)

Showalter, G. H. P. and Thomas, Leslie G. (comps.), *Church Directory and List of Preachers of Churches of Christ.* Firm Foundation Publishing House, Austin, Texas, 1949. (printed)

Story of a Church. Broadway Church of Christ, Lubbock, Texas, n.d. (printed)

Wise, Melvin J. *A History of the Pearl and Bryan Church of Christ.* Pearl and Bryan Church of Christ, Dallas, Texas, n.d. (printed)

Articles

Anon. "Christian Liberty vs. Judaistic Legalism," *Christian Courier* (Dallas), IV (January 14, 1891), p. 4.

——. "Church in Washington," *Millennial Harbinger* (Bethany, Va.), October, 1859, pp. 594-597.

——. "Eastern Texas Cooperation," *Christian Magazine* (Nashville), IV (December, 1851), p. 377.

——. "Re-baptism," *Christian Courier*, III (March 11, 1891), p. 4.

——. "Subscription List," *Millennial Harbinger*, March, 1843, pp. 137-139.

B. "Texas News," *Apostolic Church* (Louisville), VI (February, 1884), p. 30.

Bagby, W. H. "Texas Tidings," *Christian Standard* (Cincinnati), XXI (February 20, 1886), p. 61.

Banton, G. W., "News," *Christian Magazine*, V (January, 1852), p. 26.

Barnes, J. M. "Re-baptism," *Christian Messenger* (Dallas), XVI (November 12, 1890), p. 1.

Blackwell, J. W. "News," *Christian Magazine*, V (August, 1852), p. 251.

Brown, R. T. "News," *Christian Evangelist* (Fort Madison, Iowa), VI (October, 1855), pp. 478-479.

Burnett, D. S. "Progress of the Present Reformation," *Christian Preacher* (January, 1836), p. 21.

Burnett, T. R. "News Reports," *Burnett's Budgett* (Dallas), IX (July 15, 1909), p. 4.

——. "Re-Baptism," *Burnett's Budgett*, IX (July 15, 1909), p. 4.

Bush, A. J. "Texas Mission Notes," *Christian Evangelist* (St. Louis), XXVII (December 4, 1890), p. 777.

Campbell, Alexander. "Foreign Observations," *Millennial Harbinger*, June, 1859, p. 332.

―――――. "Instrumental Music," *Millennial Harbinger*, October, 1851, pp. 581-582.

―――――. "Our Position to American Slavery," *Millennial Harbinger*, February, 1845, p. 51.

Campbell, T. F. "News from the Churches,'" *Millennial Harbinger*, January, 1854, p. 57.

Chatterton, Alexander. "Elder Solomon McKinney," *The Evangelist* (Fort Madison, Iowa), XI (April, 1860), p. 186.

―――――. "no title," *The Evangelist*, XII (September, 1861), p. 503.

―――――. "Shall Christians Go to War?" *The Evangelist*, XIII (June, 1861), pp. 318-319.

Clark, N. L., "Lockney," *Gospel Review* (Dallas), I (March, 1903), pp. 37-38.

Colley, Flavil L. "Notes," *Christian Messenger*, I (October, 1924), pp. 1-3.

Defee, William. "News," *Christian Review* (Nashville), IV (October, 1847), pp. 358-359.

―――――. "News from the Churches," *Millennial Harbinger*, August, 1847, p. 480 and January, 1852, p. 60.

Dickson, James. "News from the Churches," *Millennial Harbinger*, August, 1859, pp. 479-480.

Dimmitt, E. C. "Texas State Meeting," *Christian Standard*, XXII (July 23, 1887), p. 235.

D'Spain, D. L. "News," *Christian Magazine*, V (June, 1852), pp. 175-176.

East, E. H. "A Call from Texas, *Christian Review*, IV (October, 1847), pp. 357-358.

―――――. "News," *Christian Review*, III (August, 1846), p. 191.

Elliston, J. W. "News from the Churches," *Millennial Harbinger*, June, 1852, p. 254.

Ezzell, S. R. "Texas News," *Apostolic Church*, VI (January, 1884), p. 32.

Fanning, Tolbert. "Communications from Texas," *Christian Review*, III (August, 1846), p. 191.

Gates, George. "News from the Churches," *Millennial Harbinger*, May, 1842, p. 238.

George, A. M. "Which Motive Fear or Love?" *The Gospel Missionary* (Corpus Christi), X (July 22, 1908), pp. 1-4.

Gibbs, W. L. "Come Over in the Spirit and Help Us," *Octographic Review* (Indianapolis), XXXIV (August 27, 1891), p. 2.

Giles, S. B. "News from the Churches," *Millennial Harbinger*, March, 1855, pp. 178-179, and March, 1857, pp. 176-177.

Golightly, Baxter. "My Bow," *Christian Courier*, IV (May 11, 1891), p. 220.

Gugate, Rudolph. "News from the Churches," *Millennial Harbinger*, October, 1851, p. 713.

H. A. "Co-operation," *The Evangelist*, XIII (May, 1862), pp. 209-210.

Hall, B. F. "News," *Christian Magazine*, IV (August, 1851), pp. 251-252.

―――――. "Progress of Reform," *Millennial Harbinger*, November, 1859, pp. 656-657.

―――――. "Things in Texas," *Millennial Harbinger*, February, 1850, pp. 103-104.

Harrison, George. "Longview," *Apostolic Times*, VII (September 9, 1875), p. 405.

Henderson, S., and Vinzent, C. "Cooperation in Texas," *Millennial Harbinger*, December, 1852, p. 712.

Hill, Abner. "News from Texas," *Christian Review*, I (November, 1844), p. 263.

Hill, A. C. "Sprinkling Proved by Pictures," *Millennial Harbinger*, September, 1868, p. 511.

Hobbs, A. I. "Principles," *Christian Courier*, IV (April 1, 1891), p. 1.

Homan, W. K. "Music," *Christian Courier*, XIX (November 8, 1906), p. 8.

Horn, R. C. "Letters to G. W. Elley—No. 2," *Apostolic Times* (Lexington, Ky.), VII (February 28, 1875), p. 64.

──────. "McKinney, Texas," *Apostolic Times*, VII (February 4, 1875), pp. 45-50.

Jones, E. "News from the Churches," *Millennial Harbinger*, November, 1858, p. 657.

Jones, J. R. "Trip to Texas," *Apostolic Church*, V (February, 1883), pp. 23-26.

Jordan, A. P. H. "News from the Churches," *Millennial Harbinger*, May, 1857, p. 297.

Kendrick, Carroll. "Loud Call from Texas," *Millennial Harbinger*, November, 1869, p. 651.

──────. "News from the Churches," *Millennial Harbinger*, June, 1852, p. 354, December, 1858, p. 718; October, 1865, p. 573.

──────. "Our Missionary Machinery, No. III Former and Present State Meetings, Etc.," *Christian Leader*, II (October 16, 1888), p. 1.

Lard, Moses E. "Instrumental Music," *Lard's Quarterly* (St. Joseph, Missouri), I (March, 1864), pp. 331-332.

──────. "Missionary Societies," *Lard's Quarterly*, II (July, 1865), p. 443.

──────. "The South as a Field," *Lard's Quarterly*, III (October, 1866), p. 43.

Lowber, J. W. "Ft. Worth," *Christian Evangelist* (St. Louis), XXVII (January 22, 1891), p. 61.

McCall, John R. "From Texas," *Christian Magazine*, IV (June, 1851), p. 188.

———. "News," *Christian Magazine*, IV (May, 1851), pp. 156-157.

———. "In Defense of an Innocent Man," *American Christian Review* (Indianapolis), XXIX (June 24, 1886), p. 202.

Matthews, Jewell. "Historical Sketches of the Early Church in Texas," *Christian Courier*, XLVIII (April, 1936), pp. 1-2, (May, 1936), p. 4, (June, 1936), pp. 1-5, (July, 1936), p. 1, (August, 1936), p. 1, (October, 1936), p. 1, and (November, 1936), pp. 1-2.

Meng, J. A. "Let Us Have Peace," *Old Path Guide* (Louisville), III (May, 1881), pp. 273-276.

Norton, L. R. "Worship," *Christian Evangelist*, XXVII (December 18, 1890), p. 805.

Padon, A. "News from the Churches," *Millennial Harbinger*, December, 1854, pp. 711-712.

Pendelton, W. K. "The Convention of Christian Churches," *Millennial Harbinger*, December, 1849, pp. 689-690.

Phillips, G. W. and Kidwill, W. T. "The Cause and Remedy," *The Gospel Missionary*, X (November 1, 1908), p. 1.

Pinkerton, L. L. "Instrumental Music in Churches," *American Christian Review* (Indianapolis), III (February 28, 1860), p. 34.

Ponton, Joel. "News from the Churches," *Millennial Harbinger*, June, 1842, pp. 275-276.

Ratliffe, J. M. "We Are Brethren," *Christian Courier*, IV (March 11, 1891), p. 3.

Rawlins, W. H. "News," *Christian Record* (Bloomington, Indiana), VII (July, 1849), p. 30, and (September, 1849), p. 90.

───────. "Problem in Texas," *Millennial Harbinger*, June, 1858, pp. 323-332.

Richardson, Robert. "Disciples of Christ, Christians, Reformers," *Millennial Harbinger*, April, 1845, p. 189.

Robertson, G. W. "Notes from Texas," *Christian Evangelist* (St. Louis), XXVIII (April 30, 1891), p. 287.

Sanders, B. B. "A Dead Church," *Christian Courier*, XII (October 25, 1900), p. 1.

Schug, H. L. "A Brief History of the Spanish Speaking Churches of Christ in the USA," *Cherokee Courier* (Cherokee, Texas), I (January, 1957), p. 3.

Sewell, J. P. "Southwestern Christian College," *Christian Leader and the Way* (Indianapolis), XVIII (August 2, 1904), p. 5.

Shearer, Ernest C. "The Carvajal Disturbances," *The Southwestern Historical Quarterly*, LV (October, 1951), pp. 201-202.

Shirey, R. L. "Critic Criticized," *The Gospel Missionary*, X (July 15, 1908), p. 2.

Smith, F. W. "News," *Gospel Review*, I (May, 1903), p. 31.

Srygley, F. D. "Bro. Burnett," *Christian Messenger*, XVII (March 18, 1891), p. 1.

Stamps, John. "Missionaries for Texas," *Millennial Harbinger*, March, 1850, pp. 174-175.

───────. "News from the Churches," *Millennial Harbinger*, August, 1841, p. 381.

Stout, David R. "News Report from Texas, *Millennial Harbinger*, September, 1845, p. 247.

Sweeney, Benton. "News," *Christian Evangelist* (Fort Madison, Iowa), IX (October, 1858), p. 480.

Sweet, L. J. "News," *Christian Evangelist*, VI (March, 1855), pp. 141-142; VII (January, 1856), p. 45; VIII (February, 1857), pp. 79-80.

──────. "Scyene," *The Evangelist* (Fort Madison, Iowa), X (November, 1859), p. 523.

Tant, Fanning Yater. "Concerning Our Policy," *Gospel Guardian* (Lufkin, Texas), I (May 5, 1949), pp. 2-5.

Thomas, Henry. "News," *Christian Evangelist* (Fort Madison, Iowa) (November, 1855), pp. 327-328.

──────. "News from the Churches," *Millennial Harbinger*, September, 1858, p. 54, December, 1858, p. 718, and June, 1859, p. 358.

Thornberry, James L. "Fifty Years Ago," *Apostolic Church* VII (Louisville), VI (September, 1884), pp. 20-21.

Thorp, J. L. "Fellowship," *Christian Evangelist*, VII (February, 1856), pp. 87-88.

Torrance, W. P. "Sherman," *Christian Evangelist*, VI (June, 1855), p. 287.

──────. "News," *Christian Evangelist*, VI (October, 1855), p. 479.

Updike, J. P. "On the Church," *Christian Standard*, XLII (February 2, 1907), p. 97.

Walker, Robert. "A Call from Texas," *Christian Review*, II (August, 1845), p. 191.

Wallace, Ernest. "The Comanches on the White Man's Road," West Texas Historical Association *Year Book*, XXIX (October, 1953), p. 27.

Wallace, Foy. "The Issues Before Us," *Gospel Guardian*, I (May 5, 1949), p. 3.

Webb, Felix B. "News from the Churches," *Millennial Harbinger*, September, 1850, p. 535.

White, L. S. "Brother Klingman and His Work in Japan," *Gospel Guide* (Dallas), IV (October, 1908), pp. 13-14.

Williams, Ann F. R. "News from the Churches," *Millennial Harbinger*, August, 1847, p. 480.

Wilmeth, C. M., "Notes of Travel in North Texas," *Apostolic Times* (Lexington, Ky.), VII (March 11, 1875), p. 88, (March 18, 1875), p. 100-101, and (June 17, 1875), pp. 225-226.

Wilmeth, J. B., "News from the Churches," *Millennial Harbinger*, December, 1848, pp. 705-706.

Wright, W. H. "Texas," *Christian Evangelist* (St. Louis), XXVII (January 8, 1891), p. 29.

Books

Aldrich, A. A. *The History of Houston County, Texas.* San Antonio, 1943.

Anon. *A Memorial and Biographical History of Johnson and Hill Counties, Texas.* Chicago, 1892.

------------. *Ellis County, Texas.* Chicago, 1922.

------------. *The Analytical Greek Lexicon.* New York, 1947.

------------. *The Lone Star State—Johnson and Hill Counties.* Chicago, 1892.

Baird, G. H. *A Brief History of Upshur County.* Gilmer, Texas, 1946.

Barker, Eugene C. *Mexico and Texas 1821-1835.* Dallas, 1928.

Barnes, William Wright. *The Southern Baptist Convention 1843-1953.* Nashville, 1954.

Baxter, William. *Pea Ridge and Prairie Grove.* Cincinnati, 1864.

Belcher, Joseph. *The Religious Denominations in the United States.* Indianapolis, 1855.

Boles, H. Leo. *Biographical Sketches of Gospel Preachers*. Nashville, 1932.

Bourne, Emma Guest. *A Pioneer Farmer's Daughter of Red River Valley* (Northeast Texas). Dallas, 1950.

Bowyer, John Wilson and Thurman, Claude Harrison (eds.) *The Annals of Elder Horn*. New York, 1930.

Broadway Church of Christ. *Lubbock Lectures on Mission Work*. Lubbock, 1946.

Brown, John H. *History of Texas 1685-1892*. St. Louis, 1892.

Brown, John T. *Churches of Christ*. Louisville, 1904.

Carroll, J. M. *A History of Texas Baptists*. Dallas, 1923.

Caskey, Thomas W. *Caskey's Book*. Ed. by C. G. Mullins. St. Louis, 1884.

──────. *Caskey's Last Book*. Ed. by B. G. Manire. Nashville, 1896.

Chandler, Barbara Overton and Howe, J. (eds.) *History of Texarkana and Bowie and Miller Counties, Texas-Arkansas*. Shreveport, 1939.

Clark, Randolph. *Reminiscences, Biographical and Historical*. Wichita Falls, 1919.

Cochran, John H. *Dallas County*. Dallas, 1928.

Cox, Mary L. *History of Hale County*. Plainview, Texas, 1937.

Crockett, G. L. *Two Centuries in East Texas*. Dallas, 1932.

Directory, *City of Dallas 1878-1879*. Dallas, 1879.

Dobie, Dudley R. *A Brief History of Hays County and San Marcos, Texas*. San Marcos, 1948.

Dowling, L. H. *The Christian Almanac for the Year of Our Lord and Saviour 1867*. Indianapolis, 1867.

Faulk, J. J. *History of Henderson County, Texas*. Athens, Texas, 1929.

Fort Worth City Directory—1882. Fort Worth, 1882.

Fort Worth City Directory—1907. Fort Worth, 1907.

Garden, A. W. S. *The Story of West Texas*. Hartford, Connecticut, 1915.

Garrison, Winfred Ernest and DeGroot, Alfred T. *The Disciples of Christ, A History*. St. Louis, 1948.

Hall, Alexander (ed.) *The Christian Register*. Lloydsville, Ohio, 1848.

Hall, Claude V. *The Early History of Floyd County*. Canyon, Texas, 1947.

Hall, Colby D. *Texas Disciples*. Fort Worth, 1953.

Hamrick, Alma Ward. *The Call of the San Saba*. San Antonio, 1941.

Hanfords, Albert. *Texas State Register for 1879*. Galveston, 1879.

Homan, W. K. *The Church on Trial*. Dallas, 1900.

Jackson, George. *Sixty Years in Texas*. Dallas, 1908.

McConnell, Joseph Carroll. *The West Texas Frontier*. Jacksboro, Texas, 1933.

Morris, Don H. and Leach, Max. *Like Stars Shining Brightly*. Abilene, Texas, 1953.

Nichol, C. R. (ed.) *Gospel Preachers Who Blazed the Trail*. Austin, n.d.

Ousley, Clarence (ed.) *Galveston in 1900*. Atlanta, 1900.

Paddock, B. B. (ed.) *Fort Worth on the Texas Northwest* (2 vols.), I. Chicago, 1922.

Red, W. S. *A History of the Presbyterian Church in Texas.* U.S.A., 1936.

Richardson, T. K. *East Texas, Its History and Its Makers* (2 vols.), II, Ed. by Dabney White. New York, 1940.

Schmidt, Charles F. *History of Washington County.* San Antonio, 1949.

Smythe, H. *Historical Sketch of Parker County, Texas.* St. Louis, 1877.

Thrall, Homer S. *History of Methodism in Texas.* Houston, 1872.

West, Earl Irvin. *The Search for the Ancient Order* (2 vols.), II. Indianapolis, 1950.

Weyand, Leonie Rummell and Wade, Houston. *Early History of Fayette County.* La Grange, Texas, 1936.

Young, Charles A. *Historical Documents Advocating Christian Union.* Chicago, 1904.

Young, M. Norvel. *A History of Colleges Established and Controlled by Members of the Churches of Christ.* Kansas City, Mo., 1949.

APPENDIX

I. Preachers of the Churches of Christ in Texas Prior to 1860

Most of these men preached part-time. A few preached every Sunday. A number of these preachers also served as elders, or as elders did some preaching. This list was obtained from reports from Texas which appeared in religious periodicals prior to 1860.

Anthony, Rhoddy
Appling, C. H.
Armstrong, Thomas
Baird, James M.
Baird, W. W.
Barrett, Thomas
Beebe, _____
Blackwell, J. W.
Boyter, J. J.
Burditt, W. B.
Bush, W. F.
Cain, John
Campbell, T. F.
Carrington, W. H. D.
Clark, Joseph Addison
Collins, A. G.
Cope, J. A.
Couch, J. L.
Cox, T. W.
Crisp, John
D'Spain, D. L.
D'Spain, Lynn
Daniels, R. L.
Dean, A. M.
Deboore, Ephriam
Dickson, J. A.
Dow, John
East, E. W.
Eldridge, Peter
Elliston, J. W.
Foster, _____
Gaines, W. C.
Gale, Henry
Giles, S. B.
Goodman, Z. P.
Goodnight, _____
Gough, Asher
Griffin, Thasher
Ground, Robert
Hall, B. F.
Heath, _____
Henderson, N. A. V.
Henderson, Samuel
Hill, Abner
Holbrook, David
Holloway, W. B.
Jasper, T.
Jones, E.
Jordan, A. P. H.
Kendrick, Carroll
Lovelady, James
McCall, John
McCluskey, John
McComas, Amon
Marshall, H.
Matteson, W. P.

Matthews, Clinton
Matthews, J. C.
Matthews, Mansil W.
Moore, Ephriam
Moore, John H.
Moore, L. V.
Neathry, Robert
Newman, Aaron
Padon, Alfred
Polly, H. N. O.
Ponton, Joel
Power, James M.
Prather, _____
Prince, W. B.
Rawlins, William
Rucker, Lindsey
Rucker, Lloyd
Rutherford, W.
Scruggs, James F.
Simpson, William
Slaughter, G. E.
Southern, P. F.
Stamps, John
Steward, _____
Stewart, D. K.

Stratton, F. M.
Strickland, Stephen
Stirman, William
Stout, David
Sweet, L. J.
Swinney, Benton
Swinney, T. M.
Thomas, Henry
Thompson, C. B.
Thorp, J. L.
Walker, Jesse
Walker, Robert T.
Weaver, Green
Webb, Felix
White, _____
Whitmire, John
Williams, H. L.
Williams, S. S.
Wilmeth, C. M.
Wilmeth, J. B.
Wilmeth, S. B.
Wilson, W. B.
Withers, W. K.
Wood, John M.

II. CHURCHES OF CHRIST IN TEXAS PRIOR TO 1860

Counties in which churches were located are indicated by parenthesis. Some locations are unknown. This list was obtained from reports from Texas which appeared in religious periodicals prior to 1860.

Church County	Church County
Alvarado (Johnson)	Berea
Antioch (San Augustine)	Bethany
Austin (Travis)	Birdwill's Mill
Bald Prairie (Robertson)	Black Cypress
Bastrop (Bastrop)	Boggy
Bearden	Boston (Bowie)
Beaver	Brenham (Washington)
Bellville (Austin)	Bryant's Station
Belton (Bell)	Buena Vista

Church	County	Church	County
Burnet (Burnet)		Liberty (Liberty)	
Caldwell (Burleson)		Live Oak Well (Fayette)	
Carolina		Lockhart (Caldwell)	
Cedar Creek		Lyons	
Circleville		McKinney (Collin)	
Clarksville (Red River)		Madisonville (Madison)	
Clear Springs Meeting House (Fayette)		Mantua	
Cold Springs (Dallas)		Marshall (Harrison)	
Comanche (Comanche)		Matagorda (Matagorda)	
Cross Timbers		Midway	
Dallas (Dallas)		Mill Creek	
Daingerfield (Morris)		Montgomery (Montgomery)	
Darr's Creek		Mountain Church	
Dime Box (Lee)		Mt. Enterprise (Rusk)	
Elm Creek		Mt. Moriah	
Florence (Williamson)		Mt. Pleasant (Titus)	
Forrest Grove		Mt. Vernon (Franklin)	
Fort Worth (Tarrant)		Mulberry	
Gay Hill (Washington)		Nacogdoches City (Nacogdoches)	
Georgetown (Williamson)		Oppolow Springs	
Gilmer (Upshur)		Owensville	
Grandview (Johnson)		Palestine (Anderson)	
Grapevine Prairie (Tarrant)		Pigeon Creek (Fayette)	
Hallettsville (Lavaca)		Pine Tree	
Hallonia		Pleasant Grove	
Hamilton (Hamilton)		Pleasant Hill	
Hickory Grove		Pleasant Run	
Huntsville (Walker)		Post Oak	
Independence		Prairie Creek (Dallas)	
Indian Creek		Red Oak	
Jefferson (Marion)		Rio Navidad	
Jernigan Church (Hopkins)		Round Mountain	
Jones Prairie		Rusk (Cherokee)	
Kickapoo		Ruterville	
LaGrange (Fayette)		Salado (Bell)	
Lampasas Springs (Lampasas)		Saltillo	
Lancaster (Dallas)		San Gabriel	
		San Marcos (Hays)	

APPENDIX

Church	County	Church	County
San Patricio	(San Patricio)	Union	
San Saba	(San Saba)	Uvalde	(Uvalde)
Savannah		Van Alstyne	(Grayson)
Scyene	(Dallas)	Vanzant	
Sempronius Academy		Victoria	(Victoria)
Shelbyville	(Shelby)	Weaver	
Sherman	(Grayson)	White Mound	
Shiloh		Woodlawn	
Squaw Creek	(Erath)	Yancy's Settlement	
Texanna		Yorktown	(DeWitt)
Tyler	(Smith)	Young's Prairie	
		Zion	

III. Preachers of the Churches of Christ in Texas, 1880

This list was obtained from F. M. Green, *Preachers of the Churches of Christ in the United States* (December 1, 1880).

Name	Home Town
Abney, J. A.	Lampasas
Allen, J. H.	Caddo Grove
Andrews, John	Coke
Aten, A. P.	Round Rock
Bagby, W. H.	McKinney
Bandy, H. M.	Thorp Spring
Bantau, H. D.	Millsap
Barnett, W. R. D.	
Barrett, Thomas	Gainesville
Baxter, Kirk	Dallas
Baxter, Wm. E.	Elliott's P. O.
Beard, J. M.	Bairdstown
Billingsly, C.	Buena Vista
Boyles, N. S.	Valley View
Burnett, T. R.	Bonham
Burns, C. S.	Denison
Bush, A. J.	Hallettsville
Bush, J. W.	Huntsville
Bush, S. J.	
Butler, C. B.	Sherman

Name	Home Town
Calloway, T. H.	Decatur
Carrington, W. H. D.	Austin
Carlton, Charles	Bonham
Cartwright, A.	Van Alstyne
Caskey, Thomas W.	Sherman
Castleman, J. L.	Pella
Charles, R. O.	Ennis
Chenowith, A.	San Marcos
Childers, R. P.	Mineola
Clark, Addison	Thorp Spring
Clark, Joseph A.	Thorp Spring
Clark, Randolph	Thorp Spring
Cole, B. W.	Scyene
Collings, W. G.	Tehuacana
Connell, G. F.	Buena Vista
Dabney, E .W.	Brenham
Darnall, J. R.	Weston
DeSpain, A. L.	Sulphur Springs
Dimmitt, W. C.	Sherman
Douglas, A. M.	Pilot Point
Downing, J. M.	Sherman
Downing, R. L.	Paris
Driskill, M. D.	Corsicana
Driskill, T. F.	Corsicana
Durst, J. F.	Leona
Dykes, ————	
Eaves, William	
Emerson, James E.	Eldorado
Ethridge, W. G.	Marlin
Ezzell, S. R.	Bonham
Farthing, A. G.	Gainesville
Faulkner, J. B.	McKinney
Foster, A. H.	Rockdale
Fulgham, W. G.	Hullville
Furgeson, Green	Willis
Gano, R. M.	Dallas
Gibbons, N. B.	Ennis
Gragan, L. R.	Ravenna
Gray, E. G.	Will's Point
Holloway, J. P.	Long View

APPENDIX

Name	Home Town
Holt, G. H.	Center
Hooker, J. D.	Milano
Horn, R. C.	Farmington
Huffman, N. B.	Weatherford
Jackson, A. W.	Groesbeck
Jackson, J. W.	Mt. Calm
Jasper, T.	Lewisville
Jones, Isaac	Moro
Key, C. R.	St. Joe
Keyser, James	Rockwall
King, A. D.	Center
King, John	McKinney
Kyle, A.	Ioni
Landrum, A. K.	Tyler
Lane, J. R.	Mooresville
Leak, D. A.	Melrose
Linton, W. N.	Montgomery
Lyles, W.	Mineola
Mackey, E. O.	Sandy Switch
Major, E. F.	Monroe
Marquis, A.	Weesatche
Matthews, A. C.	Giddings
Matthews, Mansil	Decatur
McIntire, Wm.	Dallas
McKinney, John	McKinney
McKinney, Wm.	Van Alstyne
McPherson, C. M.	Waxahachie
Milton, G. S.	Honey Grove
Moore, W. H.	Bremond
Moss, C. A. T.	Pleasanton
Noble, _____	Willow Hole
Northcutt, W. H.	Paris
O'Brien, B. A.	McKinney
Padon, Alfred	
Pangburn, Henry	Hutchins
Phillips, B. F.	Longview
Poe, John T.	Huntsville
Polly, H. N. O.	Rockwall
Pritchard, A. J.	Bib Valley
Ragsdale, W. F.	Tehuacana

Name	Home Town
Rawlins, J. M.	Lancaster
Reedy, T. C.	Greenville
Reeves, S. C.	Greenville
Richardson, W.	Covington
Richardson, W. P.	Cleburne
Royal, S. C.	St. Joe
Runnion, A. W.	Weston
Savage, J. W.	St. Joe
Scott, Levi	Bryan
Scott, W. H.	Denton
Scruggs, Wm.	Prairie Valley
Sewell, P. M.	Howard
Shadle, Henry	Dallas
Shaw, N. B.	
Sikes, N. B.	Groesbeck
Smith, M. H.	Savoy
Smith, M. F.	Greenville
Smith, P. T.	Plano
Southern, B. F.	Lake Ford
Stamps, W. E.	Etna
Stewart, W. H.	Thorp Spring
Stinson, W. B.	Sherman
Stirman, V. I.	Kaufman
Strickland, S.	Comanche
Surber, Green L.	Dallas
Sweeney, P. B.	Bald Prairie
Sweeney, T. M.	Palestine
Taylor, W. T.	Fort Worth
Tennison, _____	Woodbury
Theatt, U. S.	Milano
Thomas, J. W.	Waco
Thurman, W. L.	Sherman
Tyer, J. R.	Buena Vista
Veatch, S. H.	Brookland
Verna, J. C.	Gladewater
Ware, N. W.	
Warden, T. F.	Jacksboro
Weaver, G. N.	Buena Vista
Weaver, J. N.	Center
Williams, G. W.	Rockdale

Name	Home Town
Williamson, J. J.	
Willis, Pat	Hallville
Wilmeth, C. M.	Dallas
Wilmeth, J. B.	McKinney
Wilmeth, J. R.	McKinney
Young, G. P.	Jefferson

STATISTICS

I. Report by Daniel Shipman, 1879.

Daniel Shipman, long-time resident of Texas, who appeared before the U. S. Centennial Commission on September 11, 1876, said, "Nowhere on this continent does there exist a greater respect for religion and law than in my long abused state." He listed 350,000 Christian worshipers in Texas as follows:

    70,000 Baptist
    70,000 Methodist
     5,000 Old School Presbyterians
     3,000 Protestant Episcopal
     7,000 Disciples of Christ
     4,000 Cumberland Presbyterians
  140,000 Catholics
     2,000 Methodist Protestants
     2,000 Preachers
   30,000 Sunday School Scholars[1]

II. Report of Churches of Christ, Disciples of Christ, 1880.

David Lipscomb, editor of the *Gospel Advocate*, obtained these statistics from the General Missionary Society, but said they were too low.

	Texas	United States
Churches	165	4,768
Preachers	138	3,788
Members	16,500	563,928[2]

III. Report by W. R. McDaniel, 1886.

W. R. McDaniel of Thorp Spring, Texas, says, "There are 30,000 disciples according to the lowest estimate in Texas and there are more than three times

---

[1] Daniel Shipman, *Frontier Life*, p. 400.
[2] *Gospel Advocate*, February 24, 1881, p. 114.

STATISTICS

seven thousand of these who will never board the progressive car."[3]

IV. REPORT BY *Christian Evangelist*, 1890.

Church members in Texas (evidently only the Progressives were listed)—29,540[4]

V. REPORT BY *Firm Foundation*, 1891.

Church members in Texas (progressives and conservatives apparently were included)—50,000.[5]

VI. REPORT BY W. A., L. R. AND C. W. SEWELL, 1891.

These brothers formed an evangelistic team. Along with other conservative preachers, they conducted meetings during the summer in many rural localities. Generally, the progressives confined their efforts to cities and large towns.

Location	Baptisms	Members	Evangelists
Vansickle	12	50	J. A. Cathy
Coleman	10		S. N. Jones
Benjamin	1		J. M. Morton
Caldwell	0		J. I. Haden
Lisbon	26		W. F. Barcus
Blooming Grove	2		R. R. Hamlin
Canton	26	56	W. C. Holloway
			W. W. Slater
Crown Point	34		
Reagan	5		
Wooten Wells	33		
Crawford	1		
Concord	0		
Wortham	5		
North Elm	7		
Woodland	7		and a congregation
Osage	0		established
Elm Grove	1		
Marlin	2		

[3] *Ibid.*, January 27, 1886, p. 54.
[4] *Christian Evangelist*, November 27, 1890, p. 761.
[5] *Firm Foundation*, May 19, 1891.

Location	Baptisms
Durango	5
Near Comanche	12
Oak Grove	21
Clifton	20
McGregor	17
Goldthwaite	1[6]

VII. Report by J. D. Tant, 1895.

"The Institutionists lament that only 42 churches out of 500 in Texas contributed to foreign missions through the human society."[7]

VIII. Report by J. D. Tant, 1895.

"Among our 500 preachers in Texas, I can almost say five hundred meetings this year have been held at the preachers' own charges. Among our 60,000 members and 500 congregations in Texas, I feel assured I can safely say these churches have not held 50 meetings in the region beyond [evidently referring to out-of-state meetings].

"During the past ten years in Texas, I have observed by my own experience and observation of others that four-fifths of all missionary work is done by our preachers [conservatives]. I find almost in every county where I go some two or three godly men who are living on the farm and working hard for a living, and preaching around in the out-of-the-way places almost every Sunday, holding four or five meetings every year . . ."[8]

IX. Report by Texas Christian Missionary Society Convention Meeting in Gainesville, June 14-18, 1895.

. . . 100 counties in which we as a people [progressives] have no congregation or church house. Over 100 towns of 1000 population and over in which we have no church house. We have no church in all the

---
[6]*Gospel Advocate*, September 16, 1891, p. 588.
[7]*Ibid.*, March 7, 1895, p. 147.
[8]*Ibid.*, September 12, 1895, p. 590.

Panhandle country west of Quanah. Our numerical strength is from 6000 to 7500.[9]

X. REPORT BY F. M. TRIMBLE, 1896.

"I am willing to go on record as saying that preachers in Texas having no connection with anything save the church of God are baptizing ten to where the progressives are baptizing one. Why is this? They [the progressives] confine their work to towns and cities, while God's ministers are out among the people."[10]

XI. REPORT BY MISSIONARY SOCIETY, 1900.

According to reports at the National Missionary Society convention of 1900, held in Cincinnati, 59 churches in Texas contributed, 368 did not contribute.[11]

XII. REPORT BY S. R. EZZELL, 1900.

"There are about 70,000 disciples in Texas, and about 700 churches, which average 100 members per church. Total giving —$19,600, which is an average of 28 cents per member. But only about one-fifth, or 140 of the 700 churches give. These 140 churches have 14,000 members, but only one-fifth or about 2800 of the 14,000 give the $19,600 which is just $7 per member . . . We have in Texas about 450 preachers. About 200 are trying to put in all their time preaching; 150 can preach only part of their time, while the other hundred are not preaching any; some for want of support, some boycotted."[12]

XIII. REPORT BY B. B. SANDERS, 1903.

"Correct statistics of the churches of Texas have never been obtained, but approximately speaking, there are 700 churches with an aggregate membership of 90,000 . . . In 1903, 35 churches were organized, 12 churches reorganized, 36 Sunday Schools organized,

---
[9]*Texas Christian Missionary Convention*, 1895, p. 9.
[10]*Gospel Advocate*, October 29, 1896, p. 701.
[11]*Firm Foundation*, January 9, 1900.
[12]*Christian Courier*, March 15, 1900, p. 5.

4,059 additions to the various churches, and over $20,000 received for Texas Mission work."[13]

XIV. Report by T. R. Burnett, 1906.

"In claims and counter-claims, the results in Texas . . . 1906. Replies to J. D. White concerning conversions during the year—1800 by progressives, 8000 by non-progressives. By fruits shall ye know them."[14]

XV. Report by *Christian Courier*, 1906.

"From a list of 367 preachers of the Church of Christ which appeared in the Courier, only 180 claimed to be identified with organized mission work. Less than 60 of the 180 gave their full time to one congregation. Only about 80 preach regularly . . ."[15]

XVI. United States Census, 1916—United States.

	Church of Christ	Disciples of Christ
Churches	5,570	8,408
Members	317,937	1,226,028
Males	132,755	378,777
Females	185,057	554,731
Property Value	$5,644,096	$40,327,201[16]

XVII. United States Census, 1916—Texas.

	Church of Christ	Disciples of Christ
Churches	1,240	544
Reporting Debt	59—$37,779	89—$239,145
Parsonages—Value Reported	9— $9,000	71—$179,350
Expenditures Reported	431—$174,593	301—$594,604
Sunday Schools	715	554
Officers and Teachers	3,247	4,365
Scholars	38,104	49,504[17]

---

[13] Brown, *Churches of Christ*, pp. 286-87.
[14] *Burnett's Budgett*, July 15, 1909, p. 1.
[15] *Christian Courier*, October 25, 1906.
[16] *Census, Religious Bodies*, 1916, p. 142.
[17] *Ibid.*, p. 225.

STATISTICS

XVIII. UNITED STATES CENSUS, 1916—TEXAS.

	Churches of Christ	Disciples of Christ
Churches	1,240	544
Members	71,542	54,836
Male	29,445	16,572
Female	42,097	25,456
Church edifices	899	460
Halls, etc.	328	22
Value of church property	$1,376,135	$2,386,912[18]

XIX. UNITED STATES CENSUS, 1916—TEXAS.
Number of members in selected rural and urban counties

County	Churches of Christ	Disciples of Christ
Bell	1,701	1,105
Brown	761	279
Bexar	360	1,341
Cooke	896	504
Dallas	1,997	4,911
Denton	1,679	625
Grayson	2,409	1,888
Harris	220	525
Hockley	0	0
Johnson	1,447	401
Jones	794	137
Nacogdoches	400	110
Parker	1,565	289
Tarrant	2,825	2,541
Taylor	1,069	390[19]

XX. UNITED STATES CENSUS, 1916—TEXAS.
Selected Cities and Towns

Town		Churches of Christ	Disciples of Christ
Austin	Churches	1	4

[18]*Ibid.*, p. 224.
[19]*Ibid.*, pp. 311-318.

	Members	175	807
	Sunday School	100	865
Dallas	Churches	8	11
	Members	997	3,122
	Sunday School	624	21,812
El Paso	Churches	1	2
	Members	102	818
	Sunday School	84	482
Fort Worth	Churches	9	9
	Members	1,818	2,411
	Sunday School	1,391	2,379
Galveston	Churches	0	1
	Members	0	379
	Sunday School	0	225
Houston	Churches	1	4
	Members	86	469
	Sunday School	60	565
San Antonio	Churches	3	7
	Members	360	1,341
	Sunday School	140	877
Waco	Churches	1	3
	Members	150	712
	Sunday School	125	518[20]

XXI. UNITED STATES CENSUS, 1926—UNITED STATES.

	Churches of Christ	Disciples of Christ
Churches	6,226	7,648
Members	433,714	1,377,595
Urban Churches	896	2,014
Urban Members	104,571	751,915
Rural Churches	5,330	5,634
Rural Members	329,143	625,680[21]

XXII. UNITED STATES CENSUS, 1926—TEXAS.
  Number of Members in Selected Counties

County	Churches of Christ	Disciples of Christ
Bell	2,037	1,033

---
[20] *Ibid.*, p. 360.
[21] *Ibid.*, 1926, p. 840.

STATISTICS

Brown	1,502	535
Bexar	778	2,273
Cooke	1,017	400
Dallas	4,300	8,923
Denton	1,864	743
Hockley	164	0
Tarrant	3,458	6,048
Taylor	1,871	753
Johnson	1,442	381
Jones	1,474	138
Nacogdoches	514	189
Grayson	2,543	2,610
Harris	1,056	3,131
Parker	2,229	47
Jim Hogg	0	0[22]

XXIII. UNITED STATES CENSUS, 1926—TEXAS.
Selected Cities

		Churches of Christ	Disciples of Christ
Austin	Churches	3	3
	Members	294	853
	Sunday School	277	642
Beaumont	Churches	4	4
	Members	468	1,171
	Sunday School	386	1,344
Dallas	Churches	10	12
	Members	3,052	6,999
	Sunday School	2,000	3,565
El Paso	Churches	1	2
	Members	125	1,044
	Sunday School	150	891
Fort Worth	Churches	17	11
	Members	2,337	5,786
	Sunday School	1,692	4.125
Galveston	Churches	1	1
	Members	52	451
	Sunday School	75	283
Houston	Churches	7	6
	Members	959	2,886

---

[22]*Ibid.*, pp. 678-687.

	Sunday School	947	2,080
San Antonio	Churches	4	6
	Members	778	2,273
	Sunday School	677	1,740
Waco	Churches	4	3
	Members	695	1,185
	Sunday School	485	1,090
Wichita Falls	Churches	1	2
	Members	800	1,635
	Sunday School	400	1,700[23]

XXIV. UNITED STATES CENSUS, 1926—TEXAS.

	Churches of Christ	Disciples of Christ
Churches	1,286	489
Members	98,909	77,150
Church edifices	1,055	
(1,051 reported buildings worth $4,076,250)		
Debts on churches	145	
Total amount of debt	$396,376	
Expenditures		
(1,229 reported	$1,091,544)	
Sunday Schools reported	867	
Teachers	4,470	
Enrollment	63,293[24]	

XXV. CHURCHES OF CHRIST IN SELECTED CITIES, 1932—TEXAS.

	No.	
Abilene	11	(1 Mexican)
Amarillo	2	
Austin	3	
Beaumont	3	
Corpus Christi	2	
Dallas	12	(1 Hebrew Mission)
El Paso	4	(2 Mexican Missions)
Fort Worth	19	
Galveston	1	

---

[23] *Ibid.*, pp. 358-576.
[24] *Ibid.*, pp. 256-257.

Houston	6
Lubbock	4
Orange	1
Port Arthur	3
San Antonio	6
Sherman	3
Texarkana	1
Waco	5
Wichita Falls	3 [25]

XXVI. REPORT BY J. G. MALPHURS, 1937.

"The Federal Government takes a religious census every ten years. Christians are to obey ordinances of man when they do not conflict with God's orders. Brother Leslie G. Thomas, of Corsicana, Texas, has been appointed by the government to gather the reports for churches of Christ.

"Because there is no bishop or pope over the churches of Christ such a census is hard to take. There are many congregations without a located preacher to look after the matter, and unless someone in such churches takes special care to make the required report they will be left out. If all congregations will send in to Brother Thomas their report I doubt not that 'we' will make a splendid showing in the Government's report of religious conditions in America. But unless elders and preachers do their part in this matter there is a danger to this census taking. Many churches will be left out of the figures, and the Census Bureau in Washington will represent 'churches of Christ' as a vanishing religion on the American continent. If the figures represent us as having lost during the last decade, 'we' will know how to explain, but the denominations will not know, and we'll not be able to show them; the government report will be taken as final."[26]

---

[25] Glenn, E. N. (comp.), *Church Directory of Churches of Christ in USA and Canada* (Cincinnati, 1932), n.p.

[26] *Firm Foundation*, August 17, 1937.

XXVII. Report by Edgar Furr, 1940.

"There are one hundred and twenty county seat towns with congregations that have a full time preacher, sixty-six county seats with a congregation but no full time preacher, and sixty-eight county seat towns with no congregation. The total population of these sixty-eight towns is within a few souls of one hundred twenty thousand . . . only two of the sixty-eight counties do not have a neighboring county with a full time man, so we cannot say we do not know where to begin . . ."[27]

XXVIII. Report by Leslie G. Thomas, 1941.

"Inasmuch as the 1926 report gave 6,226 [churches of Christ] and the 1936 report lists only 3,815, a net loss of 2,411 for the ten year period, some questions naturally arise in the minds of interested people. Was a sufficient effort put forth to get the census, etc. . . . Hundreds of churches did not report that I know about. The main reason for not reporting seems to be that ministers of certain denominations were not in as cooperative mood in 1936 as in 1926, and that this attitude on non-cooperation extended so far that they did not even heed the earnest appeals of their own national officials to fill out the schedules so as to assure a complete report for their own denominations. . ."[28]

(All reporting churches except the Roman Catholic showed a decrease in churches and membership in 1936 compared with 1926. Some showed such a marked decrease as to evidence outright opposition to the religious census or widespread indifference. As a result, the religious census was discontinued by the United States Government.)

XXIX. Churches of Christ in Selected Cities, 1941—Texas.

	No.	
Abilene	13	(1 Mexican, 1 colored)

---
[27]*Ibid.*, April 2, 1940.
[28]*Ibid.*, June 3, 1941.

STATISTICS 365

Amarillo	4	
Austin	13	(1 Mexican, 1 colored)
Beaumont	2	
Corpus Christi	5	
Dallas	29	(1 Mexican, 2 colored)
El Paso	3	(1 Mexican)
Fort Worth	19	(1 Mexican, 2 colored)
Galveston	1	
Houston	19	(1 colored)
Lubbock	3	
Orange	1	
Port Arthur	3	(1 colored)
San Antonio	11	(3 Mexican, 1 colored)
Sherman	3	(1 colored)
Texarkana	1	
Waco	4	
Wichita Falls	3	(1 colored)[29]

XXX. CHURCHES AND PREACHERS (CHURCHES OF CHRIST), 1946—TEXAS.

White	1,980	
White (non-Bible class)	154	
Colored	54	
Mexican	14	
Total number of churches		2,203
Total number of preachers		844[30]

XXXI. CHURCHES AND MEMBERS (DISCIPLES OF CHRIST), 1947-48—TEXAS.

	1947	1948
Churches	489	501
Members	104,378	105,911[31]

---

[29] G. H. P. Showalter and Leslie G. Thomas (comps.), *Directory and List of Preachers of Churches of Christ* (Austin, 1941).

[30] Olan Hicks, *1946-1947 Yearbook of Churches of Christ* (Abilene, 1947), pp. 17-49.

[31] *1948 Yearbook of International Convention of Disciples of Christ* (Indianapolis, 1948).

XXXII. Churches and Preachers (Churches of Christ), 1949—Texas.

	Churches		Preachers
Total	1,863	Total	985
White	1,800	White	913
Colored	49	Colored	62
Mexican	14	Mexican	10[32]

---

[32]Showalter, G. H. P. and Thomas, Leslie G. (comps.), *Church Directory and List of Preachers of Churches of Christ* (Austin, 1949).

MISCELLANEOUS

I. BENEVOLENT EFFORTS

Benevolent work among the churches of Christ in Texas prior to 1906 was limited and temporary. The first effort evidently was made to pay the tuition of some orphans who attended Add-Ran College in 1877.[1] The orphans lived on an adjacent farm which apparently was organized as a home for children. In 1884 the owners of Add-Ran College met at Caldwell, Texas, with the board of directors of the "orphan school" and offered to sell the college property to the home. The proposition was accepted,[2] but never actually executed.

During the next few years, some controversy arose in the church concerning the care of orphans. In 1896, J. W. Jackson, a minister, proposed that the churches of Texas establish a home. In opposition, evangelist John T. Poe argued that ". . . God has ordained that this work be done by the church and in the church . . ."[3] Notwithstanding, a home was established by Jennie Clark at Luling in 1899[4] and continued until 1928 when it closed because of financial difficulties.[5] As indicated in the last chapter of this study, a number of homes have been established in the twentieth century which are supported by churches throughout Texas and other states.

II. DEBATES AND DEBATERS.

Although debates and debaters are often popular and emotionally appealing to people, they have not exerted a significant influence upon the development

---

[1] Young, *History of Colleges*, p. 71.
[2] Chalmers McPherson, "Our Orphan Work," *Gospel Advocate*, XXV (November 21, 1883), p. 740.
[3] *Firm Foundation*, September 15, 1896.
[4] *Gospel Advocate*, June 30, 1904, p. 413.
[5] C. C. Dye (Luling, Texas), to Stephen Eckstein, interview, April 15, 1962.

of the churches of Christ in Texas. Debating probably reached its peak in the state during the last quarter of the nineteenth century when T. W. Caskey was in his prime. In the first few decades of the twentieth century, debating waned as Texas lost its frontier characteristics and became more settled. By 1950, ministers of the churches of Christ engaged only in occasional debates. In a number of instances, these were among fellow preachers debating issues within the churches of Christ. A few of the more prominent debaters in the churches of Christ in the twentieth century were J. D. Tant, C. R. Nichol and Joe Warlick.

INDEX

A

Abilene—155, 156, 159, 160, 176, 223, 302, 306, 310, 311
Abilene Christian College—156, 307, 309, 310, 311, 317
Abney, J. A.—90, 91
Add-Ran College—125, 166, 182, 207, 212, 214, 215, 216, 217, 220, 235, 237, 269
Allen, F. W.—257
Alsup, A.—102, 247
Amarillo—173, 176, 301, 302
American Christian Missionary Society—73, 85, 229, 230
American Christian Review—220, 268
American Home Missionary—287
Anderson County—42
Angelina County—43
Anthony, Rhoddy—15
Antioch—15, 68, 90
Appling, C. H.—86
Apostolic Church—119, 206
Apostolic Times—113, 279
Arceneaux, Early—164
Arkansas Methodist—244
Armstrong County—174
Armstrong, J. N.—300, 301
Armstrong, Thomas—252
Atascosa County—62, 143, 144
Athens—91
Augustine County—43
Austin—29, 37, 56, 68, 82, 87, 129, 130, 132, 133, 134, 152, 182, 200, 207, 208, 219, 230, 237, 239, 240, 255, 308, 309
Austin's colony—14, 165
Austin County—134, 253, 264
Austin Evening News—240
Austin, Stephen F.—2, 3, 7

B

Bagby, W. H.—259
Baird, James—36
Ballinger—162, 272
Bandy, H.—166
Bantau, G. W.—63, 64
Bantau, H. D.—97, 106, 123, 126, 127, 137, 138
Bantau, J. H.—58
Baptist—3, 4, 5, 8, 13, 18, 19, 25, 33, 39, 40, 41, 48, 51, 52, 57, 59, 60, 72, 82, 89, 90, 92, 108, 113, 122, 127, 128, 136, 139, 144, 151, 153, 154, 158, 164, 167, 168, 169, 175, 176, 177, 189, 190, 193, 194, 195, 201, 202, 224, 252, 253, 254, 256, 257, 258, 261, 262, 272, 288, 310, 322, 326, 328
Baptist Observer—189
Baptist Reflector—244
Barens, J. M.—88, 158, 249, 253, 257, 258
Barrett, A. B.—116, 118, 310
Barrett, Thomas—68, 181
Barrows, J. W.—175
Bartlett—191
Bastrop—133
Bastrop County—65
Baxter, William—87, 232
Beaumont—87, 140
Bedford, Hilary G.—157, 158
Bee County—145
Beeville—39, 61, 62
Bell County—29, 63, 64, 65, 135, 192, 212, 226, 248, 268
Bell, R. C.—317
Bible Chairs—308, 309, 310
Bible Student—209, 210
Billingsley, Price—156, 223
Birdville—185
Blackwell, J. W.—42
Boles Home—321
Boles, W. F.—321
Boll, R. H.—210, 322
Bonham—14, 119, 180, 185, 212, 236, 269
Bonham, E. W.—145
Bonham, G. W.—157
Bonham News—206
Booth, H. C.—248, 281, 282
Bowie County—16
Bowser, W. P.—314
Boyter, J. J.—30, 269
Brazos County—134
Bremond Visitor—233

Brenham—20, 24, 134, 204
Brewer, Charles—317
Brewer, G. C.—317
Briscoe County—171, 172
Browder, U. M.—272
Brown, John H.—56
Brown, **John T.**—238
Brownfield—168, 320
Brownwood—157, 267
Bryan—134, 233, 236, 259, 313
Burditt, W. B.—29, 56, 62
Burleson County—57, 269
Burnet—58
Burnet County—65
Burnet, D. S.—25
Burnett, G. P.—199
Burnett, T. R.—88, 94, 95, 192, 193, 206, 207, 210, 226, 256, 261

Burnetta College—216
Burnett's Budgett—209
Buruss, M.—87
Busby, Horace—298
Bush, A. J.—91, 134, 145, 163, 236, 239, 240, 241
Bush, J. W.—58

C

Cain, J. H.—85
Caldwell County—67, 225
Campbell, Alexander—7, 10, 23, 28, 29, 32, 47, 72, 219, 220, 230, 242, 257, 263, 328
Campbell, William J.—287, 289
Campbellites—49, 54, 59, 92, 189, 190, 195, 257, 258
Canyon—309
Carlton, Charles—96, 97, 116, 212, 235, 257, 269
Carlton College—119
Carlton, D. T.—96, 249
Carnes, J. E.—140
Carnes, W. B.—155, 274
Carrington, W. H. D.—130, 136, 238, 239, 258
Carvajal, Jose Maria—7
Caskey, T. W.—107, 114, 117, 119, 194, 195, 196, 197, 198, 222, 234, 235, 236
Cass County—36
Castleman, S. F.—261

Catholicism—7, 9, 25, 54, 62, 82, 113, 122, 144, 147, 149, 181, 310, 315, 320
Center—90
Chambers County—140, 142
Chambers, E. C.—85, 86
Chambers, J. H.—175
Chatterton, Alexander—74, 75
Cherokee County—89, 91
Childers Classical Institute—156, 310
Chisholm, L. C.—143, 151, 221
Christian Chronicle—305, 315, 327
Christian Courier—209, 245, 251, 258, 259, 271, 272, 273, 275, 280, 284
Christian Echo—314
Christian Evangelist—81, 262, 268, 278
Christian Leader—273
Christian Messenger—8, 119, 205, 206, 207, 256, 258, 270, 271, 272, 275
Christian Monthly—206
Christian News Service—305
Christian Philanthropist — 30, 204, 205
Christian Preacher—183, 207
Christian Record—81
Christian Review—12, 22, 23, 31, 81, 268
Christian Science—198, 199
Christian Standard—244, 259, 268, 273, 278
Christian Student—207
Clark, Addison—77, 104, 120, 123, 125, 128, 131, 138, 194, 206, 212, 213, 257, 269, 279
Clark, J. A.—24, 29, 69, 71, 104, 105, 182, 209, 212, 213, 215, 238, 257, 274
Clark, N. L.—170, 218, 264
Clark, Randolph—77, 104, 212, 213, 257
Clarksville—3, 9, 13, 14, 16, 36, 254
Claude—174
Clay County—129
Cleburne—123, 124, 195, 315, 319
Coke County—164

INDEX

Coleman—156, 157
College Station—309
Colley, Flavil L.—297
Collin County—32, 112, 113, 114, 115, 152, 212, 226, 227, 230, 275
Colorado City—160
Colorado County—24
Comanche—55, 139
Comanche County—139
Commerce—248, 281
Concord—264
Congregational Church—100
Conroe—87, 88
Constitution for the Republic of Texas—11
Cooke County—116, 240
Corpus Christi—87, 140, 146, 178, 209
Corsicana—54, 97, 121, 122, 185, 313
Coryell County—138, 193
Cox, James F.—307
Cox, T. W.—19, 25
Crockett—63
Crockett County—41
Crockett, David—9
Crosby County—171
Cypert, Lillie—319

D

Dabney, E. W.—134, 253
Dabney, T. H.—214
Dalhart—175
Dallas—16, 29, 36, 39, 44, 49, 50, 54, 71, 87, 97, 98, 99, 101, 102, 103, 104, 112, 129, 130, 152, 182, 183, 185, 187, 194, 196, 200, 209, 210, 212, 217, 225, 234, 237, 245, 253, 258, 271, 279, 280, 297, 298, 299, 304, 305, 306, 307, 308, 317, 318, 319, 321, 323
Dallas Morning News—50
Daingerfield—17, 95
Davis, W. M.—214
Dawson—248
Dean, A. M.—29, 36, 50, 52, 125, 253
DeBoore, Ephraim—24
Deefe, William P.—8, 15, 32, 39, 42, 85

Deleon, Martin—7
Del Rio—151, 306
Denison—118, 197, 199
Denison News—198
Denton—115, 159, 185, 218, 219, 223, 247
Denton County—115, 152, 253, 261
D'Spain, B. L.—54
D'Spain, D. L.—41
D'Spain, Lynn—9, 14
DeTocqueville, Alexis—263
Dewitt County—61, 67, 143, 144
DeZavala County—8
Dickson, James—55, 92, 93, 94
Dimmitt, W. C.—116, 187, 189
Driskill, J. A.—133, 178
Driskill, T. F.—121
Dublin—185
Dunn, G. A.—124, 210, 276, 299
Dunn, James S.—102, 210
Dunn, John L.—265, 272, 307, 317
Durst, John S.—163, 181, 220, 238, 254, 279, 297
Dyches, J. F.—206, 233

E

East, E. H.—20, 24, 31
Eastland County—125
Eaves, W. H.—90
Eckstein, S. D.—316, 317, 318
Edwards County—163
Electra—304
Ellis County—54, 120, 175, 215, 298
Elliston, J. W.—51, 52
El Paso—164, 165, 315, 316
Ennis—121, 185, 245
Episcopalian—53, 90, 93, 122, 130, 150, 151
Erath County—125, 164, 218
Errett, Isaac—257
Everts, S. H.—106
Eye-Opener—210
Ezzell, S. R.—120, 152, 179

F

Falls County—136, 147

Fannin County—14, 24, 34, 119
Fanning, Tolbert—23, 29, 30, 71, 75, 76, 180, 205, 231, 257
Faris, G. A.—122, 236
Fayette County—24, 60, 67
Fife, R. H.—246
Floyd, Cass—253
Floyd County—170
Fort Worth—39, 49, 52, 53, 54, 74, 87, 97, 104, 105, 106, 109, 110, 111, 112, 129, 130, 152, 154, 194, 195, 198, 212, 213, 215, 236, 245, 253, 273, 282, 298, 299, 309, 315, 323
Fort Worth Daily Standard—198
Fort Worth Gazette—107
Fort Worth Register—108, 185
Foster, Otto—315
Fowler, James—309
Franklin, Joseph—283, 284
Fuller, W. T.—89
Furr, Edward L.—305
Fuston, Isaac—246

G

Gaines County—69, 168, 169
Gainesville—74, 202, 203, 240, 272
Galveston—87, 142, 181, 200
Galveston Evening Tribune—142
Gano, R. M.—77, 98, 100, 101, 103, 111, 125, 142, 180, 185, 217, 238, 261, 281
Garland—104
Gates, George—16
Gatewood, Otis—319, 320
George, A. M.—261, 266
Georgetown—37, 58, 135
Gibbs, W. L.—155
Giles, Samuel B.—24, 31, 39, 55, 56, 68
Gill, Jesse G.—316
Gilmer—93, 283
Glenn, E. N.—315, 316, 327
Goldthwaite—139, 305
Goliad—61, 143
Goliad County—67, 143

Gospel Guardian—324, 325
Gospel Guide—210
Gospel Missionary—209, 261, 266
Gospel Review—210
Gough, Asher—36
Gonzales County—24
Graham—128
Granbury—249
Grand Prairie—44
Gray—175
Grayson County—32, 112, 116, 218, 299
Greenville—97, 116, 120, 321
Groves, Charles—253
Gunter—119, 218, 264, 322
Gunter Bible College—218, 264, 322

H

Hale Center—302
Hale County—302
Hall, B. F.—32, 33, 47, 48, 76, 77, 98, 115, 116, 137, 226, 230
Hall, C. B.—259
Hall County—171, 172
Hall, W. E.—130, 131, 137, 236
Hall, W. H.—207
Hallam, S. K.—174
Hallettsville—60, 61, 88
Hamilton County—138, 272
Hamilton, H. H.—89, 91, 255, 258
Hamilton, J. J.—125
Hansbrough, E.—131, 192, 219
Hardeman County—91, 159
Hardeman, N. B.—303
Harding, James A.—144, 257, 286
Harding, Joe H.—100, 103, 116, 122, 149, 151, 162, 182, 183, 185, 272, 273, 300
Harlingen—303
Harris County—140, 142
Harrison County—85, 94, 200
Harvey, G. W.—264
Hatcher, William—320
Hawkins, J. T.—147
Hawkins, W. E.—157

INDEX

Henderson, Samuel — 35, 66, 67, 89
Henrietta—129
Henshaw, John—62
Hereford—176
Herndon, E. W.—149
Hicks, Olan L.—305, 306, 315, 327, 328
Higgins—175
Higgins, A. S.—176
Hill, Abner—17, 22, 23, 34
Hill County—122, 179, 261
Hill, Father—24
Hillsboro—97, 122
Hines, J. L.—313
Hobbs, A. I.—249, 250
Hoffman, G. A.—289
Hogan, R. N.—312, 314
Holloway, W. B.—41
Holsapple, J. W.—276, 281
Holton, A. R.—313
Holt's School—215
Homan, W. K.—209, 236, 237, 250, 257, 272, 275, 279
Hood County—125, 213
Hooper, Richard—39
Hopkins County—32, 34, 36, 93
Horn, R. C.—112, 113, 115, 206, 234
Houston—31, 87, 140, 141, 202, 249, 300, 312, 313
Houston County—41, 69, 89, 200
Huckaba, A. G.—221
Huff, A. C.—210
Hunt County—120, 321
Hunter, William—61
Huntington Institute—216
Huntsville—22, 39, 55, 63, 86, 254
Hutcheson, D. L.—175, 176
Hutchins County—253

I

Idalou—302
Indians—44, 45, 105, 125, 126, 138, 139, 154, 199, 202, 203, 204
Irene—261
Iron Preacher—207

J

Jacksboro—97, 128, 167
Jack County—128, 167
Jackson County—143
Jackson, H. L.—15
Jackson, J. J.—132, 259, 275
Jackson, J. W.—149, 150, 240
Jackson, O. I.—14, 15
Jacksonville—91
Jarrell, W. A.—127, 193, 195
Jasper County—24, 43
Jasper, T.—111, 253
Jefferson—40, 82
Jews—296, 316, 317, 318
Johnson, A. L.—107
Johnson County—54, 55, 123, 216
Jones, Granville—92, 240
Jones, J. R.—119, 157, 200
Jones, W. F.—140, 141
Jordan, A. P. H.—37, 40
Junction—163, 181, 220

K

Karnes County—143
Kaufman—96, 247, 276
Kaufman County—120
Keeble, Marshall—312
Kelton, J. A.—261
Kendrick, Carroll—30, 31, 42, 55, 58, 59, 63, 64, 65, 66, 69, 70, 71, 78, 80, 81, 82, 86, 89, 178, 179, 191, 204, 205, 206, 234, 237, 238
Kentuckytown Academy—212
Kerrville—150
Kidwill, W. T.—140, 266
Kimble County—163
Kingsville—146
Klingman, C. C.—318
Klingman, George—294, 311, 317

L

LaGrange—17, 60
Lamar County—16, 34, 36, 96
Lamesa—168
Lampasas—58, 65
Lancaster—36, 49, 104, 274
Lard, Moses—84, 85, 231, 242

Lard's Quarterly—84, 242
Larimore, T. B.—100, 117, 186, 187, 188, 189, 190, 248, 299
Lawson, J. H.—159, 223, 281
Lavaca County—61, 67
Ledlow, William—263
Lemmons, W. F.—210, 211
Leona—181, 254
Leon County—69, 136, 226
Ligon, D. S.—218
Limestone County—69, 179, 216
Lingleville Christian College—218
Lipscomb County—175
Lipscomb, David—105, 106, 111, 129, 137, 138, 188, 206, 233, 249, 251, 254, 256, 257, 260, 261, 264, 265, 269, 273, 279, 283, 286, 287, 288, 289, 290
Lipscomb, William—102
Littlefield—168
Live Oak—144
Lockhart—59, 60, 217
Lockney—167, 170, 171, 176, 210
Lockney Christian College—166, 170, 209, 217, 310
Lockport—37
Longview—92, 94, 159, 237, 314
Lord's Supper—249, 262, 266, 267
Louisville Plan—234
Lowber, J. W.—107, **143**, **218**
Lubbock—166, 167, 168, 169, 170, 176, 296, 301, 309
Lubbock County—302
Lutheran—150, 160
Lyles, W. A.—211, 261

M

McAllen—303
McCall, John—55, 56, 58, 230
McCarty, A. J.—136, 161, 165, 208
McCluskey, John—17, 34
McComas, Amon—36
McGarvey, J. W.—220, 250, 257, 277
McGary, Austin—77, 131, 132, 141, 207, 208, 219, 239, 249, 251, 252, 254, 255, 256, 257, 258, 260, 264, 273, 275, 280
McGregor—259, 260
McGregor Court Case—259
McKenzie Institute—254
McKinney—39, 47, 98, 112, 113, 114, 183, 196, 206, 234
McKinney, C. C.—45, 62, 151
McKinney, Collin—4, 5, 6, 16
McKinney's Landing—6, 16
McKinney, Solomon—73, 74
McKinney, William—46
McKnight, R. O.—107
McLean—175
McPherson, C. E.—109, 121, 209, 220, 237, 246, 257, 274
Maccalla, W. L.—257
Madison County—29, 57, 69, 254, 313
Marlin—136
Marshall—41, 94
Mason—150
Mason County—157, 191
Mason, J. C.—95, 141
Matagorda—87
Matteson, W. P.—42
Matthews, Mansil W.—8, 9, 17, 74, 126
Menard—163
Memphis—172
Meng, J. A.—106, 107, 274
Methodist—3, 13, 16, 18, 21, 25, 33, 45, 51, 52, 54, 56, 59, 60, 62, 71, 72, 82, 89, 90, 94, 113, 114, 115, 121, 128, 129, 136, 139, 142, 143, 144, 146, 148, 150, 151, 153, 154, 161, 169, 173, 176, 177, 193, 195, 201, 202, 204, 223, 248, 251, 252, 253, 254
Mexican—1, 6, 50, 149, 200, 201, 297, 315, 316, 329
Midland—165
Midlothian—185
Milam County—65, 135, 147
Miller, Luke—314
Mills County—139
Mills, Isaac—173
Mitchell County—159
Mineola—92, 223

INDEX

Mineral Wells—97, 127
Montgomery—88
Montgomery County—24, 85, 88, 240
Moore, Ephraim B.—17, 34
Moore, John H.—17
Morlan, G. C.—307
Morris County—94, 95
Morris, Don H.—311
Mount Enterprise—35
Mount Enterprise Academy—212
Mount Pleasant—68, 181, 185
Mount Vernon—68, 181, 276
Mulkey, James—88

N

Nacogdoches—3, 268
Nacogdoches County—14, 24, 36, 42, 43, 90
Nance, Thomas—169, 173, 174
Navarro County—54, 121, 248
Nazareth University—217
Nelson, J. B.—323
Newman, Aaron—55, 60, 67
Nichol, C. R.—122
Nicolin County—43
North, S. N. D.—287, 288, 289, 290
Norris, J. Frank—323
Norton, L. R.—245

O

O'Banion, J. W.—15
Odessa—165, 303
Officer, R. W.—171, 172, 203, 204
Oliphant, W. L.—297, 298
One Cup—262, 266, 267
Orange—314
Order of worship—209, 262, 266
Organ incident—214

P

Paden, Cline—320
Padon, A.—41
Palestine—40, 71, 245, 314
Palo Pinto County—125, 127
Paris—44, 68, 87, 96, 171, 203, 246
Parker County—125
Patroon College—216
Peak, Jefferson—50, 101
Pease, R. W.—259
Pecos—164
Pennington, David—135, 147, 148
Peoria—265, 272
Philanthropia Institute — 66, 212
Phillips, G. W.—266
Phillips, T. H.—129
Phillips, T. W.—162, 273, 282, 309
Philpot, J.—255
Plainview—169, 174
Plano—196, 213
Pleasant Grove—29, 268
Poe, John T.—77, 86, 88, 93, 101, 121, 133, 159, 233, 237, 248, 250, 258, 270, 275, 276, 279
Polk County—89
Polly, N. O.—49, 54
Ponton, Joel—19, 20, 21, 24
Post—168
Power, James—42
Poyner, J. A.—235
Presbyterian—3, 13, 14, 18, 21, 25, 39, 60, 72, 82, 89, 91, 113, 122, 128, 149, 150, 152, 153, 177, 201, 204, 245, 252, 253, 257
Presbyterian, Cumberland — 33, 41, 51, 59, 60, 120, 196

Q

Quanah—159, 308
Quinlan—321

R

Radio programs—306, 307
Ranger—125
Ratliffe, J. M.—275
Rawlins, William—49, 230, 257
Red River County—6, 10, 16, 24, 32, 34, 36, 96

Republic of Texas—7, 13, 14, 16, 20, 21, 23, 24, 27
Rice, Ira Y., Jr.—303
Rice, W. J.—266
Rio Navidad—20
Roberson, C. H.—309
Robertson County—57, 179
Rockwall—16, 196
Rucker, L. P.—19, 20, 24, 32
Runnels County—156
Rusk County—34, 35, 41, 42, 66, 89, 212
Rutersville—20
Rutherford, N. P.—39
Rutherford, T. A.—55

S

Sabine—2, 27
Sabine County—39, 43, 90
Salado—30, 63, 66, 178, 212, 293
San Angelo—161, 162, 163, 164, 176
San Antonio—7, 62, 87, 146, 150, 283, 300, 306, 314, 316
Sanders, B. B.—165, 214, 224, 241, 290
Sanders, Liff—167, 168
San Augustine—4, 13, 15, 32, 90, 268
San Augustine County—8, 14, 24, 36, 90
San Jacinto County—11
San Marcos—59, 60, 132, 133, 178
San Patricio County—20, 144
San Saba—39, 55, 58, 59
Santa Anna—11
Saunders, J. P.—212
Savage, G. W.—286
Scobey, James—109, 110
Schleicher County—164
Scott, L. W.—135, 181
Scott, Walter—328
Scruggs, James—63
Scruggs, W. C.—175
Scurry County—159
Seguin—86, 87
Seminole—168
Seventh Day Adventist—175
Sewall, W. A.—282

Sewell, C. W.—135, 138, 144, 144, 146
Sewell, E. G.—263
Sewell, J. P.—102, 146, 156, 162, 210, 301
Sewell, L. R.—143, 145, 146, 178
Seymour—155, 159, 276
Shamrock—175
Shaw, Knowles—98, 183
Shelby County—8, 36, 43, 90, 91, 216, 233, 268
Shepherd, J. W.—289
Sherman—39, 47, 116, 186, 187, 190, 195, 196, 198, 199, 247, 276, 281, 299, 307, 313
Sherman Daily Register—189
Sherrod, Paul—319
Shirey, R. L.—266
Showalter, G. H. P.—209, 217, 294, 304, 308, 310, 323
Showalter, J. T.—170, 171
Silverton—172, 173
Skaggs, W. P.—163, 164
Slaton—168
Smith, C. W.—170, 171, 178, 217
Smith, Eugene S.—306
Smith, F. W.—185
Smith, John T.—119
Smithson, J. M. F.—98, 126, 127
Smith, S. W.—166, 167, 170, 209, 217
Southern, P. F.—36, 69, 90
Southland University—219
Southwestern Christian College—219
Spain, Carl—309
Spiritualist—197
Srygley, F. D.—280
Stamps, John H.—18, 33, 34
Stephenson, George—299
Stephenville—125
Stewart, S. W.—190
Stirman, Ed.—120
Stirman, V. I.—34, 120, 180
Stone, Barton W.—5, 10, 76, 224, 328
Stout, David R.—24

INDEX 377

Strickland, Stephen—55, 58, 68, 135
Sulphur Springs—68
Sunday School — 4, 56, 100, 101, 126, 131, 133, 136, 209, 210, 211, 218, 229, 246, 262, 263, 264, 265, 291, 292, 293, 294, 296, 297, 300
Sunny Glenn Home—321
Sunset—272
Surber, Green L.—100, 137
Surratt, Judge Marshall—259
Sweeney, Benton P.—57, 62, 64, 140, 179, 270
Sweeney, T. M.—29, 180, 233, 268
Sweet, L. J.—49, 51, 54, 253
Swinney, W. L.—175, 275
Swisher County—171

T

Tahoka—168
Tarrant County—51, 52, 111, 152
Tant, J. D.—117, 132, 139, 141, 158, 159, 174, 178, 191, 215, 222, 240, 241, 245, 248, 250, 271, 273, 276, 290
Tant, Fanning Y.—324, 325
Taylor, W. Y.—106
Telegraph and Texas Register—12
Terrell—195, 224, 315
Terrell County—164, 276
Teddlie, Tillit S.—304
Temple—135, 191, 293
Texarkana—6, 95, 200
Texas Christian—209
Texas Christian Advocate—204
Texas Christian Missionary Society—132, 237, 238, 240, 241, 270, 280
Texas Christian Monthly—206, 279
Texas Christian Reformer—206
Texas Christian University—214, 215
Teaxs Presbyterian—204
Texas Wesleyan Banner—204

The Evangelist—77, 81, 205, 231
Thomas Henry—37, 55, 56, 57, 59, 61, 67
Thomas, Leslie G.—327
Thornberry, James L.—224, 284
Thorp Spring—125, 166, 207, 213, 215, 237, 274, 319
Thornton Institute—216
Thurman, W. L.—247
Titus County—36, 94, 95
Tom Green County—160
Torrance, W. P.—47
Travis County—133, 140
Trinity County—200
Trott, G. A.—259, 260
Tulia—173, 303
Turkey—171, 172
Tyler—211, 216, 272
Tyler Courier—211

U

United States Census—79, 104, 152, 287, 290, 291, 292, 293, 326, 327
Universalists—89
Updike, J. P.—285
Upshur County—42, 94
Uvalde—30, 62, 151, 164

V

Vacation Bible School—307
Val Verde County—163
Van Alstyne—16, 119
Van Zandt County—54
Van Zandt, I. L.—53, 97, 98
Van Zandt, K. M.—104, 108
Vernon—159, 276
Vickery, I. C.—222
Victoria—61, 82
Victoria County—143

W

Waco—87, 129, 137, 138, 152, 215, 233, 245
Walker County—57, 69, 88
Walker, Robert—22, 23, 24, 89
Wallace, Foy E., Sr.—303

Wallace, Foy E., Jr.—323, 324, 325
Wallace, H. H.—173
Warlick, Joe—167, 210, 263
Washington—11, 13
Washington County—18, 24, 32
Waxahachie—120, 220, 235, 246, 307
Weatherford—99, 125, 127, 185
Weaver, Greene—17, 34
Wetzel, Mrs. Jennie—174
White, L. S.—118, 297, 299
Whiteside, R. L.—266, 289
Whitmire, John—54, 55
Wilbarger County—159
Wilkinson, T. B.—223
Williams, Ann F. R.—31
Williams, H. F.—117, 283
Williamson County—134, 206
Willis, Pat—200
Wilmeth, C. M.—46, 99, 101, 103, 114, 115, 119, 142, 183, 200, 201, 202, 206, 207, 217, 227, 235, 238, 239, 257, 272, 280
Wilmeth, J. B.—29, 32, 43, 44, 45, 46, 112, 226, 268
Wilmeth, J. R.—46, 76, 112, 157, 206, 207
Wilson County—143, 144
Wilson, Homer T.—108, 109
Winkler County—304
Winston, J. S.—313
Wise County—125, 128
Wise, Melvin J.—50
Withers, W. K.—39
Wolfe, John F.—316
Wood County—91, 92, 261
Wood, E. V.—317
Word and Work—322
Wright, W. H.—100, 181

Y

Yorktown—61
Young, A. W.—127, 272
Young County—128
Young, F. S.—165
Young, M. Norvel—296, 301